# HARD BARGAINS
## THE POLITICS OF SEX

Linda R. Hirshman
Jane E. Larson

*New York   Oxford*
OXFORD UNIVERSITY PRESS
1998

Oxford University Press

Oxford    New York
Athens    Auckland    Bangkok    Bogotá    Buenos Aires    Calcutta
Cape Town    Chennai    Dar es Salaam    Delhi    Florence    Hong Kong
Istanbul    Karachi    Kuala Lumpur    Madrid    Melbourne    Mexico City
Mumbai    Nairobi    Paris    São Paulo    Singapore
Taipei    Tokyo    Toronto    Warsaw

associated companies in
Berlin    Ibadan

**Library of Congress Cataloging-in-Publication Data**
Hirshman, Linda R.
Hard bargains : the politics of sex /
Linda R. Hirshman and Jane E. Larson.
p. cm.    Includes index.
ISBN 0–19–509664–9
1. Heterosexuality—Political aspects.
2. Sex—Political aspects.
3. Sex—Political aspects—History.
4. Sex and law.
5. Sex and law—History.
6. Sexual ethics—History.
I. Larson, Jane E.
II. Title.
HQ23.H69    1998
306.76'4—dc21    98–9499

1 3 5 7 9 8 6 4 2
Printed in the United States of America
on acid-free paper

# TABLE OF CONTENTS

# ACKNOWLEDGMENTS

## LINDA HIRSHMAN

Thirty-two years ago, Professor Andrew Hacker, then of the Cornell University Government Department, assigned his senior students Betty Friedan's *The Feminine Mystique* and changed my life forever. I only hope this book will be a modest part of the work, so honorably pursued by Andrew Hacker throughout his extraordinary career, of tough inquiry in support of understanding politics.

Thanks to Edwin Curley for the introduction to Thomas Hobbes, to Lori Andrews for the reminder that a woman's reach must exceed her grasp; to the faculty and staff of Washington and Lee University School of Law, particularly the remarkable library, and to Frances and Sidney Lewis, for the Lewis Scholarship there; to the anonymous reviewers of Oxford University Press, to Helen McInnis, for her unswerving faith in the project; to Carol Rose, Carole Pateman, and Rhona Mahony for inspiration, to Randy Bezanson for faith at the founding, to the unswervingly rigorous Gloria Pollack for a "lay" reading, to Laura Fitzgerald, Richard Posner, Carol Rose, Stephen Schulhofer and David Wong for comments along the way, and to David Forkosh for keeping body and soul together.

The law faculty of Washington and Lee Law School and the Philosophy and Women's Studies communities at Brandeis University heard and commented on earlier versions.

To the memory of my friend and mentor, Jean Hampton, Hobbes scholar, game theorist, moralist, divine.

## JANE LARSON

Richard Posner, Carol Rose, Jonathan Rosenblum, Jane Schacter and Stephen Schulhofer extensively commented on a previous draft and contributed greatly to the final product. Ben Brown, Alta Charo, Mary Louise Fellows, Linda Gordon, Neil Komesar, Arthur McEvoy, Victoria Nourse, Michelle Oberman, Robin West and Joan Williams all contributed valuable insights at particular turning points in the book's development.

To all the members of the Friendly Faculty Writing Circle, and to Susan Carl, Katherine Franke and Louise Rosenblum for engaging the project. The law faculties of Washington College of Law at American University and Harvard Law School, as well as the critical race and feminist theory seminars of the Fordham Law School and the Symposium on Sexual Harassment at Yale Law School heard and commented on earlier versions of parts of the book.

Wilma Larson, Don Larson, Jennifer Larson and Elizabeth Mertz gave loving support for which I cannot credit you fully, except in my heart.

To those who formed a circle of "virtual colleagues"—the network that sustained my work and is spread throughout many places and institutions—I cannot name you all but acknowledge you as silent collaborators.

Parts of Chapter Seven were published as Jane E. Larson, "'Even a Worm Will Turn at Last': Rape Reform in Late Nineteenth Century America," *Yale Journal of Law and Humanities* (1997): 1, and are used here by permission.

Michelle Landis and Renata Scanio did yeowomen's service as research assistants. Michael Morgalla opened the door to any and every library. The University of Wisconsin Law School contributed research support and intellectual energy. Leigh Anne Sackrider did an expert job of editing. David Forkosh kept us fed and sane.

Finally, to my co-author Linda, an exemplar of the classical virtues of friendship.

And to Simon.

## INTRODUCTION: SEX IN PUBLIC

Penis. Challenging the appointment of Clarence Thomas to the United States Supreme Court on grounds of sexual harassment, star witness Anita Hill's advisors couldn't decide whether she should say "penis" in the United States Senate. Hill advisor Lloyd Cutler, white-haired and gravel-voiced Washington power broker, thought "penis" would offend the delicate decorum of the highest legislative body in the United States. Susan Deller Ross, feminist litigator, thought that if Anita Hill was going to accuse Supreme Court nominee Clarence Thomas of penis talk, the senators should hear it too. Ross prevailed.

Oral sex. Reports of the President of the United States having oral sex with a twenty-one year old White House intern bumped Pope John Paul off the front pages and preoccupied the nation in the winter of 1998. Accusations of sexual misconduct levelled at the highest political and public figure in the country pushed the subject of sex to the forefront of political debate.

Adultery. The favorite candidate to head the Joint Chiefs of Staff of the American Armed Services, Vice Chairman Joseph W. Ralston, withdrew his candidacy when information surfaced about an affair he had had thirteen years earlier, while still married to another woman. Ralston's downfall was inextricably linked to the discharge, a few weeks earlier, of the first female Air Force fighter pilot for adultery and fraternization.

Are these developments just a circus—the public spectacle of society's degradation at the end of the millennium? No. Sex occupies the center of our political life for other and better reasons.

For thirty years, since the birth of the modern feminist movement in the 1960s, women have been moving into the political system. Although women—and issues of love, sex and family—have been the subject of political governance since Hammurabi, women are entering politics now not as the objects of male sexual governance but as citizens, representatives, and voters.

With women on the political scene, the official content of politics has begun to change. Obvious changes involve, for example, women's much-reported concern for issues such as education and health care. As the developments since the hearings on Thomas's nomination reflect, however, women's presence as full participants in politics also changes the way in which love, sex, and family are regarded.

If women are political players, sexual harassment can become a civil rights violation and adultery an offense both husbands and wives can commit. The change in
the political agenda put penis in the Congressional Record.

Recognizing sex as a political subject seems easy. Politics is about power. Sexual
politics is a specific example of the general question of power: under what conditions do people seek and grant one another access to their physical selves? The
most obvious example of the politics of physical access is violence, the treatment of
which is a traditional core subject of politics.

Indeed, although until recently women could not press the legislatures formally
as political actors, anthropologists speculate that men and women have been using
the political tool of bargaining by negotiating privately over the terms and conditions of sexual access since they dropped out of the trees on the African savannah
eons ago. What has changed is that then the bargaining was private and the politics
one-sided; now the bargaining takes place as part of a shared political realm of
power, fairness, and justice. But one way or the other, sex—and bargaining—will
occur. Although there is much good recent work describing the political failures
of sexual relationships, this book is the first effort to suggest solutions within the
recognition that sex and its politics are inevitable.

We acknowledge that even in the face of the long history and powerful contemporary presence of sex in politics, to say that there is a politics of heterosexual
sexuality is still deeply controversial. Many contemporary thinkers argue that sex
can be understood only as a matter of natural biology; others, that religion has the
last word where sex is concerned. But unless sex is categorized as uniquely beyond
secular human control—unless sex is like the weather or reincarnation—sex has all
of the characteristics of a subject of politics.

This is also a book about law. In the democratic societies of the modern West,
the political conditions under which people may make claims to the bodies of others is ordinarily the subject of law. Indeed, western societies, with their democratic
processes and market economies, pride themselves on the political centrality of the
rule of law, extolling its virtues of neutrality, stability, and foreseeability. For centuries, western political thinkers have elevated the legal system over the purely political, denigrating politics as corrupt, biased and arbitrary.

Just as sex has always been the subject of politics, sex has always been the subject
of law. Over time, the legal terms of sexual exchange have defined the social rules
of sexual behavior, influenced the gender division and, ultimately, affected the relative bargaining power of persons. Because norms of sexual access are closely related to desirable sexual behavior and appropriate gender roles, the law of sex also
enters centrally into debates about these less obviously legal subjects. As the role of
women as political players has changed the content of politics, so, too, has it
changed the content of law. We focus, then, not simply on the politics of sex, but
on the political institution of sex law.

This inquiry comes at a time of extraordinary promise and danger in sex, politics, and law. Recognizing the heterosexual exchange as political forces the question of the political standards to apply. Selecting standards requires answers to fundamental questions like whether men and women are created the same or different, equal or unequal, autonomous or requiring governance. Any discussion about the relative position of men and women exposes diverse and conflicting beliefs. These conflicts arise most powerfully in consideration of the heterosexual exchange. Thus, not only is the characterization of sex as political controversial, but the political standards to be used to evaluate that transaction are also mortally contested.

In this book we argue that these issues arise with particular urgency at the end of the twentieth century because the governing political and philosophical heterosexual order is shifting foundationally. We refer to the established sexual order, the one we argue is currently in the historical process of passing away, as the "libertine" paradigm of unregulated bargains. Libertinism, with its roots in the early years of this century, had replaced an earlier sexual worldview, the "Victorian" model of virtue, or unfree bargains, a regime which began just after the American Revolution.

As with any fundamental social change, the current instability results from stress and incoherence in the existing arrangements. Much contemporary American debate about sexual politics consists of either denunciation or praise for the two prior schemes. Commentators debate whether sexual libertinism is the godless stepchild of the failed traditional family or whether the so-called 'new Victorians' are prudish, repressive and sexually self-hating. As to that debate, our purpose is not to join or to settle it, but instead to anticipate, describe and argue for the shape of the different sexual world to come, an emerging paradigm we call the era of "hard bargains." At the demise of the old order, we will argue, men and women can recognize the age-old political nature of their negotiations over sexual access as well as their more recent commitment to equality and begin to develop workable processes for resolving their differences and making a fair division of the goods of their sexual cooperation.

Finally, this book is about history. The sexual politics of the present cannot be understood without understanding where the present came from, because many sexual arrangements, including the present arrangements governing heterosexual access, are the products of history. We record both the institutional memory of the legal regulation of sex and the evolution of sexual personhood. Although important aspects of sexuality are natural and enduring, people from different eras and places will be different kinds of sexual creatures. Because sexuality is of the body, it is tempting to forget that it is also of the mind, heart, and spirit—those human capacities primarily formed by and constitutive of culture.

We also turn to history to observe the way in which particular understandings and arrangements divided up the benefits and burdens of sexual interaction, empowering or disempowering the players in their bargaining. Hammurabi's Code, prescribing the death penalty for unfaithful wives (and their lovers), for example, laid the burden of secure paternity on the married female, by making her alone responsible for marital fidelity. This law thus radically reduced a wife's bargaining power for the good of her sexual fidelity, because a husband in a regime of death penalty for unfaithful wives does not have to offer much—not even his own sexual fidelity—to get her to stay home.

We begin, therefore, with a critical interpretation of the history of sexual politics in the West, from the classical world to the present. We do not search the past for a turnkey operation of sexual regulation to import into the present; in our judgment there is no past tradition that was not deeply flawed, among other reasons for failing to recognize women as political players. Instead, we look to past models to understand what the governors of past societies considered necessary for a flourishing sexual life, at least for the members of their society recognized as persons and political players. We also seek to understand what part law played in providing good sexual lives to those elites. Because our proposal for a future sexual order includes concern for flourishing sexual lives of women as well as for men, past models may be useful as "social laboratories." We bear in mind, however, that past models assumed a gender hierarchy grounded in sex or relied on a male norm inconsistent with our assumptions of the political equality between men and women.

In our attempt to understand how past arrangements divided the pie, we do not treat the evolution to the present as inevitable. Although winners write history, critical inquiry can reveal alternative arrangements that either disappeared over time or survived within hidden subcultures. History, as opposed to the inquiries of nature or religion, is thus an account of choices made and not of determinate patterns unfolding. We also reject the current popular version of sexual history, which presumes a nice progression from sexual repression in the past toward sexual freedom for heterosexuals at the end of the twentieth century. We deny that future progress would be simply more of the same.

Viewed through the lens of politics, but without these blinders of naturalness, inevitability, and progress, the history of sexuality in the West is a story of how the meanings and place of sex in human life and culture have changed. From an aristocratic system of freedom and privilege for a few in the classical world, sexual governance moved to the reproductive family of pre-modern Europe and America, then to the intimate yet anxious romance and marriage of the nineteenth century, and finally to a hedonistic world of sexual consumption in the modern period. What the future will bring is, of course, an important concern of this book.

## SELECTING SEXUAL SUBJECTS

A study of western sexual legal regulation raises many possibilities. Several recent histories focus on the family, analyzing the network of laws that governed sexuality within the tradition of monogamous heterosexual marriage. During the centuries when sex was lawful only within such marriage, family law—the legal conditions of marriage, divorce and marital sexual obligations and permissions—was the primary regulatory scheme.

Yet the history of heterosexuality is written as much outside the law of marriage as inside. Even where sexual marriage was privileged, family law existed against a backdrop of regulation, mostly in the form of criminal law, of other sexual possibilities. Such regulation of nonmarital sex took the form of codes of prohibition, like the ancient laws against rape, fornication, adultery, sodomy, bigamy and prostitution. These regulations did more than simply buttress the marital norm. The regulation of nonmarital sex set the terms of sexual access between social actors not husband and wife. Laws regarding sex outside of marriage threatened punishment and scandal and also played a symbolic and hortatory role. Moreover, in the modern world, sex outside of marriage can hardly be ignored. Yet extramarital regulation has received much less attention.

Of all the subjects of nonmarital sex, the most attention in recent years has been paid to the regulation of homosexuality. In the arguments over what intimacies should be permitted and prohibited within the same sex, understandings of sexuality, gender, and power reaching deep into heterosexuality are also expressed. Our project is both broader and narrower than these histories of homosexuality. In this book, we discuss the regulation of same-sex activity only tangentially, and the shifting sexual possibilities of transvestism, bisexuality and so on not at all. Our focus is the regulation of sexual access between women and men. As our treatment of personhood will reveal, we fix on male-female sex not because we think heterosexuality is a category of humanity or the only natural sexual possibility. Indeed, it is a central tenet of this book that people's personhood is not congruent with their sexual identity, including their partner selection. We do not claim that people "are" "homosexuals" or they "are" "heterosexuals" or that they "are" sexual anything at all. Sexual transactions are only one part of a human life or a human's personal identity.

For most of the human species, however, there is a physical genital distinction between males and females. Moreover, the male-female distinction also divides players of observable, stable physical inequality and historical social inequality, which inequalities present specific problems of political and moral philosophy. The sexual differences across numbers in size, weight, strength, and vulnerability to childbirth and nursing present the problem of bargaining between physical unequals over a physical transaction. The cultural differences in social power, economic resources and inherited historical presumptions present the problem of bargaining between economic, social and ideological unequals over an economic, social and ideological transaction. The absence of such physical and social inequalities makes same-sex regulation different enough from the male-female exchange to warrant separate philosophical as well as historical treatment. We also are interested in the ways in which our ancestors addressed human reproduction, a question that has been foundational to western political history and philosophy. Here, too, the history and politics of the regulation of homosexuality are different enough from that of reproductive heterosexuality to justify separate treatment.

This being said, however, there are some places where the modes of sexuality meet in important ways. First, definitions of heterosexuality and homosexuality have changed over history, as they may change over the life of any individual. Wherever that fluidity affects the sexual exchange between women and men, we include it in our analysis. For example, we discuss instances where sexual regulations do not treat same-and other-sex conduct differently, as in the global use of the term "sodomy," and where ideas and practices of homosexuality shed light on our primary topic, as in the theories of ancient Greek toleration for any sexual act by a man—except for a man to play the woman. Importantly, in our analysis of sexual bargaining, the possibility of sex with another individual of the same sex operates as a kind of ever-present alternative to the heterosexual bargain, and so puts a limit on how demanding the other-sex partner can be.

In fixing on the sexual exchange between male and female, we pay special attention to four issues addressed by the sexual regulatory scheme of any era. They are rape, prostitution, adultery, and fornication.

Serious prohibitions of rape strengthen the bargaining power of the weaker sexual player by making the stronger obtain consent from the weaker rather than force the sexual transaction. The various possible incarnations of rape—stranger rape, statutory rape, marital rape, acquaintance rape, and rape by abuse of familial or professional authority—mark the boundaries of one person forcibly claiming access to another's sexual body without their consent and accordingly are central to setting the terms of such consent. The law governing forcible rape also reflects the core beliefs of a society about the role of sexual access, the privileged status of physical persons, the inclusion of females (the overwhelming majority of rape victims) in the category of persons entitled to claim that privileged physical status, and the political/social status of females and other rape victims.

Prostitution is the exchange of sexual access for money. It differs from rape because the exchange of something valuable makes it look consensual. From a bargaining standpoint, prostitution at first appears to be the purest of bargained-for sex. The purity of the prostitution example is somewhat tainted because throughout much of history prostitution has been a transaction of radically unequal bargaining power, undermining its consensual character. Yet sporadic efforts to eradicate prostitution through law have met with resistance from the prostitutes, who describe themselves in clear bargaining terms as making a good sexual bargain. Many prostitutes today make the same arguments.

Prostitution also raises the issue of what it means to sell sexuality. When noneconomic norms dominate a culture, as in historical periods strongly affected by Christian values, the attitude toward prostitution reflects the tension between a spiritual and material world view. Even in those eras like our own, which are strongly dominated by market values, the interplay of sex and commerce in prostitution raises the question of whether sex should be part of a monied economy separated from mutual sexual desire. If not, what kinds of inducements to sexual consent should be acceptable, and how or why is sexuality different from other human attributes that may (or may not) be traded in the marketplace?

The law of adultery and fornication is the purest instance of regulating sex as such, rather than sex as a form of coercion. Stripped of the background "noise" of global concerns like coercion, the law of adultery (sex by a married partner with someone not her or his spouse) and of fornication (sex outside of marriage) is evidence of the reigning ideal of the heterosexual exchange. In times when monogamous marriage is the only legitimate place for sex, therefore, we find severe prohibitions on all parties to an adulterous or nonmarital sexual exchange. Unlike rape, where a norm against violence generally produces some prohibition, and even unlike prostitution, where the cold-bloodedness of the market generates a sense of impropriety, adultery and fornication—sex, neat, so to speak—have been the subjects of the wildest regulatory swings throughout history as ideals of sexual community have changed.

Laws against adultery and fornication also affect the sexual bargain. Enforceable laws make marriage the necessary condition of sexual access; as a result, the party who benefits from the marriage bargain, which differs in different cultures, gains in bargaining power by controlling all access to legitimate sex.

Rape, prostitution, fornication and adultery. By tracing a detailed history of the philosophy and politics of the legal regulation of these subjects, we can paint a detailed picture of the place of sexuality in our larger commitments to proper human relations over the long course of western history.

## JUDGING SEX

We report the history of sexual regulation in order to judge the arrangements as political and to propose new ones. In judging sex, we apply the accepted standards of secular political philosophy as they have evolved in the western political tradition since Plato. We divide western political philosophy into three schools— virtue ethics, classical liberalism, and utilitarianism. Almost any survey of secular Western philosophy recognizes the dominance of these three schools of thought. The three traditions are distinguished by three sets of fundamental assumptions about the world. Each school makes assumptions about what it means to know anything. Each assumes an essence of human personhood. Each defines the purpose of morality or, where they are separated, of politics. As we will describe in more detail later, bargaining, our preferred tool of organizing sexuality, is not a school of political philosophy, but a means. The ends are provided by the goals and understandings of the philosophical traditions themselves.

Classical virtue ethics is the oldest secular western tradition, dating back to Ancient Greece and Rome (750 B.C.E. to approximately 430 C.E.). Virtue ethics asserts that people can have reliable knowledge of the world, including the lives and experiences of others, that there are better and worse lives, and that a good society is one that makes it possible for people to lead good lives. Virtue ethics has a generous understanding of the legitimate subjects of politics. Classical liberalism, which arose in the seventeenth century, is skeptical about each of the assumptions of virtue ethics. Classical liberals doubt that certain knowledge of the world, and particularly of the human condition or of the "good," is possible. Liberals believe that individuals are the site of human morality and can decide what is a good life only for themselves. Finally liberals believe that the core value of public institutions is to leave people as free as possible to make their own decisions about their lives. Consequently, liberalism has a narrow understanding of the legitimate subjects of politics. The third major school of western political philosophy is also the newest. Utilitarianism is attributed to eighteenth-century British philosopher Jeremy Bentham, who claimed that the goal of morality was to create the maximum human pleasure and the minimum of pain ("the greatest good for the greatest number"). Utilitarianism, like virtue ethics, thus asserts that knowledge about the human condition is possible. In evaluating the good and the bad of the human condition, utilitarians emphasize the sensations of the physical world. In politics and morality, utilitarianism counts all players equally, which permits one individual's well-being to be legitimately sacrificed for the greater good of others. Optimistic about knowledge and unrestrained by individual boundaries, utilitarianism also generates a generous understandings of the legitimate subjects of politics.

In our judgment of sex, we use principles of knowledge, personhood, and politics from each of these traditions. Throughout the book we pause to evaluate each historical regime of sexual regulation according to how well it realizes the goods of the three traditions, with particular attention to how, if at all, the regime makes it possible for the players to advance their own sexual and social interest when arranging for sex. Where appropriate, we assign a philosophical "grade" to the sexual arrangements when they first make their appearance in our historical tale. Occasionally where we require several schemes to make a clear judgment, we delay our evaluation until several regimes can be compared.

Applying the principles of philosophy, we conclude that the goods of each school can best be obtained by allowing the players themselves to bargain for the best sexual arrangement supported by legal rules to offset the worst depredations of the stronger bargainer. We call this technique "supported bargaining." In the last chapter, we set forth our proposals for such laws concerning each of our subjects of sexual inquiry: rape, prostitution, adultery, and fornication. Taken together, our proposals comprise the regime of "hard bargains."

## TELLING SEX'S HISTORY

Part One sets the stage. We set forth our methods in detail, describing and justifying the philosophical and analytic principles we use in sifting through the millennia of sex, law and politics. We expose the bare bones of the origins of enduring issues in sexual governance: hierarchy, chastity, naturalness, monogamy, and equality. Modern sexual culture has ancient roots in the classical, Jewish and early Christian approaches, in the theology of the established Catholic Church, and in the political ideas and energies of Enlightenment and Reformation Europe.

Part Two describes and evaluates American sexual regulation from the European settlement of the continent through the late nineteenth century, with particular focus on the sexual paradigm that arose from the rich political and social ferment that established American independence. The philosophy of the "republic of virtue" is exemplified by Alexis de Tocqueville's foundational political work, *Democracy in America* (1840), a work that we argue exemplifies the sexual order dominant at the critical early period of the American nation. We explore how, during the rise of the republic of virtue, philosophy, religion, law, and culture operated together to fortify the concept of "opposite sexes," to establish marriage as the only legitimate sexual partnership, and to place the nuclear family at the heart of a new social and political order. We evaluate how the virtuous republic in its prime measured up to the standards of virtue and republican values like freedom and equality. We conclude that the whole social structure of virtue weighed the sexual bargain in favor of the party with dominance within the marriage.

We reconceive the Victorian period, conventionally viewed as the zenith of virtue, as the beginning of the decline of the period of the republic of virtue. First, virtue was weakened by the problem of how "opposite" sexes could negotiate the most intimate relationships from completely different moral schemes. Then, around mid-century, the virtue republic confronted powerful egalitarian movements such as abolitionism and woman suffrage. We focus on the sexual theory of John Stuart Mill as a manifestation of the collision between egalitarian politics and hierarchical sex.

In their challenge to inequalities of sexual power that had prevailed between men and women since the ancient world, Victorian reformers, including the first American feminists, could not agree on whether to expect chastity of men or allow sexual liberty to women. Sexual purity is the image that has survived to bear the label "Victorian," but the competing candidate—free love—ultimately won the contest of history. We measure the promise and peril of both social purity and free love against the goods of western political philosophy and show how each was an effort on the part of the weaker females to gain surer ground from which to bargain with men for sex.

The transition to a libertine ideal of free love occurred gradually, its seeds beginning to blossom in the latter part of the nineteenth century and exploding colorfully in the early decades of the twentieth century when several

forces—Freudianism, a new science called "sexology," and the burgeoning consumer culture—all acted to relocate sexuality from the moral to the realm of the
physical. Part Three tells the story of the battle to define the new sexual ideal between the progressives of the eugenics movement, who treated material sexuality
as an important social force, and the liberationists, who took the physicalism of
sexuality to justify individual pleasure-seeking free of social or moral consequences. Although the experience with Nazi Germany would probably have de-
feated eugenics, the blossoming of male-female relationships at work and play
contributed to the triumph of liberationism. At the level of law and politics, we
also examine the strange disconnection between public and private as thinkers
seemed oblivious to the implications of these startling changes in social practice.
We choose the term "libertine" to describe this modern sexual ideology because
it connotes the link between a political commitment to a minimal state, particularly as concerns consensual sexual conduct, and a moral commitment to the
good of sexual hedonism and expression.

We then describe the legal and social triumph of libertine sexual deregulation
by the 1960s. We describe how the elitist American Law Institute developed a
Model Penal Code, which, along with constitutional protections of sexual integrity and a revived First Amendment, drove gaping holes in the regime of official
sexual regulation. We recount how the Kinsey Report and *Playboy* magazine articulated a new middle-class identity of sexual and consumer sophistication. We analyze the libertine paradigm as a sexual worldview characterized by dominant
norms of individualism, which paralleled a revival of rights-based individualism in
political philosophy, as represented by the work of Harvard philosopher, John
Rawls.

We address the ways in which this individualist perspective once again missed
the political lives of women. This time, rather than allocating women to one moral
and political universe and men to another as the virtue republic and social purists
had done, the governing paradigm simply turned women into men, sexually female, but with all the other characteristics of men: strength, independence, emotional control and separation from the consequences of reproduction. The refusal
to admit any female characteristic into political analysis ultimately meant the libertine paradigm could not support women's bargaining power in seeking their
share of the heterosexual exchange.

We then describe the breakup of libertinism. Corrosive pressure on the dominant worldview came from a resurgent feminism challenging the assumption of a
male norm for humanity and the myth of consequence-free sexual exchange, and
asserting a connection between unequal private heterosexual relationships and
other social inequalities superficially unrelated to sex. Simultaneously, utilitarian
values of collective well-being put external pressure on sexual freedom, with rising
rates of divorce, rape, and impoverished, female-headed families. We also analyze
the contemporary contenders to replace a libertine sexual politics. Cultural con-

servatives contend for a return to the religiously dominated republic of virtue. Libertarians claim the problem is too little rather than too much liberty and seek a more absolute libertinism, stripped of all redistributions and justified on biological grounds of natural inequality. We evaluate the effect on sexual bargaining of each alternative, with particular emphasis on the one position on which both virtue revivalists and libertarian purists agree: sex is not a subject for political resolution between two recognizably political players.

### ENVISIONING SEX'S FUTURE

Part Four sets forth our prescription for a new sexual order. We propose that the touchstone for political legitimacy requires the recognition that women are political players, that adult heterosexuality is a political relationship, and that the goal of sexual politics is neither to be the handmaid of an antique morality nor the umpire in a free-for-all between unequal players. Rather, it is the goal of living within the generous limits imposed by a flexible human nature and the social nature of the human condition, of a dignified and flourishing life. We assume that the sexual good can be known adequately to allow for theory, that human beings have both deep sexual interests and interests beyond the sexual, and that politics can support people as they negotiate over the benefits and burdens of the sexual exchange.

# PART ONE

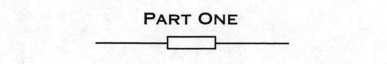

# THE ORIGINS OF HARD BARGAINS

## 2

# THE POSSIBILITIES OF THEORY

As a political subject, we would expect sexual governance to be part of the established body of political philosophy. Yet there exists only a small amount of serious explicit political analysis of heterosexuality. Given that sex matters and that all societies recognize its importance by regulating it, this scarcity of attention is surprising. The scarcity of attention is also costly because philosophy gives people their ends, both of a good life for themselves and of the purposes of a good society. In our concrete analysis of history and proposals for change, we will emphasize the technique of bargaining for sexual goods. But the goals of sexual bargaining, and, indeed, the choice of bargaining as a means, reflect ends set forth by philosophy, its definition of personhood and of a good common life.

To bring issues of sexual regulation into the mainstream of legal and political thought, we must make explicit our position on the foundational assumptions of any effort in political philosophy: knowledge, personhood, and subject matter. We assume that knowledge, including knowledge about sex, is possible; that sexual personhood is a mix of the natural and the cultural; and that male-female sex can be understood as a political relationship, even though it mostly takes place in private circumstances of one-on-one bargaining. Like any other human activity about which we make choices, sex cannot be understood without making some assumptions about each of these matters. Every historical regime of sexual regulation has rested on some such set of assumptions.

Each of our assumptions could be challenged. Is sex knowable? An important strain of modern thought asserts that knowledge is difficult, rare, and unreliable, especially about physical and psychological experience. Based on this skeptical attitude, many modern thinkers insist that no one can know what is good for another person. Sexuality, they contend, is the most elusive of all subjects of knowledge.

Is personhood, or that part of personhood involved with sex, physical and natural, or is it psychological and cultural? Sociobiology claims that a detailed set of male and female sexual behaviors is the non-negotiable natural inheritance of millennia of evolution. By contrast, followers of social theorist Michel Foucault claim that sexual personhood is an almost entirely cultural creation, endlessly constructed and reconstructed through a series of mostly psychological exchanges.

Is sex political? Even if value judgments about sexuality can be made, many believe that male-female sex is natural, wild, and not to be domesticated by any human enterprise such as law or politics. Others believe that even if sex can be regulated, only a narrow range of issues is properly subject to political judgment or political processes, and that sex is the most highly guarded of all private spheres. Still others believe that even if political governance of sex is possible and legitimate, in a secular and pluralistic society it would be imprudent to use the state to shape sexual behavior.

Do men and women engage in political bargaining over sex? It is a commonplace belief that rationality, strategy, and self-interest play little or no role in heterosexual decision-making. Passion and altruism are all there is, or they so dominate sexual choices as to leave no room for reason.

## OUR USE OF HISTORY

In defending our assumptions of knowledge, personhood, politics, and political bargaining, we are not confined to mere speculation about what they might mean if put into effect in a real system of sexual regulation. We have the historical record of experience with living in sexual regimes that rest on the different assumptions available in western philosophy. As our account of that history will show, although often inexplicit western culture has always behaved as if sex were knowable, natural and social, political, and negotiable. Virtue ethics, which characterized classical western civilizations, for example, assumes that sex exists in the natural world, that human sexuality is a mixture of bodily impulse and moral and social governance, that people can judge the relative merits of different sexual arrangements for the human good, and that sex can be the subject of collective moral and political judgment as well as of private negotiation.

Classical liberalism is the school least inclined to treat sex as political. Skeptical about what people can know of each other and of the good, and fearful of the state, classical liberalism tends to see sex as beyond reason, and hence beyond judgment or politics. Liberal sexual personhood combines materialism and self-actualization in a way that largely immunizes sex from politics. Nonetheless, in history, the early modern societies in which liberalism was born neither aspired to nor achieved a politics-free sexual regime. Instead, classical liberalism delegated governance of male-female sex to the private power of the feudal family and church, and later the individual and the market. Twentieth-century liberalism remains skeptical about politics, but assertive about the naturalness of heterosexuality. Accordingly, contemporary liberals repudiate the remnants of feudal sexual governance that survived into the Enlightenment, leaving only the individual and the market.

Benthamite utilitarianism asserts that knowledge about the human condition is possible and can be measured by the hedonistic calculation of pain and pleasure, sexual sensation and satisfaction. Lacking any public-private distinction, utilitarianism draws no limits around the proper subjects of politics. Utilitarianism can justify very coercive public governance, provided the sum total of social value

outweighs the individuals sacrificed, although other versions of the theory oppose a strong state on the grounds that individuals can best decide what causes
them pain or pleasure. In its valorization of sensation, utilitarianism might be
taken to assume that personhood is natural as opposed to cultural. But, in the
end, utilitarianism should be neutral as to whether pain and pleasure is biological
in origin or culturally constructed. Although there have been no strictly utilitarian sexual regimes in history, when liberalism moved from defending the morality of freedom and tolerance to embracing the virtue of the sexual revolution
itself, it implicitly shifted from liberal skepticism about the good to utilitarian valorization of the good in physical pleasure.

Finally, under each regime of sexual theory and in each culture, the players bargained between and among themselves. Children bargained with their parents for
leeway in choosing a spouse, wives bargained with their husbands not to patronize prostitutes, and courting couples bargained for sex outside marriage. Historical evidence of sexual bargaining is more elusive than is evidence of the law,
ideologies, or norms. Where records of such bargaining do exist, they are fragmentary and usually unofficial. Sexual bargaining mostly takes place in intimate
or familial settings, in secluded places and off the record. Nonetheless, we can
glimpse traces of sexual bargaining in works of fiction, in letters and diaries, and in
the detailed accounts of private disputes found in litigation records or newspapers.

Sexual bargaining always took place against the backdrop of prevailing law. But
other forces, including technology, ideology, and collective action, also structured
sexual bargaining. Technologies of effective contraception and medically safe
abortion, the door lock and firearms, the automobile—all these changed the
terms of male-female sex. Sexual ideologies such as celibacy, chivalry, manly self-
restraint, superior female virtue, companionate marriage, and gender equality,
tipped the balance of bargaining as well, by convincing stronger players not to use
every advantage they possess, or inducing weaker players to press their advantages.

Last, sexual bargaining also took the form of collective action, or participation
in cultural or political contests. Groups with common sexual interests acted collectively to negotiate norms, ideologies, or laws to advance their position. In the
nineteenth century, for example, middle-class women took up sex reform, a collective bargaining strategy through which they sought greater authority over the
sexual conduct of their lovers, husbands, and sons.

Each of these ways of understanding sex and its governance has drawbacks. As
the systems of sexual regulation in the ancient world reflect, classical virtue ethics
incorporated hierarchies at odds with the modern commitment to equality between men and women and between people of all ethnicities and classes. Virtue's
certainty about the good supported terrible acts of enslavement and persecution
in antiquity and Christian Europe. Liberal skepticism and individualism elevated
freedom of action so highly as to pave the way for private tyrannies and to strip

morality and politics of the language to criticize these abuses of private power. Utilitarianism elevated physical life over all other aspects of personhood and provided no sure protection against the harvesting of some persons for the use of others seeking pleasure or avoiding pain. The private setting of the bargain masked its political and social nature. Against this historical backdrop of the possibilities and pitfalls of existing philosophical traditions, we turn to our own theoretical assumptions.

### ASSUMPTIONS OF OUR ANALYSIS

#### *Knowledge Is Possible*

We assert that knowledge about the physical world is possible, and that moral knowledge about social arrangements in that world is also possible. Although the possibility of knowledge has been disputed since Plato, we are concerned only to establish that knowledge adequate for judgment of sex is possible. In our claim that knowledge necessary for our project is possible, we draw on good recent thinking in this enduring debate.

From a distance, a square tower looks round. Maybe what I mean when I say green is what you mean when you say blue. Maybe nothing exists but the inside of your own mind. These are the problems that philosophers face about the reliability of human access to the natural world. Modern thought struggles with the paradox that knowledge of the physical world can be obtained only by observation, but that induction from observation is inherently unreliable. That we see the sun rise today is no promise that it will rise tomorrow. This thoroughgoing skepticism about knowledge denies the reliability of moral, aesthetic, and psychological judgments, and makes law and even politics impossible. Why have a law against murder? Maybe the person is not really dead, and so on.

Yet people go right on making laws, running for office, and driving on the right side of the road. Contemporary philosophical work treats these behaviors as a sort of artificial social agreement to act as if there is a world and as if we all mean the same thing when we name and describe things in that world. Philosophers call these agreements, variously, "animal faith," "common sense," and "linguistic conventions." Accordingly, even if people can have no objective knowledge of the material world, our social agreement to act as if there is a material world, that we can know enough about it to legislate our conduct within it, and that we are justified in punishing deviations from the agreed conduct, is a complete substitute for certainty. In this worldview, skepticism plays the role of a healthy restraint on dogmatism and not a conclusive argument against any moral or political theory.

Michel Foucault's work opened a second modern debate that bears on the question of whether knowledge of sex is possible. Foucault argued that sex is not confined to the natural world, but rather is mostly a social construction, like language or manners. Insofar as sex is a social construction, we would not need to rely on an agreement to treat the natural world as real and knowable. Instead, we could invoke a social agreement to treat the subject of that accord—language, for example—as binding. The difference is that subjects of social agreement are usually considered more fluid than subjects of the "harder" natural world. As we discuss below, we regard sex as only partly social construct; it is also a natural fact. So the existence of any social agreement on sex cannot fully resolve the problem of knowledge for our analysis.

Even if we can know what sex is, we would still have to ask whether moral and political truth sufficient to judge sex is possible and whether sex is susceptible to governance and politics. Again, because we regard sex as a mixed natural and social reality, we avoid the argument that sex is like the weather, and thus a subject immune from moral or political judgment. The question of whether moral knowledge is possible remains, however.

Moral skepticism is as venerable as doubt about the possibility of knowledge of the physical world. Plato's *Republic*, for example, considers whether justice is anything more than the will of the strong. The Renaissance rediscovery of ancient skepticism fueled rejection of divine revelation, which had been the most assured source of moral certainty in the medieval world. Modern inquiries into the economic and psychological foundations for moral belief fuels the skepticism of late liberal theory.

In our assumption that moral knowledge about sex is possible, we ally ourselves with virtue ethics, including the revival of liberal virtue, and utilitarianism. In this we join a growing movement in contemporary moral philosophy. In the aftermath of the rejection of value relativism or neutrality, many contemporary philosophers are renewing the ancient project of describing good lives. These thinkers argue that certain conditions are common to human beings, with which any moral system must deal. Good societies are those that find stable and satisfactory solutions to the problems human face because of the kind of creatures they are. As the utilitarians correctly emphasize, people are embodied selves, and so must deal with death. Similarly, people are capable of pain, and so must deal with injury and illness. They must eat, and so are pressed by scarcity. They have language and reproduce sexually, and so must create society, including the society of the heterosexual bond. People think, create, and feel, and so must consider how to exercise their capacities for reason, invention, and emotion. From these descriptions of the human condition, contemporary virtue revivalists derive the characteristics of a human system of good and evil: avoiding untimely death, unnecessary pain, and hunger; providing the conditions of social interaction; and ensuring opportunities for exercising the capacities of thought and agency through art, politics, religion, education, and society. Over centuries of recorded history, all human systems of morality ask and answer these same questions.

In their struggle with these timeless problems, contemporary virtue revivalists advocate a plurality of values against the totalizing systems of antiquity on the one hand and the corrosive skepticism of value-relative modernity on the other. They seek a social agreement, like the agreement to treat the natural world as knowable, to treat the moral world as knowable at least to this modest extent. A world without morality is impossible to attain, they contend, and would be unbearable if realized.

Male-female sex is an obvious candidate for this "plurality of moral knowledge" approach. All humans have sexed bodies, and our survival as a species requires that at least some among the population desire the other sex enough to bring them into intimate bodily contact. Sexual reproduction means that social contact between men and women will occur, and the governance of the resulting sexual community is a human problem no moral system can avoid. Sex is also associated with pleasure and sociability, which are among the human capacities that any human morality must address. Thus people both need and want physical access to the sexual selves of others. This poses the same problems of distribution, security, and self-realization as any other instance of human physical access, such as violence or property ownership. A sexual morality may be judged according to the extent to which it helps people address the demands of reproduction and the craving for genital pleasure and the company of others.

Of course, revived virtue ethics does not have a monopoly on moral analysis. Concern with the sanctity of individual free action makes it possible to think of sexuality as a liberal moral problem and recent writing has attempted to revive the connections between liberalism and the virtue tradition. Immanuel Kant, for example, saw sexuality as risky because it caused the desiring partner to make an object of desire out of another autonomous being. Liberal thinkers thus emphasize the personhood interests at stake in a sexual transaction. Yet these efforts to make a liberal sexual morality are limited by the liberal focus on freedom as the preemptive moral issue, and by the tradition of assuming that sex falls on the private side of a line that defines the proper sphere of politics and often even of morality.

### Sexual Personhood Is Natural and Social

All moral theories include assumptions about personhood, defined as those aspects of the human condition the theory chooses to honor. Sexual personhood is an application of a larger theory of personhood.

Virtue ethics assumes that people are naturally capable of virtue in their pursuit of a good life, or of happiness, as it is sometimes defined. The tradition treats sex as an expression of innate human physicality and sociability, but also as an activity open to political and moral governance in the service of a good life and a good society.

Classical liberalism focuses on the material and willful aspects of personhood. The liberal person is defined by the boundedness of her or his separate physical body, and each body contains a separate individual will. People are opaque to one another and existentially atomistic; all cooperation is fragile, the product of negotiations leading to a consent that may be freely revoked. The liberal sexual person is similarly bounded and willful. Because liberal individualism is both physical and mental, ideas of liberal sexual personhood can either emphasize an uncontrollable physical drive or an expression of the individual's endless capacity for self-creation.

Benthamite utilitarianism similarly assumes the importance of the material self and its physical pains and pleasures. More evolved versions of the philosophy set forth a hierarchy of values of personhood similar to the virtue ethics tradition. The utilitarian person is more accessible than the opaque liberal self. The tradition honors the pleasure-seeking materialist and at the same time seeks to protect the person who experiences pain. But the collective nature of utilitarian morality can reduce sexual personhood to the person's stake in the collective good, allowing great individual sacrifice for the well-being of a whole family, a people, or a nation. At the extreme, utilitarianism can lead to a version of eugenics in which the sexual person is honored not for herself or himself, but as a carrier of a race.

Two conflicting trends in late-twentieth-century thought have produced variations on these accepted visions of personhood. Sociobiology, with some of its roots in utilitarian materialism, suggests that social behavior is the product of biological drives refined over millennia of natural selection, with certain behaviors emerging as superior to others. Such theories fell from favor after the disastrous experience with racial politics in the United States and eugenics under the Nazis. By the 1970s, however, a revived sociobiology suggested that contemporary heterosexual arrangements, particularly male dominance and female submission, are evolutionarily superior. More recent and sophisticated sociobiological accounts emphasize other human qualities, particularly cultural flexibility and altruism. On the other hand, Foucault's theory roots the sexual self in shifting social sands rather than a natural ground. Interestingly, this vision recalls the virtue ethics position favoring education and moral society as the means to construct human character.

We adopt none of these visions of personhood entirely. Instead, we assume that the sexed person is partly physical, possessing a biological sex and capacities for physical sensation, and particularly for genital pleasure. The embodied nature of the person and the boundaries of that body place limits on even the most open-ended sexual imagination. Nature also gives human beings enduring psychological and emotional characteristics that bear on sexuality, specifically the capacity for sociability, rationality, and self-interestedness. Finally, we see culture-making as intrinsic to human nature, and also the source of virtually all of the interesting details that make up the human erotic. History demonstrates too much variety in patterns of sexual orientation or standards of beauty, in the erotic associations of pleasure and pain or the charge between domination and submission, to support any view but that the natural and the social intersect in what it means to be a sexual person.

The argument between biological determinism and social construction of sexual personhood often stands in for the real argument, which is whether sex can be controlled. It is hard to overlook the cultural conservatism of many enthusiasts of sociobiology or the strong feminist-homosexual alliance behind Foucault. Contemporary philosopher David Estlund argues persuasively that these arguments must be separated in sexual debates. The natural and universal are not necessarily beyond control, nor should the cultural be assumed to be malleable. As Estlund puts it, cancer and sexism seem to be universal to the human condition, but we believe they may be eradicated in the knowable future. Tay-Sachs disease and selfishness are more common in some local cultures than others, and yet they seem to endure. In this version of the debate, we assert that enough control to be meaningful can be exerted over sexual life.

### Sex Is Political

We define the political broadly to include sexual arrangements. This accords with the vision of politics associated with virtue ethics traditions (both secular and religious) and with utilitarianism. Only classical liberalism, in its historical effort to restrain murderous political conflict, drew a line between public things and private ones, relegating sex from public politics to private morality. When twentieth-century liberalism embraced sexual libertinism, it moved sex from private morality to a kind of state of nature where no limits applied.

Once we let go of the liberal notion that only state action is political, we see that standard political issues are present in even the most private sexual exchange: multiple players seeking physical access to each other; exposure to harm; the danger of overreaching and the potential for life-altering consequences. In heterosexual exchanges, the male and female sexual players start from a baseline of physical inequality of strength, size and vulnerability to pregnancy. In contemporary society, they meet in the context of an embedded hierarchy that places one over the other because of gender. Some rules for such persons to live together justly must apply.

Those rules may be formal and prescriptive, issuing from the state in the form of laws. Prescriptive sexual governance in turn may lay down boundaries for everyone, as do the criminal laws. Or the rules may be discretionary, as are laws that provide for a civil action allowing a person to decide whether a particular sexual exchange has caused harm. Rules may be social, a form of governance based on informal sanctions and ideology. Finally, sexual regulation may take the form of deregulation, which includes the absence of regulation, and also delegation of power from the collective body of the state to the strongest private players.

Most existing analyses of sexual regulation focus exclusively on the prescriptive model of state-enforced prohibitions. Foucault, however, reframed this focus by directing attention to the multiple manifestations of sexual regulation. When a priest hears a confession of misconduct or a doctor prescribes a regimen of cold water for masturbation, Foucault observes, an act of sexual regulation takes place.

As regulation, these acts involve the criteria for political concern, even if they do not involve official state action. We have been influenced by Foucault's critical insight that sex is a product of power relations and a producer of power relations, and his exposition of the sexual politics in the most apparently private and individualistic exchanges: "My main concern will be to locate the forms of power, the channels it takes, the discourses it permeates in order to reach the most tenuous and individual modes of behavior, the paths that give it access to the rare or scarcely perceivable forms of desire, how it penetrates and controls everyday pleasure." Foucault brings to the analysis of sexuality a definition of power fundamental to any understanding of modern politics.

It is not a coincidence, we believe, that Foucault's pervasive power resembles the power analysis of our second source of inspiration, that most seminal of thinkers about power, early modern philosopher Thomas Hobbes. As in Hobbes's vision of the natural state, Foucault's power is rooted in the physical body, pervasive in all human relationships (rather than being concentrated in the decrees of the state), and set in motion by peoples' imaginings. Foucault adds to Hobbes's structure that in every transaction the more powerful player attempts to impose on the imaginings of the other players his own version of the weaker's imaginings, but this addition to Hobbes reflects the centuries of focus on the psychological that succeeded Hobbes's time. It is difficult to imagine that Hobbes, who saw the possibilities for domination everywhere, would turn away from this new source of imposition.

At the core of our project, too, is the recognition that most sex between men and women occurs in private, dispersed, and unofficial circumstances. In a variety of settings from the passionately spiritual to the grimly commercial, private parties of unequal bargaining power seek to come together to accomplish their ends. They do so through a series of decentralized and often subtle exchanges almost entirely beyond the power of the state to regulate directly. When private transactions involve people of unequal bargaining power who seek different ends, such exchanges raise the question of how the differences will be resolved. Yet the physical, psychological, and social realm of sexuality is one in which people highly prize freedom and individuality, meaning that any effort to control sex also invokes people's fiercest defense of their liberty. All of these factors present a hard problem for politics. We propose to solve these problem with the relatively recent technology of bargaining theory.

## HETEROSEXUAL EXCHANGES AS A GAME

### A Short History of Bargaining

The explicit application of bargaining theory to politics is a recent phenomenon in intellectual thought. We add to this insight recognition of the political nature of sexual exchanges, leading to our analysis of the covert and discrete process of bargaining over sexual transactions as an instance of political behavior. Since this work is so new, we will lay out our theoretical groundwork on bargaining in detail.

Bargaining theory, or game theory, as it is called, grew from the work of the mid-twentieth-century mathematician John von Neumann for the purpose of predicting peoples' self-interested, uncoordinated behaviors. Game theory was used at first mostly in economics to analyze, for instance, when businesses would choose to compete with other businesses. Recent work applies the model to other situations in which people behave rationally, including the question of how legal rules will affect choices. For example, legal scholars use game theory to predict how different rules of liability for accidents will affect peoples' decisions to take precautions. Political philosophers apply von Neumann's models to the classic social contract problem of bargaining for the formation of the state itself, analyzing how self-interested people would calculate the benefits and burdens of laying down arms and forming the state.

Game theory starts with the hardest bargaining problem where each player has a strong preference to get what she or he wants without having to deal with the other player at all. For example, in the case where two farmers live side by side, each would prefer to take all the other's crops without any payment rather than negotiate an ordinary sale of goods, even if both would be better off if they did not live in fear of one another. In sex, this most undesirable situation arises where a rapist seeks to impose himself sexually on another person without having to accommodate the victim at all. The victim, in turn, seeks to avoid the rapist altogether, if not to rape in turn. There is no acceptable private bargaining solution to this kind of situation. Accordingly, societies usually elect to restrain the predatory farmers with laws against theft, and the rapist likewise. These laws force predators into bargaining; that is, the rapist must find someone who is willing to bargain with him for sex, and the farmer to trade, meaning in both cases that he must offer to pay at least some price to gain his desired end.

Most heterosexual exchanges are not such a losing game. Assuming some quantity of natural desire, sexual bargaining between women and men more resembles the model or "game" that bargaining theorists named "The Battle of the Sexes." In The Battle of the Sexes, two players, one male and one female, would rather spend the evening together than seek satisfaction on their own. The problem is that he wants to spend the evening at a prize fight, but she prefers the ballet. Recasting this problem in sexual terms, each would prefer to have sex with the other than remain celibate or masturbate. But, for example, he prefers to have a sexual relationship on terms of her fidelity and his freedom. She, on the other hand, prefers sex on terms of equal fidelity, or even the reverse of his scenario. The Battle of the Sexes poses the question of whether they can agree at all, and if so, on what terms?

In a recent analysis of the heterosexual family, negotiations theorist Rhona Mahony applies this bargaining model to the division of labor in the home. Both husband and wife prefer living together in a well-maintained household as opposed to living alone, but they disagree about who should do the housework. Mahony shows that predicting who will do the dishes is as appropriate a subject of bargaining theory as who will lay down arms or lower a price. In applying game theory to the act of male-female sex itself, we take Mahony's work behind the bedroom door.

## The Terms of Bargaining

For bargaining to occur, four conditions must exist: people must be interdependent, their interests must conflict, they must have some options, and there must be room for agreement. All the conditions for bargaining exist in the male-female sexual exchange. Potential partners are interdependent, possess somewhat conflicting agendas, have options, and can compromise.

### Men and women are sexually interdependent

Unless people are completely indifferent to sexual experience, potential sexual partners are by definition interdependent. How interdependent they are depends, critically, on how flexible sexual desire is. If desire naturally exists, but its object and content are socially constructed, then men, women, children, and, presumably, animals, can be substituted one for the other, depending upon the circumstances. Thus creatures might need each other for sex, but males and females do not necessarily need one another.

History reflects that at least some of the content of what is felt as erotic at any time in history is a product of culture. Given this, whether the natural measure of heterosexual desire is strong, moderate, or weak is unknown. If reproduction is part of the sexual payoff, male-female coupling will be more desirable. Many cultural forces also intensify the appeal of heterosexuality. In fact, humans do reproduce sexually and have survived. Accordingly, we take the existence of the species to stand for some irreducible minimum of heterosexual desire, no matter what the cultural context.

### Men and women have some conflicting interests

Men and women may have conflicts as men and women, or as individuals. Although sociobiologists speculate that natural selection has created complementary sexual agendas of dominance and submission between males and females, females have interests that are not wholly congruent with the sociobiological view of male sexual strategies. For instance, females may need help in child-rearing, or may not want to have to market themselves sexually when old. History contains an ineradicable record of women's struggles to modify or escape from the subordinate position that evolutionary biology predicts they would embrace. Indeed, even if sociobiologists are right and women do enjoy some measure of sexual subordination, being dominated may be just one aspect of their pleasure.

Individual females may well differ concerning when, where, how often, how much, and what is the price for sex with subordination. So conflict exists between the sexual agendas of males and females. Absent or outside inherited preferences, people may also disagree on a whole range of issues that bear on a sexual agenda, like who does the housework or childcare. So conflict also may exist between individuals.

*Options are possible in heterosexual exchange*

For players to behave strategically, each must have some options. The options do not have to be either numerous or generous. To take the classic example, when a captive agrees to slavery rather than be killed, the choice of enslavement is the making of a bargain. Sex almost always involves a wider range of options than this. For instance, if the stronger sexual player prefers to have sex with a willing partner, the weaker gains in bargaining power because she can refuse consent. The strong also may be constrained by the state in the strategic uses of that superior position, by the law of rape, for instance. Or the weak may act collectively to restrain the powerful through the informal structures of civil society. If a family presses a seducer into marriage through shame, gossip, or boycott, for instance, the stronger player's advantage is diminished. The opposite, of course, is also true: The strong may use the state as an efficient enforcer of their will, or may use ideology to weaken the weak further. But in almost any scenario, there is room for at least some sexual bargaining between males and females.

*There is room to come to agreement*

Bargaining requires that there be room for agreement. In other words, can either party tolerate yielding some part of her or his optimal outcome to the needs of the other? Sociobiology denies that men and women can compromise. In the face of the inexorable pressure of natural selection, any compromise from the optimal evolutionary strategy makes the species vulnerable to extinction. In any less determinist worldview, however, people can find almost countless sexual arrangements that yield some satisfaction to each, without dying from it.

## The Background Conditions of Bargaining

Game theory does not stop at predicting when bargaining will occur. Indeed, the point of the analysis is to predict bargaining outcomes, that is, the content of the bargain that will result based on conditions at the time of negotiation. That prediction rests on understanding what would happen if the parties do not agree. Bargaining theorists such as Mahony call this the best alternative to a negotiated agreement, or BATNA. Like so much of bargaining theory, a version of the BATNA first appears in Hobbes's work. People desire to dominate each other; fearing domination, each person is motivated to attack the other; life is, famously, "solitary, poor, nasty, brutish and short." Given this fate, Hobbes predicted that people would agree to take any negotiated agreement, even at the expense of all of their liberty, because the next best alternative, the state of nature he described, was so intolerable. In the centuries since Hobbes wrote, no one has found a better way to explain the existence of the state than to compare it to the state of nature.

Mahony also notices a dynamic that Hobbes, with his focus on single transactions, missed: Once a player makes one bad bargain, she or he is weakened in future bargaining. There is a downward spiral when two unequal players meet repeatedly to bargain. For example, once a weak player bargains away a job opportunity in exchange for marital security, she is less marketable, and the stronger player can extract even greater concessions the next time. Law professor and property theorist Carol Rose adds another dimension to the problem of the downward spiral. The expectation of relative value, which can result from nothing more than the natural inequality of physical assets accelerates the process, because when women come to negotiate for a marriage bargain or for the distribution of domestic burdens, they are perceived as weak and so are challenged at every turn. (Rose uses the example of the husband who without argument shares the cooking chores with his camping buddies, but puts up a relentless fight when asked to take up slack in the household he shares with his wife.) Challenged at every turn, women will tire of fighting for the things men get without a fight. Failing to fight, women will be perceived as weaker still, and offered still worse bargains. And so the spiral goes.

In the sexual state of nature where, by definition, there is no law, sexual bargainers negotiate based on natural endowments of strength and other physical realities, from the position they occupy in a social order, and in response to the psychological value of consensual sex. In the male-female sexual bargain, women as a group are smaller and weaker than men, vulnerable in childbirth and nursing, and as a social group, poorer and less well-positioned. In short, their BATNA is generally unattractive, except for the value of their good will.

In any state other than the state of nature, social facts like economic power, cultural status, and legal rights provide a significant measure of the initial distributions of the BATNA. Accordingly, although bargaining is not law, even what seems like private sexual bargaining takes place in the shadow of the law. Any realistic analysis of sexual governance, therefore, must recognize the role of law and social facts providing the background alternatives for one-on-one sexual bargaining.

Sexual bargaining happens despite the cultural association of male-female sex with unreasoning romance and passion. Indeed, bargaining analysis and much of modern politics derives from Hobbes's attempt to understand and control violence, the most ungovernable of human passions, with its roots in anger, pride, and fear. Classic problems of bargaining theory, such as how to deter soldiers from deserting in times of paralyzing fear and mortal peril, assume people can rationally calculate even in the presence of powerful emotions. So, too, incompletely rational behavior exists even in that paradigm of rational bargaining, the marketplace. Despite examples of impulsive market behavior, no one questions the basic insight that demand usually goes down when the price goes up.

ℬℬℬ

Knowable, both natural and cultural, a subject of politics and subject to bargaining, sex between males and females is a critical element of any human society. With these assumptions, we begin our story.

## NOTES

A good treatment of the role of skepticism in modern political philosophy is William A. Galston, *Liberal Purposes: Goods, Virtues, and Diversity in the Liberal State* (Cambridge: Cambridge Univ. Press, 1991), 11, 79.

On the social constructionist view of sexual personhood, see Michel Foucault, *The History of Sexuality*, trans. Robert Hurley (New York: Random House, 1990), and on the determinist view of sociobiology, see David M. Buss, *The Evolution of Desire: Strategies of Human Mating* (New York: Basic Books, 1994).

Good summaries of the assumptions of virtue ethics, classical liberalism and utilitarianism appear in Galston, *Liberal Purposes*, Michael Sandel, *Liberalism and the Limits of Justice*, (Cambridge: Cambridge Univ. Press, 1982) and "The Procedural Republic and the Unencumbered Self," Political Theory 12/1, 1984, and Will Kymlicka, *Contemporary Political Philosophy: An Introduction* (Oxford: Oxford Univ. Press, 1990).

The chief advocates of sexual skepticism and ungovernability include Ronald Dworkin and Joel Feinberg. See Ronald Dworkin, *Taking Rights Seriously* (Cambridge, Mass.: Harvard Univ. Press, 1978), especially Chapter 10 ("Liberty and Moralism") and Joel S. Feinberg, *Harmless Wrongdoing* (Volume 4 of The Moral Limits of the Criminal Law), (New York: Oxford Univ. Press, 1988), Chapters 29 and 30.

Plato on Knowledge is *Theaetetus*, vol. 7 of *Great Books of the Western World*, trans. Jowett (Chicago: Encyclopedia Brittanica, 1952). The most thorough exposition of the unreliability of sense data in the ancient tradition was Sextus Empiricus, one of the last of the Pyrrhonian school from Roman times. See Philip P. Hallie, ed., *Scepticism, Man, and God: Selections from the Major Writings of Sextus Empirixus* (Indianapolis: Hackett, 1986); on private language (green and blue), see Saul A. Kripke, *Wittgenstein on Rules and Private Language* (Cambridge: Harvard Univ. Press, 1982).

Among the most important virtue revivalists are the liberal feminist Susan Moller Okin, classicist Martha Nussbaum, virtue theorist Philippa Foote, liberal thinker William Galston, economist Amartya Sen, and the last works of the late philosopher Judith Shklar.

Kant on male-female sex is found at Immanuel Kant, *Lectures on Ethics*, trans. Louis Infield (New York: Harper Torchbooks, 1963), 163-64.

David M. Estlund, "Shaping and Sex: Commentary on Parts I and II," in *Sex, Preference and Family: Essays on Law and Nature*, eds. David M. Estlund and Martha C. Nussbaum (New York: Oxford Univ. Press, 1997), 148, 154-55.

Foucault's quote concerning "the forms of power" and "how it penetrates and controls everyday pleasure," is found in Foucault, *History of Sexuality*, at 11.

Rhona Mahony specifies the conditions of bargaining in *Kidding Ourselves: Breadwinning, Babies and Bargaining Power* (New York: Basic Books, 1995), 37. In the legal literature, a cogent discussion of gender relations and bargaining theory is Carol Rose, "Women and Property: Getting and Losing Ground," *Virginia Law Review* (1992): 421.

Three contemporary political philosophers returning to Hobbes and applying game theory insights to the question of state formation are Jean Hampton, *Hobbes and the Social Contract Tradition* (Cambridge: Cambridge Univ. Press, 1987); Gregory S. Kavka, *Hobbesian Moral and Political Theory* (Princeton: Princeton Univ. Press, 1986); and David Gauthier, *Morals by Agreement* (New York: Oxford Univ. Press, 1987).

"The Battle of the Sexes" was first modeled by R. E. Luce and H. Raiffa, *Games and Decisions* (New York: Wiley, 1957).

The phrase "bargaining in the shadow of the law" is from a foundational work in legal sociology, Robert H. Mnookin and Lewis Kornhauser, "Bargaining in the Shadow of the Law: The Case of Divorce," *Yale Law Journal* (1979): pp. 950, 980 (legal rules as background rules for private ordering).

# 3

## REDISCOVERING EARLY WORLDS

Every story of western culture starts somewhere in the ancient Near East: in Athens, Jerusalem, and the Roman Empire, pagan or Christian. Nowhere is this more real than in political thought, where every major theme—the state, personhood, citizenship, democracy—eventually can be traced to antiquity. Each ancient culture left behind a fragmented record of how law and custom governed sex between males and females, and it is from these fragments that the legal, religious, and philosophical underpinnings of contemporary society grew. Classical Greek and Roman society organized itself around natural hierarchies, of which the sexual preeminence of men over women was fundamental. For elite men of the citizenry, sexual relations had political dimensions, and it was accepted that a good society should be organized to provide the sexual liberty, variety, and sociability necessary for their human flourishing. By contrast, for those cast as natural subordinates such as women, children, and slaves, the principal sexual as well as political virtue was fidelity. Biblical and rabbinic Jewish writings reflect an effort to set Jews apart from pagans by expecting greater sexual discipline of the covenant people, yet Jews shared with their neighbors both a regard for the earthly joys of sex and a firm commitment to gender hierarchy. Later, the strands of earthy physicality in Judaism would come to distinguish it from Christianity.

Christianity usurped these ancient traditions, and from the dissident Jesus movement to the institutional Roman Catholic Church in Europe, it is Christianity that dominates any history of western sexual regulation. Yet Christianity is itself a syncretic tradition, shaped by its incorporation of and responses to its classical and Judaic ancestors. From the outset, Jesus' followers defined themselves by an austere sexual morality that elevated celibacy over physicality and thus the mind over the body. With the rise of the institutional church, the radical meanings of this chastity were replaced by an uneasy accommodation with sex, at least within monogamous heterosexual marriage. The Church often depicted sex as defiling and guarded against its dangers (especially in the form of the female body) more than celebrated its blessings. Protestants honored sexual marriage more highly than Catholics and consequently sought to elevate the status of women to make them worthy marriage partners. Protestants also denied that marriage was sacred, however, treating it instead as a problem for human governance, a secularization that opened the door for reform of sexual regulation in accordance with human need and social condition.

With the Renaissance and the Enlightenment, secular philosophy largely replaced divine revelation as the ground of political authority. Modern political theory challenged the core concept of natural relationships of status, first on grounds of rough equality of physical strength and ultimately on grounds of moral equality. (Secular equality paradoxically derived in part from Protestant notions of the soul.) Although the inconsistency between theories of individual equality and hierarchical sexual and familial arrangements surfaced as early as the seventeenth century in the work of Thomas Hobbes, classical liberalism sidestepped the problem by casting sexual inequality into the ungovernable realm of "nature" and leaving it to preexisting non-state authorities like the Church. Later modern sexual theory developed the concept of opposite sexes, which substituted natural difference for natural inequality as the enduring basis for gender hierarchy.

Many recent inquiries into sexuality focus heavily on the past. As modern western societies moved sex out of the realm of enforced Christian morality and into a sphere of deregulated private choice, critics of tradition often looked to the distant past to criticize the present. Because the liberal state's enforcement of Christian sexual morality rested in part on the assumption that this morality was both natural and universal, one strategy of those seeking to dismantle the sexual regime has been to disprove its naturalness or universality by pointing to examples of quite different sexual codes in pre-Christian and non-Christian societies. Pre-Christian Greece and Rome especially intrigue those seeking, for example, to undermine the idea that homosexuality has always and everywhere been condemned. In 1993, challengers to the constitutionality of Colorado's anti-gay legislation called upon classicist Martha Nussbaum to give legal evidence of the moral acceptability of male homosexuality to the ancient Greeks.

We have a different purpose in revisiting these early worlds. This chapter moves selectively from Plato to the Bible to Aquinas to Hobbes to the Puritans of early modern England, offering brief sketches of crucial issues without which we believe it is impossible to understand modern thinking about heterosexuality and its regulation. This is not a history of ancient, medieval, and early modern European heterosexualities, but rather an intellectual genealogy that lays the groundwork for the chapters that follow. There is adequate evidence to support some analysis. Because, however, much material is fragmentary and deeply contested, we limit our conclusions to the core issue of sexual regulation and its effect on sexual bargaining between men and women. We will not evaluate ancient and medieval sexual codes and practices according to the ends of modern philosophies here. Virtue ethics was the only enduring secular philosophy in existence at any of the times we describe, and much of our presentation consists of an analysis of the sexual teachings in the foundational writings of virtue ethics—the works of Plato and Aristotle. To impose schools of thought from centuries later seems artificial. We focus in particular on themes and issues that resurface in American sexual regulation, which is where our historical account is heading.

## JERUSALEM, ATHENS, AND ROME

The very existence of evidence about the ancient western world is disputed. To the extent that this contested and fragmentary evidence is revealing, we find marked regularity across ancient Hebrew, classical Greek, and imperial Roman law governing male-female sex. Although there was no single pre-Christian sexual regime, elite men in these societies limited sexual access to women of their class by social and legal structures mandating virginity for unmarried girls and fidelity for married women. Wives and unmarried daughters of the citizenry or covenant people (that is, not slaves or foreigners) were forbidden to have sex with anyone other than their husbands, and a man was forbidden to have sex with another's wife or unmarried daughter. Men literally governed women's sexual bodies; the laws assured not only that men had sexual access to a range of women, but also that they could exclude other men from sexual and reproductive access to certain women. These early cultures do not appear to have been morally offended by nonmarital sex per se (as would characterize Christians, for example, in later centuries), believing instead that what we call adultery or fornication by females violated a patriarch's personal right to exclusive sexual access of his wife and control of the sexuality of the unmarried females of his household.

These societies treated a wife's betrayal and the trespass of her lover in adultery seriously. In most, a husband was expected to kill the adulterous couple without resort to law. Even after law began to replace private vengeance with public justice for crimes such as homicide, many ancient legal codes still left the husband a private option to revenge adultery by killing his wife and her lover, especially if he caught them in the act. Biblical Jewish and Roman law ultimately asserted the community's monopoly over private vengeance, criminalizing adultery as a moral offense not simply against the husband but also against the community, and punishable only by law and after trial.

The ancient laws against sex outside marriage were directed exclusively against the unfaithful wife or rebellious daughter and her lover; the adulterous husband or unmarried man, by contrast, faced no sanction for nonmarital sex (unless he chose a married woman or the unmarried daughter of the citizenry or covenant people for his sexual partner). An interesting twist on this treatment of women as sexual property is found in ancient Greek law. Although, for example, a Greek citizen could invoke adultery as his defense to murdering his wife's lover, he could not kill, nor would the state punish, the wife, although the husband could divorce her. Some classical scholars interpret this leniency toward female offenders as a reflection of an idea of moral disability. Lacking any capacity to make a moral judgment, a woman could not be held legally accountable for her sexual errors.

By contrast to the tight sexual controls on women of the covenant people or citizen class, Jewish, Greek, and Roman law and custom generally allowed men a wide range of sexual possibilities. Jewish men, for example, could keep multiple wives, maintained concubine-like matrilineal wives and bondwomen with whom they sexually consorted (like Abraham's Hagar; see Genesis 16), and there were what we might now call streetwalkers and other harlots. In addition to wives, Greek men had relations with concubines, hetaerae, and prostitutes, as well as schoolboys of the citizen class. Roman law exempted a man's relationship to concubines and prostitutes from the laws against adultery and other forms of sexual indecency. In pagan households, a master had the right to the sexual services of his slaves. The sexual pleasure of this ruling class was qualified only by restraints based on respect for the interests of other elite men to assure paternity of legitimate offspring and respect for exclusive use of women in the household.

If the ancient sex codes tightly controlled women's behavior, any defense of women's personal interests was virtually absent. This is most evident in the treatment of rape and other sexual overreachings—those heterosexual acts in which the interests of men and women most clearly clash. Adultery (to which the errant wife usually consents) and not rape (which violates the victim's will as well as her body) was the gravest sex crime. Even where rape was punished, a rapist did not pay damages to the victim; damages were paid to the husband or father whose rights to exclude other men from her sexual body had been disrespected by the violation.

The ancient regimes also imposed a hierarchical division among women based on sexual function; sexually exclusive objects like wives occupied the top rung; objects of sexual sharing like concubines and prostitutes filled progressively lower ranks. These distinctions usually reflected lines between classes as well, with wives drawn from the citizenry or covenant people, and aliens and slaves providing the shared sexual services. The lowest level of sex providers almost always were outsiders. In his speech against Neaira, a woman accused of passing herself off as a citizen and legitimate wife although she was in fact both a foreigner and a courtesan, the Athenian advocate Appollodorus, argues that the three classes of women must be kept separate: "We have courtesans for pleasure, concubines to look after the day-to-day needs of the body, wives that we may breed legitimate children and have a trusty warden of what we have in the house." Most modern interpreters treat this fragment of legal rhetoric as evidence of the legitimacy of nonmarital heterosexuality, including prostitution, and as evidence that the role of chastity in Athenian public life was to ensure the citizen class that it was reproducing itself (and no one else), passing its lands along class lines, and ensuring a steady supply of citizen warriors.

The hierarchies that are the organizing principle for ancient sex codes rested on philosophies of social order that openly acknowledged heterosexual exchange as a relationship of political consequence. The sexual relationship between males and females was one of natural, lifelong, and eternal hierarchy. Aristotle, who argued

from the natural as the standard for the moral, is perhaps the most famous exposi-
tor of this view, using the male-female relationship as the natural place to develop an ethics of inequality: "[A]s the first elements into which a living being is
resolved are soul and body, as soul is made up of rational principle and appetite,
the family of husband and wife, property of master and slave." Again, in the
*Eudemian Ethics*, Aristotle uses the husband-wife relationship to illustrate the
proper relation between a benefactor and beneficiary, noting that it would be
"ridiculous" for the beneficiary to expect an equal return of love, just as one cannot expect a god to love one as he is loved. In the *Politics*, he points to the family
as home to many relationships of inequality: A father rules his children royally
and a husband rules his wife "aristocratically," whereas brothers are like the
equals in a political commonwealth. Although Aristotle admits that both husband and wife are free, the hint of equality is trumped because "[t]he male is by
nature fitter for command than the female." Being natural rulers, Aristotle advises, men must exercise the virtues of rulers, including self-control and moderation; after all, the children one day will be citizens, and "[h]alf the free persons in
a state are women." For their part, being natural subjects, women must exercise
the virtues of subjects, principally obedience and loyalty.

Oppressive as these words from the classic age of Athens sound to modern ears,
an even more ancient storyteller in the Greek tradition—the poet Hesiod—is the
source of the Greek version of the durable belief in the sexual woman as world-
destroyer. In Hesiod's tale, Pandora, through her allures, seduces mankind into
opening a box from an angry Zeus and letting escape all the troubles of the world.

Foucault's work on the sexual culture of pre-Christian societies has popularized the interpretation that sexual relationships, including the political hierarchy
between husband and wife, rested on an opposition between activity and passivity
that applied more generally in Greek sexual morality. According to this reading,
Greeks understood both heterosexual and homosexual intercourse as an act of
one who penetrates (the active partner) and one who is penetrated (the passive
partner). The Greeks accepted male-male sexual activity, and in some instances
even praised such alliances as morally worthy. But where they enjoined celibacy
or self-control, it was because in male-male intercourse one person must play the
woman, the passive role, and this passivity is morally dangerous for a male. Boys
and youth were not stigmatized by being chosen to be the intercourse partner to
an older man, however, because it was understood that the passive male always
could switch to the active role, and was expected to do so upon adulthood. Regardless of whether all such claims can be substantiated, the many uncontested
statements from Aristotle's works, as well as the provisions of Athenian sex law
and custom, support a vision of women sealed forever into the lower ranks. In a
penetration-driven sexual morality, women could only be acted upon sexually
throughout their natural lives.

Turning to our analysis of sexual bargaining, in a world in which physical strength was celebrated, women had little bargaining power. The foundational story of Greek culture, Homer's *Iliad*, opens with a quarrel between Agamemnon, the king, and his best soldier, Achilles, over who will get Achilles's sex slave, Briseas, captured during the Trojan war, after the gods demanded Agamemnon's return of Chryseis, the sister of Briseas. Clearly, the wishes of the two females, captured and allotted to the heroes' beds, play no role at all. Even Chryseis's return was the result of a plea to the gods from her father, a priest. The sexual politics of the *Iliad* are particularly revealing in that the war began in the first place because Agamemnon was pursuing the Trojan prince Paris, who eloped with his brother's wife.

There is some evidence that Athenian women were shielded from the full force of physical dominance because their cooperation in sex was valued. In Homer's other great work, the *Odyssey*, the hero's wife, Penelope, manages to stave off the powerful men who seek to conquer her while her husband is absent in part by guile, delaying the time of her "decision" among the suitors. Guile can be a weapon only where the female's agreement to sex has value. Penelope was the wife of a great king, so she may have been particularly protected in ways that even the priests' daughters of the *Iliad* were not. But Hesiod's rabid assault on women, including the Pandora story, reflects something more than mere disdain for an object of physical conquest. If a woman's agreement to sex had no value, social commentators would not have bothered to criticize women for their shrewishness in devising "anguishing miseries for man," as Hesiod put it. Men would simply have wielded their superior strength and ignored women's sharp words or guileful stratagems.

The ideology of natural hierarchy in Aristotle and other sources ranking women according to their services to the men of the citizen class worked powerfully, however, to undo the value of female consent in sexual bargaining. Athenian women were taught to expect to consent in accordance with their place in the natural order, and men learned that any accommodation to women in order to gain consent was an exercise of their virtue as natural rulers, and not a concession to women's just claims. In this way, although Aristotle's plea to men to govern their wives "aristocratically" reined in the most extreme savagery, women might perversely have been better off in the savage world of Homer and Hesiod where there was no virtue in submission, and where their castigation for villainy and guile at least marked a kind of respect.

Compared with Aristotle, and based mostly on a dialogue about political utopia, Plato often is cited as an early advocate for sexual equality. In the *Republic*, Plato suggests that women as well as men might be the guardian rulers of the city. Plato comes close to egalitarianism when he suggests that women's physical differences from men must be limited to the tasks for which such difference is relevant: If females can do their gymnastics, they should be allowed to play. Although the *Republic* seems to suggest that equality is possible, the essay is principally concerned with the conflict between loyalty to the family or clan and loyalty to the city, or patriotism. Plato suggests that the guardians of the state must share all things in common, thus eliminating the household altogether. Platonic guardians copulate at set times and raise children collectively so that they can go back to the business of ruling the state.

Although the connection is only implicit, the *Republic* is remarkable for its hint that male sexual dominance can be solved only by replacing the sexual and reproductive family, thus abandoning intimate heterosexual community. Accordingly, despite its reputation as a work of corrosive political imagination, the *Republic* suggests no more than that there can be equality between sexually active women and men only in a context lacking intimacy. This does not solve, but merely sidesteps, the problem of two unequal players making a moral and sexual life together.

In *Symposium*, Plato addresses the subject of love directly, in what is surely the oldest explicit western theory on the subject. Through three primary speakers, he suggests three explanations. Aristophanes, the comic playwright, tells a common myth about mankind as originally being two humans joined together (whether male-female, female-female, and male-male), and posits that the dual human was split in half as punishment for challenging the gods. Love (what we would call sexual love) is the yearning for reunion with the lost half. Agathon, a young and tragic poet of the time, describes love by describing an ideal love object—young, handsome, courageous, and so on. Socrates soon dissuades Agathon of his idea, suggesting that because love is a yearning for what one lacks, under Agathon's description only the person lacking the characteristics of the love object could be a lover, that is, an ugly, old, cowardly person, a concession that Agathon is not willing to make. Instead, Socrates suggests that lovers long to possess the good, not because they are lacking in goodness, but because more of the good always will make them happy, and happiness is the highest goal of mankind. The rest of the *Symposium* is devoted to a more traditional Socratic inquiry into the nature of the good. Socrates concludes that people love by contemplating a pure beauty or goodness not corrupted by being intermingled with earthly human flesh. This ideal would come to be known in the ensuing millennia as "Platonic" love.

The connection between the discussions of sex and love in the *Republic* and the *Symposium* is not clear. The suggestion in both texts is that possessive sexual love and virtue are incompatible, whether that virtue is pure goodness in the *Symposium*, or the political virtues in the *Republic*. Socrates's rebuttal of Agathon also suggests that by casting a set of characteristics onto another person, the lover tries to possess what he is not rather than becoming it himself, which abases him by excusing him from pursuing his own full moral development. So if sexual equality is an element of political goodness (as the *Republic* suggests), possessive sexual individualism and political equality may be incompatible. But if an end to intimacy is the necessary condition for any aspiration to equality in sex, Plato's is a somewhat sorrowful vision.

From the standpoint of bargaining theory, Plato's vision of a cold equality at first looks like an improvement over natural hierarchy. Both parties to sex (Plato addresses both same-and other-sex relationships) lose the hot intimacy of possessive sexuality, seduction, and private pairing or, in the specific case of the heterosexual relationship, the reproductive family. Yet both gain virtue. In place of the passionate craving to possess a beautiful young man in the *Symposium*, the virtuous lover obtains a meritorious affection in the love of the good in the beloved and, ultimately, in the abstract form of the good not connected to any mortal human body. In place of the possessive family, the virtuous citizen in the *Republic* obtains the possibility of a good state, within which he can be a good man. Plato does not pursue, but we can recognize, the payoff to Athenian women in moving to equality and the opportunity to rule in the radical thought experiment of the *Republic*.

Plato's thought experiment was not proposed in a vacuum, however; it was posed against a social background in which women overwhelmingly were confined to the private sphere. Indeed, most scholars believe that among the citizen class in Athens during some periods, elite women were allowed outside the household only for a limited number of religious festivals. So the bargain that Plato offers citizen females in the *Republic* is the loss of everything they have known in exchange for something they have never known—a public life. He offers citizen males the loss of a piece of what they have known in their possessive relations with wives, children, and property, in return for a better version of what they have always known in an aspirational state and their roles in political governance. As between the two groups, we may predict that the females would feel their loss more keenly than the men, because people usually value what they already have—the family—more than the loss of prospects they have never known—the prospect of governance. Bargaining theory bolsters this interpretation by valuing future gains less highly than present payoffs, because of the possibility that they may never occur, and because measuring future pleasure is difficult.

In claiming that theorists of sex equality are calling for the end to all heterosexual intercourse, sexual conservatives in our own century cash in on the fact that most women will not surrender the family sphere and the limited but real power of the sexual allure they have used since Hesiod's Pandora to gain a risky and abstract prospect of equality. This calculus is blurred in modern societies of the west, because some women have public lives and most women have some political power in the form of the vote. So the magnitude of the change in their social personhood required by a unisex society is blurred. But the bargaining lesson of Plato's *Republic* is that if equality can be presented as requiring a sacrifice of sexuality and intimacy in any society with a substantial residuum of privatized and sexualized female personhood, women are unlikely to pay this high price. Only when the nuclear family and the romance of heterosexual pairing is as marginal to the lives of women as it was to the Athenian gentlemen Plato wrote for will the offer to exchange the home for the world be anything but a scare tactic.

In contrast to the sexual ambivalence of the pagans, the Jewish tradition elevated the sexual relationship of men and women, treating heterosexuality (at least within marriage) as an unambiguous blessing. It is impossible to imagine a Jewish Plato calling on the people to abandon clan loyalty in the interest of the city, or to stop copulating except with a vision of the good. So, too, scholars point out, because of the importance in Judaism of tracing the genealogy of the covenant people back to Abraham, sexual reproduction, and therefore heterosexuality, are manifestly God's will: "Be fruitful and multiply," God commanded the first man and woman at the very moment of creation (Gen 1:28). Thus Jews both valued and controlled women and their sexuality as "highly prized essentials" to fulfilling the divine purpose for the covenant people. The Hebrew Bible frankly acknowledges women's sexual needs (in Gen 3:16 God tells Eve her desire is for her husband), entitles them by law to sexual fulfillment (in both Ex 21:10 and Gen 30:14-16 a woman retains marital rights even when her husband takes another wife), and even recognizes that women harbor sexual designs (consider Potiphar's wife in Gen 39:7-18 and Lot's daughters in Gen 19:32-35). Within Jewish marriage sexual intercourse is to be free and uninhibited, except around menstruation or on certain religious holidays. Until the Essenes of the Roman period, in fact, there seems to have been no thread of sexual asceticism in Jewish culture, nor even strands of the anti-materialism evident in Plato and later in Christian asceticism. The Jewish tradition of heterosexuality is, instead, one of earthy reality.

In addition to its embrace of heterosexuality, the Hebrew Bible also contains both praise and derogation of women, a mingled message that accounts for the paradoxical estimation of women characteristic of Judaism into rabbinic times. God created Eve as Adam's companion (Gen 2:18-25), and both are made in the likeness of God. Accordingly, even the most ordinary Jewish woman has a claim to better treatment than the animals—not because of her husband's virtue, but in her own right, which is an improvement on the status of pagan women. The Bible lavishly praises the virtuous, wise, and industrious wife (Prov 12, 14, 31:10–31). Yet the Torah denigrates women in other respects. Eve plays the central role in the tale of the Fall of Man (Gen 3), the patriarch Abraham is portrayed as offering the women of the tribe to placate the needs of more powerful rulers in the region, and the moral hero Lot offers his daughters to threatening mobs (Abraham proffers Sarah in Gen 12:10–20 and Lot offers his daughters in Gen 19:4-8). Wives are included among the possessions of one's neighbor (along with his slaves, work animals, houses, and land) not to be coveted (Ex 20:17, Deut 5:21). Later biblical sources like Proverbs condemn wives as nags (Prov 21), comparing them to scorpions and dogs (Prov 26:7, 25).

Turning to the rabbinic texts, contemporary Jewish scholar Daniel Boyarin concludes that the rabbis took an "ironic double stance of both genuine empathy for women and rigid hierarchical domination of women." Boyarin notes that a Talmudic passage about the moral claims that the wronged may make when they pray to God is argued almost exclusively from examples of the claims that wives may make on their husbands. Yet Talmudic law closely confined Jewish women to a separate sphere of body and household. Although the Jews of the Roman Empire prided themselves on a sexual discipline they saw lacking in the pagan world around them, a Jewish wife could be easily put aside for another. Rabbi Hillel argued that a man could divorce his wife for any reason at all, including that she had burned the soup, and Rabbi Akiva said that a husband could put aside his wife simply because he saw another woman who was more beautiful. Yet a Jewish wife could not escape a violent or displeasing husband without his permission, but instead remained bound to marriage and family throughout her lifetime.

The many strands of Jewish tradition support several possible bargaining stances. The value of tribal reproduction gives the fertile woman some power, but that power matters little without ideological constraints on the stronger player, who can just force his own reproductive strategy. (Prohibitions on rape and seduction outside of marriage constrain this behavior to marriage, but do not otherwise rein it in.) In Judaism these constraints seem to have developed at least by the rabbinic period, with strong prohibitions on forcing sex on one's wife and exhortations to attend to the needs and desires of the weaker player. The analogy between a husband's treatment of his wife and God's treatment of the supplicant in prayer locates these constraints in the ethical construct of the Jewish God (compared with the Homeric deities), and in the Genesis story proving that even women are God's creations. Jewish sexual politics thus contained possibilities that the Greek, for all its thought experiments, did not. For the Jews, heterosexual sex always was a necessary part of any reasonable social arrangement, and the consideration accorded the weaker player stemmed not from the grace or virtue of the stronger, but from her independent connection with a divinity superior even to the strongest mortal. In this, the Jewish tradition contained some glimmerings of the much more powerful notion that would surface again in Christianity. Being God's creature commands not just minimal concern or paternal concern, by which a man may equate himself with God and deal mercifully with his inferiors, but equal concern, at least spiritually and morally. As we will see, however, when Christian equality comes into play, it carries with it the ineradicable taint of Platonic disdain for the sexual body.

Many aspects of this tapestry of ancient traditions are too distant to be relevant to modern thinking about heterosexual politics. Scholars believe the ancients controlled and sequestered their wives and daughters in part because they could not establish paternity directly. We know that they regulated sexuality from within an overarching belief in the absolute superiority of male physical strength and size, as well as an untroubled acceptance of social divisions of class and enslavement based on ethnicity, hereditary family, and the consequences of war. By contrast, moderns can control reproduction and confidently establish paternity. With the rise of industrial technology, people live more by their wits than their arms, which limits the consequences of size and strength, and hence the import of maleness. Slavery, whether from heredity or war, is morally repugnant. Thus the natural hierarchies that ordered the sexual regimes of the ancient world no longer hold political legitimacy.

Yet even this brief glimpse into the early world matters because other aspects of these ancient regimes endured in the European antecedents of modern American sex law and culture. The political vision of women as reproductive physical beings and sexual possessions, valued for their sexual beauty and fidelity, dominated by active men of superior social status, remained alive. Claims of natural hierarchy as a cover for hard bargaining persisted. What we might call the existential "problem" of heterosexuality—the ambivalence reflected in both Plato and the Hellenistic Jewish sources about merger with another through sex—also remained, and so, too, did the possible solution of achieving full humanity through celibate public life.

Aspects of the Jewish tradition also help to illuminate the sources of modern heterosexual beliefs and practices. Judaism provides an example of a gender hierarchy that did not depend either upon the conviction of women's moral inferiority (as among the Greeks) or an ascetic loathing of the sexual female body (as for Christianity), but that coexisted with a moral recognition of women as divinely conceived, human, and therefore consequential. Thus a society can respect and even honor females, and also be openly lusty in its heterosexuality, and still exclude them from full political standing. This old tradition suggests that the roots of female subordination are more complex than conventional histories allow.

## EARLY CHRISTIANS

During Jesus' life and in the first century after his death, the Christian movement was simply one of a number of messianic and millennial movements sweeping the Roman Empire. In these early years, Jesus' followers controlled no governments and had no lawmaking power. Yet early Christians marked themselves off from their pagan and Jewish neighbors by adoption of an austere sexual morality. From the beginnings of the Jesus movement, and as the Church grew in institutional power in later centuries, sexuality remained definitional of Christian identity.

Early Christians made a virtue of sexual restraint, even to the extent of celebrating celibacy as a more godly state than heterosexual marriage or any other arrangement. They tolerated marital sexuality only as a second-best alternative to celibacy. Jesus praised those who could receive this strict teaching, "who have made themselves eunuchs for the sake of the Kingdom of Heaven" (Mt 19:12), and those whose "wombs . . . never bore, and [whose] breasts . . . never gave suck" (Lk 23:29). But, in a startling departure from both pagan and Jewish law, believers forbade both women and men any sex outside of marriage—that is, adultery, fornication, or seduction. Further, Christians rejected polygamy and divorce, insisting instead upon lifelong marriage (Mt 19:4-9). The Gospels also portray Jesus as

attacking prostitution as an institution, although he did not condemn individual
harlots, and even made the scandalous suggestion that prostitutes would enter the
kingdom of heaven ahead of Jewish religious leaders (Mt 21:31-33). Christians
thus refused to accommodate the various nonmarital sexual practices commonly
permitted to Jewish and pagan men in the ancient world, practices such as multiple wives, prostitution, concubinage, and homosexuality.

In developing a distinctive Christian sexual ethic, the preference for celibacy
was of tremendous import. Jesus' call to forsake family and property (Mt 19:30;
Lk 14:26; Mk 10:29-30) was understood by his followers to mean that they should
choose celibacy and poverty to prepare for the kingdom of God. These "last days"
required sacrifices unthinkable in ordinary times. Early Christian converts walked
away from property, farming, trades. Many refused to marry, committing themselves to chastity; others, already married, lived in nonsexual unions with their
spouses. By returning to the virgin state, the celibate faithful sought to step outside
the stream of human reproductivity, thereby signaling with their bodies the beginning of the end of time. Believing that they would be the last generation before the
messianic age, human propagation no longer mattered.

It is a mistake, therefore, to see early Christian celibacy as only or mostly growing out of sexual revulsion. Celibacy was instead a means of preparing mind, body,
and soul for the end of the world. According to the Hebrew Bible, God had given
the first human beings moral freedom, but Adam and Eve had abused it. In punishment, God bound them and their generations to the wheel of sexual reproduction
and mortality (Gen 3:16-24). Jesus promised that Christians could regain what
Adam and Eve had lost, and shed their earthly burden, symbolized by their sexual
nature.

It is easiest, perhaps, to imagine why slaves and women would have embraced
such an ideal, for we know the early Church included many such socially marginalized people. For slaves and women of all classes in the ancient world, the
choice of celibacy meant a freedom unavailable anywhere else. To escape sexuality
meant to shed a servile status in which women and slaves lived for the convenience
of husbands, fathers, masters, and rulers. As religious historian Peter Brown observes, the celibate transcended the whole unequal structure of bodily existence
and dwelt instead in a spiritual realm of freedom and equality. If sexuality represented all that tightly bound the individual to the world, without sex and all that it
implied, aspects of identity as foundational as gender, ethnicity, or social class disappeared: "[Souls are] neither male nor female . . . [when] they no longer marry nor
are given in marriage" (Lk 20:35). As Brown emphasizes, the continent body was a
symbol of free choice: To renounce sexual intercourse was "to throw a switch lo-
cated in the human person; and, by throwing that precise switch, it was believed
possible to cut the current that sustained the sinister perpetuum mobile of life."

As a matter of bargaining, celibacy is a risky bargaining strategy for the weaker
player. If the stronger player places no sexual value on the weaker, and especially on

her cooperation, she is reduced in social value to the weakness of her physical body. But if it is not just the sexual body but the physical body altogether that no longer matters, an equality of souls "neither male nor female" is possible. With Christian celibacy, the Platonic bargain was again on the table: chastity for equality. This time, however, women flocked to the chance to make the trade, sacrificing known present goods for equality and, more important, the completely unknowable possibility of salvation. We can only speculate that these were truly revolutionary times.

## THE INSTITUTIONAL CHURCH

But it did not last. The radicalism of early Christianity began to erode as early as the century following Jesus' death. As generations passed and the world did not come to an end, the millennialism and radicalism of the movement faded, and Christians settled down to make a common life with their neighbors. The early Church had to invent a code of ordinary social obligation for the daily life that had little interested them before, including, importantly, sexual reproduction and household organization. Was sexual marriage godly? Was sexual activity outside of marriage permitted? Was divorce ever acceptable? Could a Christian transact with prostitutes or make sexual use of slaves? Should the roles of men and women differ with respect to these issues, and if so, how?

Twenty years after Jesus' death, Paul emerged as the principal teacher in the developing institutional church. Christian communities throughout the Mediterranean world asked for guidance, and Paul drafted a series of letters that eventually were collected in the New Testament. The Pauline letters are deeply concerned about the role of sex in Christian life. Celibate himself, Paul accepted sexual marriage and taught that those who married within the Church and refrained from extramarital sex were serving God. But he reiterated the teaching that celibacy was the more blessed state. In his letter to the community at Corinth, for example, Paul wrote that those who could not renounce sexual relations ought to marry rather than fornicate: "It is better to marry than to burn" (1 Cor 7:9).

Christians were creating scandal and controversy because of the prominence of women and people of the lower classes in the local churches, and especially the population of celibate women in these spiritual communities who lived without the discipline of a husband, father or master. In the letter to Corinth, Paul sought to make concessions and advised that Christian women must not teach the gospel and must cover their heads in church as a symbol of their natural and divinely ordained submission to men: "For man was not made from woman, but woman from man. Neither was man created for woman, but woman for man" (1 Cor 11:3-16).

Scholars argue that these accommodations to the prevailing social order were necessary if Christians were to live in this world instead of the one to come. Church leaders in the years 200-400 C.E. retreated to ancient social patterns, hon-

oring patriarchal marriage, celebrating marital sexuality, and reviving gender hierarchy. Writing about this reintegration into worldly history, Peter Brown says
that "[a] community of total celibates, and especially if it were a community in
which women and slaves realized a little of the equality promised them, in ritual
terms, at their baptism, would have been a community effectively sealed off
against the outside world."

A generation or two after Paul's letters, several of his followers wrote new letters
under his name that sought to soften some of the hostility of his stance toward
marriage and the rigor of the early movement's preference for celibacy. These
"deutero-Pauline" (literally, secondarily Pauline) letters are included in the ca-
nonical New Testament as "letters of Paul," but most modern Biblical scholars believe that only eight of the thirteen Pauline letters are authentic. A principal goal of
these forgeries was to rehabilitate Christian marriage. In the Letter to the Ephesians, for example, pseudo-Paul is positive about marriage, describing the sexual union of husband and wife as being like Jesus' love for the church (Eph 5:25-26; cf. 1
Cor 6:15-19). Importantly, this union is to be hierarchical: "[F]or the husband is
the head of the wife, as Christ is the head of the church. . . . As the church is subject
to Christ, so let the wives also be subject in everything to their husbands" (Eph
5:23-24). Timothy urges unmarried women to marry so as not to arouse controversy: "I would have the younger widows marry, bear children, rule their households, and give the enemy no occasion to revile us" (1 Tim 5:14). The later gospels,
also written many decades after Jesus' death, take up this moderating project as
well, attempting to tone down the more radical of Jesus' sexual teachings. (Although the gospels all purport to be accounts of Jesus' life and words, all were written after his death, and the later gospels are the work of believers who likely never
saw Jesus alive.) The gospel according to Matthew, for example, softens Jesus' un-
compromising position on divorce: Although divorce should remain a last resort, it
is acceptable on grounds of adultery (Mt 5:32, 19:9).

The sexual ethic of the institutional Church turned out to be just a somewhat
stricter version of traditional Jewish morality—more hostile to divorce, less cele-
bratory of marital sex, and less tolerant of extramarital sex for men through fornication, concubinage, or prostitution. Even the revisionist affirmations of sexual
marriage and reproduction, however, did not entirely erase the ambivalence toward sexuality and the body forged in the earlier phase of the Christian movement. For more than a millennium to come, most Christians would marry and
procreate, but this path always would represent some sort of human weakness.
What had been distaste for the bondage of tradition in the early years of the Jesus
movement was translated by the institutional Church into a belief that the sexual
body, especially the female body, bound the soul to sin and death.

In a related move that would shape Christian understandings of female sexuality
for centuries to come, the writers of the later gospels also made the claim that Jesus
had been born not of sexual reproduction (and thus of the sexual female body), but

instead of the virgin body of Mary. (Importantly, this claim is not made in the gospel according Mark, the earliest gospel, which scholars believe was written within a few decades of Jesus' death, but instead in the later writings of Matthew and Luke.) If the ancient world thought female sexuality was dangerous and uncontainable, a woman's body nonetheless commanded respect and even awe for its generative power. By denying women this power, the Church elevated the virgin female body over the sexual body of the ordinary Christian mother.

The final step in the transformation of Christianity from a radical and marginal sect into a powerful orthodoxy was the conversion in 313 C.E. of the Roman emperor Constantine. But it was with the influential writings of a fifth-century Church father, Augustine, that the taming of early Christian sexual radicalism was complete. Augustine forged the theological link between sin, death, and sex that would prove so potent in Catholic sexual doctrine for a thousand years to come. Augustine offered a sexualized interpretation of the creation story, arguing that the serpent had tempted Eve sexually, that she led Adam to disobey God by engaging in sexual relations not intended for them, and that in punishment God made his first children mortal. In subsequent Christian doctrine, this "original sin" becomes part of the human condition through the corruptions of sexuality and mortality, which to Augustine were evidence of the Fall of Man.

Contemporary religious scholar Elaine Pagels interprets Augustine's message as a reflection of the changed circumstances of his times. By the late fourth and early fifth century, Christianity no longer was a dissident sect, but instead the official religion of the world's greatest empire. Augustine's Church had become part of the state and, as such, was more concerned about order and political control than liberation of the soul, the body, or anything else. After Augustine, Pagels writes, liberty (and especially sexual liberty) becomes the forbidden fruit to Christians, and obedient submission their virtue.

By the late fourth century and thereafter, with the Augustinian condemnation of sex as the root of all sin, Christianity fairly can be described as hostile to sexuality. Nonetheless, the Church had come to theological terms with the pragmatic need to tolerate human sexual nature, even as it sought to control that nature by elevating monogamous, lifelong, reproductive, heterosexual marriage. With the alliance of the Catholic Church with secular power throughout the territory of western Europe, this doctrine soon became law.

These developments had profound effects on the politics of sexual bargaining. First, the requirement of matrimony, when made real, had the effect of raising the price of sexual access considerably. No longer could men make legitimate, socially sanctioned sexual bargains with women of structural social inferiority—concubines, non-citizen prostitutes, and so on. If men wanted legitimate sex, they had to marry. It is important to remember that the matrimonial price was set at whatever the law and custom established as the terms of marriage. For most of western history, those terms involved satisfying the bride's father or guardian as well as the minimal requirements set by the Church, not an arrangement particularly empowering to women. The marriage law allowed wives to be beaten, confined, and raped. Thus, although the price of sex was raised, women remained essentially the goods sold rather than the owners of their own selves. Even Christian monogamy usually was no more than aspirational; adultery continued to exist, defined in law as the crime of sex with a married woman. There were prostitutes. Even the clergy begot bastard children.

Moreover, Christianity changed the ideological bargaining chips, transforming Hesiod's powerful and dangerous bargainer, Pandora, into the Christian Eve. Pandora's offense was to make demands in return for sex, saying in essence to Epimetheus, "if you want to have sex with me, let me and my jar of troubles into your world." Against this early model of bargaining from inequality, the radical celibacy of the early Christians offered women the power of equality at the price of sex, which should have made bargaining unnecessary. In the institutional Church, however, women were stripped of the equality of celibacy by the rehabilitation of sexual marriage, a relationship defined, as Paul's letters make clear, by female obedience and exclusion. The surviving tradition of Augustinian celibacy, grounded in sexual revulsion, then denigrated the alternative source of female bargaining power, sexual allure. After Augustine, women were supposed to withhold and men to resist the sexual transaction. Even within marriage, sex was tainted. The delicate structure of Jewish tradition, with its rich opportunities for marital bargaining around the permitted and forbidden moments for intercourse, and the rabbinic injunctions to satisfy and not to force, was replaced by a crude cycle of temptation and sin. Why should a man aspire to happy consent when the whole exchange is sinful? How could a woman raise the value of her eroticism with skillful advertising when advertising was temptation to sin?

## THE NATURAL SEXUAL THEORY OF AQUINAS

By the thirteenth century and the time of Thomas Aquinas, the greatest Catholic theorist of sexuality after Augustine, there was a well-established system of church law and courts on the European continent, a system brought to England in 1066 with the Norman invasion. In England itself, church (or canon) courts and state (or law) courts were maneuvering for control of sexual matters. Fornication as well as all issues touching on marriage, including adultery, were canon law matters, but ravishment and rape, for example, remained in the hands of the state. When Aquinas reopened the issue of sexuality in Christian law and ethics in the late medieval world, he wrote in a climate of clear Church authority and established norms of heterosexual monogamy, and in response to an ongoing power struggle over sacred or secular control of sexual regulation.

Aquinas sought to reconcile accepted Catholic teachings with the newly discovered philosophical writings of antiquity, particularly those of Aristotle, whose theories had begun to reach Europe through contact with the Arab world. The

Aristotelian revival in Catholic Europe reopened the natural approach to problems of sexual morality: What is desirable (what Aristotle calls "virtuous") is to live consistently with one's natural end, or *telos*. Precedent and even Biblical text, therefore, no longer were the only sources against which the morality of a sexual act or desire could be measured; instead, Aquinas taught, we must ask what is the sexual *telos* of the human being. In this emphasis on nature, Aquinas had revived the ancient tradition of reasoning from actual earthly events and things, including from sense data. Like Aristotle, Aquinas's natural inquiries led him to conclude that human nature is revealed in man's and woman's physical activities, including the causal relationship between sex and reproduction. This naturalist methodology marks a break, critical for the history of sexual regulation, with the Platonic antimaterialism of early Christianity, as well as with Paul's and Augustine's sexual teachings. Aquinian "naturalist" reasoning helps to explain, for example, why the common law describes sodomy, referring both to oral and anal sexual acts (whether heterosexual or homosexual) that have in common only the fact that they cannot lead to reproduction, as a "crime against nature."

Aquinas departed from the prevailing orthodoxy in not regarding sexual reproduction and the human body as corrupted. The female body, the occasion for sin to Augustine, was to Aquinas the morally neutral, although naturally subordinate, physical carrier of the human reproductive purpose. Because sexual reproduction is crucial to the common good, Aquinas saw the circumstances of male-female sexual exchange—issues of fornication, marital sex, adultery, and divorce—as suitable subjects for law, something pertaining to reason and directed to the common happiness.

Interestingly, the shift toward nature and away from original sin did not change the assumptions of female subordination, proving once again that a society does not need to be hostile to the body or sexuality to support gender hierarchy. Like Aristotle and Paul, Aquinas presumed that wives belong to their husbands and daughters to their fathers. This presumption, which Aquinas treated as a natural fact, resolved for him many issues of heterosexual morality: Adultery and seduction are wrong, because a woman under her husband's or father's control either is properly loyal and submissive (that is, she displays the virtues of one whose *telos* is to be ruled) or commits the sin of disobedience.

The assumption of female submission could not, however, answer the problem of fornication, or sex with an unmarried woman of independent status. Aquinas concluded nonetheless that any sex outside of marriage was immoral. He began from the premise that reproduction is the natural end for semen, and thus emitting semen without preserving the species is a waste (unlike, for example, perspiring). From this fragile foundation, Aquinas built the case for confining semen to the monogamous heterosexual family. Because semen naturally leads to reproduction, and reproduction would be wasted without "proper upbringing" of offspring, the family is necessary. Aquinas briefly considered one alternative to the

family—leaving women with the offspring, as some animals do—but he concluded that women cannot raise children alone. Human offspring require care for
the soul as well as the body, and men are naturally better suited than women for
moral education. Thus sexually active women and men must stay together in families until their children are morally as well as physically mature.

Not even this explanation, however, fully justified marriage for life, as the
Catholic Church prescribed. Aquinas argued that sons bring their fathers a kind of
immortality and are entitled to a father's love until the father dies. Moreover, he
noted compassionately that it would be unfair for men to leave women after the
children are raised, when female youth and beauty are gone. Finally, Aquinas
explained that this reproductive, heterosexual, lifelong marriage must also be
monogamous because infidelity weakens the one-to-one relationship of marital
friendship and casts doubt on the natural desire to know one's offspring. Through
their influence on the sexual theology of the Catholic Church in the Counterre-
formation, which we take up later in this chapter, Aquinas's theories heavily influenced sexual bargaining in the modern world.

### WORLDLY NATURALISM

The rediscovery of ancient culture in the West not only produced Aquinas's
grounded and pragmatic vision of heterosexuality, it also spawned in medieval
Europe a romantic and idealistic tradition known as courtly love. First flourishing
in the twelfth-century French courts of Aquitaine, Auvergne, and Poitou, courtly
love eventually became an ideal both of masculinity and of "true love" throughout
Europe. In its appreciation for the arts of love, as well as its luxuriance in philosophical and legal debate, the courtly love tradition evokes the habits of life and
mind of the Roman Empire. Indeed, one of the classics of the tradition—Andreas
de Capellanus's treatise, *De Arte Honesti Amandi* (On the Art of Honorable Loving)—was a reinterpretation of Ovid's *Ars Amatoria* (The Art of Loving). Capellanus recorded the decisions of "courts of love" convened by noble ladies in which
they rendered advisory opinions and prosecuted knights and ladies for violating
the "rules" of love.

The courtly love tradition focused on a nobly born knight and his aspiration to
the true love of a nobly born lady. The courtly love literature honored the cultivated virtues as markers of a man's essential quality—the capacity for love, gentle-
ness, humility, veneration, constancy, and romantic suffering. The tradition held
that the inner life of emotions was a spiritually rich path to self-discovery, and romantic love was thus a civilizing force. Noblewomen played a surprising role in
this courtly culture. The literature depicts them as having the power to grant or
withhold love to men not their husbands, publicly flatters them in song, verse, and
gesture as objects of a spiritual passion elevated beyond simple lust, depicts the no-
blewoman as a governor, even if only of the Kingdom of Love, and shows her sit-
ting among a court of women as judge of the amorous behavior of men.

Perhaps most startling, the heterosexual ideal advanced by the poets and troubadours of courtly love was essentially adulterous. True love could exist only between unmarried people; the classic pair in this literature, in fact, was an unmarried knight and the wife of a great lord. If consummated, such a union was perhaps the most deadly form of treason by a vassal against his lord. One of Capellanus's dialogues concerns a debate between a nobleman and a gentlewoman. She refuses to grant him her love because she is in love with her husband and he with her. The nobleman argues that the affection between husband and wife is not the same as true love. The couple submit the dispute to the arbitration of a "court" of noble ladies in the court of Countess Marie de Champagne. As Capellanus records, the court decides that true love cannot occur within marriage:

> We state and consider as firmly established, that love cannot assert its powers between two married people. For lovers give everything to one another freely, not by reasons of force or necessity. Married people, on the other hand, have to obey each other's wishes out of duty, and can deny nothing of themselves to one another.

In courtly love, we see the emergence of what will be a durable tradition of romantic rebellion against the strictures of socially approved heterosexuality. Courtly love stands for the idea that we can find our highest and best selves through passionate commitments to love and sex that go against the grain of social convention and political duty. Sexual rebellion thus becomes a symbol not only of individual self-realization but also of political independence from the weight of feudal obligation.

At the level of canon law and religions doctrine, Aquinas's influence waxed and waned in the coming centuries, but over time a mixture of Augustinian skepticism about the legitimacy of sexual pleasure and Aquinian emphasis on reproduction as the justification for sex grew together to form the core of Roman Catholic sexual doctrine. Regardless of the diversity of Catholic practice, as illuminated by the recent work of scholars of sexual regulation of homosexuality, secular sex law largely mirrored Catholic doctrine emphasizing a hierarchy of celibacy and heterosexual monogamy throughout the medieval and early modern period in Europe. This power would not be challenged until 1517 with the publication of Martin Luther's ninety-five theses and the subsequent rise of Protestantism.

The Reformation was a radical break with preceding centuries of Catholic thought on many subjects, but Luther's writing on sex is an oddly familiar mixture of Augustine and Aquinas. Like Augustine, Luther assumed that men and women have uncontrollable desires to fornicate and that sex is morally problematical. Like Aquinas, Luther treated heterosexual desire as natural and marriage as an institution that served the common good. He even proposed marriage as an antidote to what he ferociously attacked as the hypocritical sexual indulgence of Catholic clergy and religious.

For complex political and doctrinal reasons, Luther took the position that marriage was a secular matter, resolving the ongoing jurisdictional battle between church and state in favor of state control. Luther's argument for the state is not terribly powerful, consisting mostly of the invocation of precedent in the form of the "many Imperial decrees" governing marriage. Other Protestant founders such as Calvin argued, with somewhat more support, that treating marriage as a sacrament was recent in church history and stemmed from a misunderstanding of the Bible. Whatever the justification, the implications for sexual governance of this secularization would be enormous. If it is no longer God who joins husband and wife, then it is no sin for people to put them asunder. Luther did, in fact, approve divorce when either spouse proved incapable of marriage by adultery. If the regulation of sexuality could become an ordinary matter of public policy rather than theology, things could change without threatening the very order of creation or flouting the divine will.

Luther's sexual traditionalism thus contains seeds of an individualism, hedonism, and egalitarianism that eventually would blossom into modern sexual libertinism. Luther's proposal for clerical marriage, for example, suggests that no person be asked to forgo such a good human experience. And Luther's approval of some divorce implies that marriage should satisfy the needs and desires of women and men and not, as Aquinas had insisted, simply the claims of offspring.

Luther's embrace of the benefits of sexual marriage was one of the two or three most important developments in the history of sexual bargaining in the west. By separating marriage from reproduction, and elevating its moral value as the situs for sexuality, Luther built into his sexual ethic the need for a worthy marriage partner. Protestantism is thus tightly linked with the rise of what would come to be called "companionate marriage." Invoking companionability, generations of social reformers would argue for women's education, political citizenship, economic independence, and ultimately the full range of sexual and gender liberation. Taken together, the Protestant concessions to human sexual nature proved to be social time bombs, because not only did they fit women to be suitable sexual companions for men (albeit in a male-dominant arrangement), they equipped them with the bargaining tools to challenge the very institution of male dominance itself.

Furthermore, and in fact beginning with Aquinas, the Renaissance and Enlightenment return to classical naturalism replaced a Scripture-based morality in virtually all areas of human life. Later, just as the "naturalness" of monogamy had made the moral argument for Christian restraint in Aquinas's eyes, the very naturalness of fornication and adultery would make the moral argument for libertinism. Finally, and perhaps most important, Protestantism's claims of the primacy of individual conscience dangerously disrupted not only the hierarchy of the Catholic Church, but all received hierarchies, including that most ancient hierarchy of gender. The egalitarian promise of early Christianity surfaced once again.

In 1588, the Roman Catholic Church called the Council of Trent in order to deal with the challenge of Protestantism. The Tridentine doctrinal reforms included, among many other matters, sexual regulations, officially interpreted in the treatise *De Sancti Matrimonii*, which would serve as a standard Catholic guide to marriage until the mid-twentieth century. The Council of Trent not only did not liberalize doctrine (and thus sex law in still predominantly Catholic Europe), but returned the Church to a view more like that of Augustine. The Church abolished clandestine marriage, which defiant children had used to contract love-match marriages without parental approval. The details of marital sexuality, including such minutiae as coital position, became matters of religious doctrine. The insistence on clerical celibacy hardened and the Church stepped up its attacks on prostitution and homosexuality. The reforms also reaffirmed the divinely inspired natural order of the marital family: If there is to be sex, there must be reproductive sex; if there is to be reproductive sex, there must be sexual marriage; and it is the act of reproducing that determines a woman's position in God's creation.

The most socially constricting aspect of Catholic doctrine was this naturalization of the consequences of reproductive sex. In bargaining terms, the reaffirmation of Aquinas's belief that sex must be reproductive and that women are the natural and ordained rearers of children made a lifetime of service the price to women of heterosexual sex. This tilt in the relative bargaining positions of men and women was immunized from political debate by the claims to natural origins. As the current claims of sociobiologists reflect, there is little room for bargaining where the act is part of an immutable biology. In response to the latent liberation in Protestantism, the Reformation and Counter-Reformation struggles established the Roman Catholic Church as the center of doctrinal sexual conservatism for the coming centuries.

## EARLY MODERN ENGLAND

Along with classical philosophy and Christian doctrine, the third source of western sexual regulation is the Enlightenment. Between 1600 and 1700, the scientific theories of Boyle, Newton, Galileo, and Descartes critically changed European thought about the natural world. The new science conceived of a physical world animated not by God, but rather by inexorable natural laws setting matter in motion. Before this intellectual sea-change, many thinkers had seen matter as imbued with spiritual qualities, even divine purpose. The new materialism stripped the physical world of this other-worldly halo. Among the scientists participating in what would amount to an intellectual revolution, Aquinas's suggestion that semen had purpose, for example, was unthinkable. Semen might have color, taste, smell, or touch, but lacked a divine or a natural mission. As historian of science Margaret Jacob puts it, in the Enlightenment "nature was mechanized."

This demythologizing of the natural world greatly reduced religion's explanatory role in the West, and hence its moral authority. If the natural world could be reduced to its earthly materials, so, too, might human beings. Once humans were pulled back from the angels into the material realm, the struggle between matter and spirit in sexual morality, so much the center of the christianized Aristotelianism of Aquinas, or of Luther's struggles with the meaning of marital sexuality, changed.

No one played a greater role in translating these scientific insights into political theory than the English philosopher Thomas Hobbes. In his works, particularly *Leviathan*, a crucial foundation of modern politics, Hobbes asserts that people are but matter in motion, and our human desires but "motion . . . toward something which causes it." For Hobbes, goodness does not exist apart from desire; indeed, "whatsoever is the object of any man's appetite or desire that is it which he for his part calleth good; and the object of his hate and aversion, evil." From this description of people as little more than appetitive entities in pursuit of their desires, Hobbes drew his most famous axiom: Man seeks above all else his own good. From this insight into human nature, Hobbes worked out an imaginative sociology: Roughly equal to others in the dominant virtues of strength and cunning, man not only seeks but reasonably hopes to attain his own good. From these assumptions, Hobbes thought that people would be striving constantly to kill one another, creating an intolerable "state of nature." In the end, driven by the unbearable life their uncooperativeness had created for them, people would sit down and negotiate to cede all their political authority to a central state.

Interestingly, Hobbes did not see women and men as fundamentally different in this regard: "[T]here is not always that difference in strength or prudence between the man and the woman as that the right can be determined without war." Thus Hobbes has a just claim to be the first philosopher after Plato to have contemplated the possibility of equality between the sexes.

Nonetheless, Hobbes's work also contains the seeds of political understanding of what would happen if the sexes were not equal. In addition to his work on the state formed from bargaining among equals, he writes also of a Commonwealth by Acquisition, in which a socially or physically stronger player bargains with a weaker, offering protection from the rigors of the state of nature. In exchange, the weaker player submits to be ruled by the stronger in the new "commonwealth," with the terms of the commonwealth determined by the relative inequality of the two parties. Hobbes speculates that the sexes may be equal, but if the sexes prove to be unequal, the commonwealth by acquisition would supply a solution to their need to cooperate. Hobbes's acceptance of the legitimacy of a ransom agreement reflects that his theory would allow even the most rapacious arrangement to qualify as a "bargain."

For historical as well as intellectual reasons, the breakthrough in Hobbes's thinking did not shore up the absolutist governments he seemed to be defending. Instead, other political thinkers building on his work, chiefly John Locke, substituted an optimistic vision of human behavior in the state of nature, creating a more appealing picture of life without the state. Against this not unattractive alternative to the state, Locke and others argued, people would agree to a state only if the state treated them well, mostly by leaving them to their individual life plans. This line of thought produced the philosophy we now call classical liberalism, which would ultimately shape sexual regulation in the West. Given the subsequent influence of classical liberalism on politics, it is important to note that although this philosophy is popularly conceived in the optimistic and liberating version associated with Locke, its heart is in the darker vision of Hobbes, who explicitly contemplated the legitimacy of the most savage bargains, both private and official.

Although their thinking would play a major role in the evolution of sexual understanding and regulation, none of the early classical liberal philosophers devoted much attention to either the politics or the morality of male-female sex. After briefly contemplating the possibility of gender equality, Hobbes simply drops the subject, and Locke rather abruptly asserts that the rule of husbands over wives must be "founded in nature." As a matter of social practice, according to historian Lawrence Stone, English attitudes toward sensuality in the early modern period were freer than in most parts of Europe, and ideas of romantic love were newly important. Stone describes, for example, a "staggering" number of sexual cases in the English canon courts for the whole range of sexual misbehavior, including fornication, buggery (male-male intercourse), incest, adultery, and bigamy. So, too, the English of the early modern period married rather late: Applications for marriage licenses reflect an average bride of twenty-four years and a groom of twenty-eight years. There also was a high rate of illegitimate births, an unfailing sign of nonmarital sex. Because the English church had separated from Rome before the Tridentine reforms, English law never forbade clandestine marriage, leaving social space for couples to marry for love even without parental consent.

Although Enlightenment philosophy was inexplicit or laconic about gender relations, the same period saw some stirrings of a popular and explicit political debate about gender. Beginning in 1541 with the publication of *Schoolhouse for Women*, a lively discussion began in the pamphlet press and continued for over a century, a phenomenon now referred to as the *Querelle des Femmes*. Male critics in the *Querelle* portrayed women as shrews and seductive sirens; female defenders responded with arguments of women's virtue and against stereotyping their gender. Most radically female pamphlet writers blamed women's faults on men themselves. These attacks on women may have been reactions to the growth in female bargaining power stemming from the liberating currents of the Reformation and Enlightenment. Certainly the female participants in the *Querelle* represent a new level of independence and literacy.

Despite the increasingly liberal regime of early modern England, the common

law of coverture restricted married women's capacity for any independent economic activity. Family property laws in the sixteenth and seventeenth centuries
continued to favor husband and father, and legal treatises and popular literature
reflect that a husband could beat his wife for "proper correction." And if early
modern England celebrated female seductiveness, it also strove to maintain a double standard of sexual behavior. Law and custom tolerated male but not female infidelity in marriage, in part because the former did not threaten legitimate
inheritance. Among the arranged marriages of the aristocracy, married men kept
lower-class mistresses, and their wills reflect many gifts to illegitimate children.
Prostitution boomed, especially in the bigger towns, and particularly in London
where, Stone records, there were 20,000 to 30,000 bachelor apprentices.

Perhaps most important, the early centuries of modern Europe were the occasion for a foundational shift in the long tradition of female lustiness in the West. In
antiquity, the Roman poet Ovid had discussed whether sex was enjoyed more by
men or women, and the mythical Tiresias suffered blinding at the hands of Juno by
taking the position that women enjoyed sex more. Most ancient thinkers believed
that female orgasm was necessary to conception; given that the connection is substantially less observable (and, we know now, nonexistent) than that between reproduction and the male orgasm, beliefs about the power of female orgasm
actually reflect beliefs about female sexuality rather than bedrock biology. At the
beginning of the English Renaissance, men still treated women as creatures of insatiable lust. One such commentator, Thomas Wythorne, credited women with
the ability to "overcome 2, 3 or 4 men in the satisfying of their carnal appetites." In
1621, Robert Burton asked, "of women's unnatural, insatiable lust, what country,
what village does not complain?"

In a pathbreaking study of the social construction of sexual anatomy, social historian Thomas Laqueur uses a story about a man who had sex with what he
thought was a corpse to illustrate what he calls the "reorientation" in the sexual
functioning of men and women that began in the early eighteenth century. After
the "corpse" turned up not only alive but pregnant, the man claimed he thought
she was dead when he had sex with her. Before the early 1700s, Laqueur contends,
no one would have believed this story, thinking that female orgasm was essential
for generation. However, according to Laqueur, near the end of the Enlightenment this changed as medical science and those who relied on it ceased to regard
the female orgasm as biologically significant. Thus a "corpse" could become pregnant.

This picture of bawdy Enlightenment England is punctuated by the rising influence of Puritanism in the mid-seventeenth century. During the 1650s when
they ruled England, the Puritans banned entertainments like cockfighting and the
theater, and revived the death penalty for adultery after centuries of lax canon law
jurisdiction. Although only one poor soul was executed under the law, it is worth
noting that the condemned was female. Thus, when the first waves of English set-

tlers left for America in the 1600s, they carried with them an unsettled set of attitudes about sex between men and women. Protestantism, secularism, and the printing press had begun to transform social thought, and basic units of social organization like marriage and family were evolving, although the progress of change varied among different classes of society. Some sexual offenses continued to be treated seriously by the law, regardless of the regime in control: Rape, for example, was severely punished both in Puritan and Restoration England. Adultery, by contrast, was quite a different offense under the different regimes: Under the Crown, it was a canon law violation, punished only by shaming and religious sanction; under the Puritans, adultery was a capital offense tried in the secular law courts. Within this larger picture, depending on when settlers departed England for America and which group within English society it represented, quite divergent patterns of sexual regulation would be carried across the ocean—all under the name of "English" or "common" law.

## NOTES

Philosopher Terence Irwin defines the period of "classical thought" to the time from Homer (750 B.C.E.) to the death of Augustine, 430 C.E. Terence Irwin, *Classical Thought* (New York: Oxford Univ. Press, 1989), 1. Within that frame, classical philosophy was most fully developed in the fifth and fourth centuries, B.C.E. The Hellenistic Age dates from the death of Alexander in 323 B.C.E. and ends at the beginning of the Roman Empire in 31 B.C.E. Although Israelite beginnings are open to question, Biblical pre-exilic Jewish settlements date back at least to the middle of the second millennium B.C.E. The era of Talmud stretches from the destruction of the second Temple by the Romans in 70 C.E. to 640 C.E. Louis M. Epstein, *Sex Laws and Customs in Judaism* (New York: Ktav, 1968).

Evidence of Hebrew, classical Greek, and Roman imperial law is fragmentary and open to competing interpretations. This is especially true with respect to questions of private life. The Old Testament, for example, the best record of ancient Hebrew culture, may be the most argued-over historical record ever. Setting aside disputes over its divine authorship, the Hebrew Bible existed only in oral form for centuries (and perhaps millennia). No one knows who wrote it down, much less whether they wrote it down accurately, still less whether what was recorded reflects the reality of ancient events. Even the generous evidence of material life in the extant Hebrew Bible—cities, battles, architecture, taxes, farming practices—often comes from sources of other and neighboring cultures, like the Hittites and the Egyptians. Although many scholars describe Near Eastern archeology as surprisingly consistent with the biblical text, others equally strongly disagree. Ancient Jewish culture also spanned millennia and took place in diverse material contexts—rural and urban, literate and unlettered. Unlike the classical cultures, Judaism did not generate a body of organized philosophical speculation; beliefs must be inferred from the patchy and contested history of biblical stories and pronouncements, at least before the Rabbinic period of lawgiving.

Evidence about early Greek antiquity similarly rests on oral sources, as, for example, the heroic poems of Homer and Hesiod, from which the Pandora references are taken. Hesiod, *Works and Days*, in *The Poems of Hesiod*, trans. and ed. R. M. Frazer (Norman: Univ. of Oklahoma Press, 1983), 99. The first arguably reliable evidence of Greek law does not appear until the sixth century B.C.E., although later sources like Aristotle refer to earlier lawmakers, such as Dracon and Solon. The best source on the Greek sexual regulation we address is the record of advocates' speeches in sex cases from the notoriously litigious Athens of the classical era. See David Cohen, *Law, Sexuality and Society: The Enforcement of Morals in Classical Athens* (New York: Cambridge Univ. Press, 1991), 98–109. Like all litigation records, however, this evidence suffers from partiality, overstatement, and hearsay and, as Cohen's work reflects, is highly disputed. Roman legal history sources are perhaps the most conventional because they consist of imperial decrees laying down formal rules of law. Even when the content of the law is clear, however, what remains elusive is how law was or was not enforced, and how the governed as opposed to the governors understood the law's meanings.

For all these cultures of antiquity, the available evidence is mostly prescriptive rather than descriptive. From such records we can learn what the governors of a society thought sexual practice should be, what they regarded as natural or immutable about sexuality, and what they feared as dangerous or threatening about human sexual nature. But it is impossible to know from such sources how the ordinary man, woman, or child judged any particular sexual arrangement or act, nor how diverse individuals or groups thought about sexuality as part of self or society.

Many Greek and Roman legal principles persisted little changed into American law. The idea that a husband who kills his wife and her lover after finding them *in flagrante delicto* has shaped the enforcement of murder laws in the United States to the modern day. The notion that errant women of the elite classes have diminished moral agency and thus are less morally culpable for sexual wrongdoing than their male partners remains a powerful subtext in popular attitudes and law enforcement.

The Appollodorus quote is from Demosthenes, LIX 118–122, and cited in W. K. Lacey, *The Family in Classical Greece* (London: Thames and Hudson, 1968), 113.

Aristotle's discussion of gender appears mostly in Books I and II of the *Politics* and Books V and VIII of the *Nicomachean Ethics*. See also *Eudemian Ethics*, Book II. Aristotle, *Works of Aristotle*, complete trans., ed. Jonathan Barnes (Princeton: Princeton Univ. Press, 1984).

Foucault's discussion of the regulation of sexuality in classical Greece appears in Michel Foucault, *The Use of Pleasure, Vol. II: The History of Sexuality*, trans. Robert Hurley (New York: Random House, 1990).

The images of women in pre-Classical antiquity are from Homer, *The Iliad*, trans. Robert Fitzgerald (Garden City: Anchor Press, 1975), Book I, and Homer, *The Odyssey*, trans. Robert Fitzgerald (Garden City: Anchor Press, 1963), Book I.

Plato's discussion of sex and love appears in two dialogues: the Republic and the Symposium. Plato, *Dialogues of Plato*, trans. Benjamin E. Jowett (New York: Washington Square Press, 1980).

Our interpretation of the *Republic* rests on a reading of the texts suggesting gender and sexual equality, the description of an utopian society in which the household itself is eliminated, and the fact that the suggestion of common child-bearing and-rearing is textually placed right after the argument for gender equality.

The description of Jewish women as "highly prized essentials" in the Biblical and rabbinic Jewish periods comes from Daniel Boyarin, *Carnal Israel: Reading Sex in Talmudic Culture* (Berkeley: Univ. of California Press, 1993), 48, 77. On this point, see also Genesis 1:27, 17 and Howard Eilberg-Schwartz, *The People of the Body: Jews and Judaism from an Embodied Perspective* (Albany: State Univ. of New York Press, 1992), 22. The description of the rabbinic attitude toward women as combining empathy and domination is from Boyarin, *Carnal Israel*, 108.

On the relationship between early Christians and their pagan neighbors, see generally Robert L. Wilken, "Pagan Criticism of Christianity: Greek Religion and Christian

Faith," in *Early Christian Literature and the Classical Intellectual Tradition*, ed. Robert L. Wilken and William R. Schoedel (Paris: Editions Beauchesne, 1979), 117–34; Robert L. Wilken, *The Christians as the Romans Saw Them* (New Haven: Yale Univ. Press, 1984)

On the attraction of early Christianity to women, see Elizabeth Clark, "Ascetic Renunciation and Feminine Advancement: A Paradox of Late Ancient Christianity," in *Ascetic Piety and Women's Faith: Essays on Late Ancient Christianity* (Lewiston, N.Y.: Mellen Press, 1986), 175–208.

Our political interpretation of the meaning of sexual celibacy draws from both Peter Brown, *The Body and Society: Men, Women, and Sexual Renunciation in Early Christianity* (New York: Columbia Univ. Press, 1988), and Elaine Pagels, *Adam, Eve, and the Serpent* (New York: Random House, 1989). The "perpetuum mobile" quote is from Brown, *Body and Society*, 84–85. Brown also is the source of the account of the necessity for Christians to integrate their sexual and household practices with those of surrounding communities (54).

Those letters known to be authentically Paul's are Romans, 1 and 2 Corinthians, Galatians, Philippians, 1 Thessalonians, and Philemon. Virtually all scholars agree that Paul did not write 1 and 2 Timothy or Titus, and most scholars think that he also did not write Ephesians, Colossians, or 2 Thessalonians. See Pagels, *Adam, Eve, and the Serpent*, 23, and David L. Balch, *Let Wives Be Submissive: The Domestic Code in 1 Peter* (Chico, Calif.: Scholars Press, 1981). The "forgeries" characterization is made by Pagels, *Adam, Eve, and the Serpent*, 23–24.

The account of the emergence of the story of the virgin birth is from Elaine Pagels, *The Origin of Satan* (New York: Random House, 1995), 77, citing Raymond E. Brown, *The Birth of the Messiah: A Commentary on the Infancy Narratives in Matthew and Luke* (Garden City, N.Y.: Doubleday, 1977).

The political interpretation of Augustine's re-reading of the Creation story is from Pagels, *Adam, Eve, and the Serpent*, xxvi, 97–101.

On Church sexual teachings and secular law in medieval Europe, see generally James A. Brundage, *Law, Sex, and Christian Society in Medieval Europe* (Chicago: Univ. of Chicago Press, 1987). On the division of jurisdiction over sexual matters between canon and secular courts, see Norma Adams and Charles Donahue, Jr., eds., *Select Cases from the Ecclesiastical Courts of the Province of Canterbury c.1200–1301* (London: Selden Society, 1981), introduction, 57, 81–88, 96, 99.

On the sexual theory of St. Thomas Aquinas, see *On the Truth of the Catholic Faith*, book 3: *Providence*, trans., Vernon J. Bourke (New York: Doubleday, 1955), pts. I and II.

On courtly love, see Andreas de Capellanus, *The Art of Courtly Love*, ed. and trans. John Jay Parry (Edinburgh: Edinburgh Univ. Press, 1971). Ovid's *Ars amatoria* (The Art of Loving), the inspiration for de Capellanus, was an argument for adultery intended to instruct its readers in the ways by which men could seduce women. In the late twelfth century, probably between 1184 and 1186, Ovid was reinterpreted by one Andreas de Capellanus—Andreas the Chaplain—in a Latin treatise called *De Arte Honesti Amandi* (On the Art of Honorable Loving). The debate over love in marriage (or not) comes from ibid., book I, ch. I, dialogue 7. An argument for taking the jurisdiction of love and the women's courts seriously as jurisprudence is Peter Goodrich, "Law in the Courts of Love: Andreas Capellanus and the Judgments of Love," *Stanford Law Review* 48, (1996): 633.

On the sexual teaching of Martin Luther, as well as competing Protestant interpretations of marriage as secular or sacred, see Eric Fuchs, *Sexual Desire and Love: Origins and History of the Christian Ethic of Sexuality and Marriage*, trans. Marsha Daigle (New York: Seabury Press, 1983), 143–44; Brundage, *Law, Sex, and Christian Society*, 553.

On the Tridentine reforms, see ibid., 564.

The "mechanized nature" quote is from Margaret Jacob, "The Materialist World of Pornography," in Lynn Hunt, ed., *The Invention of Pornography: Obscenity and the Origins of Modernity, 1500–1800* (Cambridge Mass.: Zone Books, 1993), 157.

The Hobbes quotes are from Thomas Hobbes, *Leviathan*, ed. Edwin Curley (Indianapolis: Hackett, 1994), ch. 6, para. 7; ch. 14, para. 8 ("the object of the voluntary act of every man is some good to himself"). The interpretation of Locke draws from John Locke, *Two Treatises of Government*, ed. Peter Laslett (Cambridge: Cambridge Univ. Press, 1960), book 2.

On social conditions in Renaissance and early Enlightenment England generally, see Lawrence Stone, *The Family, Sex and Marriage in England 1500–1800* (New York: Harper and Row, 1979), 519–22; Jacob, in Hunt, *Invention of Pornography*, 159; Don Herzog, *Happy Slaves: A Critique of Consent Theory* (Chicago: Univ. of Chicago Press, 1989), 45. On the *Querelle des Femmes*, see Katherine Usher Henderson and Barbara F. McManus, *Half Humankind* (Urbana: Univ. of Illinois Press, 1985), 51 n.4, Herzog, *Happy Slaves*, 46 n.10.

On the emergence of the companionate marriage ideal, see Stone, *Family, Sex and Marriage*, chap. 8; Herzog, *Happy Slaves*, 61–62. But on continued restrictions on women's status, particularly within marriage, see Stone, *Family, Sex and Marriage*, 195–202 (16th century) and 330–34 (17th century); Henderson and McManus, *Half Humankind*, 29, 51.

The Wythorne and Burton quotes are cited in Stone, *Family, Sex and Marriage*, 495. On medical views of the necessity of female orgasm for reproduction, see Thomas Laqueur, *Making Sex: Body and Gender from the Greeks to Freud* (Cambridge, Mass.: Harvard Univ. Press, 1990), 2–3.

The secular punishment of adultery began under Cromwell and was abandoned in the Restoration. See Geoffrey May, "Experiments in the Legal Control of Sex Expression," *Yale Law Journal* 39 (1929): 219, 239–44.

# 4

## AMERICAN BEGINNINGS

Colonial America was a far more varied world than the familiar image of Pilgrims landing at Plymouth Rock. Even if we focus only on the European colonizers of the continent who would eventually found the United States, a comprehensive account of their American beginnings would include not only the Puritans of New England, but also English seekers of land and profit in Virginia, Spanish settlements in those parts of Mexico that are now California, Texas, and the American Southwest, Quakers in Pennsylvania, and Dutch communities in New York.

Even among outposts established by a single European nation such as England, American colonies were settled at different points of the founding nation's own history, and thus each imported a different version of the law of the mother country. Settlers to the English colonies came from varied backgrounds and for diverse purposes, from idealistic to worldly. Finally, colonies had varying degrees of independence or dependence on England, with some that were proprietary, some royal, and some corporate. Throughout the seventeenth century in England, Enlightenment materialism undermined divine authority for law and morality, but no such segregation had yet officially occurred at the time the boats sailed for Massachusetts Bay and Virginia. Accordingly, Christian teachings about sexuality imbued colonial American law.

Two colonies of English origin, Massachusetts and Virginia, left remarkably intact legal records still available to scholars. The following chapter explores sexual regulation in these colonies, but these two examples do not exhaust the seeds of the American experience. We focus on English colonies because these had the greatest lasting influence on what became the law of the United States, a law principally derived from English common law, although regionally influenced by Spanish and French law. Yet even Massachusetts and Virginia differed markedly, suggesting something of the true diversity of early American life in the European settlements.

Massachusetts and Virginia mingled strong English cultures with surprising freedom from London's political control. Legal historian Lawrence Friedman likens the initial system to the business charter of a trading company. The royal charters that created Massachusetts allowed the Puritan settlers to profess their own beliefs and develop their own politics and laws, as long as they did not contravene

"the Lawes and Statutes of England." Even this potential restriction was not enforced, according to Friedman, because in the early years England was indifferent
about governing its North American colonies. At first, a London home office
managed Virginia, but by the late 1630s Virginians were making their own local
laws.

Naturally, Massachusetts and Virginia colonists brought to the settlements a cultural memory of the English law they had known, and frequently referred in their
governance to Sir Edward Coke's treatise on English common law. But much of
that cultural memory was based on local law from particular counties or regions of
the colonists' origin, and not the common law laid down by the King's courts. Reflecting this, newly established colonial institutions differed notably from the complex and elaborate system of canon and law courts, Parliament, and monarchy in
England. Massachusetts records reflect the informality and commingling of functions characteristic of young governments. Meetings of the "general court" (the
governing body) often convened in a private home, and this single body performed at turns the executive, judicial, and legislative functions of governments.
Separation of function, formality and regularity of procedure, and organizational
depth emerged slowly, and only as the colony itself became a more established and
complex social world. In Virginia, too, a single body both made rules and decided
cases.

## TWO VERSIONS OF AMERICAN SEX

### Massachusetts

Puritan settlers brought to New England the family-centered social organization
of Protestant Europe, with its emphasis on reproductive marriage as the place and
purpose for sexuality. Settlers of the early Massachusetts colonies in Middlesex,
Plymouth, and Suffolk typically migrated in families, in a balanced ratio of women
to men, and tended to come from one region of England and a single social class.
The Puritans emigrated to establish a purer church and a godly community to
serve as a moral model for the world, a "city on a hill." This social and ideological
unity brought an unusual degree of homogeneity and closeness to Puritan settlements.

Sexual morality was a serious concern, and the close-knit and densely settled
character of New England towns and villages made it easy for the community to
enforce sexual norms. Communities often prescribed severe penalties, but in practice punished more leniently. Although, for example, the informal governing body
of Massachusetts Bay prescribed the death penalty for adultery in 1631, there is
only one reported instance of execution for the crime. Legal records are filled,
however, with reports of colonists being whipped, fined, and asked to atone publicly for fornications, adulteries, and other sexual offenses. Historian Edmund
Morgan observes that "[t]he Puritans became inured to sexual offenses, because

there were so many." Morgan describes three intertwined features of the Puritan approach to sexual regulation: They punished sexual transgressions frequently but lightly; they encouraged people to marry young; and they urged married couples to intense and interdependent cohabitation, including sexual community. From these patterns of legal and social discipline, Morgan concludes that the Puritans were practical and realistic about sex—not freedom-loving to be sure, but not "the sad and sour portraits which their modern critics have drawn of them."

Such determined regulation of sexuality reflected Puritan theology. The sin of any member of the commonwealth, if not repented, might lead God to punish the entire community. All sins had to be punished and repented to reconcile the individual to the community, and thus the community to God. As Calvinists, Puritans believed that since the Fall, sin (and especially sexual sin) was inevitable because human beings could not obey God's will perfectly.

Although sin was wrong and to be punished, sex criminals generally were not different from the rest of the community. Once punished, and assuming true repentance, the community readily reintegrated the lawbreaker without much stigma. Court records reflect many prominent people charged with fornication, for example, who reappear shortly thereafter in the public records holding positions of public trust and responsibility.

In 1642, following a scandalous case in which a man sexually abused three girls under the age of ten years, the Puritan governors elaborated the sex crimes prohibitions. They set penalties for rape, which previously had not been specified: Death for statutory rape (with the age of consent set at ten years), death for rape of a married woman, and death or, at the judge's discretion, some other "grievous punishment," for rape of an unmarried woman. Making rape a capital offense conformed with seventeenth-century English common law. Yet of seventy-two rape prosecutions recorded in New England during this period, half the defendants were convicted, but only six men actually were executed for the crime.

Massachusetts prosecuted fornication more often than any other sex crime. Based on a 1642 law, both men and women could be punished for fornication by whipping or fines. In Middlesex County from 1649 to 1699 there were 162 fornication cases; in the more populous neighboring Suffolk County (which included Boston) there were 151 fornication prosecutions in the years 1671 to 1682 alone. Fornication usually was detected by the birth of a child outside of marriage, or a comparison of the date of marriage with the childbirth date of a newly married couple. A neighbor or family member also might come upon a couple in a field, barn, or other secluded place, or a parent or master might report the fornication of a daughter or a female servant to the authorities, particularly given a pregnancy.

Economic motive as much as moral outrage drove this vigorous prosecution of fornication. The community feared not only the wages of sin, but also the expense of supporting a child born outside of marriage. Prosecuting a single mother for fornication could force her to name the father of her child; likewise, penalties for men often included an adjudication of paternity and an order to pay child support. Women were somewhat more likely than men to be charged with fornication.

The authorities prosecuted both married and unmarried copulators for fornication, although couples who had later married tended to be punished more leniently. Courts usually fined a married couple whose premarital intimacy had been detected by the early birth of a child, but more often ordered a whipping for unmarried offenders. Because of this intense attention to fornication, the rate of premarital sex probably was relatively low. Less than one-tenth of brides were pregnant at the time of marriage in the seventeenth-century Puritan colonies, a rate that would not rise significantly until the eighteenth century.

As the seventeenth century waned, however, Puritan fervor moderated, and so did this vigorous regime of sex law. In 1654, Massachusetts substantially reduced the likelihood of conviction for adultery (still a capital offense on paper) by requiring two witnesses at the trial. In 1694, they reduced the penalty for adultery further; thereafter, "a man . . . found in bed with another man's wife, the man and woman so offending, being thereof convicted, shall be severely whipped, not exceeding thirty stripes." This gradual liberalization did not herald a libertine society. At the end of the century, Massachusetts still called for death in cases of forcible or statutory rape. In 1699, the law also threatened "lewd" persons with shackles and whipping. Although the law did not define "lewdness," the crime probably included prostitution and public indecency. No Massachusetts law specifically prohibited prostitution; rather, as at English common law, the prostitute was treated as a vagrant, one of the various sorts of persons whose appearance, speech, or conduct disturbed the public peace. Then as now, deciding who was "disturbing the peace" gave authorities sweeping discretion and powers of harassment. The American colonies and states did not prohibit prostitution as such until the nineteenth century.

### Virginia

If the Puritans migrated mostly in families and for reasons of religious aspiration, settlers of the southern colonies were disproportionately male and migrated to find land and economic opportunity. Virginians tended to settle on dispersed and isolated farms rather than in the dense, family-centered towns and villages common to New England. Many southern immigrants were indentured servants, workers who had sold their labor for a period of years to pay passage from England, introducing class division into the very foundations of the region's social order. Later, as racial slavery replaced indentured servitude, the southern colonies faced not only class and race but also sexual issues not explicitly known to English law.

Settlers reached James Bay in 1610. In 1619, a Royal Charter decreed that the law and institutions of England (both common law and equity) governed the Virginia colony, and ordered the death penalty for murder, rape, arson, and adultery. Further, the church wardens of every parish were directed to present to the county court at least yearly "any person [who] . . . shall abuse themselves with the high and foule offences of adultery, whoredome or fornication," and ordered such persons punished "according to the meritt of the cause." By contrast to England during these same years, where adultery, fornication, incest, and bigamy were ecclesiastical matters, Virginia from the outset punished fornication and adultery as civil offenses, sometimes by fine or whipping, sometimes by public penance in church in the English fashion. Adultery seems never to have been punished by death, as the royal charter provided.

Colonial Virginia courts only occasionally prosecuted free persons for fornication and adultery, although servants regularly faced fornication charges. For fornicating with a servant woman, a servant man or free man suffered a fine or extra years of service. But the statute books attended closely to both crimes, tinkering constantly with the prescribed penalties for "scandalous liveing in adultery and fornication." Typical penalties were fines (to be paid in pounds of tobacco or, as the market economy grew, in pounds sterling), loss of political privileges, and whippings. In most instances, defendants had the option to pay the fine or, if unable to pay, to accept whipping or imprisonment. Judged by the fines imposed over the seventeenth century, colonial Virginia seemed to regard adultery as about twice as bad a crime as fornication.

In 1696, Virginia legislators voiced frustration with the failure of the laws to deter consensual sexual misconduct; paradoxically, they responded by further reducing punishments. The available evidence of sexual behavior in early Virginia suggests that this frustration was warranted: Rates of premarital pregnancy in the southern colonies were much higher than in New England; by the eighteenth century, 30 percent of southern brides were pregnant at the wedding.

Not until the late seventeenth century did Virginia law note for the first time "women of ill name and reputation." The church could publicly admonish persons who kept or frequented such women, followed by legal punishment on the grounds that the prostitute and her patron also had committed adultery. (Colonial laws sometimes use the term "adultery" generically to denote any nonmarital sex.)

Only rape remained severely punished, and courts imposed these punishments most savagely on the enslaved. Colonial Virginia defined forcible rape as in England as "unlawful and carnal knowledge of a Woman by Force and against her Will." The prescribed penalty was death. The law proscribed statutory rape as a felony, defined as "unlawful and carnal know[ledge] and abuse [of] any woman child." The age of consent was ten years, as at common law. Yet Virginia did not often prosecute rape, and when it did, many of the cases involved transgression of class or race barriers. During the eighteenth century, the General Court (which had jurisdiction over felonies, except rape or attempted rape committed by slaves) tried only eight cases of rape, and of these, acquitted five defendants: two of the convicted men were hanged, and the governor pardoned the third. Historian Hugh Rankin reports that a "number of slaves" were tried for rape during this same period in the county courts of summary jurisdiction. In most cases, Rankin reports, authorities hanged the convicted slave, but on one occasion the governor pardoned an enslaved man upon petition of his owner. Historian Arthur Scott concludes that the county courts frequently tried slaves for rape, and virtually all cases involved a white victim. Virginia sometimes castrated enslaved men convicted of rape under a 1723 statute that allowed dismemberment of a slave in any fashion "not touching life, as the said county shall think fit." After 1769, slaves no longer were subject to castration as a generally applicable legal penalty, except upon conviction for raping or attempting to rape a white woman.

A racial dimension of American sex law appears in other ways from the earliest years of Virginia history. In 1630, one Hugh Davis was sentenced "to be soundly whipped, before an assembly of Negroes and others for abusing himself to the dishonor of God and shame of Christians, by defiling his body in lying with a negro." Throughout the seventeenth century the Virginia assembly enacted many and varied laws aimed at interracial sex. The fine for fornication was doubled if interracial. The assembly declared that the child of an enslaved mother was a slave, no matter what the race of the father. In 1691, the assembly prohibited interracial marriage, initially punishable by banishment. A white woman was fined if she bore an illegitimate child by a black or mulatto man; if unable to pay the fine she could be sold into servitude for five years. Although any child born to a white woman was free, a mixed-race child born to a white mother was placed in indentured servitude. Despite this harsh and growing web of prohibition, interracial unions were common; at the end of the seventeenth century, more than one-fifth of children born outside of marriage in Virginia were of mixed race.

These various anti-miscegenation statutes were a new kind of sex law. English law at the time of the establishment of the American colonies did not ban either interracial sex or marriage. There is some evidence that the Puritan colonies punished interracial couples more severely than others for fornication, but the crime was not different in character from that of other unmarried sex partners. Racialist societies, however, depend upon sexual rules. Given patterns of enforcement over the coming centuries, scholars conclude that this new species of law was intended to keep white women and African-American men apart and, at the same time, not to interfere with white men's sexual use and abuse of African-American women. Interpreting the state's 1705 antimiscegenation statute, the Virginia Supreme Court ruled the law was designed "to punish and deter women from that confusion of species, which the legislature seems to have considered an evil." Because racial purity requires common biological lineage, control of sexuality and reproduction are core political problems for societies organized around racial principles. Typically this means sexual control over women. We have seen how in ancient Athens this translated into a legally elaborated distinction between sexually available women and sexually prohibited women based on membership in the citizen class. In the American South, this meant limiting access to whiteness, and thus prohibiting white women to nonwhite men. Scholar Tessie Liu describes white women in such colonial settings as "the biological gate to whiteness," and typically both law and social norms constrain and police their sexual conduct accordingly.

White men could have been similarly scrupulous about maintaining racial boundaries by restricting their own interracial sexual conduct. But in Virginia and throughout the slave South, white men, and especially men of the slaveholding class, simply were not prosecuted under the anti-miscegenation laws they had enacted. In fact, in decreeing that the child of a slave woman also was a slave, the law created economic incentive for white men to exploit female slaves.

A violent culture of rape fear and retribution further controlled and sexually isolated white women from African-American men. Although a slave convicted of rape or attempted rape of a white woman in colonial Virginia was subject to castration, the later penalty for black-on-white rape in the Southern states was death. By contrast, the rape of a female slave was not a crime. An antebellum legal scholar explained that slaves, as the property of their owners, have no independent rights under law, "except such as are necessary to protect [their] existence." Because forcible rape did not necessarily threaten the life or limb of the female slave, it was no crime. Only the master could claim protection under the law, and then only for trespass or damage to his property. (Obviously, then, the law did not protect an enslaved woman from rape by her owner.)

## JUDGING PURITAN AND VIRGINIAN SEX AS BARGAINING STRUCTURES

Even apart from the intersection of race and sex, the examples of colonial Massachusetts and Virginia present enlightening comparisons in sexual regulation. Massachusetts Bay transplanted extreme Protestant believers of the emerging bourgeoisie of London and the mercantile centers of Enlightenment England. Migrants to Virginia came much more from the nobility—recipients of royal favor in the form of grants, or younger sons of well-born families. Along with their indentured servants and the exploding population of enslaved Africans, the South created a feudal system on the wane in England itself. Heavily Anglican rather than Puritan, the Virginia colonists were Protestant as much by historical accident (English Protestantism became official when the Pope forbade the divorce of Henry VIII) as by conviction. Virginia was much more like the libertine Tudor and Stuart society than was Puritan Massachusetts.

Massachusetts, by contrast, regarded itself and behaved like a "Godly Commonwealth," a tightly-knit society in which one person's sin could threaten the salvation of all. Within this close community, the heterosexual, monogamous, companionate marriage built into Protestantism by Luther's sexual teachings was the heart of Puritan social order. One can only speculate that, to these religious nonconformists challenging an ancient and hegemonic Catholic tradition, driven across the sea like Moses's Israelites fleeing Pharaoh and in search of a new Canaan, the family was a bulwark against a disorder that must have loomed as large as the surrounding forests. Protestant reduction of Christian sexual expectation from the unattainable celibate ideal of the Catholic clergy to the acceptance of marital sex ought to have loosened sexual mores, yet Puritan sexual regulation revealed the unexpected harshness of this new ideal of marital sexual community.

The centrality of family to Puritan culture is paradoxical, however, because, forests aside, Massachusetts was in many ways a homogeneous community like the city of Plato's *Republic*. In such a setting, the nuclear family probably is not needed to preserve moral or political order. Indeed, the one-on-one sexual exchange is not the only solution to the disorder of desire in *any* intensely communal and idealistic society. Among the early Christians, for example, collective sex, if confined to reproduction as Augustine taught, would have quenched unproductive lust and allowed children to be raised communally. The choice to cure sexual "burning" by heterosexual marriage or celibacy reflects how limited were the sexual and social imaginations of even radical Christians. Yet as Puritanism evolved from a communal theocracy to an ordinary secular society in the eighteenth century, the family remained the center of social discipline. Not until the religious revivals of the early nineteenth century would radicals uncouple the idealizing and communal impulses latent in Puritanism from the family, producing an explosion of experimentation with alternative models of social and sexual organization. Although the familial assumptions of the Puritan founding concealed this possibility for more than a century, in New England (and its cultural offspring, upstate New York) the radical implications of Puritan culture fertilized the soil for such utopian sexual experiments.

By contrast, like Catholicism before the Reformation in Europe, Virginia had neither the initial unity nor the experimental impulse of Massachusetts. Linked by class and racial caste, the Virginia aristocracy built a framework of sexual regulation directed at the preservation of caste and aristocracy rather than the nuclear family. The marital couple was not the vital core of this social order, and so Virginians could and did live with laxer sexual strictures. The heart of the sexual order was a man with his official wife and children, and also his lower-status female sexual partners (in this case, indentured servants or slaves) producing increasing numbers of offspring to increase his material wealth. This resembles nothing so much as the ancient world, in which the polygamous patriarch lived in an extended household with his high-status wife and tribally pure children, as well as his foreign or servant women producing recognized offspring. Like Hagar, the latter were subject to being sold down the river.

In this sense, the corrosive political changes of individualism and egalitarianism that flowed from thinkers like Hobbes and Locke into the political and religious reform movements of the late 1700s and early 1800s failed to penetrate the world of the American South until imposed from outside by force of arms in 1865. The South resisted religious reforms like Methodism, for example, because the ideal of the racial equality of souls easily led believers to support abolition. Nor did woman suffrage, born of abolitionism and rooted in Protestant reform, come naturally to the slave states. Even after slavery, the South's religious and political isolation thus cut off its sexual organization from reform. Wrested by arms from its pseudo-feudalism of race, the white South simply came to rest at the next most repressive sexual structure, the publicly-enforced patriarchal family that northern thinkers had already begun to question. Whatever the content, then, the constant in Virginia is the collective investment in the most powerful available structures of patriarchal governance. A century later, all the states that voted not to ratify woman suffrage were from the south.

In this brief history of the sexual politics and laws of Massachusetts and Virginia, we see examples of each of the main structures of sexual governance in America—Massachusetts' structure of publicly-enforced private rulership within the monogamous family, and Virginia's public rulership within a patriarchy that transcends family.

In important ways, both colonial Massachusetts and Virginia were societies of a particular time, and so do not warrant for our particular purposes a full-blown philosophical analysis of their sexual regulation. After a time, national secular life succeeded the Godly Commonwealth in Massachusetts. And alongside the rest of America, free men and women, even in slave-holding Virginia, began to partake in the nineteenth-century republic of virtue, which is the first distinctly American sexual regime. Accordingly, we reserve an extended evaluation of American sexual regimes against the standards of philosophy for the developments after independence. However, the strong Protestant family of Massachusetts and the powerful caste system of colonial Virginia do represent strands that flowed into the larger national picture and warrant at least a brief evaluation.

As to ends, Massachusetts pressed people to marry. Insofar as the community of marriage presents an opportunity for flourishing lives, it meets the standards of virtue ethics. As we have seen, the classical version of the family was of questionable appeal to modern minds; Plato thought it inconsistent with equality and patriotism and Aristotle thought it a perfect vehicle for natural inequality. Nonetheless, membership in a family does give people an opportunity for a social life as well as a chance to govern children and attempt to live in peace with one another. Modified by Protestant notions of equality and companionability, Puritan marriage was probably more consistent with the individualism and equality of classical liberalism than any prior regime. Finally, although conceived more than a century before Bentham, marriage might even have been a hedonistic advantage; even in the libertine twentieth century, sex surveys reveal that married people have sexual intercourse more often than their unmarried counterparts. The legacy of the English common law of marriage, however, casts a shadow on this happy picture. Life was particularly not flourishing, free or equal for the marginalized and often persecuted minority, especially women, who remained single.

The philosophical status of Virginia is harsher, still. White women were further from the Protestant notion of companionability and equality, and often isolated from all society on far-flung plantations or farms, with little opportunity for a flourishing life as the ancients understood it even in its least demanding form. They were powerfully morally implicated in the management of a society of chattel slavery. The machinery of oppression largely directed at slaves also restricted their freedom, and access to the hedonistic sexuality of monogamy was limited by their competition with a completely disempowered slave class.

Because colonial Massachusetts and Virginia were so different, they also present us with an opportunity to compare how society establishes the framework for unofficial male-female sexual bargaining. The Puritans did not disfavor sex; they favored marriage. Consequently, almost every adult married. This rigorous enforcement of heterosexual monogamy made marriage the minimum price for sexual access. The value of that price support depended entirely upon the conditions of marriage, which were established by law. The model of common law marriage imported by the Puritans permitted marital rape and battery, gave the husband either outright ownership or legal control of family wealth, and made exit through divorce virtually impossible. Because marriage favored men, wives paid a higher price for sexual access than did husbands. This regime also stripped adults who happened to be or wanted to remain unmarried of most of their social status: For example, the Puritans were most likely to accuse a single woman who owned property of witchcraft. But for women who wished to have children, the marital regime provided valuable aid. Because sex was confined, spouses were available. Few babies were born outside of marriage. There was almost no prostitution.

The Virginia system of racially organized aristocracy distributed sexual power differently. The presence of an unprotected class of enslaved girls and women available for sexual harvesting created for much of the population a sexual state of nature. For African-American women, there was virtually no sexual bargaining with white men. Between enslaved men and women, traditional norms that had governed heterosexual exchange before transportation were weakened or disrupted by forced emigration. Slave status either prohibited or made provisional (in light of the ever-present possibility of separation through sale) stable adult relationships like marriage. Law and custom forbade white women to deal with whole groups of available male sexual partners, forcing them to bargain with only the strongest group—white men. Moreover, the presence of a class of sexual slave labor lessened the power of white women, for example, to bargain for marriage, and births outside of marriage were much more common than in Puritan New England. The white woman's most potent sexual bargaining chip was her whiteness and her fertility. Given this, it is understandable why the sex act that Virginia lawmakers sought most to control was reproductive sex between a white woman and a man of color, enslaved or free.

## THE AGE OF REVOLUTION

After 1700, England's influence over the distinctively American colonial cultures and legal systems grew, remaining strong well into the eighteenth century, even in the face of the Revolution. First, facing growing political resistance from the colonies, England made a policy choice in the mid-1700s to govern its North American possessions more closely. The Crown began to require the colonies to send a copy of all laws to London for approval or disallowance. The exchange between colony and mother country flowed both ways, with artifacts of English culture (manufactured goods, fashions, newspapers) traveling back across the Atlantic to America.

Second, England was caught up in the profound transformations of the Enlightenment and these currents also flowed from England to America. In the end, the Enlightenment probably had more revolutionary impact in a young America than in an entrenched England. On both sides of the Atlantic, empiricism in science, Protestantism in religion, materialism in philosophy, market capitalism in economy, and the printing press in popular culture were changing a feudal Christian society into a materialist secular one. Corrosive new ideas of political authority and social equality ate away at the divinely or naturally ordained hierarchies that had structured the ancient and medieval worlds. Protestant hostility to arranged marriage and support for companionate matches slowly altered bourgeois desires and expectations of marriage and family life, including the ways that husbands and wives emotionally and sexually related.

Even as men no longer explicitly dominated women, with the rule of love replacing authority, gender roles began to separate. Historian Thomas Laqueur finds that in the late 1700s,

> [A]natomists for the first time produced detailed illustrations of an explicitly female skeleton to document the fact that sexual difference was more than skin deep. Where before there had been only one basic structure, now there were two.

In the ancient and medieval worlds, to be a man or a woman was to hold a social rank and assume a cultural role, not to be born into one or the other of two incommensurable sexes. Before the Enlightenment there was no doubt that women and men differed bodily and that women were inferior to men, but no one thought females were fully realized beings of a different physiology than men, a different human species, so to speak. So, for example, women were thought to have the same genitals as men, except internal rather than external: The vaginal sheath was a reversed penis; the labia a foreskin; the uterus a scrotum; the ovaries a

pair of testicles; and the clitoris the sensitive head of a penis. In a profound transformation of knowledge, Enlightenment science began to develop new names for
male and female genitals and new images of these organs as anatomically distinct.
From this scientific rethinking grew the popular and political view of two stable
and opposite sexes. After the eighteenth century, gender—that is, the political,
economic, and cultural lives of men and women—was grounded in sexual biology rather than classical or Christian metaphysics of social function.

As Laqueur emphasizes, the biological immutability of sexual difference conve-
niently arose at the very moment when western political orders had broken apart
and were redefining themselves. The force of custom, social function, or divine order that had justified the patriarchal family since time immemorial no longer suf-
ficed to justify unequal social relations. Power now had to be justified. No longer
could it be argued that men rule because women are by nature or scripture morally inferior. Biologism, or opposite sexes, worked to preserve male dominance by
resting the differences between men and women on discoverable biological
grounds and not potentially undefensible political grounds. Thus Enlightenment
discourse revised the rhetoric but not the reality of sexual politics. As in political
discourse more generally, consent rather than natural hierarchy became the basis
for unequal human relationships.

A competing explanation for inequality could have been that there was no consent, only conquest, as in Hobbes's *Commonwealth by Acquisition*, but sexual conquest was an unsatisfying love story in the age of consent theory. There was no
record of actual consent to hierarchy in some remote state of nature, producing the
problem of why women would consent to a relationship of enduring sexual subordination, such as marriage as defined by the common law. Consent could be hy-
pothesized, if it could be argued that consenting is the kind of thing a reasonable
creature would do in particular circumstances, but only very different creatures
would reasonably agree to divide the world between them so as to create such unequal conditions and prospects. Thus the ideas of political consent and opposite
sexes were a felicitous coincidence.

## THE REPUBLIC OF VIRTUE

In this setting of shifting political theory, the American colonies revolted against
England. In 1789, after a brief period under the Articles of Confederation, the
revolutionaries established a strong federal government under the United States
Constitution. Despite the break from England, the legal culture of a century and a
half was too strong to break. To common law lawyers, for whom prior decisions
are the substance of law, a shortage of cases would have been crippling. Reluctant
to try to build a new body of substantive law from the ground up, state courts in
the early years of the new republic cited more English than American cases. Even
new statutes enacted by the legislatures tended to adopt familiar English legal
principles and patterns.

The publication in the United States of Sir William Blackstone's *Commentaries on the Laws of England* had as much effect on American legal history as all the debate over whether to adopt or reject English common law. First published in England in 1765-69, Blackstone, an English judge and legal scholar, sought to reduce to clear and unqualified maxims what he considered to be the essence of the common law. Despite errors, omissions, oversimplifications, and fabrications, Lawrence Friedman notes that Blackstone "manage[d] to put in brief order the rank weeds of English law." Blackstone was simple, comprehensive, and authoritative. The first American edition of the treatise (1771) was an immediate bestseller. Further, in many states and territories, legislatures did not compile or distribute records of laws made and so lawyers had virtually no other legal materials available. Friedman observes of early American lawyers, "[T]hey used [Blackstone's] book as a shortcut to the law; and Blackstone was English to the core."

The 1803 edition of Blackstone (the edition most widely used in the United States) contributed several lasting innovations to sex law. Regarding the law of husband and wife, Blackstone characterized the common law as providing that "the very . . . legal existence of the woman is suspended during marriage." A woman upon marriage no longer could exercise the ordinary legal powers of an adult, including many forms of property ownership and the capacity to contract. Further, a husband could physically chastise his wife as necessary for her due correction because he was legally responsible for her misdeeds. Blackstone suggested that a wife who killed her husband should be treated as a regicide (the subject who kills the King) and thus subject to the most painful form of capital punishment known to the law. By comparison, Blackstone stated that a wife's adultery mitigates her murder to the lowest degree of manslaughter if her husband has killed her in the heat of passion.

Blackstone also introduced into American law British jurist Sir Matthew Hale's suspicions about the credibility of women who make charges of rape. "[R]ape is a most detestable crime," Hale wrote, "but it must be remembered that it is an accusation easy to be made, hard to be proved, but harder to be defended by the party accused, though innocent." To decide whether a complainant's testimony was "false or feigned," Blackstone recited Hale's cautions that juries be instructed to consider whether the victim "be of good fame." Until well into the twentieth century, American juries in many jurisdictions were so instructed, with judges formulaically citing Hale's "easy to be made, hard to be proved" maxim.

This legal continuity with England understates, however, the degree to which post-revolutionary America was a unique and radically new society. There were no kings, no nobles, and, for free white men, no relationships of status. There was no entail and no primogeniture assigning property to oldest male heirs. The disestablishment of the church, however, had the most powerful influence on the shifting sexual landscape of this era because once disestablished, civil enforcement of explicitly religious strictures lost legitimacy. State legislatures stopped enacting

new morals laws in the early national period, and officials tended to enforce existing laws desultorily or not at all.

Stripped of so many lineaments of social hierarchy, the United States of the late
eighteenth and early nineteenth century must have looked like a society that could
fly apart at any moment, even after almost two centuries of relative modernity in
England. The intimations of class warfare in the early republic did not add to confidence in the stability of the American experiment. Fears about disorder drove intellectuals, politicians, and lawmakers to concern themselves to an unprecedented
degree with issues of virtuous citizenship and vicious self-interestedness, a movement we now call the civic republican revival.

By contrast to the earlier Puritan world and to the social discourse of the latter
half of the nineteenth century, however, this anxiety about virtue focused on public or civic virtue rather than sexual purity. Civic republicanism drew heavily from
the classical ideal of the virtuous citizen, restrained in his individualism and devoted to the well-being of the city. American civic virtue, however, did not derive
exclusively from Greece and Rome. Virtue in the civic republican ideal had many
varied sources and meanings. There were the classical virtues of excellence, including military heroism and male friendship in the political world; there also were
the Protestant virtues of self-discipline, piety, and frugality.

Historian Gordon Wood has convincingly argued that, as the period of independence played out, the commercial and impersonal public world superseded the
virtuous republic. As the fever of revolution began to pass, problems of economic
self-interest and the institutions necessary to fund the national economy moved to
center stage. Norms of public behavior shifted from the republican ideal of the
selfless public servant to the dominant construct of individualistic entities striving
for self-interest and kept in check only by canny constitutional structures. Virtue
did not disappear, however. With little room for civic virtue, the public culture increasingly cultivated and encouraged the concept of private virtue.

And it is here that virtue begins to intersect with gender. The private realm of
family fell increasingly to wives and mothers as economic and political life moved
out of the household. Stripped of compelling sexual claims by the invention of
female indifference, the association of females with morality grew stronger, not co-
incidentally liberating men to pursue self-interest in public. It is within this framework and with the rise of secular and commercial life that questions of sexual
morality grew more heavily charged with national interest. An early sign of the
linkage between sexual behavior and the fate of the nation appeared in Alexis de
Tocqueville's analysis of sexual relations in his landmark book *Democracy in
America*.

## Notes

The best general history of American law is Lawrence M. Friedman, *A History of American Law*, 2nd ed., (New York: Simon and Schuster, 1985). An impressive social history of

sexuality in America is John D'Emilio and Estelle B. Freedman, *Intimate Matters: A History of Sexuality in America* (New York: Harper and Row, 1988). Neither book, however, is a legal and philosophical history of sex. Friedman examines the law on various sexual subjects as examples of larger legal trends, but the scope of his work is too broad to permit of extensive analysis of the particulars of sex law. Similarly, although D'Emilio and Freedman refer to governing law and political theory throughout their study, the role of these subjects in a social history is of necessity limited. But the following chapters have been greatly influenced by these two works and we acknowledge our special debt to these scholars.

The Massachusetts charter is found in *The Federal and State Constitutions, Colonial Charters, and Other Organic Laws of the States, Territories and Colonies Now Or Heretofore Forming the United States of America*, vol. 3, ed. Francis Newton Thorpe (Charter of Massachusetts Bay, 1629) (Washington, D.C.: Government Printing Office, 1909), 1846. The requirement of colonial conformity with English law is from Friedman, *A History of American Law*, 48, and the meeting of the colony's general court and early legislative and adjudicative functions are described on pp. 39, 40.

On Puritan sexual regulation, see generally Edmund S. Morgan, "The Puritans and Sex," in *The American Family in Social-Historical Perspective*, ed. Michael Gordon, 3rd. ed. (New York: St. Martin's Press, 1983), 311. The "sad and sour" quote is on p. 312. On Puritan governance and belief generally, see Edmund S. Morgan, *The Puritan Family: Essays on Religion and Domestic Relations in Seventeenth-Century New England* (Boston: Trustees of the Public Library, 1944), 7. On the social status of those charged with fornication, see D'Emilio and Freedman, *Intimate Matters*, 15, 23.

The following are the biblical sources of Puritan sex law: Adultery and fornication are prohibited by the Bible; see Exodus 20:14, Leviticus 20:10, Deuteronomy 22:22 (adultery), and 1 Thessalonians 4:3 (fornication). The Bible prescribes capital punishment for adultery (as well as homosexuality and bestiality) in the nation of Israel at Leviticus 20:10, 13, and 15–16. The biblical requirement of two witnesses for a conviction of adultery is found at Deuteronomy 17:6: "A person shall be put to death only on the testimony of two or more witnesses; he must not be put to death on the testimony of a single witness."

On the death penalty for adultery enacted by the 1631 Massachusetts legislature, see 1631 Records of the Colony of Massachusetts Bay, New England, 92, sec. 26–(12). On the treatment of adultery as a crime against morality in U.S. law, see, e.g., *State v. Holland*, 145 S.W. 522, 523 (Mo. Ct. App. 1912) (describing ecclesiastical roots and the separate legal evolution of the crime of adultery in what would become the United States). On the penalties actually imposed on adulterers in the Puritan settlements, see John Demos, *A Little Commonwealth: Family Life in Plymouth Colony* (New York: Oxford Univ. Press, 1970), 152–58.

On Puritan penalties for forcible and statutory rape, see Edwin Powers, *Crime and Punishment in Early Massachusetts, 1620–1692: A Documentary History* (Boston: Beacon Press, 1966), 264–67; Lyle Koehler, *A Search for Power: The "Weaker Sex" in Seventeenth-Century New England* (Urbana: Univ. of Illinois Press, 1980), 94. On the rate of execution for rape, see Koehler, *A Search for Power*, 95.

On the Massachusetts laws against fornication, see D'Emilio and Freedman, *Intimate Matters*, 22; Demos, *A Little Commonwealth*, 152–58; Laurel Thatcher Ulrich, *Good Wives: Image and Reality in the Lives of Women in Northern New England, 1650–1750*, 1st ed. (New York: Knopf, 1982). On the patterns of fornication prosecutions, see Roger Thompson, *Sex in Middlesex: Popular Mores in a Massachusetts County, 1649–1699* (Amherst: Univ. of Massachusetts Press, 1986), 10–11; Ethan Cohen, "Groping in the Dark: The Use of History in Rights Analysis as Viewed Through a Study of Fornication

Prosecutions in Colonial Massachusetts," unpub. ms., 1991) (on file with authors), 45. On the detection of fornication, see Emil Oberholzer, *Delinquent Saints: Disciplinary Actions in the Early Congregational Churches of Massachusetts* (New York: Columbia Univ. Press, 1956), 132, and Thompson, *Sex in Middlesex*, 38, 35. On the economic motives underlying fornication prosecutions, see ibid., 22, and Cohen, "Groping in the Dark," 50. On the actual patterns of punishment, see ibid., 55. On the rate of premarital pregnancy, see D'Emilio and Freedman, *Intimate Matters*, 10, 22.

On the crime of "lewdness" and prostitution laws (or lack thereof in Massachusetts), see Barbara Meil Hobson, *Uneasy Virtue: The Politics of Prostitution and the American Reform Tradition*, 2nd ed. (Chicago: Univ. of Chicago Press, 1990), 32–33.

The Virginia General Assembly formally adopted the English common law in 1660–61, Hening, II Statutes at 43 (1823) in accordance with the Royal Charter. The death penalty for murder, rape, arson, and adultery is found in *Virginia Colonial Decisions*, vol. 1, Introduction by R. T. Barton (Boston: Boston Book Company, 1909), 164, and described by Arthur P. Scott, *Criminal Law in Colonial Virginia* (Chicago: Univ. of Chicago Press, 1930), 4. Scott claims Virginia never imposed the death penalty for adultery (277). On fornication, see Hening, I Statutes at 433 (1692) (1823), Act II. On the civil nature of these offenses in Virginia, see *Virginia Colonial Decisions*, 168; Scott, *Criminal Law*, 277. On the 1657 penalties for adultery, see Hening, I Statutes at 433 (1657) (1823). On the 1691 penalties, see Hening, III Statutes at 71–75, 888 (1691) (1823) (fornication) and Hening, III Statutes at 71–75 (1691) (1823) (adultery). On the 1696 penalties, see Hening, III Statutes at 137–38 (1696) (1823); III Statutes at 361 (1705) (1823). On the 1792 penalties, see Rev. Code of Va. at p. 276 (1792) (fornication and adultery).

On the harsher punishments imposed for sexual conduct with slaves or servants in Virginia see Scott, *Criminal Law*, 279. For exemplary statutes, see Hening, I Statutes at 252–53 (1642–43) (1823); Hening, I Statutes at 438 (1657–58) (1823); Hening, II Statutes at 114–15 (1661–62) (1823); Hening, III Statutes at 136–40 (1696) (1823).

On rates of premarital pregnancy in the colonial American South, see Daniel Scott Smith, "The Long Cycle in American Illegitimacy and Prenuptial Pregnancy," in *Bastardy and Its Comparative History* ed. Peter Laslett et al. (Cambridge, Mass.: Harvard Univ. Press, 1980), 369; Daniel Scott Smith and Michael Hindus, "Premarital Pregnancy in America, 1640–1971: An Overview and an Interpretation," *Journal of Interdisciplinary History* 5 (1975):537.

"Women of ill fame and reputation" first appear in the Virginia statutes in 1691, see Hening, III Statutes at 74 (1691) (1823) (frequenting the company of women of ill fame and reputation).

Rape was made a felony without benefit of clergy by the British Parliament at 18 Eliz. 1, ch. 7 (1576). See also Sir Edward Coke, *Institutes of the Laws of England*, pt. 3, ch. 11, the most commonly used legal treatise in colonial Virginia before the publication of Blackstone's *Commentaries* in the United States in the 1750s. See *Virginia Colonial Decisions*, 192 (up until the end of the 17th century, the Acts of the General Assembly existed only in manuscript form and most colonial Virginia lawyers relied instead upon Coke). According to Coke, rape is felony by common law, declared by parliament to be the unlawful and carnal knowledge of any woman above the age of ten years against her will, or of a woman child under the age of ten years with her will, or against her will, and the offender shall not have the benefit of clergy. Coke, *Institutes of the Laws of England*, pt. 3, ch. 11. On the application of this statute in colonial Virginia, see Hugh F. Rankin, *Criminal Trial Proceedings in the General Court of Colonial Virginia* (Charlottesville: Univ. of Virginia Press, 1965), 219.

On the racialized nature of rape prosecutions in colonial Virginia, see ibid., 220–22, and Scott, *Criminal Law*, 207–8. County courts were justice of the peace courts with jurisdiction over small civil law cases and misdemeanor crimes. Common law procedure was to be used, but the process was criticized for "looseness and extreme lack of formality in the court." *Virginia Colonial Decisions*, 199. These courts had broader jurisdiction over serious crimes charged against enslaved persons, than crimes of free persons, especially the rape of white women. See Scott, *Criminal Law*, 45–47. On the castration penalty, see Rankin, *Criminal Trial Proceedings*, 221, citing Hening, IV Statutes at 132 (1723) (1823) (permits dismembering); Hening, VIII Statutes at 358 (1769) (1823) (castration unlawful, unless in the case of rape of a white woman).

On the whipping of Hugh Davis for "lying with a negro," see Hening, I Statutes at 145–46 (1823), cited in Edmund S. Morgan, *American Slavery, American Freedom: The Ordeal of Colonial Virginia* (New York: Norton, 1975), 333. On the doubling of fines for interracial fornication in Virginia, see Scott, *Criminal Law*, 281, citing Hening, II Statutes at 170 (1661–62) (1823), and Morgan, *American Slavery, American Freedom*, 335–36.

On the punishment of white women who bore mixed-race children in Virginia, see Scott, *Criminal Law*, 283; Hening, III Statutes at 86–87, 453–54 (1691) (1823) (child to be bound until 31 years of age); Hening, VIII Statutes at 134 (1705) (1823) (servitude until child's majority).

On the 1691 Virginia prohibition of interracial marriage, see Hening, III Statutes at 86–87 (1823); Hening, III Statutes at 453–54 (1823).

On miscegenation at common law, see Harvey M. Applebaum, "Miscegenation Statutes: A Constitutional and Social Problem," *Georgia Law Journal* 53 (1964):49. For a historical background of Virginia's anti-miscegenation law, see generally Walter J. Wadlington, "The Loving Case: Virginia's Anti-Miscegenation Statute in Historical Perspective," *Virginia Law Review* 52 (1966): 1189 Through the mid-1960s anti-miscegenation and fornication statutes directed at interracial couples still existed and were enforced in many states. They were declared unconstitutional in *Loving v. Virginia*, 388 U.S. 1 (1967), and *McLaughlin v. Florida*, 379 U.S. 184 (1964).

For discussion of the social control functions of anti-miscegenation laws, see generally Karen A. Getman, "Sexual Control in the Slaveholding South: The Implementation and Maintenance of a Racial Caste System," *Harvard Women's Law Journal* 7 (1984): 115. For a discussion of sexual relationships between white women and black men, see James Hugo Johnston, *Race Relations in Virginia and Miscegenation in the South, 1776–1860* (Amherst: Univ. of Massachusetts Press, 1970), 175–81, 263–67; Morgan, *American Slavery, American Freedom*, 336; A. Leon Higginbotham, Jr., *In the Matter of Color: Race and the American Legal Process: The Colonial Period* (New York: Oxford Univ. Press, 1978), 46.

The Virginia Supreme Court decision interpreting the state's 1705 anti-miscegenation law is *Howell v. Netherland*, Jefferson 90, 90 (Va. 1770) (interpreting Virginia Act of 1705, ch. 49, sec. 18).

On the role of sex law in racialist and colonial societies, see generally Tessie Liu, "Teaching the Differences Among Women from a Historical Perspective: Rethinking Race and Gender as Social Categories," in *Unequal Sisters: A Multicultural Reader in U.S. Women's History*, ed. Vicki L. Ruiz, and Ellen Carol DuBois, 2nd ed. (New York: Routledge, 1994), 571. On the penalties of death and sexual mutilation imposed upon black men accused of raping white women, see sources cited above, and Getman, "Sexual Control," 134.

On the views of white Virginians concerning African Americans, see Herbert Gutman, *The Black Family in Slavery and Freedom, 1750–1925* (New York: Vintage Books, 1977), 11–22, 51, 270–76 (Southern American attitudes); Winthrop D. Jordan, *White Over Black: American Attitudes Towards the Negro, 1550–1812* (Chapel Hill: Univ. of North Carolina Press, 1969) (English origins of American attitudes). On the views of white Virginians concerning white women who had sex with African-American men, see Gutman, *Black Family*, 300, 338–39. For a discussion of the legally constituted economic incentives to exploit enslaved women in the American South, see generally Higginbotham, *In the Matter of Color*, 44.

On the lack of rape protections for enslaved women, see "Race, Racism, and the Law," *Harvard Women's Law Journal* 6 (1983): 103, 106 n.13, 118 n.92. The antebellum legal scholar quoted is Thomas R. R. Cobb, *An Inquiry into the Law of Negro Slavery in the United States of America* (Philadelphia: T. and J. W. Johnson and Co., 1858), quoted in Willie Lee Rose, *A Documentary History of Slavery in North America* (New York: Oxford Univ. Press, 1976), 196, 199. Cobb is also the source for a master's remedies for rape of his female slave. See ibid., 203.

On British control of colonial American lawmaking, see Friedman, *A History of American Law*, 48.

On the dominance of English law in the early American courts, see ibid. 112. On Blackstone's common law and the treatise's influence in America, see p. 21. The "ranks weeds" quote is on p. 21. The "English to the core" quote is on p. 112. For Blackstone on coverture, see William Blackstone, *Commentaries on the Laws of England* (St. George Tucker ed.), ch. XV, pt. III, 441–45. For Blackstone's adoption of Hale on rape, see Sir William Blackstone, *Commentaries on the Laws of England* 210–15 (1802), 210–15, and Sir Matthew Hale, *The History of the Pleas of the Crown* (1678; 1800, 627. For Blackstone on killing an adulterous wife, see Blackstone, *Commentaries* book 4, pp. 191–92 and book 3, p. 140.

On the new anatomical and political idea of "opposite sexes," see Thomas Laqueur, *Making Sex: Body and Gender from the Greeks to Freud* (Cambridge: Harvard Univ. Press, 1990), 4, 6, 152, 157, 161.

On civic republicanism in American history, see Gordon S. Wood, *Creation of the American Republic, 1776–1787* (Chapel Hill: Univ. of North Carolina Press, 1969).

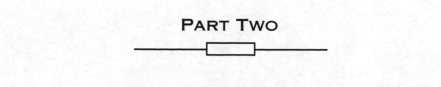

# PART TWO

# THE RISE AND FALL OF
# THE REPUBLIC OF VIRTUE

# 5

## FEMALE VIRTUE AND PUBLIC ORDER

Two generations after the American Revolution, French aristocrat Alexis de Tocqueville set out to explain American democracy to Europeans as they struggled
through their own revolutionary times. In *Democracy in America*, Tocqueville wrote
the definitive analysis of democratic society and government at the very moment
when such new societies were being founded throughout the West, framing an account of the workings of democratic life that has lasted to the present day.

### "TO THE SUPERIORITY OF THEIR WOMEN"

Unlike theorists such as John Locke in the tradition of classical liberalism,
Tocqueville did not accept a rigid division between politics and the rest of society.
He believed that social behaviors, which he called *moeurs* or mores, were the
foundation for public and political activity. Social relations influenced politics,
with the whole spectrum from the public to the private fusing in a complex inter-
mingling of cause and effect. Accordingly, to understand democratic politics in
America's early national period, Tocqueville delves into racial history, patterns of
child-rearing, games and recreation, architecture, poetry, and the influence of the
common-law tradition.

Because he was not imprisoned by the public-private divide, Tocqueville also
recognized the importance of gender and sexual relations for the new society he
described. In erasing the boundary that classical liberalism draws between politics
and society, Tocqueville thus evoked the ancient virtue tradition; paradoxically,
that classical insight accounts for much of the durability and modern relevance of
his work. Where other nineteenth-century "travelogues" of British and European
visitors to America are today little more than caches of evidence for historians,
Tocqueville continues to be a vital part of the conversation about democracy and
American distinctiveness.

Tocqueville opens his discussion of sex and gender in America in a manner
typical of this work as a whole, by criticizing European mores. Europeans, he contends, make the terrible error of unisex thinking:

> There are people in Europe who, confounding together the different character-
> istics of the sexes, would make man and women into beings not only equal but
> alike. They would give to both the same functions, impose on both the same du-

ties, and grant to both the same rights; they would mix them in all things—their occupations, their pleasures, their business. It may readily be conceived that by thus attempting to make one sex equal to the other, both are degraded, and from so preposterous a medley of the works of nature nothing could ever result but weak men and disorderly women.

Considering the time in which Tocqueville wrote—the 1830s—and the specific audience to which he addressed *Democracy in America*—the Second French Republic—the idea that European society was then threatened with sexual sameness seems overstated, to say the least. Yet since the seventeenth century, Enlightenment developments had at least opened the question of proper gender roles to European thinkers. Leading political theorists from Hobbes to Rousseau and Locke tried to finesse the egalitarian implications of liberal philosophy and the social consequences of companionate marriage with arguments of "natural" male preeminence. Their own premises of the innate equality and freedom of human beings rendered this resort to a natural or God-given hierarchy unpersuasive, however, even to societies still determined to uphold the unequal treatment of men and women.

Signs of the sexual revolution to come had already surfaced in England with the publication in 1792 of Mary Wollstonecraft's *Vindication of the Rights of Women*, a work of scandalous import at the time. Although Tocqueville did not visit England until two decades later, he could not have missed the ongoing furor over Wollstonecraft's work, as it was deeply enmeshed in the Anglo-French debate over the French Revolution, Tocqueville's chief concern. And in intellectual and reform circles, Wollstonecraft's life as much as her thought was the subject of gossip and debate years after her premature death in 1797.

Wollstonecraft, part of a circle of liberal reformers in England, first entered political debate with *Vindication of the Rights of Men*, a response to English conservative Edmund Burke's attack on the French Revolution. *Rights of Women*, her argument for women's participation in the Enlightenment project, was provocatively dedicated to Charles Talleyrand, the French Minister of Education, as Talleyrand pressed the cause of free male public education to the French National Assembly. Wollstonecraft advanced the idea, now quite tame, that reason is not gendered and that women should be educated as well as men. More radically, she applied the arguments of classical liberal philosophy and revolutionary politics to contend that men's rule in the private sphere of the family was just as artificial as had been the aristocratic rule in the public sphere so recently overthrown in France.

Wollstonecraft was part of the same English reform culture that produced Jeremy Bentham and many radical Christian thinkers. At the time of Tocqueville's visit to England, religious and philosophical reform was at a fever pitch. The unitarian and utilitarian reform circles in England in which Wollstonecraft had participated then included other early feminists such as sociologist Harriet Martineau and the woman who would become John Stuart Mill's companion and inspiration, Harriet Taylor.

It is more likely, therefore, that Tocqueville's denunciation of European "confounding ... of the sexes" is not a description of the actual conditions of European society, but an alert response to a threatening development within classical liberal thought. Like many philosophers, such as Locke, who argued that men are rulers within the family by virtue of their greater physical strength, Tocqueville tried to forestall the ominous consequences of Enlightenment philosophy and democratic politics for gender and sexual relations. His attack on social "mixing" of the sexes is a rhetorical posture, and one he repeats throughout *Democracy in America*: He sets up Europe, and particularly France, as the example of the discarded model of an authoritarian politics and a libertine society, in order to compare it to his preferred American model of a liberal politics and an authoritarian society. Thus the feint concerning European sexual sameness serves mainly to introduce Tocqueville's main point—his praise of the American gender system.

Americans, unlike their degraded European counterparts, Tocqueville continues, are firmly wedded to opposite sexes: "[They] admit that nature has appointed wide differences between the physical and moral constitution of man and woman." Nature's plan for these different tools is to give them "diverse employment," carefully "dividing" their duties into two "clearly distinct lines of action" in "two pathways" that are always different. Regardless of whether such constitutively different creatures ever could be equal, Tocqueville disclaims any such intent, declaring that Americans accept that "the natural head of the conjugal association is man." Democracy, he insists, does not mean the abrogation of sexual authority:

> [T]he object of democracy is to regulate and legalize the powers that are necessary, and not to subvert all power. . . . Nor have the Americans ever supposed that one consequence of democratic principles is the subversion of marital power or the confusion of the natural authorities in families.

Tocqueville does not explain how it is that this gender hierarchy survived the liberal assault on natural orders of inequality. But, he assures us, this "natural authorit[y] in [democratic] families" is not simply a usurpation of women's rights; rather, the hierarchy is validated by the mechanism of female consent. American women, Tocqueville writes, "attach a sort of pride to the voluntary surrender of their own will, and make it their boast to bend themselves to the yoke." What a European husband could command based on authority, the American wife yields from love and respect.

The key difference between the American and European gender orders, Tocqueville concludes, is that "[although] Americans do not think that man and woman have either the duty or the right to perform the same offices ... they show an equal regard for both their respective parts." This is proven, he asserts, by the fact that the Americans do not recognize a sexual double standard in law: They punish the seducer as much as his victim and treat rape as a capital crime. Thus protected in their sexual chastity, American women are elevated to the moral and intellectual level of men, even if they remain social inferiors. By contrast, according to Tocqueville, European men pretend to be women's slaves but never actually treat women as equals, seeing them instead as seductive but imperfect creatures. By this point in Tocqueville's exposition, we pause to note, the imaginary unisex players of his opening complaint against Europe have disappeared entirely. In their place, Tocqueville offers a romantic vision of seductive women and cavalier men.

It is worth noting that Tocqueville's formulation of the virtuous and independent, yet voluntarily submissive American woman contains certain dangerous possibilities for his larger project. In his picture of virtuous American women and dissolute French aristocrats, Tocqueville gives powerful support to the leveling idea that moral character is neither genetic nor gendered, but instead socially constructed. Thus, the American culture of free girlhood, divided spheres, and evenhanded sex law produces women who "often exhibit a masculine strength and understanding and a manly energy." Although American women "generally preserve great delicacy of personal appearance . . . [they] sometimes show that they have the hearts and minds of men." The French system of chivalry and pretended devotion, by contrast, produces women "futile, feeble, and timid." Although Tocqueville never raises the issue, the social construction of gendered moral character in the two cultures seriously undercuts his central claim to natural conjugal authority.

Winning this battle of sexual ethos implicates the future of democracy, Tocqueville tells us. Indeed, he directly attributes American ascendance to this proper ordering of the sexes: "[I]f I were asked . . . to what singular prosperity and growing strength of that people ought mainly to be attributed, I should reply: To the superiority of their women." Too often understood as little more than a fond, paternalistic compliment, Tocqueville's oft-quoted phrase is a crucial link in his political analysis of the workings of viable democracy: "Whatever affects the condition of women, their habits and their opinions," he writes, "has great political importance in my eyes."

But why is a radical submission of women either necessary or sufficient for democratic strength and prosperity? Elsewhere in *Democracy in America*, Tocqueville reexamines a range of traditional relationships of hierarchy and authority—representative and citizen, master and servant, officer and soldier, and even most presciently, black and white—and shows himself to be open to all kinds of new social arrangements. If these other structural pillars of the feudal social order can be sacrificed, why does Tocqueville single out female submission alone as the foundation stone that must be preserved for the sake of the republic?

Understanding the role of female virtue is important because the voluntary submission of American women solves a problem that preoccupies Tocqueville throughout the two volumes of *Democracy in America*: How can order be maintained in a free society when the deferences of custom and authority have been discarded?

> [Stripped of] the instinctive, disinterested, and undefinable feeling which connects the affections of man with his birthplace [and] a taste for ancient customs and a reverence for traditions of the past . . . [,] [e]pochs sometimes occur . . . when the old customs of a people are changed, public morality is destroyed, religious belief shaken, and the spell of tradition broken.

Then ominous disorder looms. Much as he admires America, Tocqueville sees that the young nation's democratic enterprise is perilous; if tradition fades and the discipline required for self-government fails, all that is left to ensure order is fear. "It cannot be doubted that the moment at which political rights are granted to a people that had before been without them is a very critical one. . . . [T]here is nothing more arduous than the apprenticeship of liberty."

Even on the hopeful ground of America in the 1830s when Tocqueville landed, his uneasiness and anxiety were shared by many ordinary Americans. The virtuous republic of George Washington had already been surpassed by the commercial society of Andrew Jackson, and the American people had begun to fear that they would betray their inheritance of liberty by the surrender of vigilance and abandonment of republican virtue for the temptations of profit.

This anxiety grew out of the changes and dislocations that accompanied the dramatic expansion of the market economy in the first decades of the nineteenth century, drawing young men from the country into the city, pulling farmers out of self-sufficiency and into the money economy, and fueling financial speculation. "Should our grand experiment of self-government ultimately fail," said one commentator, "it will doubtless be because our prosperity is greater than our virtue can bear." Images of decline and corruption dominated discussions of the state of the republic: "There is no charm in free institutions to sustain themselves and to bless a nation," warned another. The struggle between liberty and power, the dangers of corruption, and the ultimate threat of political tyranny—in short, what had been at stake in the American Revolution itself—were again hanging in the balance as Jacksonian America struggled to make sense of deep economic and social transformations then underway.

Democracies are not without weapons in this battle against temptation, and in exploring the political and legal structures that might assist the new American democracy in its arduous apprenticeship of liberty, Tocqueville consistently invokes the stabilizing role of female virtue. Tocqueville's account of the connection between female virtue and public order in America begins in Puritan New England: "[I]t is there that the solution of the great social problem which the United States now presents to the world is to be found." He approvingly notes that Puritan legislators invoked the deity and forbade any other worship. Drawing their statutes from the Old Testament, they punished with death the crimes of blasphemy, sorcery, adultery, and rape. Idleness, fornication, and drunkenness were unlawful.

Tocqueville frankly acknowledges the anomaly of such religious law in a free society. Completely contrary to the opinion of European democrats, however, in Tocqueville's America religion is the very ground of democratic order:

> [T]he character of Anglo-American civilization . . . is the result of two distinct elements, which in other places have been in frequent disagreement . . . the spirit of religion and the spirit of liberty. . . . Liberty . . . considers religion as the safeguard of morality, and morality as the best security of law and the surest pledge of the duration of freedom.

Religion governs men's unchecked designs, restrains them from making the unjust and inequitable demands that their self-interest would allow, and makes them submit to the laws of the state below as to the deity above. Religion does this in part by making people believe in immortality and so offsets the destructive materialism of a commercial society that encourages the taste for physical gratification:

> This taste, if it become excessive, soon disposes men to believe that all is matter only; and materialism, in its turn, hurries them on with mad impatience to these same delights; such is the fatal circle within which democratic nations are driven round.

Religion also plays a role in forming the personal character required for self-government. By answering the hard questions about God and human nature—questions beyond the ability of most people to resolve alone—religion relieves people of the temptation to plead moral impotence. Such moral feebleness enervates the soul and prepares a people for servitude, Tocqueville claims, because they come to fear their own unbounded independence.

The most interesting aspect of this analysis of the means by which a democracy can arm itself against disorder is not Tocqueville's emphasis on Puritan religion, however; rather, it is his invocation of "puritanism" in the colloquial sense of sexual repression. Why did the laws of the New England colonies that ground Tocqueville's faith in the American experiment focus so powerfully upon sex? (Half the death penalty crimes he approvingly cites from the Puritan regime were sex crimes.) If, as Tocqueville claims, theological skepticism, materialism, and greed are the destroyers of democratic society, one might think that laws regarding usury, predatory dealing, or sumptuary excess would be more to the point. In light of the feminization of virtue, moreover, the Puritan sex laws, which differed from their centuries-old European precedents in treating male and female sexual misconduct similarly, would not suit the new order.

Tocqueville's move from approving sexual restraint generally to elevating a female sexual virtue reflects the change from the virtue-laden Puritan ideal and its later counterpart, civic republicanism, to the disorderly commercialism of the new age. Tocqueville emphasizes female sexual virtue because he differs from the Puritans in believing that religion often is not strong enough to restrain men from temptation. Rather, religion works through the agency of women, just as American preachers and sentimental writers of the period suggested. "[Religion's] influence over the mind of woman is supreme," writes Tocqueville, "and women are the protectors of morals." Women protect morals by creating a peaceful home: "[W]hen the American retires from the turmoil of public life to the bosom of his family, he finds in it the image of order and of peace." Where the home is peaceful, Tocqueville concludes, men accustom themselves to moderate their political opinions. In Europe, by contrast, "almost all the disturbances of society arise from the irregularities of domestic life."

Despite their vital role as guarantor of public order, Tocqueville admits, women must weep. They are "confined within a narrow circle of domestic life, and their situation is in some respects of extreme dependence." To be a successful democracy is to be both a religious and mercantile nation; religious communities require monogamous marriage as the guarantee of the purity of women's morals, just as trading nations require monogamous marriage so that the household may be orderly and prosperous. "[I]n America the independence of woman is [thus] irrecoverably lost in the bonds of matrimony," he concludes.

If the goal is to preserve woman's role as exemplar of religious self-abnegation and republican sexual discipline, one might think that an explicit regime of force, fear, and authority would be the best solution. But Tocqueville is above all a realist about post-Enlightenment politics. The French and American Revolutions are not about to go away, and so certain social relationships of force and fear cannot be reconstructed. Indeed, Tocqueville wrote *Democracy in America* largely to convince his fellow French aristocrats to stop fighting the democratic tide and turn instead to managing the waves of social change that accompany the spread of political egalitarianism. Accordingly, he acknowledges that women cannot be compelled to take on this role but must be persuaded to assume their burdens voluntarily, as an expression of their own will. Paradoxically, in Tocqueville's account, it is the very autonomy and independence of young American women that allows them to choose this surrender freely:

> [A]mong almost all Protestant nations young women are far more the mistresses of their own actions than they are in Catholic countries. In the United States the doctrines of Protestantism are combined with great political liberty and a most democratic state of society, and nowhere are young women surrendered so early or so completely to their own guidance.

American girls are educated to such strength of will and character so as to surrender the amusements of an unfettered girlhood in order to follow "the only path that can lead to domestic felicity," by submitting "without complaint to the austere duties of their new state."

The problem is not only the practical one of how to oppress in a culture of freedom. This freedom-loving society also must somehow convince a creature cast as a superior moral actor, who has tasted liberty in her independent child-hood, to exercise her moral excellence, but only from a position of subordination. Accomplishing what Tocqueville admits is "so much abnegation on the part of woman" turns out to require what becomes a uniquely pervasive form of domi-nance in the modern world—the social construction of women's sacrifice as con-sent. Tocqueville thus presages an insight that feminist political theorist Carole Pateman comes to generations later: Consent has deteriorated into ideology, not only in democratic political theory but also in the law of sex, and particularly as concerns rape. The consent constructed by ideology cannot be distinguished from habitual acquiescence, assent, silent dissent, submission, or even enforced submis-sion. In making this point, Pateman points to the obvious question raised by Toc-queville's harsh description of marriage: Why would a young and independent woman voluntarily consent to a society of free males, each governing a hierarchi-cal and monogamous household confined by laws and mores that strongly enforce female sexual restraint? Because to do otherwise, answers Tocqueville, "put[s] in jeopardy . . . her social existence":

> Upon her entrance into the world a young American woman finds these no-tions firmly established; [she sees that] she cannot depart for an instant from the established usages of her contemporaries without putting in jeopardy . . . her so-cial existence [and so she] consents . . . voluntarily and freely enters upon this en-gagement. She supports her new condition with courage because she chose it.

Although Tocqueville generally eschews undemocratic notions like forced obedience, the sanctions he approvingly describes for females who withhold their consent are not trivial—loss of peace of mind, honor, social respect, and identity. These are not the death penalties of Puritan New England, but they are hardly to be treated lightly. Yet Tocqueville calls such socially coerced consent "free" and "voluntary."

To further cement the women into his construction of a politics of sexual hier-archy and marital fidelity, Tocqueville also invokes the positive and powerful promise of romantic love. Unlike European aristocrats with their arranged mar-riages, he notes, Americans can marry for love. Somewhat counterintuitively, he argues, this bow to passion actually promotes sexual restraint before marriage. This is not because inflamed lovers will not try to gain sexual access without marriage. Rather, American women, knowing that men are free to marry them regardless of money, family, or station, will not be fooled into believing the greatest seductive ploy of traditional societies—that men love them but cannot marry them. Accord-ingly, the targets of seduction will be more resistant to male wiles. After marriage, Tocqueville continues, those who have married for love will not be unfaithful. This optimistic view does not rest on the lasting nature of love, but on the separate spheres doctrine, which will keep women confined to the household and men to the market, minimizing their opportunities for misbehavior. Nothing he says should be interpreted as requiring sexual fidelity of men, Tocqueville hastens to add; after all, "[t]he equality of conditions cannot . . . ever succeed in making men chaste." In fact, because virtuous wives will not be available for dalliances, he predicts there will in fact be "a great number of courtesans." Prostitution should not be a grave concern, however, because it is less dangerous to a democracy than is the political intrigue that preoccupies men under authoritarian governments.

After invoking social stigma, romance, and reason as ways to gain female consent, Tocqueville proposes in the end what subsequent history will prove was the hardest lure of all for women to resist: American women consent to their sacrificial role because they have better moral characters than men. If American men are driven by their passion for wealth and thus risk all other values for fortune (including not only liberty but also their humanity), women's desires "seem to contract with their fortune as easily as they expand." In short, women have the virtue of moderation that men lack. And so they submit for the sake of the whole.

Tocqueville thus lays out the blueprint of a gender hierarchy suited to a free society, what we will call the "republic of virtue." Free women, treated as equal moral and intellectual players, consent to subordinate themselves to cloistering in the home and exclusion from public life. So willing are they to yield their fates to their husbands that they end up subordinated and living in fever-filled cabins on the western frontier, all in the interest of democracy. Charged with responsibility for the moral well-being of society, these bearers of piety and purity do not even object when their husbands resort to prostitution because they know it is not as bad as treason.

## SEX LAW IN THE REPUBLIC OF VIRTUE

A host of social institutions established and enforced the sexual regime that Tocqueville at once described and prescribed. Sex law was not central to the project of female virtue. Rather, virtue was principally enforced by a combination of mores and exhortation, and by the indirect impact of economic sanction. Almost immediately after its translation into English, for example, *Democracy in America* was adopted as a school text in many American states.

When Tocqueville landed in America in the early 1830s, Massachusetts regulated few sexual acts. Forcible rape was forbidden. The age of consent was ten years. Adultery was prohibited, and, if an adulterous couple later tried to marry, it was considered polygamy. Unmarried sex constituted fornication, but the offense was neither seriously prosecuted nor penalized. Other sexual misbehavior was lumped together in a generic prohibition of lewd and lascivious behavior or of being a lewd and lascivious person. Prostitutes might be imprisoned either for lewd and lascivious behavior or as a "common night-walker."

In Virginia, forcible rape and sex with a child under the age of ten was prohibited. Adultery and fornication were criminal, but the laws were enforced against free men and women only sporadically. Indeed, until 1849, Virginia required fornication or adultery to be proved by the testimony of two witnesses, a rule of evidence not imposed on other crimes.

In addition to the old colonial settlements, by the time Tocqueville came to America new states, of which Illinois is typical, had been entering the union for a generation. The laws of the Northwest Territory governed Illinois until 1815, when the territorial assembly attempted to gain greater control over lawmaking. A lawyer named Pope compiled the laws of the Illinois territory, and Judge Samuel D. Lockwood wrote a supplementary criminal statute, which lasted essentially intact throughout the nineteenth century. Illinois law of the 1830s prohibited forcible rape and sex with a girl under ten years, but required corroborating evidence before conviction. Illinois prohibited men and women from living together outside of marriage, but cases from later in the century reflect that adultery and fornication were unlawful only if "open and notorious." The territorial legislature passed a law in 1807 concerning vagrants, which law enforcement used against prostitution.

As these state examples reflect, the structure of sex law in the early republic was relatively laconic. But this was not a libertine period or one of unregulated sexuality. The reported decisions (limited to cases on appeal) in Massachusetts, for example, include several instances of criminal prosecution for sexual offenses. Notably, the opinions do not differ in tone from other decisions, suggesting that sex crimes were neither unusual nor of any heightened concern. Most sex cases appealed raised the most ordinary of legal issues, such as relevancy of evidence and the elements of criminal intent. Issues of critical social import did occasionally surface in the decisions, but the courts' language does not hint at controversy. In 1839, for example, the Massachusetts Supreme Court definitively interpreted the adultery statute to apply to a married man's infidelities. The decision is important in sexual history, but the opinion itself is an uninteresting exercise in statutory interpretation devoid of commentary on the social import of what the court is ruling. By the end of the nineteenth century, this would change as sex law became a crucible for political reform energies.

It was not sex crimes but the common law doctrine of coverture that was the most powerful legal tool for the enforcement of female virtue. Coverture, usually traced at least to the Norman conquest of England, treated husbands and wives as one person at law, that person being the husband. Under the doctrine of coverture, a husband and a wife could neither testify against nor contract with one another. The wife could not sue or be sued by a third party, she had a limited capacity to make contracts and wills, and all of her personal property, gifts, assets, and earnings belonged to her husband. Although a married woman retained technical ownership of real property, her husband managed the land.

As described in Chapter 4, the "fresh start" that the American Revolution provided to the common law was abandoned soon after independence, and the nation-builders turned to Blackstone for the framework of an American legal system. Blackstone's distillation of the doctrine of coverture and other sex law was more severe than contemporary English common law, particularly with respect to wife-beating. Even Blackstone, however, asserted that a wife recently had been given "security of the peace against her husband." Yet many mid-nineteenth-century American cases explicitly authorized a husband's violence against his wife as needed for private governance. In an 1868 North Carolina case, a husband's battery of his wife was not chargeable as assault on the grounds that "every household has and must have a government of its own, modeled to suit the temper, disposition, and condition of its inmates . . . and we will not interfere or attempt to control it." Many divorce cases from this early period include testimony of appalling physical abuse with no record of criminal prosecution for the family violence.

## SEX LIFE IN THE REPUBLIC OF VIRTUE

What we call the republic of virtue other historians describe as the Cult of True Womanhood or the ideology of domesticity. American society before the Civil War glorified domesticity as women's arena of achievement and fulfillment and romanticized the companionate family. Sentimental novels, popular magazines, religious tracts and sermons, public lectures, and advice books counseled both women and men on the duties and responsibilities of their roles in this emerging social order. This popular literature of domesticity was tremendously successful, in terms of both sales and suasion. Social historian Ann Douglas notes that in the 1850s, the sales of all the works by Hawthorne, Melville, Thoreau, and Whitman did not equal the sales of one of the more popular domestic novels.

These domestic advisors urged women to protect their families from men's worldly ambition and materialism by making home a haven for the piety, self-sacrifice, and emotion increasingly absent from public life:

> We go forth into the world, amidst scenes of business and pleasure . . . [and] we behold every principle of justice and honor disregarded, and good sacrificed to the advancement of personal interest; and we turn from such scenes with a painful sensation, almost believing that virtue has deserted the abodes of men; again, we look to the sanctuary of home; there . . . disinterested love is ready to sacrifice everything at the altar of affection.

Advice writers also urged young men with aspirations in the commercial economy to marry and settle into a virtuous household. An unmarried adult man seemed dangerously unanchored, lacking any female moral counterweight to balance his acquisitive, restless, and aggressive masculine nature. Together, this interlocking system of male and female roles created the separate spheres system: Middle-class women focused on nurturant activities centered around home, children, husband, and church; men lived everywhere else, returning to the shelter of the household for restoration and the gentle influences of piety and purity.

What trust, what confidence, has not God reposed in woman. To man he con-
fides the enterprises of virtue, the labors of government, the conduct of armies,
the mysteries of science, the glorious conquests of eloquence; whilst to woman
he trusts man himself.

The insistence on "opposite" sexes and "separate" spheres translated into gendered boundaries drawn around fundamental aspects of human nature. The newly
emerging profession of medicine made a cottage industry of theories about the
biological differences of women and men, adding scientific weight to the ideology
of domesticity. Physicians emphasized the inferiority of the female brain and her
reason, the physical weakness of her body, and the delicacy of her nervous system.
Historian Stephanie Coontz has collected a sampling of these medical opinions: In
1847, Dr. Charles Meigs described the female to his gynecology class as having "a
head almost too small for intellect and just big enough for love"; in 1849, Dr. Frederick Hollick announced that "the Uterus, it must be remembered, is the controlling organ in the female body, being the most excitable of all, and so intimately
connected, by the ramifications of its numerous nerves, with every other part."
Professor M. L. Holbrook summed up the emerging scientific view neatly in a review of medical research from 1820 to 1870: "It is as if the Almighty, in creating
the female sex, had taken the uterus and built up a woman around it." These descriptions of the female constitution were even more sexualized than those of the
ancient world. Importantly, though, this conception of female sexual nature was
maternal rather than carnal. This reduction of women to their sexual organs led to
the emerging belief that all female ailments could be cured through those organs.
It is in this period that clitoridectomy (surgical removal of a woman's clitoris) first
began to be performed in the United States to "cure" women of various physical
and psychological disorders.

Among the human capacities that shifted from human to female in this era were
piety and virtue, both qualities of core moral, philosophical, and political significance since ancient times. The feminization of virtue was linked to the Great
Awakening, an evangelical revival in New England and upstate New York in the
early part of the nineteenth century. American women responded fervently to the
evangelists' message that, as historian Nancy Cott puts it, "women were made for
God's purposes, not for men's." Preachers spoke of women as moral beings responsible not only for themselves, but also for "effectual reformation . . . in every department of society. . . . [A]ll virtues, all vices, and all characters are intimately
connected with the manners, principles and dispositions of our women."

American women responded by forming moral reform societies that energeti-
cally sought to purify society. Perfectionist and absolutist, these reform organizations were militant in practice and frequently focused on issues of sexual morality.
The Female Moral Reform Society founded in New York in the 1830s, for example, aggressively campaigned against the double standard and men's licentiousness.
Through such organizations, historian Carroll Smith-Rosenberg concludes, oth-

erwise politically disenfranchised women claimed the right to judge public policy for themselves, to criticize the prevailing social morality, and to attack the sexual hypocrisy of their male governors.

After the 1840s, however, virtue increasingly was a personal quality confined to private relations. Further, the pursuit of virtue became not just a woman-friendly domain, as under the evangelical influence, but a peculiarly female domain. Eventually, as Coontz describes, "the concept of virtue was totally trivialized by its nearly exclusive association with women's sexual purity." No longer would women and men spar with the sharp words and biting sexual parries characteristic of the English *Querelle des Femmes.* The "scold" was now the very antithesis of womanhood, no longer the fearsome defender of her sex. Instead, a True Woman's power could be exercised only through her ability to sway her husband and sons:

> She must rely upon the strength of others; man must be engaged in her cause. How is he to be drawn over to her side? . . . It must be by conformity to that character which circumstances demand for the sphere in which she moves; by the exhibition of those qualities which delight and fascinate.

In the emerging Victorian world, a woman's personality not only differed fundamentally from a man's, it also revolved around men, being defined by its capacity to gently influence him.

If domesticity undermined middle-class women's role in public life and social reform, it improved their status and quality of life in the home. British and European visitors commented on the social courtesy accorded women in America. "I have nowhere seen woman occupying a loftier position," Tocqueville observed. Even Tocqueville's feminist counterpart, visiting sociologist Harriet Martineau, described marriage in America as "more universal, more safe, more tranquil, more fortunate than in England." Within marriage, women gained greater control over reproduction and sexual relations. The explicit legal and social approval of wife-beating by husbands was undermined, if not wholly repudiated. Woman's role as moral educator and guardian of her family led to an expansion of interest in female education, and her identification with religiosity led to a more active role in the churches.

But Martineau also puts her finger on the heart of the dilemma of domesticity for Victorian women: "[I]ndulgence is given her as a substitute for justice." Despite their elevation, society respected and protected women only insofar as they complied with an exacting ideal of virtuous and submissive womanhood. The glorification of domestic femininity was tightly bound to a correspondingly harsh condemnation of those women who strayed outside the bonds of patronage and dependence. This definition of "true womanhood" denied not only the economic reality of those who were not middle-class, but ultimately the very womanliness of those who worked outside of the home as well as of enslaved women. Therein lies the poignancy of abolitionist and former slave Sojourner Truth's challenge to this class-bound definition of womanhood in asking, "Ar'n't I a Woman?"

An especially rigid set of mores confined female sexual conduct. Popular and prescriptive literature advanced the norm of female purity, arguing that women lacked much sexual desire and had greater capacity than men to control their feeble passion. Older images of women as carnal and disorderly disappeared; the new ideal of femininity was essentially "passionless." British doctor William Acton, a widely read authority in America, described most women as "happily not troubled with sexual feelings of any kind." For those women who were troubled by such feelings, the advice literature warned of the dangers of falling from purity, even by such chaste means as masturbation.

Intense social stigma attached to extramarital pregnancy as a sign of premarital sex. For a middle-class woman, even the suspicion of premarital sex could destroy her reputation, ruining her chances for marriage. Despite more open sexual relations with men, poor and working-class women also bore alone the consequences of premarital pregnancy and sexual disrepute. With few wage labor opportunities that could support an independent woman (not to mention her child), a woman who could not marry often resorted to prostitution in order to live.

Under these pressures the rate of premarital pregnancy fell steadily. At the end of the eighteenth century, 30 percent of brides bore a first child within eight and a half months of the wedding. By the middle of the nineteenth century, the rate was 10 percent. The behavioral change seems to have come more quickly to the middle class; according to historian Christine Stansell, premarital sex between engaged couples remained acceptable among the white working class until at least the Civil War.

If female purity and male protection were the pillars of the republic of virtue, a woman without a home and family to protect her was fair game. Poor women may not have aspired to strict middle-class standards of sexual respectability but they were especially vulnerable to abuse because their sexual integrity was not regarded as worth defending. We do not know whether sexual predation increased during this era, but we have ample evidence that public concern about it grew, especially among middle-class women. Moral reform societies publicly condemned seducers and actively lobbied state legislatures to make seduction a crime. In 1841, women sent some 40,000 signatures to the New York legislature in support of an anti-seduction law; other states registered similar petition drives in these years. Sentimental novels, like Lydia Maria Child's *Rosenglory*, as well as political tracts like Margaret Fuller's *Woman in the Nineteenth Century*, attacked seduction and also the social hypocrisy that tolerated male sexual liberty but ostracized women for the same acts. Child and others took up the cause of "fallen women," publicly championing notorious cases of women who murdered lovers who had seduced and abandoned them.

In the civil courts, litigation of the tort of seduction increased, especially claims brought by working-class families on behalf of their daughters. The seduction action originated in a father's right to dispose of the services of his daughter, services that her lover had unlawfully commandeered and therefore must pay for. In a social structure in which so much rested on female chastity, seduction—particularly under the promise of marriage—came to be seen as a grievous injury to the life prospects of a woman herself, potentially keeping her from marriage and thus from her role as a fully adult woman in her culture. Although the damages awarded in such cases ostensibly remained linked to the father's loss of services, juries tended to focus on the family's loss of honor and the woman's loss of reputation. Seduction was among the most common of civil actions litigated in nineteenth-century courts.

By the time of the Civil War, the edifice of mores for a private world of sacrificing women was fully in place. With the republic of virtue, we come to the first fully American regime of sexual regulation since the European settlement. We turn, then, to an evaluation of the politics of sex in this first distinctively American sexual state.

## JUDGING SEX IN THE REPUBLIC OF VIRTUE

As a sexual regime the republic of virtue made marriage both the necessary and sufficient condition for sex. For women, any sex with men outside of marriage was prohibited by law as well as the tight corset of mores. From the standpoint of marital sexual bargaining, the balance of power between women and men in this world resembles Puritan Massachusetts. In both societies, bargaining theory's best alternatives to a negotiated agreement of marriage were either shameful and criminal behavior or celibacy. These were the only alternatives. Under such a regime, men and women can be expected to marry in proportion to the level of heterosexual desire they feel, plus their fear of penalties for sex outside of marriage. Although personal sexual history is elusive, some records from the past—letters, diaries, even a medical survey questioning women born early in the Victorian period—allow us to test this prediction. These scattered records indicate deep anxiety associated with heterosexual relations for women because of stigma and dread of pregnancy, fears that often led them to deny their sexual desires, even where permitted inside of marriage. On the other hand, men and women of the period also expressed passionate sexual feelings and described sexual pleasure in courting as well as marriage. Given this intensified climate of both desire and fear, we might conclude that criminalizing adultery and fornication accounted for at least some of the decisions to marry.

Ideology and economics also played a role. The culture had inherited a weighty tradition of Christian preaching for monogamy and reproductive sex. Women who did not marry had few choices of paid work, and even fewer jobs were open to unmarried women with children. If sex, religion, and money were not sufficient pressures toward marriage, there was an avalanche of secular exhortation to the bond directed at those perceived to be "holding out," particularly bachelors in the early period and independent women at the century's end.

The marriage that was woman's citizenship in the republic of virtue was not always a bad sexual bargain. A strong norm of married sex creates certain predictable bargaining outcomes. First, when two parties come together to negotiate for sex, players intent on marriage can count on strong social support for their bargaining stance of sex for marriage. A strong marriage norm prevents the weaker player from having to give away everything to get into the marriage. If, as has been the case for much of history, even bad marriages are better for the weaker player than life in the sexual state of nature, then marriage benefits the weaker player, just as Hobbes's state benefits the weaker player. One might argue that this was the case in colonial Virginia, where women, the weaker players, would have benefited from a more compelling marriage norm. In Chapter 4, we saw that the powerful matrimonial norm in Puritan New England paid off for women in its support for child rearing, its discouragement of their need to resort to prostitution and in fewer unwanted births outside of marriage. If, however, life in the state of nature is not otherwise too bad, a strong marriage norm, standing alone, does not favor either party. To ascertain the effect of a pro-marriage regime, we must inquire into who benefits most from the substantive good that marriage distributes. When we examined Puritan marriage, we noted that marriage itself was a mixed bargain. There was no crime of marital rape and so women not only were forbidden to have sex outside of marriage, they were forbidden to resist sex within marriage. With virtually no possibility of divorce, a wife could not escape a brutal or worthless husband. For women at either end of the economic spectrum—propertied women and wage-earning women—coverture put a steep price on marriage, allowing husbands to claim and control the fruits of female wealth and labor. Compared to this, the alternative of single life in the godly community might not have been so bad. So the strong marriage norm in Puritan Massachusetts seemed to tilt the bargaining toward the males in the heterosexual exchange.

The rapaciousness of Puritan marriage, however, was substantially constrained by strong Protestant norms of equality in salvation and fidelity, and by the demands on all adults of a colonial settlement. The development into the republic of virtue made matters much worse for women and better for men, because it enshrined a radical inequality in the ideology of marriage itself. We have seen how the burden of salvation, and the accompanying burden of fidelity, and, indeed, all moral rectitude, was redistributed from the egalitarian Puritan ideal onto the woman alone. Moreover, we have seen how the necessity for inequality in marriage was built into the very concept of marriage itself. Finally, we have seen how the moral responsibility for the inequality was not borne by the stronger males, but redistributed to the women in the form of the self-inflicted wound of their freely-given consent. As a last measure, the survival of the republic was made to rest on female subordination.

Such a marriage construct leaves women with no bargaining power at all, and they exercised none. Hemmed in by coverture, socialized into submission, charged with the moral and political survival of their nation, women were stripped of even the religiously-based entitlements they had enjoyed since Old Testament times.

Although men at first appear to have been almost completely liberated to self-ishness in the market and licentiousness in the whorehouse, the republic of virtue also constrained men's bargaining options. The disciplining force of the economy toward sobriety, ambition, and industry was powerful. As we will see in later chapters, in the later Victorian period the machinery of virtuous sexual constraint directed to women eventually would be turned on men as well.

Virtue politically justified this tightly bound world of sexual choice, and so we ask first how virtue ethics would judge the republic. From the public virtue of civic republicanism in the 1770s to the domestic sexual virtue of the 1830s, virtue ethics theories share a common core. They ask what the highest purpose of a person is and then evaluate political arrangements according to whether they advance the end specified. The classical virtue of the ancient Greeks took politics and philosophy as the highest human end. Christian virtue sought salvation.

The American republic of virtue was less aspirational. After the experiences of the French Revolution and the failed Articles of the Confederation, American political thinkers were skeptical about men's virtue (and men were their principal concern). Left untended in a democracy, they feared men's selfishness, aggression, materialism, and inclination to faction.

Faced with men's reluctance to embrace political virtue, one solution would have been to abandon democracy. But, as Tocqueville pointed out, the revolutions of the Enlightenment era could not be undone. Accordingly, as Tocqueville and the American Founders agreed, freedom, like virtue, may be treated as aspirational. Tocqueville's post-revolutionary virtue of freedom was imperfect but, as is now the cliche, it was better than any other system of politics.

Moreover, American political thinkers did not forgo all hope for a regime in which stable, other-regarding citizens would also care for the common weal. Liberal individualism and egalitarianism having dissolved the traditional community of neighbors and clan, the only remaining basis for community was the sexual family. In addition, the emerging world of capitalism and commerce required a stability not usually associated with bachelor households, and men were more likely to accumulate wealth beyond their own needs if they could be convinced to adopt a class of dependents. As Foucault described it, semen—the fluid of sex—replaced aristocratic blood as the marker of class membership. Needing guarantors of virtue but skeptical of men's capacity, social and political thinkers gave women the responsibility.

Measured against its classical antecedents, this distinctly American republic of virtue offered women better lives than ancient republics did. In the classical world, the political regime enjoined men to seek virtue but excluded women from this fundamental work of citizenship; creatures of passion in a regime of reason, women properly were kept illiterate and cloistered. In the American republic, women still had to accept monogamy, cloistering, and exclusion from politics. But another political value—freedom—had sprung up to join the virtue of ancient times. With not one but two political virtues to distribute, the male rulers could share virtue with the females. Men claimed freedom, since the Enlightenment the preeminent political virtue, but women assumed the work of virtue in its feminized expression of chastity, piety, stability, and altruism.

Exemplifying virtue is not a bad fate. There is dignity in the role of bearer of national virtue. In accordance with the Protestant ideal of companionate marriage, women in the republic could have sex (at least with their husbands) and also have virtue, clearly an improvement over Christian chastity regimes. Where the republic of virtue fails by the classical measure of virtue ethics is that women were never allowed to govern and thus could not cultivate the true attributes of political virtue. Unfree in both the public and private spheres, women did not govern themselves. Nor did they rotate into the government as male Athenian citizens did, and so they did not develop the virtues of self-disciplined and patient rulers in a system in which they recognize that one day they will be the governed. Women did not cultivate the practical wisdom necessary to govern free and equal peers who must be understood and educated to the rulers' ends. They did not learn liberality in figuring out how to reconcile means and ends in a limited universe of possibilities. Females did not experience the intense sexual friendship that linked mind and body, as the highest ancient construction of male-male sex was conceived.

Some thinkers argue that women really ruled the republic of virtue from within the family. With the rise of the companionate family, women educated and reared children, promoted religion, art and morality, and cultivated these sensibilities in their materialistic and individualistic husbands. From the standpoint of classical virtue, however, ruling the weak does not qualify as an exercise of political virtue because it does not require the highest political virtues of foresight, prudence, and rhetoric. Only dealing with people similar in power and who may themselves one day occupy the seat of governor cultivates such habits of character. Moreover, the "kitchen goddess" idea substantially overstates the power of virtuous women within the nineteenth-century family, a realm walled in by economic dependency and social repression and beyond the reach of ordinary legal protections against rape and battery. Either women did not have to account for family successes or failures such that the virtues of responsibility were denied them, or they bore those responsibilities, especially for the husband's sexual fidelity, without the power to rule him.

Turning to the modern philosophies, classical liberalism is skeptical about knowing the good for others, takes the physical individual as the unit for moral responsibility, values autonomy and freedom, and limits the state to the task of preventing people from harming one another. The republic of virtue fails on each of these counts.

First, the virtue republicans presumed to know the content of the good. Conventional claims that women were paragons and that men lacked virtue assigned meaning to the good, as did the assumption that marital sex should be a good and fulfilling experience. Worse, male thinkers, lawmakers, and experts presumed to know what constituted a good life and good sex for someone other than themselves, a presumption constitutively at odds with liberal skepticism about knowing other people. So, too, the fundamental liberal restraint on legislating the good—that the rules should apply to those making the laws as well as to those subject to them—was absent in a regime in which men prescribed rules for women. In fact, some men also were sexually restrained; for example, men who wanted a married woman faced the prohibition against adultery, but a married man who wanted to fornicate with an unmarried woman was generally tolerated despite the law on the books, and there were few laws against prostitution at all. Further, the exacting demands of sexual respectability consigned many women (and especially poor, nonwhite, or sexually disgraced women) to a netherworld where they were available for virtually unpoliced sexual connection with wandering men. Thus the male governors prescribed a monogamous sexuality and then imposed it on their wives, but not themselves.

Women could not freely act on their own concept of the good and the substantive good that the governors prescribed for women was political and sexual self-sacrifice, exactly the opposite of the individual self-actualization that drives liberal theories of personhood. Thus the ideal of female good was fashioned not in their own interest, but instead to serve the interests of the male governors, the children, the economy, and the nation.

Finally, the state enforced this female ideal despite the liberal prohibition against conscripting people to act affirmatively for the good of others. Women who desired independent lives and a free choice of sexual partners (and the men who wanted to be with them) were driven to enter marriages of legal submission, political inequality, and sexual fidelity so that male citizens could lead individualistic, egalitarian, and competitive lives without creating social disorder. From the standpoint of the final criteria of negative liberty, the republic of virtue failed as a liberal project.

Judged from the standpoint of utilitarianism, these same sexual arrangements are not so obviously flawed. Utilitarians believe that it is possible to know what is good for people, the good consisting of the presence of pleasure or the absence of pain. Because there is nothing constitutively wrong with sacrificing one person to the greater utility of another, the subordination of women in the republic of virtue was not automatically suspect.

A well-ordered republic can be a pleasant place for its citizens. The republic of virtue aspired to a political order that would allow some freedom and equality without having the society deteriorate into the terror of the French Revolution. Further, women in the republic enjoyed the security of lifelong marriage, economic provision for their children, and the pleasures of courtesy, indulgence, and protection. Finally, although women did not enjoy freedom, they did enjoy the feeling of virtue. The pains of sexual frustration, economic dependency, and lack of physical security, however, offset these pleasures.

The republic of virtue also failed to provide values that utilitarianism shares with liberal individualism. First, the regime did not count women's own perceptions of their well-being, instead prescribing what was good for them. Insofar as people are themselves the most reliable source of information about what pleases and pains them, that is a drawback. Rulers who make decisions without input from their subjects make mistakes. Second, even if the rulers did not make mistakes, their decision-making deprived women of the pleasures of feeling in control of their fate, and made them fearful in having to trust instead in the goodwill of others.

Finally, the republic of virtue was not grounded in utilitarian understandings of the good. Even if the rulers knew that the regime reduced women's well-being by more than the pleasure realized by others, the system nonetheless would have survived. The republic's goal was not the greatest good for the greatest number; the regime did not really count women as utilitarian players but instead as virtuous altruists. A small improvement in the well-being of the liberated males would have justified even great sacrifices by the subordinated females.

In the end, the republic of virtue could not be justified by any prevailing political concept of human well-being. In early-nineteenth-century sexual arrangements, separate spheres and female difference kept turning up not as superior virtue or "opposite natures," but rather as inferiority. That inferiority could not be reconciled with the currents of political equality that had been running heavily since the Enlightenment. The only question was when that flood would wash over the most private of nineteenth-century political arrangements, the high walls of the middle-class household.

## NOTES

On the apprenticeship of liberty see Alexis de Tocqueville, *Democracy in America*, vol. 1 trans. Henry Reeve (1840; New York: Vintage Books, 1945), 250, 251–52.

On European "confounding . . . of the sexes," see ibid., vol. 2, third book, ch. 12. On Wollstonecraft and her political writings, see Mary Wollstonecraft, *A Vindication of the Rights of Men, in a Letter to the Right Honourable Edmund Burke; occasioned by his reflection on the Revolution in France* (London: J. Johnson, 1790); *A Vindication of the Rights of Women*, ed. Carol H. Poston (1792; New York: Norton, 1975). On Taylor and Mill, see John Stuart Mill and Harriet Taylor Mill, *Essays on Sex Equality*, ed. Alice S. Rossi (Chicago: Univ. of Chicago Press, 1970), 20. On the American commitment to opposite sexes, see Tocqueville, *Democracy*, vol. 2, third book, ch. 12. Also found in ibid. are: the "natural head" language, the "object of democracy" quote, the observation that American women "attach a sort of pride to the voluntary surrender of their own will," the "equal regard for both their respective parts" quote, and statements on the lack of a sexual double standard in America and on the moral and intellectual equality of American women.

On the contrasting character of American and French women, and on American women's "masculine strength," etc. see ibid.

The "to the superiority of their women" quote is from ibid.; the "whatever affects the condition of women" quote is from ibid., ch. 9.

On the anxieties of Jacksonian America, see generally Karen Halttunen, *Confidence Men and Painted Women: A Study of Middle-Class Culture in America, 1830–1870* (New Haven: Yale Univ. Press, 1982); Marvin Meyers, *The Jacksonian Persuasion: Politics and Belief* (Stanford: Stanford Univ. Press, 1957). For economic changes in the era, see generally Douglass C. North, *The Economic Growth of the United States, 1790–1860* (New York: Norton, 1966). The "prosperity is greater than our virtue can bear" assessment is quoted in Fred Somkin, *Unquiet Eagle: Memory and Desire in the Idea of American Freedom, 1815–1860* (Ithaca: Cornell Univ. Press, 1967), 32. The "no charm in free institutions" quote is from Artemus Bowers Muzzey, *The Young Man's Friend* (Boston: J. Munroe, 1838), 116, cited in Halttunen, supra. *Confidence Men.*

Tocqueville's references to the Puritans are in *Democracy*, vol. 1, ch. 2. The argument for the restraining power of religion and its essential role in democratic order is found in ibid., vol. 2, second book, ch. 15. See also ibid., vol. 2, first book, ch. 5, on the restraining power of religion.

The "women as protectors of morals" quote, the peaceful home observation, and the "domestic disturbances" claim about Europe are all from ibid., vol. 1, ch. 17. The confinement of American wives to a "narrow circle of domestic life" quote is from ibid., vol. 2, third book, ch. 10. On the reasons for the requirement of monogamous marriage and the "irrecoverabl[e] loss" of independence in the "bonds of matrimony," see ibid. On the liberality of the education of American girls and young women, see generally ibid., vol. 2, third book, ch. 9; quotes are from ibid., ch. 10. The "so much abnegation on the part of woman" quote is from ibid.

The Pateman reference is to Carole Pateman, "Women and Consent," *Political Theory* 8 (1980): 149, 150. The "supports her new condition with courage because she chose it" quote is from Tocqueville, *Democracy*, vol. 2, third book, ch. 10. On the resistance of American women to seduction, the role of companionate marriage and separate spheres in preventing adultery, and reasons for tolerating men's resort to prostitution, see ibid., ch. 11. On women's better moral character, see ibid., ch. 12. On women's virtue of moderation, see ibid., ch. 10. On women's self-sacrifice taking them to fever-filled cabins on the western frontier, see ibid.

Massachusetts sex law in the 1830s: Rev. Stats. Mass. sec. 18, p. 718 (1836) (forcible rape); Rev. Stats. Mass. 125, sec. 18, p. 718 (1836) (age of consent); Rev. Stats. Mass. 130, sec. 1, p. 739 (1836) (adultery); Rev. Stats. Mass. secs. 2–3, p. 739 (1836) (adulterers who seek to marry commit polygamy); Rev. Stats. Mass. 130, sec. 5, pp. 739–40 (1836) (fornication punished by two months' imprisonment or $30 fine); Rev. Stats. Mass. 130, sec. 4, p. 739 (1836) (lewd and lascivious behavior); Acts and Resolves of Massachusetts, 1834, ch. 151, secs. 2–3, pp. 190, 192 (common night-walkers).

Virginia sex law in the 1830s: Rev. Code Va. 1819, vol. 1, ch. 158, p. 585 (prohibiting forcible rape and sex with a child under age of 10); Rev. Code Va. 1819 vol. 1, ch. 141 pp. 555–56 (adultery; fine of $20 per offense); Rev. Code Va. 1819 vol. 1, ch. 141, pp. 555–56 (fornication; fine of $10 per offense); Rev. Code Va. 1819 vol. 1, ch. 141, p. 554 (oath of two or more witnesses or the confession of party required as evidence for fornication or adultery); Acts of the State of Virginia 1847–48, ch. 8, p. 110 (free persons should not commit adultery, etc.; no further mention of need for two witnesses).

Illinois sex law in the 1830s: Crim. Code 1833, Fifth Division, sec. 48, p. 179 (forcible rape); Crim. Code 1833, Fifth Division, sec. 48, p. 179 (age of consent); Crim. Code 1833, Fifth Division, sec. 49, p. 179 (in rape case, no need to show emission of semen so long as there is other evidence of violence); Crim. Code 1833, Eleventh Division, sec. 123, p. 198 (adulterous cohabitation). The "open and notorious" requirement is discussed in *Searls v. People*, 13 Ill. 597 (1852) (adultery); 1807 Laws of the Indiana Territory vol. 1, ch. 82, sec. 1, p. 566 (vagrancy defined as being a person whose livelihood is made by gaming, who is wandering, who has no honest calling or no visible means of support).

Among the pedestrian issues raised in early- to mid-nineteenth-century Massachusetts sex crime appeals include problems of relevancy of evidence, e.g., *Commonwealth v. Merriam*, 31 Mass. (14 Pickering) 518 (1833) (did evidence of the defendant's earlier dalliances with the adulterous partner prove dalliance on the litigated occasion), and whether the element of criminal intent had been proved, e.g., *Commonwealth v. Mash*, 48 Mass. (7 Metcalf) 473 (1844) (does mistake of fact about husband's survival negate element of intent to commit adultery by marrying a second time). Among momentous decisions with little fanfare, see *Commonwealth v. Call*, 38 Mass. (21 Pickering) 509 (1839) (criminal adultery statute applies to infidelities of married men). Cf. *Commonwealth v. Lafferty*, 47 Va. (6 Gratt.) 672 (Va. 1849) (wife's unmarried lover not guilty of adultery, but only of fornication).

Although Blackstone allowed that wives "have security of the peace against her husband," William Blackstone, *Commentaries on the Laws of England*, 444–45, many nineteenth-century American cases reflect the opposite view, authorizing a husband's moderate physical violence against a wife. See, e.g., *State v. Rhodes*, 61 N.C. 453, 457, 459 (1868) ("every household has and must have a government of its own, modelled to suit the temper, disposition, and condition of its inmates . . . and we will not interfere").

On the literature of domesticity, see Nancy F. Cott, *The Bonds of Womanhood: "Woman's Sphere" in New England, 1780–1835* (New Haven: Yale Univ. Press, 1977), 69. The "altar of affection" quote is found in Kirk Jeffrey, "The Family as Utopian Retreat from the City," *Soundings* 55 (1972):28 (emphasis in original). On advice to young men, see Stephanie Coontz, *The Social Origins of Private Life: A History of American Families 1600–1900* (London and New York: Verso, 1988), 213. On sales of works by Hawthorne, Melville, Thoreau, and Whitman in the 1850s, see Ann Douglas, *The Feminization of American Culture* (New York: Knopf, 1977), 96, 254.

The "what trust, what confidence" quote is collected in Mary P. Ryan, *The Empire of the Mother: American Writing About Domesticity, 1830 to 1860* (New York: Institute for Research in History and Haworth Press, 1982), 50. On women's less lustful nature, see Nancy F. Cott, "Passionlessness: An Interpretation of Victorian Sexual Ideology, 1790–1850," *Signs* 4 (Winter 1978): 219, 221.

On "separate spheres," see Carl N. Degler, *At Odds: Women and the Family in America from the Revolution to the Present* (New York: Oxford Univ. Press, 1980), 9, 298. In using the term "separate spheres," Linda Kerber helpfully insists on distinction between "an ideology imposed on women, a culture created by women, [and] a set of boundaries expected to be observed by women." Linda K. Kerber, "Separate Spheres, Female Worlds, Woman's Place: The Rhetoric of Women's History," *Journal of American History* 75 (1988): 9, 17 (emphasis in original).

On the role of doctors and other experts in the ideology of domesticity, see generally Carroll Smith-Rosenberg, "The Female Animal: Medical and Biological Views of Woman and Her Role in Nineteenth-Century America," *Journal of American History* 60 (1973):334. The "a head almost too small" quote is collected in Richard W. Wertz and Dorothy C. Wertz, *Lying In: A History of Childbirth in America* (New York: Free Press,

1977), 58. The "uterus . . . is the controlling organ in the female body" is collected in Barbara Ehrenreich and Dierdre English, *For Her Own Good: 150 Years of the Experts' Advice to Women* (Garden City, N.Y.: Anchor Press, 1978), 108. The "taken the uterus and built the woman around it" quote is collected in William and Robin Haller, *The Physician and Sexuality in Victorian America* (Urbana: Univ. of Illinois Press, 1974), 49–50 (all emphases in original). These quotations were gathered by Coontz, *Social Origins*, 222–23. On clitoridectomy in America, see G. J. Barker-Benfield, *The Horrors of the Half-Known Life* (New York: Harper and Row, 1976), 117, 120.

On republicanism, see generally Linda K. Kerber, *Women of the Republic: Intellect and Ideology in Revolutionary America* (Chapel Hill: Univ. of North Carolina Press, 1980). On evangelicism and American women, see Cott, "Passionlessness," 225. The "effectual reformation . . . in every department of society," quote is from ibid., 225, n. 17, quoting Thomas Gisborne, *An Enquiry into the Duties of the Female Sex* (London: T. Cadell Jun. and W. Davies, 1787), 2–3, 187, 193.

On moral reform societies and their sexual agenda, see Carroll Smith-Rosenberg, "Beauty, the Beast, and the Militant Woman: A Case Study in Sex Roles and Social Stress in Jacksonian America," in *Disorderly Conduct: Visions of Gender in Victorian America* (New York: Knopf, 1985), 109, 128.

On the shift from public virtue to sexual virtue, see Coontz, *Social Origins*, 213. Catherine Beecher on "submission" is quoted in Kathryn Kish Sklar, *Catherine Beecher: A Study in American Domesticity* (New Haven: Yale Univ. Press, 1973), 83. The "she must rely upon the strength of others" quote is from Thomas Dew, *Southern Literary Messenger* 1 (1835): 495.

The observations of Alexis de Tocqueville and Harriet Martineau on American marriage are found in Tocqueville, *Democracy*, vol. 2, p. 224, and Harriet Martineau, *Society in America* (New York: Saunders and Otley, 1837), 296. On women's gain in control over reproduction and marital sex, see Daniel Scott Smith, "Family Limitation, Sexual Control, and Domestic Feminism in Victorian America," in *A Heritage of Her Own: Toward a New Social-History of American Women*, ed. Nancy F. Cott and Elizabeth H. Pleck (New York: Simon and Schuster, 1979), 222. On changes in attitudes toward wife-beating, see generally Reva B. Siegel, " 'The Rule of Love': Wife Beating as Prerogative and Privacy," *Yale Law Journal* 105 (1995): 2117. On expansion in women's education and property rights, see generally Degler, *At Odds*. On women's greater power in the churches and the popular culture, see generally Douglas, *Feminization*. The "indulgence instead of justice" quote is from Martineau, *Society in America*, 292.

On changes in views about the carnal nature of women, see Kerber, *Women of the Republic*, 193; Cott, "Passionlessness." Acton is quoted in D'Emilio and Freedman, *Intimate Matters*, 70. On warnings to women against sex, including masturbation, see, e.g., Nicholas Francis Cooke, *Satan in Society (By a Physician)* (1871; New York: Arno Press, 1974); Mary Grove Nichols, *Lectures to Ladies on Anatomy and Physiology* (Boston: Saxton and Peirce, 1842). On the social stigma attached to extramarital pregnancy, see D'Emilio and Freedman, *Intimate Matters*, 77.

For views on the sexuality of poor white women, see Christine Stansell, *City of Women: Sex and Class in New York, 1789–1860* (New York: Knopf, 1986), 20–30. On sexual abuse of enslaved women, see Deborah Gray White, *Ar'n't I a Woman? Female Slaves in the Plantation South* (New York: Norton, 1985), 164–65; Paula Giddings, *When and Where I Enter: The Impact of Black Women on Race and Sex in America* (Toronto and New York: Bantam Books, 1984), 85–90; Elizabeth Fox-Genovese, *Within the Plantation Household: Black and White Women of the Old South* (Chapel Hill: Univ. of North Carolina Press, 1988), 192–241.

On rates of premarital pregnancy at the end of the eighteenth century, see Ellen K.

Rothman, *Hands and Hearts: A History of Courtship in America* (New York: Basic Books, 1984), ch. 1. On comparative rates of premarital pregnancy at mid-nineteenth century, see Daniel Scott Smith and Michael Hindus, "Premarital Pregnancy in America, 1640–1971: An Overview and an Interpretation," *Journal of Interdisciplinary History* 5 (1975); 537; Daniel Scott Smith, "The Dating of the American Sexual Revolution: Evidence and Interpretation," in *The American Family in Social-Historical Perspective,* ed. Michael Gordon (New York: St. Martin's Press, 1973), 321.

On white working-class norms about premarital sex between engaged couples in the antebellum era, see Stansell, *City of Women,* 83, 90, 93, 254 n. 35.

On women's organized lobbying for seduction laws, see Lori D. Ginzberg, *Women and the Work of Benevolence: Morality, Politics, and Class in the 19th-Century United States* (New Haven: Yale Univ. Press, 1990), 77–78. On public support for individual "fallen women," see, e.g., Lydia Maria's Child's 1844 advocacy for Amelia Norman, described in Carolyn L. Karcher, *The First Woman in the Republic: A Cultural Biography of Lydia Maria Child* (New Haven: Yale Univ. Press, 1994), 327–28. On litigation of tort causes of action for seduction, see generally Constance Backhouse, *Petticoats and Prejudice: Women and Law in Nineteenth Century Canada* (Toronto: Women's Press, 1991), 40, 62; Jane E. Larson, " 'Women Understand So Little, They Call My Good Nature Deceit': A Feminist Rethinking of Seduction," *Columbia Law Review* 93 (1993): 374, 381–401; M. B. W. Sinclair, "Seduction and the Myth of the Ideal Woman," *Law and Inequality Journal* 5 (1987): 33.

The reference to a medical survey done of women's sexual history and feelings, questioning women born in the early part of the nineteenth century, is to the work of Dr. Clelia Mosher, discussed in Rosalind Rosenberg, *Beyond Separate Spheres: Intellectual Roots of Modern Feminism* (New Haven: Yale Univ. Press, 1982), 179–86; Degler, *At Odds,* 262–64; and D'Emilio and Freedman, *Intimate Matters,* 74–77. On the passions and pleasures of heterosexual connection amongst Victorians, see Karen Lystra, *Searching the Heart: Women, Men and Romantic Love in Nineteenth-Century America* (New York: Oxford Univ. Press, 1989), and D'Emilio and Freedman, *Intimate Matters,* 74–77.

As Foucault described it, semen—the fluid of sex—replaced aristocratic blood as the marker of class membership. See Michel Foucault. *The History of Sexuality: An Introduction* (New York: Vintage, 1990), 124.

# 6

## CHALLENGING THE REPUBLIC OF VIRTUE

Thirteen years after Tocqueville proclaimed the superiority of self-sacrificing American wives, a group of women met in Seneca Falls, New York, to consider the "social, civic and religious conditions and rights of woman" and reject their domestic martyrdom. This first official gathering of what would become the women's rights movement resulted from the refusal of powerful men within abolitionist organizations to recognize female delegates and officers or to allow women to make speeches in public. The meeting at Seneca Falls made history, not least for being the first public demand for the vote by an organized group of women in America.

### DIVORCE AND PROPERTY: THE MOVEMENT FOR LEGAL REFORM OF MARRIAGE

The vote remains the emblem of nineteenth-century feminism; of equal importance, however, are the struggles of many of these same women against aspects of the sexual order of virtue. The *Declaration of Rights and Sentiments* adopted at Seneca Falls not only demanded the vote for women but condemned the unjust conditions of marriage and divorce and the sexual double standard. The Seneca Falls assembly addressed their sisters directly, calling for women "no longer [to] publish their own degradation by declaring themselves satisfied with their present position, nor their ignorance, by asserting that they have all the rights they want." Like the exclusively male franchise, the sexual order of virtue rested upon the segregation and submission of women, as well as the belief that this arrangement was either natural or necessary. The *Declaration*'s signers urged women to regain self-respect, without which they had been "willing to lead a dependent and abject life," to reject "the circumscribed limits which corrupt custom and a perverted application of the Scriptures have marked out for her," and, in direct contradiction to Tocqueville's exhortation, to move into "the enlarged sphere which her great Creator has assigned her." As a political vision for change, women's claims for equality in public life thus coincided in the *Declaration* with demands for a better deal in the sexual exchange with men. If liberal principles and democratic practice mandated women's inclusion in political and economic life, so, too, the rules of justice that governed human relations in public should apply to private quarters.

The same religious piety and moral fortitude that made Tocqueville confident in the superiority of American women had driven those women to radical breaches of the social order he had entrusted to their care. In the mid-nineteenth century, currents of social change again linked America and England. Radical Christian movements like Quakerism, Methodism, and various strands of religious evangelism grounded this ferment. Quaker elevation of the dictates of inner conscience over external ritual or orthodox belief gave spiritual dignity to the flouting of tradition and custom. The fervor of evangelism cast social activism as a matter of redemption from sin. From the emerging liberal philosophy-religions like Unitarianism came the message that human beings could aspire to perfection in this world and need not wait for the next. The American Transcendentalists had a romantic vision of the divinity in human beings.

In America, this rich mixture of thought and belief found a unified message in the demand to end the sin of racial slavery. The moral imperative not to compromise with sin led religious abolitionists (known as "Garrisonians" after the prominent leader William Lloyd Garrison) to abandon the perhaps more politically pragmatic goal of gradual abolition and to call instead for an absolute and immediate end to slaveholding. Inner conviction compelled many religious women to speak out against slavery, despite the fact that a woman's raised voice in a public meeting could trigger angry rebukes or even a street riot. When not only slavery's defenders but also abolitionist allies resisted women's antislavery activism as unfitting to her gender, the "woman movement" was born. Simultaneously, in England, an educated class learned of arguments for women's rights from sources other than abolitionism, especially French and English socialism and utopianism.

As we described in Chapter 5, male-headed, monogamous marriage was the central institution of the republic of virtue, in which women were expected to sacrifice personal autonomy, economic liberty, bodily integrity, and political authority to ensure the stability and well-being of society. Besides being the only legitimate situs of sex, marriage also was the single most important source of women's economic support. The best-paid wage labor was closed to women workers, and the jobs that were available paid poor and uneducated women less than subsistence. Occupations open to middle-class women, including dressmaker, governess or companion, shop clerk, teacher, or nurse, also were poorly paid as well as rare. Getting and staying married was thus a necessity for women, not just her civic duty or the fulfillment of the romance of the newly companionate family. But once married, the common law stripped women of ownership or control over property.

Such an arrangement for access to sexual and material sustenance contradicted nineteenth-century America's vision of itself as a society of liberty, equality, individualism, and mobility. Accordingly, when egalitarians began to discuss women's rights one might have expected them to challenge first of all the feudal, religious institution of marriage. When the debate over women's status erupted in the early nineteenth century, however, the participants were working against two centuries of Puritan heritage and a burgeoning tradition of sentimentalized domesticity. Puritanism meant that sexuality could be discussed only with extreme discretion, and the romanticization of family life was an ideal that women as well as men aspired to. So, too, the construction of women as the bearers of virtue was a double-edged sword: Women's goodness gave them a place at the table of moral debate, but female authority could be exercised only through persuasion of the husbands, sons, and fathers who represented them in the trading places of power. Thus any claim that women should set the moral tone of society tended to deteriorate into discussions about how women might be made into fit companions for their mates. Feminist Amelia Bloomer, for example, argued passionately throughout the 1850s in the women's rights publication *Lily* to broaden woman's sphere and deepen her educational opportunities, but her best argument was the need to fit woman for her role as mother of the race. Thus when nineteenth-century feminism was born, prudery and domesticity limited the depth of analysis of sexual politics.

Although there was a persistent undercurrent of dissatisfaction with the sexual bargain of virtue, the first public attacks on marriage arose not over the fairness of making inequality the condition of adult female sexuality. Instead, reformers took aim at issues at the margins of marriage—divorce, child custody, and married women's economic rights. First and foremost, women's advocates challenged the legal doctrine of coverture by which a woman upon her marriage was said to be civilly dead.

Even these moderate challenges rent the sexual ideal. Married women's property reform aimed to improve the negotiated agreement of marriage. If women could keep the property they earned or inherited, the content of that marriage would change, even if the laws of fornication and adultery continued to support marriage as the only place for legitimate sexual satisfaction. After property reform, if a husband wanted to control and enjoy his wife's property, he would have to bargain for the arrangement. If the wife chose to do so, she could use that bargaining chip to negotiate over other issues in their common life such as alcohol consumption, sexual mutuality, or joblessness. Similarly, making divorce available made exit from marriage possible, and the existence of exit puts an absolute limit on how rapacious a bargain can be. If divorce is an option, the best alternative to a battering spouse would be life alone, not more life with the battering spouse.

The shape of marriage reform, however, remains a powerful reminder of how little women's interests drove even empowering legal change. Fathers who wished to avoid costly estate arrangements to bypass profligate or untrustworthy sons-in-law were key advocates of property reform, and so it was decades before the property of women without rich fathers (i.e., wage earners) was protected. By century's end, men and women could escape unsupportable marriages by divorce and women had some hope of keeping custody of their children. Yet the limited economic opportunities for women outside of marriage still made the alternative very unattractive.

The public struggles of the Englishwoman, Caroline Sheridan Norton, and her husband George Norton opened the almost century-long property reform movement. In 1827, Norton, the dull and clumsy heir to an aristocratic title and fortune, fell in love with and married Caroline Sheridan, a well-connected woman with a great taste for society and a biting wit. Only nine years later, their unfortunate marriage exploded in a series of lawsuits and public disputes. Norton barred his wife from the door, secreted their children, and sued the prime minister for an adulterous relationship with her. For the next twenty years, Caroline Norton was exposed to the full impact of common law marriage. She could neither divorce George Norton nor testify in her own defense in the adultery litigation. She could not compel her husband to support her while they were separated, nor legally enforce his promises to do so when they negotiated a private settlement. Worst of all, she was powerless to force him to allow her to see her young sons.

As befit a descendant of the playwright Richard Brinsley Sheridan, Caroline Norton turned her private suffering into public performance by writing a series of widely circulated pamphlets. *English Laws for Women in the Nineteenth Century* (1854) attacked the injustice of the law governing married women's property; *A Letter to the Queen on Lord Chancellor Cranworth's Marriage and Divorce Bill* (1855) assailed the provisions of a parliamentary proposal to allow men to divorce their wives for adultery with no comparable remedy for women. If women were not to be left at the mercy of unreliable men like George Norton, Caroline Norton argued, they must be allowed to divorce and remarry, and also to possess their own property or work for a living wage. If an adulterous wife is rightly to be discarded, why not an adulterous husband?

Norton's pamphlets set fires in English reform circles. By using her personal misfortune as the basis of a political critique, Norton collapsed the boundary between the private sphere where civil law did not reach, and the public domain, where men made and enforced law. Against arguments that woman's higher nature suited her only for teaching or other motherly pursuits, Norton posed Lockean claims of the natural right of woman to labor and to profit by her labor. Petitions to Parliament succeeded pamphlets, as reformers took up the cause. Opponents of the irrationality and injustice of coverture joined forces with more conventional law reform organizations interested in rationalizing the murky contradictions of law and equity that governed married women's property rights. This coalition effort brought a bill before the Parliament in 1857 to expand married women's property rights.

In these same years, reformers had set their sights on another institutional remnant from feudal times in England, the ecclesiastical monopoly over dissolution of marriage. By coincidence, in 1856–57 a Royal Commission was studying proposals to establish civil divorce in British law. The increasing secularization of society and the impropriety of the legislature occasionally acting as a judicial body to grant a private bill for divorce—not the claims of women—had fueled calls for divorce reform. Once the general question of the proper grounds for divorce was opened, however, reformers interested in equalizing the sexual exchange rushed in with their own views of what made marriage intolerable. Accordingly, when the Divorce Act of 1857 proposed to punish only adulterous wives with divorce, declining to allow women the same remedy against an adulterous husband, the proposed law was met with scalding criticism. The ensuing parliamentary and public debate starkly revealed the grounding of marriage in ancient assumptions of gender hierarchy. This new clarity fueled the women's rights and sexual reform movements.

Members of Parliament quickly detected the radical possibilities in both proposals, defeating the property bill and severely limiting women's access to divorce. Lawmakers increased some property protections for deserted wives, but not until the Married Women's Property Acts of 1870 and 1882 would married women in Britain gain a reasonably full measure of autonomy with respect to property. What these two early and unsuccessful legislative attempts did accomplish, however, was to place the subject of women's status squarely on the table in the culture and politics of nineteenth-century England.

Although many supporters of marriage reform were little interested in sexual justice, all the strands of support that coalesced for these bills were products of the continuing unfolding of Enlightenment political thought. Once the secular state had displaced the church as the ultimate authority in issues of human governance, even marriage could be the subject of political debate. Once all men were presumptively equal and consent the only legitimate basis for authority, even the conditions of the male-female sexual exchange could be democratized.

The winds sweeping one common law system also stirred another. Mary Wollstonecraft's *Vindication of the Rights of Women* reached America in 1792. A generation later, Scottish utopian Frances Wright transplanted the British infusion of Enlightenment egalitarianism and Unitarian radicalism to American shores, establishing a community in Nashoba, Tennessee, founded on utopian principles of free love and interracial union.

The early transplants to America took root. In 1836, twelve years before the Seneca Falls meeting, another immigrant, the Jewish Ernestine Rose, presented the first petition to the New York legislature for married women's property reform. Two years later, native-born Quaker Sarah Grimké published the first sustained defense of women's equality by an American, *Letters on the Equality of the Sexes, and the Condition of Woman.*

Although inspired in part by the English movement, marriage reform in America was distinctive for its legal and political heritage of secularism. Property rights were of preeminent importance, as was personal dignity and security. Divorce, by contrast, was less a focus in America than in Britain, perhaps because liberalization came more easily to the decentralized system of state law. Because marriage law had been canon law in England, this meant that there was no English common law of divorce for American courts to adopt. Marriage and divorce law had never been in the hands of an ecclesiastical establishment in the U.S. Accordingly, following the Revolution the states had made their own laws on the subject. There were many states in which divorce was almost unknown (except, as in England, for special acts of the legislature), but the availability and grounds for divorce in other states ranged widely, with adultery, desertion, and extreme cruelty common grounds. The most liberal divorce laws grew out of the Puritan tradition of contractual marriage in New England. South Carolina, by contrast, permitted not a single divorce until almost mid-century, reflecting its feudal traditions of organic and enduring hierarchy and authority.

The acceptance of a cruelty ground for divorce was part of a broader attack on the customary and lawful power of a husband to physically discipline his wife. The antebellum temperance movement first raised the issue of wife-beating, classing it among the great evils of alcohol, causing men to abrogate their duty to act as responsible protectors and household heads. Temperance newspapers, poems, songs, and novels featured heart-rending accounts of women and children terrorized, maimed, and killed by drunken husbands and fathers. The Seneca Falls *Declaration* also attacked the chastisement prerogative:

> In the covenant of marriage, she is compelled to promise obedience to her husband, he becoming, to all intents and purposes, her master—the law giving him power to deprive her of her liberty, and to administer chastisement.

The objection here is cast in quite different terms, however, describing the right of private violence as an unjust political imposition on the wife's person.

The *Declaration* also challenged the inequity of existing divorce laws more broadly as "framed . . . wholly regardless of the happiness of women." In other of her political writings, Elizabeth Cady Stanton advocated divorce reform and regularly compared the relationship of husband and wife to that of master and slave: "The right idea of marriage," she wrote, "is at the foundation of all reforms." Stanton went further in her critique and insisted that a wife had a right "to her own person" and "the control of her own body," by which she meant the right not only to be free from violence but to refuse to have sex with her husband. These ideas were too radical for Stanton's feminist allies. A decision was made not to raise the issue of marital rape at the 1860 national women's rights convention, although Lucy Stone wrote in a private letter that "it is clear to me, that question underlies the whole movement, and all our little skirmishing for better laws, and the right to vote, will yet be swallowed up in the real question, viz: Has woman a right to herself?"

By the period 1860-1900, most states allowed some battered wives to divorce their husbands for cruelty. The rate of divorce grew faster than the population in these decades, and the number of cruelty cases outstripped any other statutory basis for divorce except nonsupport. The wife had to claim violence amounting to "extreme cruelty," and not all personal violence amounted to cruelty. For example, a Massachusetts state court in 1867 denied a divorce to a woman who alleged her husband shut her arm in a door and bit her, deprived the wife and her children of furniture and food for weeks at a time, and, after a reconciliation, again resumed beating her. Judges grew more liberal as the century wore on in their interpretation of what amounted to cruel treatment, eventually even recognizing mental and sexual cruelty. An Illinois state court held in 1886 that although repeated instances of shoving, hitting, and kicking might not themselves be cruel, the fact that a husband refused to speak to his wife for a period of two years and six months, although still living with her, amounted to extreme cruelty: "[I]t was great wrong for the husband . . . to remain silent, in comparison with which the bruises made upon her person by his hand and foot are as nothing." Husbands, too, could seek divorce on the ground of cruelty, and in increasing numbers they did so. Typical is a case from Kansas in which the court held that it was extreme cruelty for the wife to write anonymous letters to a clerk in her husband's office charging criminal intimacy between her husband and the clerk's wife, and to send a similar letter to the newspapers for publication and to other employees in the husband's office.

The erosion of the common law chastisement prerogative was more general than just divorce law. Legal historian Reva Siegel claims that by the 1870s there was no judge or treatise writer in the United States who recognized a husband's legal right to physically chastise his wife. Several states had enacted statutes specifically to prohibit wife-beating. Massachusetts, a liberal state with a strong women's rights movement, was the first in 1871 to repudiate the common law right of chastisement in the case of *Commonwealth v. McAfee*. A husband hit his drunk wife in the face and head; she fell, struck her head, and died. At his trial for manslaughter, the husband asked for and was refused a jury instruction that he had a legal right "to administer due and proper correction and corporeal chastisement on his wife." The Massachusetts Supreme Court affirmed his conviction on the grounds that "[b]eating or striking a wife violently with the open hand is not one of the rights conferred on a husband by the marriage, even if the wife be drunk or insolent." Nonetheless, the Massachusetts legislature refused to enact a law that would have allowed a battered wife to obtain a court order preventing a husband convicted of aggravated assault from coming near her or her children without permission or requiring him to pay the family reasonable support.

Although states abandoned the chastisement doctrine, "marital privacy" emerged as a new rationale for continuing law enforcement reluctance to treat wife-beating as a criminal assault. "Once translated from an antiquated to a more contemporary gender idiom," Siegel argues, "the state's justification for treating wife beating differently from other kinds of assault seemed reasonable in ways the law of chastisement did not." If wives no longer were subjects in their husband's Hobbesian commonwealth by acquisition, neither were they subjects of civil society entitled to ordinary legal protections. The new frame around such abuse was fashioned from a concept of the family as a political unit immune from the ordinary precepts of politics, like the state's monopoly on violence.

American reformers were both more at ease and more successful in pressing for married women's property rights, the other aspect of the marriage reform agenda. In the earliest periods of American history, various legal accommodations had eased tensions around the property question. From the colonial period on, many jurisdictions allowed married women the legal power to do business under what were known as "feme sole trader" statutes, by which a husband gave public permission for his wife to conduct her affairs as if she was an unmarried woman. Propertied women who were widowed often declined to remarry, retaining their legal powers. Historian Suzanne Lebsock documents that in Petersburg, Virginia, of ninety women widowed in their thirties from 1784 to 1850, the remarriage rate was less than one-third; for women widowed in their forties, the rate was less than 10 percent. The most eligible widows, younger women with the most wealth, were the least likely of all to remarry. For the very wealthiest women with access to lawyers, English and American courts long had been willing to use equity powers to provide married women some control over inherited property in the form of trusts and separate estates. But in the Jacksonian era American law turned against equity for reasons unrelated to sexual politics, and the movement for statutory reform of married women's property rights grew.

Proponents of property rights made common cause with reformers seeking to rationalize the law more generally. Law reformers wanted to fuse law and equity to eliminate the confusion and complexity that arose from the existence of two distinct and often contradictory bodies of law, a phenomenon especially marked in the area of married women's property. In the United States, this reform was called the Field Code movement, named for a leader in law reform, David Dudley Field. When New York enacted the Field Code just prior to the Seneca Falls convention, the state codified some of the trust principles from equity that had allowed wealthy women to protect their interests in real and personal property. The middle class supported the new laws because the expensive and elaborate requirements for drawing up an enforceable equitable trust for a married woman had been elitist. Creditors and businessmen also supported reform because they resented married women's legal incapacity to enter into enforceable debts. And finally, in keeping with the growing financial uncertainties of capitalist markets in these years, some husbands saw the benefits of placing family property in the hands of their wives, thus shielding it from creditors.

The first statues proposed in New York did not address a married woman's right to keep her wages, and thus mostly benefited women of property. Even in this limited form, it took more than half a century for a majority of American states to enact married women's property acts. Thus for the majority of American women, the strictures of coverture that Blackstone described continued to govern their economic rights in marriage throughout the century.

## HEARTS AND MINDS

Along with the legal struggle to reform marriage, a pitched intellectual battle also brought down the republic of virtue, just as ideas had been constitutive of the paradigm in the first place. In this fight to control the terms of understanding both sex and gender, high honors go to John Stuart Mill, utilitarian philosopher and English politician. After reading his essay *On the Subjection of Women* in 1869, Elizabeth Cady Stanton wrote to him: "I lay the book down with a peace and joy I never felt before, for it is the first response from any man to show he is capable of seeing and feeling all the nice shades and degrees of woman's wrongs."

In recent years, feminist philosophers have criticized Mill for his failure to challenge the naturalness of the female domestic role. Yet in its time and in its scope, *Subjection* was a critical breakthrough in the sexual politics of the modern West. Mill had been exposed as a youth to the best of reform thinking, becoming a member of the Unitarian religious and utilitarian political circles early in his life. His first article (1824) criticized the radical philosophy magazine *Westminster Review* for stereotyping women and constructing a female ideal of sentimentalism and altruism completely at odds with the ideal of male moral character. Some years later, Mill met and began a lifelong relationship with Harriet Taylor, then a married woman. Soon after meeting, Mill and Taylor collaborated on *Essays on Marriage* (1832). In his contribution to the collaboration, Mill articulates for the first time the themes he would develop in later works: The inequity of married women's legal disabilities; the status deficit of single women; the ideal of a marriage of equals; the servitude of indissoluble marriage. Taylor's essay, although not a complete defense of sex equality, is the more radical, particularly in her advocacy of a purely voluntary marriage, dissoluble at will.

Contemporary Millian scholarship endlessly debates Taylor's influence on Mill. A crucial question is whether Taylor wrote or collaborated in Mill's next effort, the anonymous *Enfranchisement of Women* (1851). Regardless of authorship, *Enfranchisement* matters for two reasons: First, it is the product of the American Women's Rights Convention in Worcester, Massachusetts, and thus exemplifies the transatlantic nature of the nineteenth-century debate over sexual politics; second, it articulates the theoretical relationship between public equality in the political realm and private equality within marriage. The year *Enfranchisement* was published Mill and Taylor finally married. On the occasion of their marriage, Mill wrote a formal protest against the laws that would govern their relationship. He sought to renounce:

The whole character of the marriage relation as constituted by law ... for ... it confers upon one of the parties to the contract, legal power and control over the person, property, and freedom of action of the other party, independent of her own wishes and will. . . . [H]aving no means of legally divesting myself of these odious powers . . . I feel it my duty to put on record a formal protest against the existing laws of marriage.

*Enfranchisement* quickly became a best-selling pamphlet in the United States, and Mill's marital protest was widely discussed.

When Mill stood for election to the British House of Commons in 1865, he became the first candidate to make woman suffrage part of his platform. Throughout his legislative career Mill advocated woman suffrage and married women's property rights, but his political efforts confined sexual revolution to the public sphere. (Mill played no role, for example, in the 1866 parliamentary battle over the coercive medical examination of prostitutes, which lit the fuse of English sexual reform for the coming decades.) In 1869, Mill published the magisterial treatment of gender equality, *The Subjection of Women.*

*Subjection* sets forth the best liberal arguments for gender equality. Its analysis justifies the radical suffragism and moderate sex reform that ultimately would prevail in both American and Britain. Like the political vision of suffragism, however, *Subjection* is incomplete as an analysis of male-female sexual politics: Its focus is public and sexual relations are largely private; its proposals for action are voluntaristic, where heterosexuality is marked by compelling drives and coercive moves; its concern with sexual behavior is indirect (child-rearing), whereas sexual practice raises many political issues besides children. Accordingly, after giving this great work its due, we turn in chapter 7 to the other two political sex reform movements of the period, social purity and free love.

Mill's challenge begins with the issue of knowledge, dragging into the light of argument the assumptions that support old orders. The subjection of women is almost universal in both geography and history, Mill observes, thus "the burthen is hard on those who attack an almost universal opinion." Why is this so? In every other school of western philosophy, the burden of proof lies on the advocate; criminal prosecutors, historians, everyone asserting the truth of something ordinarily must go first. But where the subjection of women is concerned, Mill complains, the attackers must go first and prove a negative—that the subjection is not just—which is the hardest proof burden of all. Even if "the a priori presumption is in favour of freedom and impartiality . . . [and] [i]t is held that there should be no restraint not required by the general good," when it comes to the subjection of women it is those who support subjection who get the benefit of belief. Mill says that he accepts that he must prove the negative and anticipate and answer every argument that defenders of subjection may make.

Mill makes some assumptions that favor his position. He will not concede the force of the argument from tradition, and so refuses to treat the duration or ubiquity of women's subjection as an argument for its justice. If the practice had been started after a thorough review of all the different possibilities in constituting society, Mill asserts, tradition might be convincing. But because people have never tried any other arrangement, a defense based on longevity or widespread adherence is just theoretical. This is an astute move, but it is hardly epistemologically neutral: Mill simply chooses to favor reason over tradition as a source of moral knowledge. In a truly open argument, his presumption of reason would itself have to be defended.

Mill also refuses to credit "the law of the strongest" as an argument for women's subjection. Mill argues first that abandoning the position that might makes right is a "fortunate" mark of progressive civilization. He observes that England is so far from the law of the sword that perhaps Englishmen have forgotten how influential physical strength can be in establishing initial political arrangements. In these observations, Mill clearly assumes that defenders of the status quo will be reluctant to rest their case for the subjection of women on force.

Mill still must address the most potent argument for women's subjection, that from nature. In the nineteenth-century struggle to redistribute sexual power, the claim that the gender hierarchy was natural and thus immutable was the most persuasive position against change. For almost two centuries, the move to naturalism had deflected the possibilities for gender and sexual relations embedded in Enlightenment and Protestant egalitarianism. Sexual naturalism had its roots in biblical revelation, but by the eighteenth and nineteenth centuries biological explanations from science were increasingly invoked. As Charles Darwin wrote in the handbook for all such arguments *The Descent of Man*:

> Woman seems to differ from man in mental disposition, chiefly in her greater tenderness and less selfishness. . . . The chief distinction in the intellectual powers of the two sexes is shewn by man's attaining to a higher eminence, in whatever he takes up, than can woman—whether requiring deep thought, reason, or imagination, or merely the uses of the senses and the hands.

When joined with the ideology of domesticity, the move to nature reinforced the political legitimacy of male rule within and without the family. "Opposite sexes," by virtue of their biological differences, constituted distinct creatures who occupied "separate spheres" of human function, but who nonetheless were joined by natural sexual attraction into a relationship properly governed by a rule of love instead of justice. If love unites the interests of men and women, and husbands and fathers are the natural heads of households, men can be trusted not only to govern the household but also to represent women's and children's interests in the political realm. This vision of the natural family denied women's self-interestedness and romanticized the self-interestedness of men into benevolence.

Sex reformers before Mill had dealt with the natural family argument in several ways. First, they cast their complaints in the language of overreaching and did not challenge the structure of marriage as a private, unequal sexual arrangement.

In arguing to limit a husband's access to his wife's body, for example, marriage reformers recounted cases of horrendous violence and abuse. Critics of the husband's unqualified dominance in the family argued for liberalized divorce, for a
mother's right to her children, and for legal intervention in domestic violence as
solutions, rather than attack marriage itself. Caroline Norton, for example, believed that women were men's natural subordinates and opposed woman suffrage.
But when men failed to protect their female dependents as they ought, Norton
insisted, the state had an obligation to do so by allowing divorce, granting married
women full property rights, and defending a mother's rights to her children.

The success of the overreaching strategy relies upon the assumption, dating
back to Aristotle, that the inequality of marriage is not tyranny but a morally
bounded form of rulership. Aristotle characterized the proper political relationship of husbands to their wives as one of aristocratic rule that stopped well short of
slavery. Likewise, the marriage reform argument in the nineteenth century was
that some husbands were not good governors but instead brutes, and the state must
step in to protect helpless dependents. Within this frame of argument, reformers
sought changes in the legal regulation of sexuality to bring laggard behavior into
conformity with an ideal type, but never challenged the "music" of the separate
spheres, the concept that men and women have differing life roles but a common
fate in the joint enterprise called marriage.

The acceptance of difference and dominance in these disputes eventually would
founder on the close ties between sexual reform and abolition. Unlike the monar-
chical and aristocratic claims of right overturned by the Enlightenment political
revolutions, which rested heavily on history or the Bible, sexual hierarchy like racial slavery was a claim of natural right. Defenders of slavery argued that the physical nature of the races differs, that whites are more fit to rule than blacks, that blacks
are incapable of self-governance, and that this natural inferiority and superiority
has persisted since time immemorial and is immutable. Sexual hierarchs claimed
that the physical nature of males and females differs, that men's nature is dominant
and women's submissive, that men always have governed women, and that this is
the condition of mutual happiness.

Not surprisingly, then, Mill's answer to the argument from nature begins with
an invocation of the antislavery sentiment dominant in England by the latter half
of the nineteenth century:

> Was there ever any domination which did not appear natural to those who pos-
> sessed it? ... Did not the slaveholders of the Southern United States maintain the
> same doctrine, with all the fanaticism with which men cling to the theories that
> justify their passions and legitimate their personal interests? Did they not call
> heaven and earth to witness that the dominion of the white man over the black
> is natural, that the black race is by nature incapable of freedom and marked out
> for slavery?

Mill also acknowledges the democratized version of hierarchy posed by thinkers like Tocqueville, who were his contemporaries: "But, it will be said, the rule of men over women differs from all these others in not being a rule of force: it is accepted voluntarily." First, Mill answers, some women do in fact object. More important, he disputes the consent by articulating the now unfashionable, but not necessarily unfounded notion of false consciousness. The ideology of the republic of virtue and the material conditions of nineteenth-century sex law make women believe that they are behaving voluntarily, he argues:

> All causes, social and natural, combine to make it unlikely that women should be collectively rebellious to the power of men. . . . The masters of women wanted more than simple obedience, and they turned the whole force of education to effect their purpose. It would be a miracle if the object of being attractive to men had not become the polar star of feminine education and formation of character.

In this aspect, Mill observes, male dominance and female subjection are different from other forms of social subjugation. And it is here that he finally reaches the particular politics of male-female sex:

> Men do not want solely the obedience of women, they want their sentiments. All men, except the most brutish, desire to have, in the woman most nearly connected with them, not a forced slave but a willing one.

In sum, the desire for companionate marriage carried with it the temptation to try to control the heart and mind of the partner. Mill may have fallen into the naturalistic trap he criticizes in the defenders of patriarchy; as we have seen, the institution of companionate marriage is relatively recent in western history. Although there is talk since Aristotle about marriage being an aristocratic rather than a tyrannical rule, there is little evidence before the eighteenth century of any widespread idea that the bonds of marriage are those of affection rather than duty, authority, and interest. But Mill sees more than just the false consciousness of companionate marriage at work in sexual subjection. He invokes the arguably natural force of heterosexual attraction to argue that women's own interests—"the natural attraction between the opposite sexes"—makes them desire to please men, and makes men want to convince women to want to please them. Nonetheless, whether his argument rests on nature or merely on facts from his own historical context, Mill's point about the political dynamic of companionate desires remains valid.

Mill then proceeds to set forth his own, mostly libertarian, proposal for a new form of male-female sexual union: "Freedom of individual choice is now known to be the only thing which procures the adoption of the best processes, and throws each operation into the hands of those who are best qualified for it." Generalizing from the overthrow of feudalism and racial slavery, he concludes that "we ought not to ordain that to be born a girl instead of a boy . . . shall decide the person's position through all life." All that is required for choice to replace coercion is for men to stop trying to convince women that subordination is either natural or in the female self-interest, and for women to be educated as to their true interests.

Anticipating the Tocquevillean argument that anarchy would result if women were allowed to follow their own inclinations rather than civilizing men and bringing virtue to the republic, Mill turns the naturalist argument on its head. If women are naturally wives and mothers, he asserts, they do not need to be forced into such roles by law and education. This is a weak argument, as Mill acknowledges, because laws are not made for the virtuous majority, but for the deviant few. Thus the issue of what world would ensue if no laws governed the male-female sexual union remains unanswered. Mill takes a stab at it: Women will not marry if they cannot obtain equal conditions; if men insist on inequality as the condition of marriage, women will bolt. Here, Mill's assumptions of the naturalness of freedom and equality again surface, forcing him away from the politically more palatable position that women might continue to play their accustomed role even without force. Rather, he leaves open the much more threatening possibility that substantial social disorder might result from the thoroughgoing application of equality to heterosexuality.

Mill goes on to rebut several other commonplace defenses of marriage as it had been established by common law and custom. First, he answers the "but I really love my wife" argument by observing that much marital affection rests on feminine wiles, which is the response of the disempowered, and not on male virtue. If women stop flattering men, men are not likely to remain so loving and generous to their mates. Next, Mill disputes the claim that women really rule the household as the "power behind the throne." He observes that a wife's advice to her husband is often flawed because she is sequestered from the real issues of the world. To answer the claim that all joint enterprises must have a head, Mill asserts that there is no reason this head must always be the man; authority can rotate, rest on the most able person, or be settled by agreement. Finally, Mill, the lover of liberty, asserts that the family cannot be the school of virtue for democratic citizens if it rests on an arbitrary despotism.

Even as corrosive and original a thinker as Mill, however, ultimately failed to see the connection between the unequal private contract of marriage and the background conditions of women's place in the larger society. Although he recognized that women often marry men older and richer or more enterprising than they, he remained sanguine that free and equal relationships could emerge from private bargaining between such parties. Further, Mill approved the traditional division of marital labor whereby the woman "superintends the domestic expenditure," including "the physical suffering of bearing children and the whole responsibility of their care and education in early years," describing it as the "most suitable division of labour between the two persons." Thus Mill's own assumption of natural freedom misses entirely the coercion of private bargaining that might lead women to choose domesticity, even if society prescribed no particular fate for them at all.

This easy assumption of free choice accords with Mill's faith in liberty and equality as the natural condition of human beings, but is inconsistent with his recognition of culture as the constitutive force in forming women's behavior and the role of law as the constraint on the most savage impulses of nature. In proposing free sexual unions, Mill fails to address the continuing effects of culture on women ("the artificial state superinduced by society disguises the natural tendencies of the thing which is the subject of observation"). Indeed, although Mill generally denies the naturalness of nature, he assumes in the end that women are naturally domestic. So, too, in anticipating the happy evolution of English culture to the point where physical superiority no longer is a legitimate basis for political rule, Mill ignores the critical role of law in restraining violence and threat in private relationships.

For a man involved in one of the most notorious love affairs in all of Victorian society, Mill is frustratingly silent on the subject of sex itself. He could not marry the object of his desire until Harriet Taylor's husband died. It seems safe to assume, then, that Mill did not believe that monogamous marriage was the only outlet for heterosexual desires. Accordingly, he was perhaps less concerned with the specifically sexual oppression of forcing women (and to lesser degree, pressing men) into hierarchical marriage as the only legitimate channel of satisfaction.

In the end, the only explanation for this silence may be that Mill was a philosopher of social and not sexual equality. The failure to focus on sex, or on culture and the impact of unequal bargaining power means, however, that even Mill misses huge pieces of the political picture. As we will see in the following chapters, even after legal reforms and changes in material and cultural worlds, men and women continued to agree to sexual arrangements of deep inequality. Social change would surge past Mill's reformed marriage to sexually open and informal relationships of temporary duration, yet these relationships remained light years away from Mill's happy companionship of educated equals. We are left to explain why male–female sexual bargaining did not change in the ways an unsentimental material philosopher like Mill would have anticipated.

## NOTES

The Declaration of Sentiments and Resolutions, Seneca Falls (1848) is reprinted in *Feminism: The Essential Historical Writings*, ed. Miriam Schneir (New York: Random House, 1972), 76.

On the importance of evangelism and abolitism to the emergence of the woman movement in America, see generally Blanche Glassman Hersh, *The Slavery of Sex: Feminists–Abolitionists in America* (Urbana: Univ. of Illinois Press, 1978).

On the controversy surrounding women's public speaking, see ibid. at 2, 6, 10.

What twentieth-century readers know as the "women's rights movement" or "feminism" was called the "woman movement" in the nineteenth century. To ask "the woman question" was to consider any of the broad range of issues related to women's status, rights, and role in society, from suffrage to property, citizenship, wages, sexual mores, and participation in positions of public influence from law-making to the ministry.

On English sources for women's rights in socialism and utopianism, see Barbara Taylor, *Eve and the New Jerusalem: Socialism and Feminism in the Nineteenth Century* (New York: Pantheon, 1983).

Modern historians characterize the early-nineteenth-century family in England and America as principally bound by ties of romance and affection. See, e.g., Randolph Trumbach, *The Rise of the Egalitarian Family: Aristocratic Relations in Eighteenth-Century England* (New York: Academic Press, 1978), 97 (by 1790, three out of four marriages were made for love) (England); Lawrence Stone, *The Family, Sex and Marriage in England 1500–1800* (London: Wiedenfield and Nicholson, 1977), 392 (same); Carl N. Degler, *At Odds: Women and the Family in America from the Revolution to the Present* (New York: Oxford Univ. Press, 1980), 14 (America). For a critique of these views, see Susan Moller Okin, "Women and the Making of the Sentimental Family," *Philosophy and Public Affairs* II (1982): 65.

Amelia Bloomer's ideas are found in D. C. Bloomer, ed., *Life and Writings of Amelia Bloomer* (1895; rpt., New York: Shocken Books, 1975).

On Caroline Norton, see Mary Lyndon Shanley, *Feminism, Marriage, and the Law in Victorian England, 1850–1895* (Princeton, N.J.: Princeton Univ. Press, 1989), ch. 1, citing *English Laws for Women in the Nineteenth Century* (1854), 160–61, 167–68, and *A Letter to the Queen on Lord Chancellor Cranworth's Marriage and Divorce Bill* (1855), 150–51. Technically, George Norton sued the Prime Minister for "criminal conversation," a common law tort.

On the married women's property and divorce reform efforts in Britain, see Shanley, *Feminism, Marriage, and the Law,* 31–47.

Grimké's essay is reprinted in Schneir, ed., *Feminism: Essential Historical Writings,* 35.

On legislative divorce in America, see generally Richard H. Chused, *Private Acts in Public Places: A Social History of Divorce in the Formative Era of American Family Law* (Philadelphia: Univ. of Pennsylvania Press, 1994). On conditions and grounds for divorce, see generally Marylynn Salmon, "Divorce and Separation," in *Women and the Law of Property in Early America* (Chapel Hill: Univ. of North Carolina Press, 1986), 58–80; Michael S. Hindus and Lynne E. Withey, "The Law of Husband and Wife in Nineteenth-Century America: Changing Views of Divorce," in *Women and the Law: A Social-Historical Perspective,* vol. 2: *Property, Family and the Legal Profession,* ed. D. Kelly Weisberg (Cambridge, Mass.: Schenkman, 1982), 133, 135.

On temperance literature, see Barbara L. Epstein, *The Politics of Domesticity: Women, Evangelism, and Temperance in Nineteenth-Century America* (Middleton, Conn.: Wesleyan Univ. Press, 1981), 109–10.

Stanton's equation of marriage with slavery and her claims of a wife's right to her own body comes from the *Declaration of Sentiments and Resolutions, Seneca Falls* (1848), 76, 82. The Stanton quote is from *Lily,* Nov. 1851. The Stone letter is quoted in Hersh, *Slavery of Sex,* 66.

The Massachusetts case holding that not all spousal violence amounts to cruelty for purposes of divorce is *Bailey v. Bailey,* 97 Mass. 373, 380 (1867). The case about refusal to speak as cruelty is *Sharp v. Sharp,* 116 Ill. 509, 6 N.E. 15, 21 (1886). The Kansas case about the wife's slanderous letters as cruelty is *Carpenter v. Carpenter,* 2 Pac. Rep. 712 (Kan. 1833). On the cruelty ground generally, see Robert L. Griswold, "The Evolution of the Doctrine of Mental Cruelty in Victorian American Divorce, 1790–1900," *Journal of Social History* 19 (1986): 127, 132–35; Robert L. Griswold, "Law, Sex, Cruelty, and Divorce in Victorian America, 1840–1900," *American Quarterly* 38 (1986): 721, 723; Robert

L. Griswold, "Sexual Cruelty and the Case for Divorce in Victorian America," *Signs* II (1986): 529, 529–32. See generally 2 Chester G. Vernier, *American Family Laws* 66 (Stanford: Stanford Univ. Press, 1938) (state-by-state listing of statutory definitions of cruelty ground for divorce). On the incidence of the cruelty claim, see Griswold, "Law, Sex, Cruelty, and Divorce," 722.

Reva B. Siegel's article on wife beating is " 'The Rule of Love': Wife Beating as Prerogative and Privacy," *Yale Law Journal* 105 (1996): 2117, 2129. *Commonwealth v. McAfee* is reported at 108 Mass. 458, 459, 461 (1871) and discussed in Siegel, " 'The Rule of Love,' " 2131–32. On the effects of the companionate marriage ideal on willingness to treat wife beating as assault, see ibid., 2120.

On married women's property rights in equity, see generally Salmon, "Divorce and Separation." On widows' reluctance to remarry, see Suzanne Lebsock, *The Free Women of Petersburg: Status and Culture in a Southern Town, 1784–1860* (New York: Norton, 1984), 26–27. On married women's property reforms in America, see generally Norma Basch, *In the Eyes of the Law: Women, Marriage and Property in Nineteenth-Century New York* (Ithaca: Cornell Univ. Press, 1982) and Lebsock, Free Women of Petersburg, 54–86.

The Stanton letter to Mill is quoted in Alma Lutz, *Created Equal: A Biography of Elizabeth Cady Stanton* (New York: John Day, 1940), 171–72.

Harriet Taylor Mill and John Stuart Mill, *The Enfranchisement of Women* (1853; London: Virago, 1983). Mill's attempted renunciation of his marital rights is quoted in Friedrich A. von Hayek, *John Stuart Mill and Harriet Taylor: Their Correspondence and Subsequent Marriage* (London: Routledge and Kegan Paul, 1951), 168.

*Essays on Sex Equality,* by John Stuart Mill and Harriet Taylor Mill, ed. Alice S. Rossi (Chicago: Univ. of Chicago Press, 1970) (including *The Subjection of Women* (1869). Mill's "burthen of proof" quote is in *Subjection*, 126; his argument for a presumption in favor of freedom, 126–27; his refutation of the argument from tradition, as is his invocation of choice, 129–31; his refutation of the argument from force, 131, his invocation of women's sentiments, 141.

The Darwin quote is from Charles Darwin, *The Descent of Man* (1871; Princeton, N.J.: Princeton Univ. Press, 1981), 326–27.

For a discussion of the claim that men could adequately represent the interests of their wives and children, see Okin, "Women and the Sentimental Family," 74. On Caroline Norton's views of men as women's natural protectors, see Shanley, *Feminism, Marriage, and the Law*, 17–18, 26.

Mill on the supposed "naturalness" of racial slavery is found in *Subjection*, 137–38; his refutation of women's "voluntary" assumption of subordination, 140–42; the "willing slave" quote, 140; the quote arguing that gender should not determine fate, 143–44. Mill on no need of laws, 154; on the "naturalness of woman's role as wife and mother, 178.

Susan Moller Okin, *Justice, Gender and the Family* (New York: Basic Books, 1989), sees the shortcoming of Mill's liberalism on pp. 20–21.

Mill's division of labor argument is found in *Subjection*, 178. Even here, however, one must commend the generosity of spirit in which Mill writes; he notes that if women tried to pursue their talents outside the domestic sphere, the likeliest outcome would be to add to rather than replace their existing responsibilities (see ibid., 178), a social development now widely described as the "Second Shift."

The "artificial state" quote is from ibid., 202.

## 7

## EQUAL FREEDOM VERSUS EQUAL COMMITMENT

"Victorianism" is more a symbol than a word. It serves as shorthand for a familiar description of an era, and also an unquestioned judgment of it. To invoke "Victorianism" is to speak the vocabulary of a libertine culture, part of the language we use to explain ourselves to ourselves. But like most symbols, "Victorian" simplifies the complicated history of nineteenth-century sexual politics, focusing on the movement known as "social purity" and, as we will see, not doing justice even to that piece of the story.

Social purity sought to impose on both men and women the high standards of sexual morality assigned to the idealized female citizens of the republic of virtue. Although in theory no more radical than Tocqueville's republic of virtue, only social purity is painted as repressive and hypocritical. In part this may be because history contains so few actual attempts to legislate aspirational sexual beliefs. But Victorianism also undoubtedly suffers because social purity intended these sexual rules to apply evenhandedly to both sexes. To affect the well-being of people whose personhood truly matters brings home the costs of any sexual regime, whatever its actual or aspirational benefits. Another Victorian sex reform movement, free love, also sought to bring parity to the conditions of male-female sex, but proposed to encourage human sexual self-realization by abandoning marriage altogether. Free love is remembered as the direct ancestor of modern sexual libertinism, but it is social purity that deserves the lion's share of credit for dismantling the republic of virtue by attacking its patriarchal underpinnings. Encompassing strains of social purity, free love, and Millian social reform, the Victorian era is best understood as the period of the breakup of the republic of virtue.

Contemporary disputes over why virtue failed are almost as political as the period itself. Modern sexual liberals tell a Millian story of naturally free human beings struggling against a repressive social order that attempted to contain adult sexuality inside the male-headed, monogamous and heterosexual marriage. Sexual libertarians and Freudians have their own versions of the natural, invoking a powerful force of sexuality that burst the bounds of a propriety doomed from the beginning by its inconsistency with natural drives.

Cultural conservatives like William Kristol attribute the decline of the sexual monopoly of marriage to "women's liberation." If America is ever to flourish according to Kristol, American women must live up to Tocqueville's "flattering portrait" of them as the guarantors of democratic virtue, by "grasp[ing] . . . the necessity of marriage, the importance of good morals and the necessity of inequality within marriage."

Our own reading of history suggests that neither a repressive social order nor boundless sexual nature took the heart out of the republic of virtue. Instead, as Kristol observes, it was the revolt of women. Women's revolt involved a range of overlapping and sometimes inconsistent ideologies and strategies. At turns, Victorian women and their allies fought through the suffrage movement to achieve the Millian goal of equal public status, through the social purity movement to bring parity to the private world of sex and marriage, and to abandon marriage altogether for a spiritualized "free love."

Although the two explicitly sexual movements—social purity and free love—often are posed as opposites in history, they were branches from the same root. Both impulses derived their power from a modern aspiration to male-female parity and a romantic notion of an idealized sexual fulfillment. Free love, like social purity, opposed prostitution, denounced the double standard and other expressions of male sexual dominance, criticized traditional marriage, and aspired to a society in which women as much as men decided about when and how sex happened. Because free love and social purity shared foundational commitments to sexual equality and fulfillment, liberationist free love resembled repressive purity more closely than either movement resembled the public-sphere feminism of suffrage and liberal equality.

Yet this repositioning may overstate the case. Suffrage feminists, too, adopted the sex reform agenda in substance, if not always in emphasis or style. But if suffrage is the child of classical liberalism, social purity and free love reflect the egalitarianism and perfectionism in moral reform movements like abolition, as well as the aspiration to romantic love and companionate marriage growing out of the Protestant Reformation. This equality and romanticism fused in an aspirational ideal of parity and passion in the male-female sexual connection.

Sex reformers saw male-female sex as a means by which the spiritual bond between partners could be spoken and strengthened. If the traditional Christian chastity view had been that sex, being primarily of the body, dragged the soul down to its level, this new ideal elevated the body through an intense spiritualization of the erotic. It was an egalitarian ideal in advancing the claim that women must control their sexual bodies. Elizabeth Cady Stanton said in 1853 that "the right idea of marriage is at the foundation of all reforms. . . . [M]an in his lust has regulated long enough this whole question of sexual intercourse." The revulsion against a wife's legal duty to submit to intercourse was especially strong in free love and social purity, where it was routinely described as "sexual slavery." Thus it was a core principle that women must not be compelled to sex, that men must allow women's sexual needs and rhythms to set the pace, and that wives must be allowed to limit sex in order to avoid unwanted childbirth. The determination to allow women to control sex did not grow out of a revulsion toward sexuality, but instead from the contrary desire to make female sexual pleasure possible by stripping away the history of compulsion, fear, and physical burden.

Purity and free love advocates published dozens of marital advice and physiology books in which they openly acknowledged women's sexual desire. Dr. Elizabeth Blackwell, prominent purity activist and popular speaker, disputed the fallacy that men's sexuality was more powerful than women's, but also insisted that women could enjoy intercourse only if they truly wanted it. Blackwell emphasized that if a woman had not been injured by too-frequent childbirth and could choose when sex happened, "increasing physical satisfaction attaches to the ultimate physical expression of love." Men were counseled that women's sexuality was different from theirs, and that consent and willingness was essential for mutual pleasure.

The ideology of nineteenth-century sex reform is evident not only in the marital advice literature but also in the commitment to sex education (referred to as "moral education"). Reformers urged women to educate themselves and their children in order to lay the groundwork for happy marriages and an end to sexual hypocrisy. Women established Moral Education Societies in cities and towns throughout the country, adopting the slogan, "No Secrets." Both free love and social purity were haunted by the sexual hypocrisies of the republic of virtue. The distance between the ideal of separate but equal spheres and the reality of familial gender hierarchy, between the notion of female authority through virtue and the reality of men's persistent sexual license, and between the claim of equality and the tolerance for a sexual double standard convinced many nineteenth-century women that a just sexual relationship could be had only by tearing away all mystifications. Sex reformers sought to replace nature and sentimentality with an open, rational, and scientific perspective on gender, sex, and family. "If we are to compel a radical change in the wifehood and motherhood, women should know themselves thoroughly in all that pertains to the varying attributes of girlhood, wifehood and maternity," said Dr. Anna Densmore, speaking to a popular audience in a series of scientific lectures for women in 1868. In this desire for sexual truth and reason, conventional reticence about public discussion of sex came to imply, in the words of historian William Leach, "an unjust, authoritarian system of relations in which certain groups and classes monopolized truth and power, in which men wielded undisputed authority over women and nature itself held a mystifying dominion over human life."

If social purity envisioned sex reform as establishing the conditions of equal commitment within a marriage, free love sought an end to traditional marriage and equal freedom to choose and discard sexual partners. Free love did not mean license, but a deep commitment to self-restraint and a belief that love must be the basis of all sexual exchange between men and women. As free love advocate Ezra

Heywood summarized the sex reform impulse, the goal was "to promote discretion and purity in love by bringing sexuality within the domain of reason and moral obligation."

Idealistic and romantic, free love and social purity little resemble the openly materialistic sexuality of early modern England, also a product of the impulse to strip away mystification and secrets surrounding sexual behavior and morality. Yet although informed by this more sophisticated picture of the ideological currents sweeping the nineteenth century, our story ultimately returns to the delayed impact of the freedom, individualism, and egalitarianism of classical liberalism and the other consequences of the Reformation and Enlightenment.

## SOCIAL PURITY

The origins of social purity, like free love, are in the period before the Civil War. The movement did not peak, however, until the last half of the nineteenth century. Once again, events in Britain led the way. In 1864 and 1866, the British Parliament enacted the Contagious Diseases (CD) Acts providing for the forced inspection, detention, and medical treatment of women in certain military districts who were suspected as prostitutes. By this law, the British government in effect recognized the legitimacy of prostitution and sought to assure that soldiers and sailors could find "clean" women to pay for sex. With the potent accusation that the government was thus "licensing," if not outright legalizing "vice," British feminist Josephine Butler launched a public campaign to repeal the CD Acts. The resulting effort linked middle-and upper-class feminists and reformers with radical workers' organizations and social nonconformists. Opposing prostitution in all forms, the antiprostitution movement compared the sale of sexuality to the sale of the person in slavery. The movement that grew out of opposition to the CD Acts was called "the new abolitionism," and, indeed, many activists came to antiprostitution from antislavery work, including the influential abolitionist, William Lloyd Garrison.

The exigencies of the Civil War led some American doctors to make similar proposals to inspect and license prostitutes in the United States. In the 1870s, medical and public health officials revived licensing as a proposed solution to municipal vice problems. Inspired by Josephine Butler's work in England, the American antiprostitution movement that emerged in response also drew on the indigenous tradition of moral reform campaigns against prostitution in the 1830s. Feminists again allied with the clergy and social reformers to use the issue of prostitution to attack tolerance for male sexual license. Thus was born the movement that came to be known as "social purity."

Social purity rested on a bedrock of moderate and conservative women reformers, in particular the members of the Woman's Christian Temperance Union and the General Federation of Women's Clubs. In the last quarter of the nineteenth century, these public-spirited women committed themselves to social and moral change ranging from child labor and child care to consumer protection, temper-

ance, women's education, sex education, municipal sanitation, and prison reform. In the area of antiprostitution, the purity coalition beat back American
initiatives to legalize prostitution and, by the mid-1880s, had definitively de-
feated regulated prostitution in the United States.

Antiprostitution in both in England and America broke the polite conspiracy
of silence surrounding sexual exploitation and commercial sex amongst middle-
class Victorians. Silence, once considered the appropriate method of dealing with
sexual immorality, was recast as neglect or collaboration. Women in the early suffrage movement had feared to air publicly issues of sexual abuse and injustice such
as rape in marriage. Now, through the purity movement, women and men who
did not otherwise see themselves as radicals entered into a profound and sustained
public debate over sexuality. Not until almost a century later with the modern
feminist movement would the Anglo-American world again see such intense debate over sexual politics.

The social purity attack on prostitution has been well documented by modern
historians. Despite this story of grass-roots activism, some have argued that
nineteenth-century women mostly shied away from directly confronting sexual
abuse and exploitation. They argue that middle-class feminists projected the
problem outward by focusing on prostitution as the quintessential crime against
women. Although prostitution was a highly visible symbol of the era's sexual
politics, women of this period also were activists on a much broader range of issues of sexual access, including rape, incest, workplace harassment, and sexual
abuse by professionals. Perhaps the most dramatic example of purity's impact on
sexual regulation was the sustained legislative campaign to raise the age of consent in the law of rape. In the period 1885-1900, this campaign not only strengthened rape laws in the majority of states, but stripped any lingering legitimacy
from the traditional apologies for perpetuating the sexual double standard in law.

Age of consent first emerged as an issue closely connected to antiprostitution.
In 1885, one year before Parliament repealed the CD Acts in deference to social
purity pressure, the London reform newspaper the *Pall Mall Gazette* published an
exposé of child prostitution titled "Maiden Tribute of Modern Babylon." The series documented the abduction, imprisonment, drugging, enticement, and sale of
poor and working-class girls into prostitution in London. In one sensational in-
stallment, editor William Stead wrote about how he had purchased a thirteen-
year-old girl from her mother for the price of five pounds. The series electrified
the British public. A quarter of a million people flocked to a public demonstra-
tion in Hyde Park to demand passage of a bill to raise the age of consent that Parliament had stalled for years.

As with married women's property and divorce, an ancient legal doctrine took
on volatile new meaning in a charged political environment. English common
law had for centuries equated the forcible rape of an adult woman with sexual intercourse with a female child. Indeed, with respect to a range of issues concerning

the power to consent, and long before modern notions of childhood as a time of innocence, the law had acknowledged that children lacked many of the physical, mental, and moral resources of adults. To protect the young from their own bad choices, as well as from manipulation and exploitation of their immaturity by others, the law stripped underage persons of the power to make consequential decisions. These ancient rules remain good law to this day. For example, a minor cannot be held to a contract nor waive a legal right; importantly, neither can an underage child consent to sex. For most legal purposes in the nineteenth century, the common law designated twenty-one years as the age of full moral capacity. But for purposes of rape law, a female child was protected only under the age of ten years. This "age of consent" was adopted along with the common law of rape by the newly formed United States and later codified in state criminal statutes. In most parts of this country in the late nineteenth century, the age of sexual consent for girls was ten years. (In Delaware it was seven years.) Rape standards concerned only females because rape at common law was defined as a crime committed against a female person.

Establishing a statutory age for purposes of rape defines when a defense of consent may be raised. If a child is underage, it does not matter that she agreed to, or even actively solicited, sex with the defendant; liability for rape can be established by the mere fact of the sex itself, with or against her will. But if the alleged victim is over the statutory age, she must meet the more restrictive definition of forcible rape in order to challenge a particular sexual act. A charge of forcible rape usually requires that the complainant refute a defense of consent. Until twentieth-century rape reforms, courts typically required evidence of overwhelming force and utmost resistance as proof that a victim had not consented, making consent a formidable and often insurmountable defense.

The rhetorical "hook" for the American age-of-consent movement was not child prostitution, as in Britain, but the fact that the age of consent in commercial transactions was markedly more protective than the standard in the law of rape. As purity leader Dr. Elizabeth Blackwell bluntly put it, "The present [age of sexual consent] amount[s] virtually to the protection of children only of the years during which the physical abuse of children is so brutal an offence as to excite indignation even among the majority of persons of vicious life." The law recognized that a boy required years of education, nurturing, and experience to develop the intellectual, moral, and emotional strength and judgment to fit him for the economic responsibilities of adult manhood. But to function as a woman, a girl needed only reach the age at which she could be sexually penetrated without grievous physical injury. The markedly lower standard of protection for girls making sexual decisions communicated a powerful message about the law's gendered vision of personhood and moral value: Men and boys had a moral and rational existence, but girls and women existed only as material creatures for sexual function.

To purity reformers, this disparity in legal ages of consent also reflected the elevation of property interests over moral or personal interests. To thus elevate the sphere of market activity dominated by men over the sexual and familial arrangements that determined women's well-being violated the "separate but equal" argument that had justified the republic of virtue. By the late nineteenth century, the intellectual assumptions underlying *Democracy in America* were standard cultural fare; women's sphere of family, church, and charity was as important to social order as the public sphere of politics and markets. How, then, could such legal favoritism be reconciled with Tocqueville's claim that, despite submission in marriage, Americans still regarded women as the moral and intellectual equals of men?

Upon reading the Stead exposé and discovering that U.S. law provided even less protection to girls than did British law, Frances Willard, the charismatic national president of the Woman's Christian Temperance Union (WCTU), adopted the cause. Beginning in 1885, the WCTU launched a national campaign to seek legislation in all states and territories to raise the age of sexual consent. In the latter part of the nineteenth century, the WCTU was one of the few organizations that credibly could have undertaken such an ambitious state-by-state campaign for legal reform. The Union was the largest women's organization in the nation, and the first mass (as opposed to elite) political organization for women in American history. There were 150,000 dues-paying WCTU members in 1892, almost ten times as many members as belonged to the largest woman suffrage organization.

The push began in earnest in the 1886 legislative sessions in state capitols throughout the country, as purity activists drafted a model statute establishing eighteen years as the statutory age of consent and drew up petitions to solicit mass support for reform legislation. The WCTU petitioned the legislatures with vigor, using petitions in the way that modern interest groups use public opinion polls to register with politicians the strength of feeling among their constituents on a particular issue. Other lobbying tactics included visits to legislators and attendance at hearings and debates; solicitation of personal letters from eminent citizens; public education, including mass meetings and speeches by nationally known speakers; and efforts to persuade the press to run favorable coverage at critical moments in the legislative process. In the Texas age-of-consent campaign, one legislator is reported to have said that "he would vote for anything if only the women of his district would let him alone."

Although formally in the role of supplicant to their male legislative representatives as they petitioned, visited, and wrote, women reformers did not hesitate to threaten, scold, and shame legislators just as voters might. The WCTU national newspaper, the *Union Signal*, proposed, for example, to expose and publicize any legislator's opposition to the proposed rape reform, commenting that "[t]he record will be of singular value if carefully preserved and used at future elections." True to their word, the newspaper printed the names of legislators who spoke or voted against age-of-consent legislation, and quoted from opponents' speeches in careful detail. When angered or disappointed by adverse action, campaign leaders often commented bitterly on the argument that women did not need the vote to involve themselves in politics because fathers and husbands would serve as their protectors: "You take the role of protector," they countered, "but then you abuse it."

This rhetoric of protection was an elegant subversion of the separate spheres ideal. At once it justified women's entry into the masculine sphere of politics and appealed to the gender identity of men in the legislatures. In reminding legislators of their duty to protect women, and in particular of the importance of sexual self-restraint as an aspect of manhood, women reformers made support for protective sex laws a test of masculinity. The argument was possible because since the time that Tocqueville expressed the vision of men as driven by uncontrolled desires that could be reined in only by relentless enforcement of female virtue, the Victorian period had seen a shift in the middle-class ideal of manliness. Men were urged to control their passions and impulses by force of will. This shift reflects a growing uneasiness with the arguments of an earlier era that male authority was natural; indeed, even Tocqueville had admitted that in a democracy, "a husband's power [will be] contested." But a man who could master his desires through strong character provided a new, merit-based justification for male social, political, economic, and familial authority. The self-contained man demonstrated that he was fit to assume the patriarchal role of protector and governor of his wife, children, servants, and employees. Male legislators might therefore be pressed to vote against their immediate sexual interests to express loyalty to this higher gender ideal. As the age-of-consent battle reflects, this shift in the ethos of masculinity had egalitarian implications for sexual politics because it required men to exercise virtue, just as the separate spheres ideology long had required of women. Where Tocqueville urged virtuous women to submit to licentious men on the threat that otherwise the men would destroy the republic, Victorian manliness extracted sexual restraint in exchange for the male right to govern. The sexual hierarchy remained constant, but the degree of inequality was subtly moderated.

Given the extraordinary legislative success of the age-of-consent campaign, as well as the surprisingly muted opposition to it, this strategy proved effective, at least for a time. In the first two years of the state-by-state campaigns, twenty states or territories passed laws to raise the statutory age. In 1889 the reformers won a symbolically important victory in persuading Congress to raise the age in the District of Columbia from ten to sixteen years. By 1895 twenty-three states and territories had raised the age to sixteen years or more, and by 1900 thirty-two states had done so. Eleven states and territories had set eighteen years as the age of consent, including, notably, the states and territories that had adopted some form of limited or full woman suffrage. By the turn of the century only three southern states still retained ten years as the statutory age.

As this record of political success suggests, legislative opposition to the reform, although manifest, was subdued and mostly futile. The reform magazine *Arena* arranged to have a constituent write a personal letter to every state legislator in the country to ask him to state his position on raising the age of consent to the age of majority (i.e., twenty-one years). Of more than 9000 letters sent, only two opponents of the proposal were willing to go on the record in response. Supporters, by contrast, flooded the magazine office with replies. The tense silence of opponents suggests that it had become politically dangerous to fight social purity, or to defend either the double standard or the traditional sexual liberties of men. The process of sexual egalitarianism that had begun with Millian liberalism and opposition to the CD Acts in England already had changed the terms of public discourse and pushed these arguments out of the mainstream.

Indications of opposition to strengthening the law of statutory rape can be gleaned, however, from the scrupulous records that activists kept of state legislative debates. Careful attention to these arguments in opposition matter, not because they were effective (they were not), but because they reflect tension between the ideal of sexual restraint and the inadmissible social reality of exploitation, a tension present in sexual history from antiquity to the present day. Opponents to the age-of-consent campaign invoked arguments from sexual "nature," arguments from the morality of sex or punishment, prudential arguments based on the possibility of abuse of law, and modern-sounding arguments of sexual liberty and gender equality. Some of these arguments hearken back to the "good old days" when male sexual liberties were taken as natural and necessary; others give us a peek into our own times when sexual libertinism is defended as resistance to overweening state power or as the only consistent expression of gender equality.

The argument from nature combined a moral naturalism that dates back to Aristotle with a physical naturalism that is specifically a product of Enlightenment materialism and the nineteenth-century infatuation with "science." The physical naturalist claim was that there is a bedrock of sexual predation in the male constitution and the law should reflect this natural order: Men are entitled to sexual access because of naturally exigent, masculine, sexual needs. Opponents defended the right of young men to "sow their wild oats" or spoke of a man's "sex necessity."

Victorian naturalists also saw a natural moral hierarchy between the sexes. They could not follow Aristotle and insist that all women were morally inferior to all men, for that would have been inconsistent with the elevation of female virtue in the prevailing gender ideology. Rather, they argued that only some women were naturally morally inferior and thus proper sexual targets. In defining this subordinate group, other natural categories—race and class in particular—substituted for the natural category of gender. Thus some southern legislators referred to the "undue sensuality" or "early sexual maturity" of African-American and Mexican-American girls, suggesting that these females did not deserve the sexual respect men rightly accorded to "respectable" girls and women. Other law-makers claimed that young working women had loose morals. In many state legis-latures, opponents referred to underage prostitutes whose debauched condition justified any man's sexual use of them. Unlike the "boys will be boys" argument of the physical naturalists, however, the moral naturalists at least recognized the personhood of females by the implicit concession that sexual access to girls and women must be justified as a proper use of another human being—even if the race and class justifications seem to the modern reader to be deeply suspect. Some op-ponents were simply offended that women might attempt to dictate men's sexual conduct.

The second class of argument embraced morality rather than trying to trump it with arguments from nature. From this perspective, demanding sexual restraint of men and boys and sexual protection for girls was not unnatural, but simply unnec-essary, unjust, or unwise. One version of this argument was that raising the age of consent above ten or twelve years was unnecessary because physical maturity is the same as moral maturity. Once girls reach puberty they are ready for sexual activity. Advocates intoned that "nature fixed the age of consent" or delivered lengthy ex-positions of the biological imperative of physical maturity as the threshold of moral and intellectual competence. They commented favorably on the impact of puberty on the "emotional nature," "ratiocinative faculty," and "logical prowess" of young girls, arguing that these females were fully competent to handle sexual solicitations. Although the moral maturity argument partook to some extent of physical naturalism as a basis for morality, it also recognized that for a sexual act with a female to be proper she must consent to it, thus lifting girls and women out of the category of objects for the use of others. The impact of classical liberal as-sumptions had begun to erode the last bastion of natural hierarchy.

Going further, other opponents of the reform argued that even if physical ma-turity is not equated with moral maturity, it still was imprudent to penalize such acts because the punishment was disproportionate to the wrong. Many states, par-ticularly in the South, had prescribed the death penalty for the crime of rape out of largely imaginary fears of interracial rape. Such harsh punishment seemed to many legislators a horrifying consequence when applied to white boys and men. Even outside of the highly racialized context of the South, a common argument was that statutory rape was simply not as bad a crime as forcible rape and should not lead to death, and perhaps not even to imprisonment. Other legislators asked if it was fair for a boy or man who went "innocently" into a brothel to find himself li-able on a charge of rape for having sex with an underage prostitute. In response to such concerns, many states raised the age of sexual consent but also prescribed less severe penalties for statutory than for forcible rape.

A variation of the prudential argument was that "designing and dissolute" girls and women would blackmail boys and men if rape laws were strengthened. In every state legislature this was by far the prevailing argument against raising the age of consent. "Unchaste" girls and young women—specifically "scarlet women," "[w]orking girls . . . urged on by designing mothers," "lecherous, sensual negro wom[e]n," and "inmates of houses of ill-fame"—would use tougher statutory rape provisions to "seduce young men into criminal intercourse and afterwards blackmail their victims." Stronger laws, it was predicted, would "send youths to the gallows, and fill our penitentiaries with immature boys."

A few legislators suggested that the claim for protective sex laws and women's equality was inconsistent: Women want to be placed on an equal footing with men, why should they have this special protection? A legislative supporter of age-of-consent reform tried to explain the thinking of his colleagues: "It is simply the unformed but influential fact in men's minds that they were willing to vote for the protection asked, but only on terms that women should relinquish all claims to a wider sphere of activity."

Although the claim that equality means that women must "play by the same rules" is familiar and persuasive to modern readers, this argument was less common in the late nineteenth century, perhaps because of the widespread acceptance of fundamental sexual differences. Nonetheless, a Kentucky lawmaker defended his state's statutory age of twelve years as a fair balance between the interests of the "young girl" and the "male member of society, who is also worthy of protection." Both male and female feel sexual desire, he argued, and the law should not impose differential penalties upon them for participating in the same sexual act.

Few women or men in the nineteenth century directly challenged age-of-consent reform as an intrusion on personal sexual liberty of either girls or adult men and boys. In 1898, however, free love advocate Lillian Harmon spoke to a British reform group in opposition to protective sex laws. On the basis of biography, we may speculate that Harmon intended to include statutory rape laws in her criticism: At the age of sixteen years, she had been imprisoned in Kansas for her non-state, non-church marriage to Edwin C. Walker, aged thirty-seven years. In her speech, Harmon argued against legal "protection" from certain sexual relations and in favor of the liberty to make sexual "mistakes," including the mistakes of youth:

> I consider uniformity in mode of sexual relations as undesirable and impracticable as enforced uniformity in anything else. For myself, I want the right to profit by my mistakes. If I inadvertently place my hand in the fire, I shall take the liberty to withdraw it; and why should I be unwilling for others to enjoy the same liberty? If I should be able to bring the entire world to live exactly as I live at present, what would that avail me in ten years, when, as I hope, I shall have a broader knowledge of life, and my life therefore probably changed?

As we discuss below, these statements do not mean that free lovers like Harmon were unconcerned about the same issues of sexual abuse and injustice as social purity. They believed, however, that the state had no role to play in enforcing sexual rights and wrongs, subscribing instead to a libertarian or voluntarist ideal of social change.

Through the age-of-consent arguments both pro and con, purity—an uneasy alliance of Christian chastity, republican family order, and egalitarianism—opened a public debate about the terms of sexual access within the hidden world of the virtuous republican family. Stories of girls wronged by boyfriends, stepfathers, employers, and neighbors abound in the literature. Women and girls, reformers suggested, confronted greater sexual danger in the institutions most revered as centers of safety and moral authority than in the streets or from strangers. Reformers recounted incidences of incest, acquaintance rape, workplace sexual harassment, and sexual exploitation within professional relationships. The campaign thus addressed sexual transactions of inequality that would not again attract sustained public attention for almost another century.

There were no legal categories by which to classify these acts of inequality and so they were difficult to describe, much less challenge. American criminal law had been codified from the English common law. Within its ancient and patriarchal framework, if a sexual violation did not fit into the category of forcible rape or statutory rape, it was a wholly lawful act. The legal definition of forcible rape itself was narrowly drawn, failing to cover many instances of coercive and nonconsensual sex. Even with respect to that narrow category of sex crimes that the criminal law did recognize, the attitude toward enforcement was equivocal at best, and more often frankly hostile. Within the framework of existing law, therefore, setting a high age of consent was a strategy for effectively "criminalizing" whole categories of acts not yet treated as sexual crimes, at least for a group of especially vulnerable victims (girls and young women). By expanding the definition of statutory rape (a strict liability offense), reformers could import through the back door more liberal definitions of prohibited sexual acts, and of consent and nonconsent as it applied in existing rape law. In other words, by prosecuting all instances of sexual wrong committed against a girl or young woman as statutory rape, the powerful consent defense in the law of forcible rape could be neutralized. We suggest that reformers grasped the inadequacy of existing sex law and, by raising the age of consent, sought to ameliorate the difficulty of proving rape.

If this strategic interpretation of the age-of-consent initiative is correct, the scope of rape reform aspired to by social purity was almost as sweeping as that eventually accomplished by the modern rape reform movement. As we will see in later chapters, twentieth-century rape reformers directly confronted the assumptions and values embedded in restrictive rape laws and assailed the victimization of adult and married women, as well as girls and young women. The political effort required was enormous, the legislative battles exhausting and intense, the reformers' claims often viewed as extreme and controversial, the organizational resources demanded staggering, and the outcome only partially successful. At the time of the social purity movement a century earlier, it is uncertain whether even the powerful women's organizations aligned with the purity agenda could have achieved such political success with a similar strategy of direct challenge.

Although the age-of-consent initiative achieved spectacular short-term results, over the longer course of time it fell short. After the fervor of the lobbying campaigns cooled, legislators, prosecutors, police, and courts crippled the tougher statutory rape laws. The reform effort had mobilized the lobbying power to enact new laws, but they failed to sustain effective legislative and enforcement monitoring. Some states, either by statute or common law rule, introduced new requirements that the young victim demonstrate her previous chastity to claim protection under the toughened laws. Other states denied protection to "promiscuous" girls, and some jurisdictions recognized a "mistake of age" defense.

Social purity targeted more than prostitution and statutory rape for legal reform. The Christian virtue strand of the purity movement also produced an explosion of sex law that would match the political successes of the egalitarian strand. By the end of the nineteenth century, the statute books were heavy with elaborate and detailed sexual proscriptions, reflecting the vigorous sexual politics of the period. The combination of denigration of sexual desire and calls for its control are not different in kind from what had been expected of females since the early part of the century. But the enforcement on men and the explicit expression of the repressive agenda in law made manifest the strangeness of the assumptions that long had been applied unexamined to women, giving the word "Victorian" its pejorative connotation.

The Young Men's Christian Association of New York, for example, went after obscene literature, culminating in the 1873 enactment of the federal Comstock Act "for the Suppression of Trade in, and Circulation of Obscene Literature and Articles of Immoral Use." The law was named for its most prominent advocate, self-appointed crusader Anthony Comstock, and forbade the mailing of obscene, lewd, lascivious, and indecent writing or advertisements, including material about and articles for contraception and abortion. Unlike the age-of-consent activists, Comstock not only lobbied for stronger laws, but also organized aggressively to enforce them. Acting as an unpaid postal inspector, and with the aid of eager volunteers in local Societies for the Suppression of Vice, Comstock succeeded in banning sexual material from the mails and from public sale and display, ranging from "French" postcards to birth control devices. Throughout the 1880s and 1890s, Congress further strengthened the Comstock law and the courts upheld its constitutionality. By the end of the century, seven states had passed "little Comstock Acts" directed at newsstand and street sales of sexually explicit materials.

Another mark of the intensification of sexual regulation during this period is the campaign to criminalize abortion, beginning in about 1840. During earlier periods of American history, abortion had been both legal and tolerated by custom. The common law rule that came with the colonists to America permitted abortion before "quickening," that point in time when the pregnant woman feels the fetus move (around five months). By the mid-nineteenth century, sharply de-clining birth rates signalled that many married women were turning to abortion. Historians estimate that the rate of abortions per pregnancy in that period was comparable to the rate today. Abortion services and abortifacient products were widely advertised in the popular press; in 1840 in New York City alone, approxi-mately 200 full-time abortionists openly conducted business.

Between 1850 and 1880 states and territories for the first time enacted criminal laws against abortion before quickening. In this new criminal regime, abortion was not a form of homicide, but rather a less grave injury to the person of the fetus. Nonetheless, even this marked a sharp departure from the common law tradition. The campaign to criminalize abortion was led by physicians through the fledgling American Medical Association as part of a move toward professionalization and monopoly over the practice of medicine. As an emerging profession, allopathic (or "regular") physicians sought to cut out competition from "irregulars," especially midwives and other lay healers who provided most of the abortions as well as de-livered most of the babies.

These crusading physicians attacked abortion as medically harmful and abor-tion providers as quacks whose methods and practices could not withstand the probing light of modern science. In the realm of public opinion, the "regulars" po-sitioned themselves as experts whose opinions should be taken as authoritative on the whole range of social issues relating to public health and the body, especially female sexuality and its relationship to woman's proper role. Because physicians sought both respect and business primarily from the middle class, their advice tar-geted middle-class women as in special need of professional guidance. The doctors described the freedom with which this class of women resorted to abortion as self-ish, "unnatural," and a violation of their responsibility as citizens of the republic of virtue. In 1871, the American Medical Association's Committee on Criminal Abortion described the woman who sought an abortion:

> She becomes unmindful of the course marked out for her by Providence, she overlooks the duties imposed on her by the marriage contract. She yields to the pleasures—but shrinks from the pains and responsibilities of maternity; and, destitute of all delicacy and refinements, resigns herself, body and soul, into the hands of unscrupulous and wicked men. Let not the husband of such a wife flatter himself that he possess her affection. Nor can she in turn ever merit even the respect of a virtuous husband. She sinks into old age like a withered tree stripped of its foliage; with the stain of blood upon her soul, she dies without the hand of affection to smooth her pillow.

The anti-abortion campaign dovetailed with Comstock's campaign against birth control information. Federal and state Comstock law prosecutions targeted advertisement, sale, or distribution of abortifacient medicines or instruments.

The powerful impact of all strands of social purity—from the egalitarianism of women's moral reform to Comstock's Christian chastity— is written all over the laws of Massachusetts, Virginia, Illinois, and Wyoming. Sex law, once limited to prohibiting adultery, rape, and whoredom or lewd behavior, by the end of the nineteenth century ran to pages of elaborate and detailed prohibitions. Over the course of the century, Massachusetts, for example, greatly expanded the simple Puritan prohibitions. Massachusetts legislated against abortion ("attempt to pro-cure miscarriage")in the 1840s, becoming the first state in the nation to enact a criminal law that dealt directly and exclusively with the subject. It was a signal of things to come. In 1845, responding to two notorious cases in which criminal charges had been dismissed because abortion before quickening was no common law crime, the legislature made attempted abortion a misdemeanor, with the provision that should the aborted woman die, the crime was a felony. In 1847, Massachusetts made the knowing advertisement of abortifacients or abortion services a minor crime, and, in 1879, strengthened its policy by enacting a Com-stock law with clauses directed at the sale and advertisement of abortifacients. Where once the state had condemned "common night walkers," in response to the antiprostitution movement of the 1880s the state passed a group of laws di-rected at the entire commercial enterprise of prostitution. It became unlawful to induce any person under the age of eighteen years to have unlawful intercourse, to own property used for such acts, to send a female to a house of ill fame, or to detain her once there.

In Virginia, too, prohibitions of prostitution and obscenity, abduction for sex or concubinage, and an anti-abortion law first appear in the statute books by the late 1840s. In the succeeding decades, Virginia elaborated its sex laws, criminaliz-ing seduction, enacting a little Comstock Act against the trade in obscene materi-als, and strengthening penalties for adultery, fornication, and keeping a house of prostitution or lewdness. In 1866, the state raised the age of consent to twelve years, in 1896, to fourteen years, and in 1916, to fifteen years.

Race was deeply woven throughout Virginia sex law. Following emancipation, Virginia abolished its separate penalty schemes for crimes by free and enslaved persons, but not the race line as applied to sexual conduct. The law continued to forbid a white to marry a "negro," or for any person to perform a ceremony of marriage between a white and a "negro" person. As of 1873, such intermarriage was punishable by up to one year imprisonment and a fine of up to $100. As a measure of the enduring significance of race (even as compared with the escalat-ing concern for sexual morality), consider that adultery and fornication carried only a minimum fine of twenty dollars. Clearly, if one were inclined to have sex with a man or woman of another race, it was cheaper to burn than to marry in Virginia. Rape prosecutions in the state also reflect an intense concern to control race through sex law. A black man convicted of the rape or attempted rape of a white woman was sentenced to death. The state-imposed death penalty was complemented by an uncontrolled culture of lynching, particularly when a black man was accused of rape. According to one recent survey, more than 700 black men accused of raping white women were lynched in the South between 1882 and 1930.

In 1867 and 1871, Illinois, too, passed tough anti-abortion laws, criminalizing the sale and advertising of abortifacients, and providing that if the woman died as a consequence of the procedure the abortionist would be tried for murder. The influence of social purity is evident in an 1874 "emergency" statute to prohibit cities and towns from licensing prostitution or inspecting the prostitutes for disease, a response to the St. Louis experiment in regulating prostitution. Every few years for almost a generation, antiprostitution crusaders put some new prohibition concerning prostitution on the statute books, focusing in particular on coerced prostitution, or "white slavery." In 1874, for example, Illinois prohibited abduction of "an unmarried female of chaste life" for prostitution or concubinage; in 1887, they extended the prohibition to the enticement of a woman into prostitution or the detention of a woman by force or debt in a brothel. In 1889, the legislature went further and enacted an elaborate pandering statute that forbade the use of promises, threats, violence, or any other device or scheme to induce a woman into prostitution or to imprison a woman in a brothel. In 1887, the age of consent went from ten to fourteen years, and in 1905, to sixteen years. Two years later the state forbade seduction of an unmarried female under eighteen years, but required corroboration of the complainant's testimony and made subsequent marriage a bar to prosecution.

Beginning in the latter part of the nineteenth century, states carved out of the western territories began to participate in national political struggles, including the battles over women's rights and sex reform. Wyoming, for example, was among the first jurisdictions to allow women to vote, and so adopted many of the reforms on the purity agenda. Early on, the territory had adopted the common-law definition of rape, including ten years as the age of consent. In 1891, the state raised the age to eighteen years. Seduction under promise of marriage was a misdemeanor, but subsequent marriage was a bar to prosecution. Adultery and fornication were criminal only if the man and woman lived together openly. Wyoming legislators moved against abortion in 1870 by amending the poisoning statute to include any attempted or completed abortion that resulted in the woman's death. Women who aborted illegitimate issue were added to the anti-infanticide statute prohibiting concealment of the birth of an illegitimate child. By 1890, abortion of any quick fetus was manslaughter. In that same year, Wyoming lawmakers adopted an unusual provision creating criminal liability for a woman who agrees to an abortion after quickening. Pursuant to the social purity view of women as less culpable than men in sexual error, criminal laws against abortion never held the aborting woman liable; only the abortionist and any person procuring the abortion for a pregnant woman were subject to the laws. Before 1890, Wyoming had regulated prostitution only indirectly under its vagrancy statute ("leading an idle, immoral or profligate course of life"). Reflecting growing concern, the territory criminalized prostitution in 1890, and in 1921 enacted further provisions to suppress the trade.

By the early decades of the twentieth century, sex reform began to recede as political activism on what came to be known as "the girl problem" reflects. Beginning in about 1900, states began to punish girls for underage sexual activity in the name of "protection," creating juvenile status offenses that judged girls delinquent for "precocious sexuality." Enforcement of the delinquency laws fell most harshly on poor and immigrant girls. Ironically, it turned out to be mostly girls rather than men who were placed in state custody to prevent underage sex. Sex reformers became more conservative, nativist, and racist, and retreated from openly feminist positions. The reform-minded women who, in the 1870s and 1880s, pressed to strengthen laws against sexual abuse of girls now joined in the establishment and administration of the new juvenile courts and reformatory institutions to which these girls were committed as delinquents. Having failed in the end to seize power over men's sexuality through legal reform, middle-class women came to lay the heaviest hand on those who were the supposed beneficiaries of their concern. As historian Christine Stansell puts it, reformers made the "language of virtue and vice into a code of class."

## FREE LOVE

Free love contended with social purity for the affiliation of that broad range of religious and reform-minded people committed to equality and romantic sexuality. Grounded in the same critique of marriage as the egalitarian strain of social purity, free love cast off marriage instead of trying to reform it. Although free love never commanded a mass following nor saw its vision translated into law, the movement created a moral language for a sexual ideal that would come to dominate in the twentieth century. Free love championed a positively erotic, romantically charged, companionate, and committed relationship between men and women outside the state-defined boundaries of lifelong marriage. The relational pattern of serial monogamy in current adult heterosexual behavior originates here. Yet in its own era, free love remained on the margins, even of the reform community.

As early as the 1820s, Scottish immigrant Frances Wright lectured on free love and women's rights throughout the United States. Wright spoke against public enforcement of monogamy through law, and also, and more radically, the private oppression of marriage itself. Marriage was an immoral relationship tantamount to legalized prostitution, she argued, because it meant sexual slavery for women, encouraged husbands to sexual license, and permitted sex without love between spouses. Starting from a core assumption of the primacy of human autonomy, Wright typified free love thinking in advocating choice of sexual partners, the right to change partners at will, and the positive value of sexual pleasure without reproduction. In the antebellum years, Wright and other free love radicals established utopian communities, some of which flourished briefly and all of which broke apart from internal conflicts. Fanny Wright's name became synonymous with sexual immorality; "Fanny Wrightism" was a potent charge routinely thrown at women in the early feminist movement who dared criticize sexual inequality in marriage.

Free love emerged from its obscure bohemian precincts in the 1870s with the explosion onto the American scene of Victoria Claflin Woodhull. Woodhull, product of the utopian religious movement of spiritualism, popularized free love ideas in a series of public lectures and through her national newspaper, *Woodhull & Claflin's Weekly*. Notorious and charismatic, Woodhull advanced the erotic as a positive and spiritual human force ("the instinct that creates immortal souls") and stressed the importance of free choice to sensual satisfaction and sexual morality. In the name of marriage reform, Woodhull denounced sexual compulsion of wives: "I would rather be the labor slave of a master, with his whip cracking continually about my ears, than the forced sexual slave of any man a single hour." She also was explicit about the need for men to recognize women's sexual needs and rhythms. True to her word, Woodhull lived openly with a man not her husband. Shocking as she was, when Woodhull spoke in public the halls were filled to overflowing, and at least half the audience was female.

Woodhull's free love advocacy immediately conflicted with the brand of social purity championed by Anthony Comstock. At first, free love seemed helpless to resist the purity steamroller, particularly the criminal prohibitions of obscenity, which were used to prosecute their proselytizing books and magazines. Fighting back, Woodhull sought to use scandal as a technique to weaken her purist adversaries. Most infamously, she broke the story of the Reverend Henry Ward Beecher's affair with one of his parishioners, Elizabeth Tilton. Beecher's church investigated the charges and, in 1875, Tilton's husband sued Beecher for criminal conversation and alienation of affections in a sensational trial that scandalized America. This tactic of exposing sexual hypocrisy was also used by social purity egalitarians. Harriet Beecher Stowe's book exposing the romantic hero Lord Byron for his incestuous relationship with his half-sister, for example, caused almost as much controversy as Woodhull's exposé. Both Woodhull and Stowe attacked male vice with the aim of exposing the double standard. As Paulina Wright Davis put it, they "took hold of those men whose souls are black with crimes and who should be torn from their thrones of the judgment of woman's morals and made to shrink from daring to utter one word against any woman so long as they withhold justice from her." Woodhull was briefly imprisoned on federal charges of sending obscene material through the mails (the muckraking article that began the Beecher-Tilton scandal). Although she eventually was acquitted, she emigrated to England and withdrew from the political world.

Free love persisted despite persecution and its sexual radicalism, largely because its ideal of choice invoked powerful currents of American individualism and libertarianism. Free love could never be dismissed as foreign to American values, shocking as the philosophy was to conventional values. After Woodhull, Ezra Heywood began the New England Free Love League, and after Comstock had Heywood jailed, Moses Harmon took up the cause with his journal *Lucifer, the Light Bearer.*

Free love ideas smoothly overlapped with the beginnings of American cultural bohemianism, centered in Greenwich Village in the decade before World War I, and also with other political and social movements like socialism, anarchism, feminism, and birth control. Like free lovers, the bohemians valorized choice in sexual matters. From the serial monogamy of free love, it was not a long distance to the nonexclusive sexual ethic of the bohemians. It is in this mutation that the term "free love" came to have its contemporary connotations of hedonism, promiscuity, and libertinism, as opposed to the intensely moral and spiritualized sexual values of the nineteenth-century movement.

Anthony Comstock was not slow to see the liberating possibilities in the burgeoning movement to allow accessible birth control, and he targeted Margaret Sanger for prosecution. Comstock arranged for Sanger's arrest, but she fled to Europe. Comstock then brought Sanger's husband to trial for distributing one of her pamphlets in an effort to force him to reveal his wife's whereabouts. When his conviction brought Margaret Sanger home to the United States, the proposal to try her on federal obscenity charges lit a fire of protest in radicals, socialists, intellectuals, and academics. Faced with such opposition, the U.S. Attorney dropped the charges rather than risk making Sanger a martyr.

This defeat marks a change in the prevailing sexual paradigm, one well illustrated by comparing the vision of male-female sex implicit in Sanger's approach to birth control with that associated with the earlier sex reform movements. Social purity and free love had supported birth control, but only through what they termed "voluntary motherhood," or the right of wives to refuse sex to avoid children they did not want. This demand to control the timing of pregnancy depended upon giving women control over the timing of sex, folding the far more radical demand of bodily self-possession into the less controversial insistence that female reproductive health be protected against the ravages of too-frequent childbearing. Although by the mid-nineteenth century middle-class married couples increasingly used contraception and abortion, both social purity and free love argued for voluntary motherhood over what they termed "artificial contraception" such as condoms and abortion. Birth control devices and abortion freed wives somewhat from reproductive consequences (albeit with serious health risks) only by making them increasingly available to sexual demands at any time. Only voluntary motherhood actually shifted sexual power from man to woman, or required intense cooperation between sexual partners for contraceptive success. Only voluntary motherhood, therefore, suited the relational ideal of sexual parity and mutual commitment so cherished by these early sex reformers. Even liberals such as women's rights pioneer Elizabeth Cady Stanton saw abortion not as an avenue of woman's liberty, but evidence of "the degradation of woman" within marriage.

Sanger's approach to birth control, by contrast, abandoned any effort to reform or constrain men. By placing mechanical control over reproduction directly into women's hands, it liberated women for nonmarital sex, especially premarital sex, and opened the door to sexual experimentation by lowering the cost of "mistakes." But it also restricted the amount of sexual responsibility men were expected to take. Sanger's approach rejected the constrained and spiritualized eroticism of Victorian love, embracing instead a healthy, vigorous, natural view of sex as an animal urge shared by women as well as men. Thus dawned the libertine period, the third of our historical regimes of sexual regulation in America.

Not until the 1960s did libertine sexual values command the majoritarian support that the WCTU and Comstock's Anti-Vice Societies had organized for purity values in the latter decades of the nineteenth century. Nonetheless, something changed between the prosecutions of Victoria Woodhull in the 1870s and of Margaret Sanger in 1915. Although officially excluded from the public realm, free love fundamentally changed the language of sexual personhood, replacing purity's collective and communal moral responsibility for sexuality with a new vision of individual and hedonistic self-fulfillment. Such individualist values had been central to the laissez-faire economic liberalism of the nineteenth century. But under the virtue republican and Victorian social purity orders, that individualism had stopped at the kitchen door. Even John Stuart Mill had assumed that women naturally and altruistically would take up the task of social reproduction through childbearing, childrearing, housekeeping, and charity, and would order these worlds on communal and moral grounds. By extending individualism into the male-female sexual exchange, free love arguably changed sex more than any political movement or regulatory legislation could have. Historians John D'Emilio and Estelle Freedman conclude that the sexual revolution presaged by the free love movement took place within the confines of the private world, as people decided privately to limit their families and later to pursue sex outside of marriage without ever confronting the massive cultural changes these private decisions eventually would produce.

Although nineteenth-century free love eventually merged into twentieth-century libertinism, it is important to note that early proponents fiercely resisted any equation of their philosophy with promiscuity, lust, or license. Being based on love and equality, free love was not a sexual free-for-all; its advocates saw individual self-control as the necessary counterbalance to the corrosive effects of free sexual choice. This was their alternative solution to the tension between liberty and virtue in a democracy. Where Tocqueville had established balance by creating two gendered poles, free love sought to establish the balance within each individual. Free love thus allowed people who would have flinched at a completely individualistic, pleasure-seeking political morality a middle ground on which to stand: They could support the idea of sex outside of marriage, but all in the name of women's social equality, romantic love, and an elevated personal morality.

These antistate and individualist assumptions meant, however, that free love ultimately would turn the corner to libertinism. The valorization of the sexual component of romantic love and the overriding commitment to consent and sexual self-actualization forced a break with the communal virtue of virtue republicanism and social purity. If consent is the measure of sexual morality, structural and collectivist avenues to sexual exchange such as marriage and age of consent will fall morally short. Rule-based systems are general in application and can never assure perfect consent in every instance. By this exacting standard, nothing but a purified and privatized regime of individual consent to sexual partnering with no restrictions on exit ultimately would suffice. Any abrogation of sexual liberty became an immoral oppression of the best parts of the human spirit.

## JUDGING THE COMPETING SEXUAL SCHEMES

Contemporary libertines shiver at the word "Victorian," but a key focus of reform in that era was to control sex in the interests of women, not to deny either the urgency or pleasure of sexuality. To employ sexual constraint as a strategy for woman's liberation is counterintuitive to readers attuned to the modern feminist movement, which has equated greater sexual liberty with advances in women's status. But consider that in historical periods when women have had the least social authority and political rights, they have been seen as having far more powerful sexual feelings and desires than men. Only in the nineteenth century when women began to assert political and social authority was female sexual restraint established as a respected social norm. This seeming paradox should lead the reader at least to question the commonplace wisdom that Victorian sexual restraint was a mark of subordination rather than a strategy for empowerment. Historian Joan Kelly argues that historical eras traditionally labeled as "progressive" by historians are not always periods of progress for women, and may in fact bring greater restriction to their lives. The opposite also seems to be true, at least of the Victorian period. This historical period labeled "repressive" was one in which women successfully employed social and state controls over private sexual oppression, particularly within middle-class marriage. As historian Carl Degler puts it, "as a class, women would have a tendency to move in this direction [of sexual restraint] if only because sexuality was the primary source of women's subordination to men; the very institution in which the subordination of women to men was most clearly accomplished."

Against the background of the republic of virtue, any shift of the burden of sexual chastity from women to men served an egalitarian end and empowered women to bargain for something better than the ancient inequality of the double standard. Other aspects of the sex reform agenda—the age-of-consent issue, for example—strengthened women's bargaining power by challenging the legitimacy of sexual access to the young, a structurally disempowered player. Once the young and dependent were out of bounds, heterosexual men had to focus their sexual needs on the adult women to whom they were married or could be married. The antiprostitution movement served a similarly strategic end: Women opposed the "medical" legitimation of prostitution in part because they did not want their husbands given permission to seek sexual satisfaction outside of marriage.

The absence of a crime of marital rape makes this strategy of forcing men into marital sex risky for women, but note that social purity also employed a third bargaining strategy, the ideological campaign for husbandly restraint and deference to the sexual rhythms of the wife. By linking husbandly restraint to the erotic rewards of consensual sex, purity proposed a new sexual bargain: Stay home and treat us right, and we will have good sex together.

But this strategic agenda contrasts sharply with other, less strategic commitments. Opposition to birth control and abortion did not equally divide the sexual burden between men and women, but instead further disempowered women. The triumph of Comstock's anti-contraception campaign represented a rejection of women's offer of better sex for more restraint, and Comstock's anti-obscenity and anti-abortion laws sought chastity with no corresponding payoff in sexual equality or mutuality, an unattractive offer for both women and men.

In its varied commitments, social purity was an anomalous mixture of strands of western political thought from virtue ethics to liberalism to utilitarianism. Christian chastity, with its rhetoric of "purity" and "beastliness," is rooted in the platonic idea of the superiority of the spirit over the body. Like later virtue thinkers from Aquinas to Tocqueville, purity saw the natural and virtuous setting for the human sexual capability as monogamous heterosexual marriage. But unlike their Christian and virtue republican counterparts, the egalitarian strain of purity wanted to jettison the gender hierarchy that had been accepted as divinely ordained, natural, or necessary to marriage. In this claim for sexual fairness, purity was not "Victorian" in the Tocquevillean sense so much as a true child of classical liberalism. Indeed, in shining the light of egalitarianism deeply into the sexual marriage, these reformers were more liberal even than John Stuart Mill, whose works are silent on that hidden part of the marriage bargain. Finally, in publicizing sexual suffering—the pain of rape, the damage done to exploited children and youth, the social indignity of sexual dispossession in marriage and prostitution—purity articulated utilitarian concerns in the realm of sex, a form of political argument that would grow greatly in importance to women's politics in the late twentieth century.

But if purity drew part of its understanding from each of the available political theories, the movement also missed critical insights these theories offered. In all previous virtue traditions, marriage rested on male governance. In attempting to separate inequality from monogamy by insisting on a single standard of sexual restraint, purity overlooked or underestimated the social and the natural forces that would reproduce the ancient hierarchical arrangements. Even if allegiance to

Christian chastity created agreement on the husband's abstention from prostitution, for example, when push came to shove on other matters of dispute between a married couple, the wife's economic and social inequality in the public sphere and her natural state of inequality with regard to physical size, strength, and childbearing, made her a weak bargainer within the private sphere of marriage. A woman in this disempowered position rarely could make the most potent threat of all—exit. Even if "separate but equal" valued and dignified women's roles and thereby encouraged parity between husband and wife, in the end it was more significant that neither Christian nor republican virtue provided reliable arguments against hierarchy as such.

The flaw of social purity politics was thus the flip side of Mill's mistake. Purity tried to force equality on the sexual transaction within marriage without addressing the next circle of inequality within the home or the outermost circle of inequality in the public sphere. Mill, on the other hand, powerfully challenged public inequality, less successfully invoked norms of friendship and companionate marriage against the inequalities within the home, and left the core of sexual hierarchy untouched.

Just as important, purity undervalued the "pleasure" half of the utilitarian calculus in their focus on the pain of sex and through their association with the anti-physicalism of Christian chastity. As a result, and despite the broad promise of "no secrets," calls for restraint and an end to sexual pain easily translated into denial of sexual satisfaction, making sex a sterile zone. As we will see in coming chapters, this impoverishment would imprint the libertarian dismantling of the purity regime of regulation. Those who sought to remove restraints came to believe that sexual pain was the necessary price for the return of sexual pleasure. Sadly, the possibility of a sexual regime of pleasure without the pain so vividly backlighted by social purity came to seem a utopian dream.

Free love passionately denounced sexual pain but opposed legal reform as a restriction on human sexual freedom. Personal self-restraint was the ideal. Free love leader Moses Harmon, for example, was monogamous in marriage as well as abstinent with alcohol, although he vehemently opposed legal efforts to regulate either matrimony or liquor. His daughter, Lillian Harmon, condemned rape as a violation of a woman's right of self-ownership, and thought that the "undue prominence" of sexuality unreasonably restricted the social, economic, and political activities of women in the world. Yet she trusted to changes in informal norms and social morality rather than the reform of coercive law to lessen these constraints on women's security and activity.

Free love idealists were thus naive about the impact of private power on male-female sexual bargaining. With no legal strictures and no ideology other than individual freedom and hedonistic self-actualization, free love had no institutions and few arguments in favor of anything but the will of the strong. Even the commitment to sexual satisfaction for females as well as males dissolved under the argument that the sexual satisfaction of the strong cannot be sacrificed to the nonsexual interests of the weaker players. And, as free love slid into libertinism, the ideals of self-discipline that made the movement morally palatable at the end of the republic of virtue disappeared.

Insofar as free love had a bargaining strategy, it was articulated by the liberal suffragists. Like the free love advocates, liberal feminists hoped to position women as men already were in Enlightenment political theory—as rational, interest-maximizing players pursuing individual rather than family or community interests possessing personal rights enforceable against others rather than personal duties owed to others. In pursuit of this end, liberal feminists sought suffrage and property rights as their primary political goals. With the vote, women could express political interests separate from those of fathers and husbands. With economic agency, women could live independently and seek individual happiness and self-realization. Although suffragists joined sex reformers in decrying "crimes against women," their preferred political remedy for endemic sexual injustice was liberalized divorce. To these liberal feminists, reformed sexual relations meant equal and reciprocal duties within the ongoing relation of marriage. But more important, it meant the right to break that relation when the bargain went bad. In short, the solution to bad men was for women to leave them and live independently.

Like social purity, the liberals also failed to acknowledge fully the pleasure-seeking part of the sexual dynamic. Where sexual pleasure was associated with pain (as sex under conditions of inequality was), or where sexual pleasure required background arrangements of stability (as a free market does), they could not explain the willingness of many women to forgo liberty or equality in exchange for sexual pleasure.

From a bargaining standpoint, the "emancipation" strategy also overlooked the role that social inequality and the physical burdens of childbearing and childrearing would play in women's bargaining with men for their rational self-interest. The romantic lives of many of the era's female sexual pioneers—Frances Wright, Victoria Woodhull, and Mary Wollstonecraft, for example—are sad testaments to the fate of even the strongest and bravest of women in an unregulated regime of private bargaining with structurally stronger players. Wollstonecraft threw herself off a bridge to her death when she was abandoned by the lover who had impregnated her. Wright could not face childbearing outside of wedlock and ultimately married. Cabined in this private relationship, she spent the rest of her life struggling in lonely isolation with the economic exploitation authorized by that marriage, cut off from political support. Woodhull left the United States under the cloud of the Beecher-Tilton scandal, married, remained in England, and never again spoke out on free love.

As historian Elizabeth Clark emphasizes, this liberal emphasis on sexual freedom and a working definition of the male-female union as a voluntary alliance of equals also made the continuing dependency of many mothers and children seem shameful. In political terms, this preoccupation with individual freedom prevented liberals and free lovers from developing an agenda that could put communal support and resources behind those who bore the burden of reproduction.

But before we can assess more completely the successes and failures of the children of free love, we must examine the long period of its hegemony—the libertine twentieth century.

## NOTES

The Kristol quotes are from William Kristol, "Women's Liberation: The Relevance of Tocqueville," in *Interpreting Tocqueville's Democracy in America,* ed. Ken Masugi (Savage, Md.: Rowman and Littlefield, 1991), 480,491.

D'Emilio and Freedman also argue for a close link between social purity and free love. See John D'Emilio and Estelle B. Freedman, *Intimate Matters: A History of Sexuality in America* (New York: Harper and Row, 1988), ch. 7.

Stanton on "the right idea of marriage" is quoted in Ronald G. Walters, *The Anti-Slavery Appeal: American Abolitionism After 1830* (Baltimore: Johns Hopkins Univ. Press, 1976), 81.

The Blackwell quote is from Elizabeth Blackwell, "On the Abuses of Sex—II. Fornication," in Erna Olafson Hellerstein et al., eds., *Victorian Women: A Documentary Account of Women's Lives in Nineteenth Century England, France, and the United States* (Stanford: Stanford Univ. Press, 1981), 179–80. See also Elizabeth Blackwell, *The Human Element in Sex: A Medical Inquiry into the Relation of Sexual Physiology to Christian Morality* (London: J. and A. Churchill, 1884).

On the Moral Education societies and "No Secrets" as the reformers' ideal of sexuality, see William Leach, *True Love and Perfect Union: The Feminist Reform of Sex and Society* (New York: Basic Books, 1980), ch. 2. The Densmore quote is from "Lectures of Dr. Densmore," *Revolution,* March 19, 1868 (emphasis in the original). These are cited in Leach, *True Love.* The "mystifying dominion" quote is from ibid., 42–43. The Heywood quote is in ibid., 42.

On antiprostitution in England, see generally Judith R. Walkowitz, "Male Vice and Female Virtue: Feminism and the Politics of Prostitution in Nineteenth Century Britain," in *Powers of Desire: The Politics of Sexuality,* ed. Ann Snitow, Christine Stansell, and Sharon Thompson (New York: Monthly Review Press, 1983), 419; Judith R. Walkowitz, *Prostitution and Victorian Society: Women, Class, and the State* (Cambridge: Cambridge Univ. Press, 1980). On the international movement against legalization or regulation of prostitution, see generally David J. Pivar, *Purity Crusade: Sexual Morality and Social Control, 1868–1900* (Westport, Conn.: Greenwood Press, 1973).

On antiprostitution in the U.S., see generally Barbara Meil Hobson, *Uneasy Virtue: The Politics of Prostitution and the American Reform Tradition,* 2nd ed. (Chicago: Univ. of Chicago Press, 1990); Ruth Rosen, *The Lost Sisterhood: Prostitution in America, 1900–1918* (Baltimore: Johns Hopkins Univ. Press, 1982). On the legalization controversy in America, see William W. Sanger, *The History of Prostitution: Its Extent, Causes, and Effects Throughout the World* (1858; rpt., New York: Arno Press, 1972), appendix pp. 694–95, and John Chynoweth Burnham, "The Medical Inspection of Prostitutes in America in the Nineteenth Century: The St. Louis Experiment and Its Sequel," *Bulletin of the History of Medicine* 45 (1971): 203.

General information about the WCTU is taken from authors' research in the Frances E. Willard archive, National Woman's Christian Temperance Union, Evanston, Ill., and the following published sources: Frances E. Willard, *Glimpses of Fifty Years* (Evanston: Woman's Temperance Publication Association, 1889), Ruth Bordin, *Woman and Temperance: The Quest for Power and Liberty* (New Brunswick, N.J.: Rutgers Univ. Press, 1981), Ruth Bordin, *Frances Willard: A Biography* (Chapel Hill: Univ. of North Carolina Press, 1986); Mari Jo Buhle, *Women and American Socialism, 1870–1920* (Urbana: Univ. of Illinois Press, 1981). All quotations of Frances Willard are taken from her presidential addresses to the annual meetings of the WCTU 1885–98, articles in the WCTU national newspaper from the same period, or Willard's speeches as collected and reprinted in Amy Rose Slagell, "A Good Woman Speaking Well: The Oratory of Frances E. Willard" (Ph D. dissertation, University of Wisconsin, 1992), 37.

On the claim that prostitution was the preeminent concern of social purity, see Ellen Carol DuBois and Linda Gordon, "Seeking Ecstasy on the Battlefield: Danger and Pleasure in Nineteenth Century Feminist Sexual Thought," in *Pleasure and Danger: Exploring Female Sexuality,* ed. Carole S. Vance (Boston: Routledge and Kegan Paul, 1984), 31, 32–33. Elizabeth Pleck disputes this claim, arguing that although prostitution was the favored symbol of woman's sexual victimization, nineteenth-century feminists also were activists on issues of rape. See Elizabeth Pleck, "Feminist Responses to 'Crimes Against Women,' 1868–1896," *Signs* 8, (1983): 451, 469.

On the age of sexual consent in early British and European law, see Statute of Westminster I, 1275, 2 Edw. 1, ch. 13, and 18 Eliz. 1, ch. 7 (1576) (Britain); James A. Brundage, *Law, Sex, and Christian Society in Medieval Europe* (Chicago: Univ. of Chicago Press, 1987), 311 (Europe). On the legal incapacity of youth generally, see Homer H. Clark, Jr., *The Law of Domestic Relations in the United States* (St. Paul: West Publishing, 1968), sec. 8.1, p. 230. The rape statute quoted is the Statute of Elizabeth.

On the first statutory rape statutes in the states of the U.S., see 75 C.J.S. Rape sec. 13 (Brooklyn: American Law Book, 1952); 65 Am. Jur.2d Rape sec. 15 at 768–71 (Rochester: Co-operative Publishing, 1972). On the gender-specificity of rape law, see 75 C.J.S. Rape secs. 1,7 (Brooklyn: American Law Book, 1952). On the transformations in rape doctrine associated with the modern rape reform movement, see generally Leigh Bienen, "Rape III—National Developments in Rape Reform Legislation," *Women's Rights Law Reporter* 6 (1980): 170, and Susan Estrich, "Rape," *Yale Law Journal* 95 (1986): 1087.

For a more detailed account of the age-of-consent reform movement, see generally Jane E. Larson, " 'Even a Worm Will Turn at Last': Rape Reform in Late Nineteenth Century America," *Yale Journal of Law and the Humanities* 9 (1997): 1. The "protection of children" quote is from Emily Blackwell, M.D., "Another Physician Speaks," The Shame of America—The Age of Consent Laws in the United States: A Symposium, *Arena* 12 (Jan. 1895): 192, 213. The "he would vote for anything" quote is from Helen H. Gardner, "A Battle for Sound Morality, Final Paper," *Arena* 14 (Nov. 1895): 401, 409 (report of Helen M. Stoddard, President, WCTU of Texas). The success of the age-of-consent reform is chronicled in Susan B. Anthony and Ida Husted Harper, eds., *The History of Woman Suffrage,* vol. 4 (1882–1900); rpt., (New York: Arno Press, 1969), 465–1011.

On the manliness ideal, see generally Norman Vance, *The Sinews of the Spirit: The Ideal of Christian Manliness in Victorian Literature and Religious Thought* (Cambridge: Cambridge Univ. Press, 1985); Anthony Rotundo, "Learning About Manhood: Gender Ideals and the Middle-Class Family in Nineteenth-Century America," in *Manliness and Morality: Middle-Class Masculinity in Britain and America, 1800–1940,* ed. J. A. Mangan and James Walvin (New York: St. Martin's Press, 1987), 37–40, 43–46. Tocqueville on the contest to a husband's authority is from Alexis de Tocqueville, *Democracy in America,* vol. 2, trans. Henry Reeve (New York: Modern Library, 1981), ch. 9.

Opponents' arguments to age-of-consent reform are recorded in a series of articles published in *Arena* throughout 1895: "The Age of Consent: A Symposium," *Arena* 12

(April 1895): 282; Edgar Maurice Smith, "Laws Governing the Age of Consent in Canada—A Comparison with Those of the United States," *Arena* 13 (June 1895): 88; "Opposing Views by Legislators on the Age of Consent—A Symposium," *Arena* 13 (July 1895): 209; Helen H. Gardner, "A Battle for Sound Morality; or, The History of Recent Age-of-Consent Legislation in the United States, Part II," *Arena* 14 (Sept. 1895): 1; Helen H. Gardner, "A Battle for Sound Morality, Part III," *Arena* 14 (Oct. 1895): 205; Helen H. Gardner, "A Battle for Sound Morality, Final Paper," *Arena* 14 (Nov. 1895): 401.

On the ubiquitous blackmail argument, it is routinely claimed that stronger sex laws of any character will lead to extortion, although evidence is rarely offered for such assertions. Even so, skepticism about the credibility of female accusers has led to lackluster enforcement of criminal sex law from the common law era—see Anna Clark, *Women's Silence, Men's Violence* (London: Pandora Press, 1987), 52–55; Frank McLynn, *Crime and Punishment in Eighteenth-Century England* (London, New York: Routledge, 1989), 106–8—to the present: see Susan Estrich, *Real Rape* (Cambridge: Harvard Univ. Press, 1987), 17–19, 25, 114 n. 41 (describing prosecutorial practice of dismissing or downgrading rape complaints that meet the legal definition of the crime due to skepticism about victims' credibility before a jury). With respect to statutory rape in particular, such blackmail fears persisted well into the modern era. The Model Penal Code Commentary, for example, suggests that the blackmail threat is especially serious in cases of statutory rape. See American Law Institute, *Model Penal Code* (St. Paul: West Publishing, 1985), sec. 213.6, comment at 421. Until recent decades it was a standard jury instruction in rape cases that the charge of rape is easy to make and hard to prove, and harder for the accused to defend. See Leigh Bienen, "Mistakes," *Philosophy and Public Affairs* 7 (1977): 224, 234 (paraphrasing Sir Matthew Hale). Research about the prosecution of rape has demonstrated that myths about women's sexual dishonesty continue to play an important role in the way judges, juries, and the public hear women's accusations of sexual wrongdoing. See Toni M. Massaro, "Experts, Psychology, Credibility, and Rape: The Rape Trauma Syndrome Issue and Its Implications for Expert Psychological Testimony," *Minnesota Law Review* 69 (1985): 395, 417–24; Morrison Torrey, "When Will We Be Believed? Rape Myths and the Idea of a Fair Trial in Rape Prosecutions," *Univ. of California at Davis Law Review* 24 (1991): 1013, 1027–31, 1040–57.

Harmon's speech is reprinted in Lillian Harmon, "Some Problems of Social Freedom" (1898), in *Freedom, Feminism, and the State: An Overview of Individualist Feminism*, 2nd ed., Wendy McElroy (New York: Holmes and Meier, 1991), 119. On the controversy surrounding Harmon's non-state marriage, see Hal D. Sears, *The Sex Radicals: Free Love in High Victorian America* (Lawrence: Regents Press of Kansas, 1977), 81–86.

The prevailing legal definition of forcible rape in the nineteenth century was carnal knowledge (i.e., sexual intercourse) with a mature female "without her consent" or "against her will." In evaluating the evidence offered when a rape defendant claimed consent and the alleged victim denied it, courts of the period collapsed the idea of "consent" into the notion of "force," holding that where there was sufficient force there could be no consent, but where force was not substantial consent would be presumed. Courts also tested an alleged victim's claims of nonconsent by examining the intensity of her physical resistance. If she had offered "utmost resistance" and persisted "to the last," she would be believed. But if at any time during the attack she had acquiesced—succumbing to fear, for example, or to a sense of futility in further struggle—the court would find that she eventually had consented to the act. See generally Leigh Bienen, "Rape I," *Women's Rights Law Reporter* 3 (1976): 45. Coercion by the exercise of legitimate authority (i.e., the command of a father, employer, or professional), or in a social relationship (i.e., acquaintance rape) was not understood as the use of "force," and there was no distinct category for sexual assaults by employers or sexual abuse by professionals. Early criminal incest statutes were primarily directed at incestuous marriages and childbearing rather than protection against intrafamilial child sexual assault. See Sanford H. Kadish, ed., *Encyclopedia of Crime and Justice* (New York: Free Press, 1983), 880, 881–82. On enforcement, see, for example, Peter W. Bardaglio, *Reconstructing the Household: Families, Sex and the Law in the Nineteenth-Century South* (Chapel Hill: Univ. of North Carolina Press, 1995).

On the promiscuity defense in statutory rape law, see Michelle Oberman, "Turning Girls into Women: Re-Evaluating Modern Statutory Rape Law," *Journal of Criminal Law and Criminology* 85 (1994): 15, 31–36. Many such requirements were removed as part of the rape reforms of the past generation on the rationale that supported rape-shield statutes more generally. Currently the law of a majority of states refuses to recognize a reasonable mistake as to age as a defense to a charge of statutory rape. See Richard Singer, "The Resurgence of Mens Rea II: Honest But Unreasonable Mistake of Fact in Self Defense," *British Columbia Law Review* 28 (1987): 459, 470; Bruce R. Grace, "Ignorance of the Law as Excuse," *Columbia Law Review* 86 (1986): 1392, 1416 n. 15. But the debate over whether such a defense should be recognized continued into the twentieth century. The Model Penal Code provided that an honest but unreasonable mistake of fact would negate criminal liability. American Law Institute, *Model Penal Code* (Philadelphia: Institute, Proposed Official Draft, 1962), sec. 204. Regarding statutory rape, the Model Penal Code gives a defense of reasonableness if the girl's age is above ten years, but not if her age is lower. See ibid., sec. 213.6(1).

The Comstock law is at 42 Cong., sess. III, ch. 258 (1873). On the Comstock law and its use against birth control, see John Paull Harper, " 'Be Fruitful and Multiply': Origins of Legal Restrictions on Planned Parenthood in 19th Century America," in *Women of America: A History,* ed. Carol Ruth Berkin and Mary Beth Norton (Boston: Houghton Mifflin, 1979), 245, 246.

The campaign to criminalize abortion is detailed in James C. Mohr, *Abortion in America: The Origins and Evolution of National Policy, 1800–1900* (New York: Oxford Univ. Press, 1978); Carroll Smith-Rosenberg, "The Abortion Movement and the AMA, 1850–1880," in *Disorderly Conduct: Visions of Gender in Victorian America* (New York: Alfred A. Knopf, 1985), 217; and Brief of 281 American Historians, filed *amicus curiae* in Webster v. Reproductive Health Services (no. 88-605, July 3, 1989), reprinted in *Public Historian* 12 (Summer 1990): 57.

On the declining birth rate in mid-nineteenth-century America among white women, see Daniel Scott Smith, "The Dating of the American Sexual Revolution: Evidence and Interpretation," in *The American Family in Social-Historical Perspective*, ed. Michael Gordon (New York: St. Martin's Press, 1973), 321 (in 1800, the average white woman had seven births; by 1870, the birth rate for this group of women was five; by 1900, it was 3.5 children). On the abortion rate at mid-century, see Mohr, *Abortion in America*, 50. On the openness of the abortion trade at this time, see, for example, ibid., 48–52, on evidence from New York City.

The "smooth the pillow" quote is from W. L. Atlee and D. A. O'Donnell, "Report of the Committee on Criminal Abortion," Transactions of the American Medical Association 22 (1871): 241, quoted in Smith-Rosenberg, *Disorderly Conduct*, 236–37.

On the 1845 and 1847 changes in Massachusetts law concerning abortion, see Mohr, *Abortion in America*, 121, 130–32, 221, citing Acts and Resolves of the General Court of Massachusetts in the Year 1845, p. 406 (Boston, 1845) and citing Acts and Resolves of the General Court of Massachusetts in the Year 1847, pp. 365–66 (Boston, 1847). The 1879 "Little Comstock Act" is described in ibid., 221, citing Carol Flora Brooks, "The Early History of Anti-Contraceptive Laws in Massachusetts and Connecticut," *American*

*Quarterly* 18 (Spring 1966): 3–23. Antiprostitution laws enacted include Acts and Resolves of Massachusetts, 1886, ch. 329, sec. 3, p. 307 (enticing minor); Acts, 1886, ch. 329, sec. 5, pp. 307–8 (maintaining house of prostitution); Acts, 1888, ch. 311, secs. 1–2, p. 352 (sending person to and detaining person in house of ill-fame).

On Virginia law at mid-century, see Acts of the General Assembly of Virginia, 1847, at 110–12, ch. 8, secs. 6–7 (1847) (keeping house of ill-fame and importation, etc., of obscene materials); ibid., at 970, ch. 3, sec. 16 (1847) (abduction for purposes of prostitution); ibid., 1847–48, at 96, Criminal Code, Title II, ch. 3, sec. 9 (1848) (abortion). On mid-century reforms, see ibid., at 110, ch. 8, sec. 1 (1847) (adultery and fornication); ibid., (lewd and lascivious cohabitation); ibid., 1872–73, at 178–79, ch. 192, secs. 1–3 (seduction). Changes in the age of consent are found in ibid., 1865, at 82, ch. 14, secs. 15–16 (to 12 years); ibid., 1895–1896, at 673–74, ch. 611, sec. 1 (to 14 years); ibid., 1916, at 809, ch. 479, sec. 1 (to 15 years). Code of Va. 1873, Title 54, ch. 192, secs. 6–7, pp. 1207–8 (adultery, fornication, lewd behavior); secs. 8–9 (whites marrying negroes and the performing of the ceremony) establish both the crimes and penalties. On the death penalty for black-on-white rapes, see Karen A. Getman, "Sexual Control in the Slaveholding South: The Implementation and Maintenance of a Racial Caste System," *Harvard Women's Law Journal* 7 (1984): 115, 134. The statistics on Southern lynchings come from Stewart E. Tolnay and E. M. Beck, *A Festival of Violence: An Analysis of Southern Lynchings, 1882–1930* (Urbana: Univ. of Illinois Press, 1995), 91–92.

On the 1867 and 1871 Illinois laws against abortion, see Mohr, *Abortion in America*, 205–6, citing laws as collected in Eugene Quay, "Justifiable Abortion—Medical and Legal Foundations, Part II," *Georgia Law Journal* 49 (1961): 395, 465, 467. In 1827 Illinois had enacted a law making it a misdemeanor to administer a poison for purposes of procuring a miscarriage, but scholars believe this law was an anti-poisoning law directed at protecting women's health and not an anti-abortion measure. See Mohr, *Abortion in America*, 25–26, citing Illinois Revised Code of 1827, pp. 130–31. The emergency statute intended to prevent regulated prostitution is Laws of Illinois, 1874, ch. 24, secs. 217–18, p. 248 (1874). The 1874 abduction into prostitution law is Laws of Illinois, 1874, ch. 38, sec. 1, p. 352 (1874). In 1879, the legislature made it unlawful to maintain a boat for purposes of prostitution, Laws of Illinois, p. 110 (March 31, 1879). The 1887 laws against enticing a woman into the trade or into the state for purposes of prostitution, and against detaining a woman in a brothel, is Laws of Illinois, pp. 170–71 (1887). In 1889, the legislature also made it unlawful to allow a female under the age of eighteen years to live in a brothel, Laws of Illinois, 1889, p. 112 (June 3, 1889). In 1909, the legislature made it a crime to use debt to detain a woman in a brothel, Laws of Illinois, 1909, p. 179 (July 1, 1909). The various pandering statutes are Laws of Illinois, p. 47 (1889); Laws of Illinois, 1909, p. 180 (July 1, 1909). On seduction, see Laws of Illinois, p. 148 (1899). The age-of-consent reforms are Laws of Illinois, p. 171 (1887) (to 14 years); Laws of Illinois, p. 193 (1905) (to 16 years).

On Wyoming laws, see Laws of Wyoming, ch. 3, sec. 27 (1870) (rape); Laws of Wyoming, ch. 3, sec. 108 (1870) (seduction); Laws of Wyoming, ch. 3, sec. 109 (1870) (adultery and fornication). The 1891 age-of-consent reform is Laws of Wyoming, ch. 6 (1890–91) (amending sec. 27) (to 18 years). The anti-abortion reforms are Laws of Wyoming, ch. 3, sec. 25 (1870) (death of woman); Laws of Wyoming, ch. 3, sec. 26 (1870) (concealment); Laws of Wyoming, ch. 3, sec. 19 (1890) (death of quick fetus). On criminal liability for the aborting woman, see Mohr, *Abortion in America*, 219, citing law as recorded in Quay, "Justifiable Abortion," 395, 464, 520. On prostitution, see Laws of Wyoming, ch. 3, sec. 125 (1870) (vagrancy). The 1890 reform is Laws of Wyoming, ch. 3, secs. 78–79 (1890), and the 1921 statute is Session Laws of Wyoming, ch. 98 (1921).

On the transformation of the age-of-consent movement in the twentieth century, see generally Mary E. Odem, *Delinquent Daughters: Protecting and Policing Adolescent Female Sexuality in the United States, 1885–1920* (Chapel Hill: Univ. of North Carolina Press, 1995); Ruth M. Alexander, *The "Girl Problem": Female Sexual Delinquency in New York, 1900–1930* (Ithaca: Cornell Univ. Press, 1995); Mary E. Odem and Steven Schlossman, "Guardians of Virtue: The Juvenile Court and Female Delinquency in Early 20th-Century Los Angeles," *Crime and Delinquency* 37 (1991): 186; Steven Schlossman and Stephanie Wallach, "The Crime of Precocious Sexuality: Female Juvenile Delinquency in the Progressive Era," *Harvard Educational Law Review* 48 (1978): 65. The "code of class" quote is from Christine Stansell, *City of Women: Sex and Class in New York, 1789–1860* (New York: Knopf, 1986), 66.

On Frances Wright and free love, see Taylor Stoehr, *Free Love in America: A Documentary History* (New York: AMS Press, 1979), 8, 278. On Wright generally, see Celia Morris Eckhardt, *Fanny Wright: Rebel in America* (Cambridge, Mass.: Harvard Univ. Press, 1984). On early nineteenth-century utopian communities, see D'Emilio and Freedman, *Intimate Matters*, 113–16.

Victoria Woodhull's quotes on sex are from Stoehr, *Free Love*, 364, 366, and Emanie Sachs, *"The Terrible Siren": Victoria Woodhull (1838–1927)* (New York: Harper and Bros., 1928), 219. On Woodhull's popularity as a public speaker, see Carl N. Degler, *At Odds: Women and the Family in America from the Revolution to the Present* (New York: Oxford Univ. Press, 1980), 257, 276. On the Beecher-Tilton scandal and Woodhull's role in it, see Robert Shaplen, *Free Love and Heavenly Sinners: The Story of the Great Henry Ward Beecher Scandal* (1954), and Laura Hanft Korobkin, "The Maintenance of Mutual Confidence: Sentimental Strategies at the Adultery Trial of Henry Ward Beecher," *Yale Journal of Law and the Humanities* 7 (1995): 1. The original story is printed at Victoria Woodhull, *Woodhull & Claflin's Weekly*, Nov. 2, 1872. The end of Woodhull's story is described in Shaplen, *Free Love*, 162–64. On Harriet Beecher Stowe's revelations about Lord Byron, see Leach, *True Love*, 58. The Pauline Wright Davis quote is from *Letter of Davis to Woodhull* (1872), quoted in Leach, 58.

On the Greenwich Village bohemians, see Ellen Kay Trimberger, "Feminism, Men, and Modern Love: Greenwich Village, 1900–1925," in Snitow et al., eds., *Powers of Desire*, 133.

On Margaret Sanger, birth control, and the Comstock Law, see C. Thomas Dienes, *Law, Politics and Birth Control* (Urbana: Univ. of Illinois Press, 1972), 82–83. The prosecution of Margaret Sanger is reported at *People v. Sanger*, 222 N.Y. 192 (1918). The application of the Comstock law to mailing of birth control information, advertisements, or devices was struck down in *United States v. One Package*, 13 F. Supp. 334, aff'd 86 F.2d 737 (2d Cir. 1936).

On voluntary motherhood, see Gordon, *Woman's Body, Woman's Right,* chs. 5–6; Linda Gordon, "Why Nineteenth-Century Feminists Did Not Support 'Birth Control' and Twentieth-Century Feminists Do: Feminism, Reproduction, and the Family," in *Rethinking the Family: Some Feminist Questions*, ed. Barrie Thorne and Marilyn Yalom (New York and London: Longman, 1982), 40; Linda Gordon, "Voluntary Motherhood; The Beginnings of Feminist Birth Control Ideas in the United States," *Feminist Studies* 1 (Winter-Spring 1973): 5–22. The Stanton quote is from E.C.S., "Infanticide and Prostitution," *Revolution* 1 (Feb. 5, 1868): 65.

For an example of the shift towards a libertine sexual ideal, see Margaret Sanger, *Happiness in Marriage* (1926; New York: Blue Ribbon Books, 1931). For a critical view of the new sexual ideal, see Christina Simmons, "Modern Sexuality and the Myth of Victorian Repression," in *Passion and Power: Sexuality in History*, ed. Kathy Peiss and Christina Simmons (Philadelphia: Temple Univ. Press, 1985), 157.

The D'Emilio and Freedman argument on the privacy and covertness of the sexual revolution of early-twentieth-century America is found in *Intimate Matters*, chs. 10–11.

Joan Kelly's argument about periodization is found in Joan Kelly, "Did Women Have a Renaissance?," in *Women, History, and Theory: The Essays of Joan Kelly* (Chicago: Univ. of Chicago Press, 1984), 19–20. The Degler quote on the politics of sexual restraint is from Degler, *At Odds*, 257, 258. For this historical interpretation of Victorian sexual "repression," see also Simmons, "Myth of Victorian Repression," 157; Daniel Scott Smith, "Family Limitation, Sexual Control, and Domestic Feminism in Victorian America," in *A Heritage of Her Own: Toward a New Social-History of American Women*, ed. Nancy F. Cott and Elizabeth H. Pleck (New York: Simon and Schuster, 1979); 222, 230; and Nancy F. Cott, "Passionlessness: An Interpretation of Victorian Sexual Ideology, 1790–1850," *Signs* 4 (Winter 1978): 219–36.

Clark on liberal divorce reform is from Elizabeth B. Clark, "Matrimonial Bonds: Slavery and Divorce in Nineteenth-Century America," *Law and History Review* 8 (1990): 25, 43.

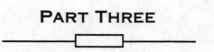

# PART THREE

# THE RISE AND FALL OF LIBERTINISM

## 8

# THE ORIGINS OF LIBERTINISM

The gap between those who came of age in the 1890s and those who were young adults in the 1920s is as great as that between any two other generations in the nation's history. On one side stand the last children of the Victorian world; on the other the first inhabitants of a new regime that became the basis of contemporary sexual culture. During this stretch of years all of the forces that make up a sexual paradigm—social behaviors, intellectual understandings, and legal rules—changed or moved toward change. Sexual behavior changed first and probably most. Immigration, industrialization, urbanization, and consumer culture created a new world of sexual possibilities. Sex became a means of self-expression crucial to personal identity. But theory also was in play. From the publication of Darwin's key works in 1859 and 1871, to the new models of human sexuality put forward by British psychologist Havelock Ellis and Austrian physician Sigmund Freud at the turn of the century, the rationalist ideals of nineteenth-century sex reform mutated into the biologically determined demands of a primal sex drive.

Law, however, lagged behind the emerging paradigm, and judges and legislators fought a reactionary battle throughout much of the first half of the twentieth century to contain the emergence of sexual liberalism. Only in the 1950s and 1960s did law approach conformity with an already-changed sexual culture.

We consider the 1920s as prologue to the 1950s and 1960s, part of a continuous historical progression away from the Victorian regime and toward the third regulatory order in American sexual history, the libertine. This periodization cuts against the traditional template that divides twentieth-century American history into uniform, decade-long segments, each with a distinct sociological character. Although the historical accident of a global economic crisis followed by world war slowed the ascendance of the libertine paradigm in the 1930s, '40s, and '50s, the sexual revolution that we locate by convention in the 1960s really began some forty years before. By the early 1970s American society came as close as it ever has to a regime of pure libertinism in sexual regulation. And as soon as it came into sight, the regime began to fall apart.

The early decades of the twentieth century mark the beginning of sexual modernity. In contrast to the prior century, American culture of the 1920s is recognizably our own in terms of social manners, leisure habits, and sexual values and practices. In the words of historian Paula Fass, "the decade sits solidly at the base of our culture."

But if it is easy to detect the cultural changes in this period, scholars are at something of a loss to explain exactly what caused changes of such scope and consequence. Historians point to dramatic economic and demographic shifts, including the growth of industrial and corporate work forces and the decline of small-scale and independent entrepreneurship, the entry of women in large numbers into the work force, the growth of a consumer and leisure economy, emigration out of the American South and immigration from overseas, continued decline in birthrates, and expanding opportunities for middle-class women.

These answers may explain everything, but they reveal much less. Why did increasing scale, complexity, and rationalization of the capitalist economy lead men and women to turn away from public and family life, and toward romance as a source of personal identity? Why did immigration lead to a culture-wide shift in sexual mores rather than a plurality of competing cultures? Why did women's growing independence translate into claims for sexual expression rather than for sexual power? We cannot offer a comprehensive account of how or why these forces converged to displace a Victorian paradigm that only a generation before had been at its apex, but we contend that changes in intellectual understandings of sex, gender, and romance must be added to the moving forces behind the social, economic, and demographic trends of the era.

Nowhere in the new era was the divide between the present and the past, the modern and the outdated, more apparent than in sexual behavior. Among working-class youth in the cities, a marked sexual openness and the growth of heterosexual socializing was common as early as the 1890s. At the time, political and cultural elites saw these looser sexual mores as evidence of the inferiority of the lower classes, a problem to be solved by social reform activity, and not an arrow pointing to their own future. Few middle-class Victorians could have imagined that the flamboyantly dressed factory girls sashaying down the streets of gilded age New York were foreshadowing a transformation soon to come to their own milieu. But by the 1920s, both the ideology and practice of sexual freedom had swept up middle-class youth and increasingly dominated both popular and intellectual culture.

The new sexual openness was felt everywhere. F. Scott Fitzgerald's *This Side of Paradise* (1920) tells a much different story of the girl who "falls" before marriage than did the melodramatic Victorian novels of seduction and betrayal. As Fitzgerald described her, the girl of the 1920s was "lovely and expensive and about nineteen." An even more compelling defense of the claims of the heart over sexual convention is found in Edith Wharton's novel, *The Age of Innocence* (1920). "Are you very much in love with her?" the scandalous Ellen Olenska wistfully asks Newland Archer about his fiancée. Newland reddens and answers, "As much as any man can be." Ellen is disappointed, "Do you think there is a limit?" "To being in love?" Newland asks, "If there is I haven't found it." Ellen then "glowed with sympathy," and sighed, "Oh, it is really and truly a romance!" summarizing the sexual morality that would soon tempt her toward an affair with the affianced Newland.

There were new scripts for men and women in real life as well as in the novels. Flappers expressed youth's defiance of the staid and prudish manners of their Victorian parents in favor of a tolerant peer culture and a new ideal of femininity that accepted some sexual experimentation by girls as normal. Birth rates were falling among middle-class women and rising among unmarried women. Unhappily married wives sued for divorce at an unprecedented rate, and the still-married longed for romance, pleasure, and fun with their spouses. The sensual and the sexual were markedly more visible in commercial films, books, songs, magazines, and leisure activities as people looked to popular culture for "modern" models of who to be and how to behave, particularly with the opposite sex.

Naturally these changes were controversial. Sexual issues dominated public discussion in the 1920s much as they do in our own time. Magazines were filled with debate over the new sexual climate with the doomsaying of conservatives matched by giddy predictions by liberal intellectuals. Margaret Sanger, Havelock Ellis, and Ben Lindsey asserted that the young were laying the basis for a whole new social order. The young had been a problem in American society before, as evidenced by an earlier generation's campaign to raise the age of sexual consent and the establishment of juvenile reformatories for girls and young women "in trouble" by reason of promiscuity or pregnancy. But in the 1920s, it was the wild children of the middle class who captured the society's horrified and fascinated gaze. Lindsey said in 1925 that the behavior of the young in this age was "unlike any revolt that has ever taken place before. Youth has always been rebellious. . . . But this is different. It has the whole weight and momentum of a new scientific and economic order behind it."

## SEX AS ROMANCE, IDENTITY, AND CONSUMPTION

The door opened for nonprocreative, nonmarital sex between women and men in the early twentieth century. Historical explanations for this sexual revolution tend to emphasize the role of a small cultural and political avant-garde living, writing, and carrying on in Greenwich Village. These bohemians, heirs to the earlier tradition of free love, pioneered a radical social vision in which nonmarital and even casual or promiscuous sex was accepted. Many of the bohemians were women, and they called themselves "feminists" to differentiate themselves from the social purity positions of the nineteenth-century woman movement. They insisted that sexual desire was as foundational to a woman's character as to a man's, and argued for female "sex rights" and a single standard of sexual morality for both sexes.

In the women's rights and moral reform movements of the late Victorian period, women who pursued an active public life ordinarily did so at the expense of marriage and children. Many women college graduates, professionals, and political leaders in the years 1870–1910 had remained unmarried. In contrast to this choice between work and love, women bohemians often were ambitious artists and activists, and also committed to creating new categories of sexual relationship outside the traditional poles of monogamous marriage or promiscuous prostitution. This meant romantic friendships and sexual unions between women, as well as heterosexual connections. As with the free lovers of an earlier generation, their personal relationships were a means of practicing politics. Despite their tiny numbers, this avant-garde strongly influenced the cultural debate over sexuality in the 1910s and 1920s. In part, this is because they were the sons and daughters, runaway husbands and wives, of the middle class, and thus carried more than their demographic weight in social influence. In addition, they were writers, artists, and activists by vocation, and thus especially articulate promoters of their ideals.

The work of Daniel Scott Smith and a new generation of social historians suggests that the seeds of this sexual revolution lie earlier in history in the peer culture of working-class youth beginning in the 1890s. Only later did these cultural patterns seep into the middle class, and thus into the historical memory of later generations.

Historian Kathy Peiss argues, for example, that the commercialization of working-class leisure in the 1890s and 1900s was key to sexual liberalization. Entrepreneurs created urban public amusements such as dance halls, amusement parks, theaters, cabarets, cinemas, and nightclubs where entertainment and sociability were a commodity to be sold. In these venues, socializing between the sexes was part of the amusement offered. In pursuit of this atmosphere, these businesses encouraged dating and close dancing, and permitted women to smoke, drink, dress in flashy clothes, and use risque language in the company of men. Girls and unmarried young women now socialized as boys and married men of their class traditionally had, in a peer culture centered on the streets and in dance halls, bars, and theaters. The chance to meet men, flirt, and pair off was the chief attraction for young women. In describing working women's leisure culture at the turn of the century, New York City reformer Belle Lindner Israels succinctly and ruefully commented: "No amusement is complete in which he is not a factor."

In a major change, women were welcomed and even sought after as customers in these new leisure venues. Before this time, public amusements had been geared primarily to men, and young men and women were expected to be chaperoned whenever they spent time together. Middle-class men and women might go to the theater or a concert together, or attend a private dance, but the urban nightlife was a world for men and their less-than-respectable women companions. So, too, the workingman's tavern, lodge, or saloon was off-limits to wives and daughters.

The novelty of young women's enthusiastic patronage of entertainment businesses was possible only because they had increasingly become wage earners. Although most young single women, native and immigrant, continued to live as daughters in the family home, their economic contributions brought them some measure of freedom from the strict patterns of parental supervision common to both rural life and the old country.

This sexualization of the social world extended from leisure activities into work. Between 1880 and 1920, the proportion of all women who were in the work force rose 50 percent. The greatest increases were among middle-class women, married as well as single. When women joined the office, factory, or retail store, they entered a world in which women and men worked side by side, sharing daily experiences as well as time on and time off.

This commonality of experience undermined the sex segregation that had supported Victorian constraint. Because Victorian women and men often were strangers to one another, the relaxed and informal social life of both sexes tended to be single-sex: friendships between women often were more romantic and intense than marriages; men, too, turned to their own sex for the daily forms of sustaining companionship in fraternal lodges, civic clubs, unions, political parties, and bars. In the new era, by contrast, romantic and sexual relationships with the other sex assumed a central place in the emotional lives of both women and men.

Middle-class reformers, including settlement workers, juvenile-court advocates, doctors, lawyers, and government officials, saw this as a dangerous flirtation with sexual ruin, coming too close to narrowing the distance between the daring "good-time girl" and the prostitute. This reform elite sought to shore up a flagging Victorian morality in the face of rebellion and leaned especially hard on working-class, immigrant girls. Reformers found allies in the families of these young women who were troubled and confused by their daughters. Sexual behavior was the crux of the anxiety, but young women's fascination with dress and appearance, late hours, use of slang, casual or disrespectful manner, drinking and smoking, and desire to keep their wages for personal consumption also created conflict in traditional families and communities.

The movement of black women from southern rural to northern urban areas in the Great Migration, often unaccompanied either by family or men, generated specific kinds of sexual and social anxiety. Sympathetic reformers regarded black women as particularly vulnerable to procurers and prostitution, and operated rescue missions and other programs to assist and protect female migrants to northern cities by offering temporary shelter, employment counseling, and instruction. In 1909, W. E. B. DuBois listed eight homes in African-American communities dedicated "to rescue girls who are already fallen into vice, or liable to." Less compassionate observers, however, saw black female migrants as a dangerous source of urban sexual degeneracy.

For all the dangers, real and imagined, the appeal of the dance hall world to the young working woman is easy to appreciate. It was a world of personal freedom, the one place where she could escape the weight of a social identity that tied her tightly to family, job, class, and ethnic community. A stylishly dressed, sexually attractive, socially skilled girl could reinvent herself. Jane Addams wrote that it was hard for a girl thrilled by "city excitements and eager to share them, to keep to the gray and monotonous path of regular work." This bursting of old barriers also attracted middle-class women. Through higher education, reform activism, feminist ideas, and labor force participation, middle-class women were developing a skeptical view of the idealized Victorian woman. Being a wife and mother no longer constituted the horizon of their aspirations. The popular culture called them "New Women," independent, modern, bold, athletic, and sexual.

By about 1910, working-class amusements were spreading to the middle class. In cities, cabarets featured jazz music and close dancing. The new Hollywood film industry constructed lavish theaters to appeal to an upscale audience and marketed movies saturated with romance and sensuality. The glamour, fun, and freedom of the new lifestyles pulled young, middle-class women, even those with few of the political or career aspirations of the New Woman, out of their homes and into the clubs. Ready-made clothing and mass-marketed cosmetics made the latest styles available at prices within the reach of all classes, and women began to spend more and more time and money on their appearance. The amount spent nationally for personal consumption almost tripled between 1909 and 1929, with the biggest increases for things like clothes, personal care, furniture, cars, and recreation. What resulted was the jazz, gin, bobbed hair, short skirts, and back-seat sexual experimentation that have become emblems of the age.

If this commercialized culture led women to link freedom to men and consumerism, this was simply one piece of a larger cultural and economic trend. Where the entrepreneurial and early industrial economy of the nineteenth century had emphasized thrift, self-restraint, and sobriety, the maturing capitalist economy of the early twentieth century depended upon consumption. Accordingly, it emphasized the virtues of indulgence, gratification, and pleasure.

This economy pressured women who earned lower wages than did their male social companions. In earlier eras, courtship typically had taken place in the girl's family home and under her parents' watchful eyes. With the emergence of public amusements, courtship became dating, which not only removed young women from the sexual supervision of their families, but introduced a new element of economic obligation into the relationship. Under the new "treating" system, the young man was expected to pay for the expenses of the date. "Treating" made it possible for young women to spend many more evenings out than their limited wages could have allowed. But this dependency on male companions also made women more vulnerable to sexual pressure and demands. In one study of girls judged sexually delinquent in New York State during these years, many reported being raped, molested, or coerced into sexual relations by a male partner or acquaintance. There is some evidence that middle-class men deliberately used their economic clout to take sexual advantage of working-class women. One study of female delinquents in New Haven, Connecticut, concluded that the male students of Yale University habitually used the town's working-class girls in this way.

Some women fully participated in this culture of "treating," trading sexual favors for entertainment, gifts, and attention. These were called "charity girls," to differentiate them from professional prostitutes. For most young women and men, however, the new dating culture with its uncertain boundaries demanded more delicate negotiations to balance sexual respectability and sociability.

Changes in mores led to changes in behavior. Rates of premarital intercourse among women went up sharply beginning in 1890 and reached a peak in 1920, where the rate remained constant until 1960. In 1920, the rate of premarital intercourse was roughly 50 percent for all women born after the turn of the century. Among women born before 1900, the comparable rate was 25 percent. Two-thirds of married women born between 1910 and 1919 had had sex at least once before marriage, compared with one-half of married women born between 1900 and 1909. This greater sexual accessibility changed the conduct of young men, who appear to have frequented prostitutes less than had men of an earlier generation having instead sex with their female social companions.

Although the rate of premarital intercourse for women was high, sexually active women tended to reserve intercourse for the man they expected to marry. By the new standards, premarital intercourse was acceptable if confined to a relationship of love and commitment. In less serious relationships, most young people stopped at "petting" (deep kissing, entwined bodies, partial undress, and even some genital touching). The premarital sexual ethos thus reverted to patterns of colonial America, where "bundling" was acceptable and pregnancy before marriage far more common than it had been throughout the nineteenth century.

## PUBLIC MORALITY AND PRIVATE LICENSE

The core issues of sexual politics for Victorians had been private oppression and the double standard. Their intellectual arguments, social visions, political activism, and legal reforms centered on unjust sexual power and the unmasking of hypocrisy, particularly among the governors of the society. The trajectory of sexual politics shifted in the new century.

The legal debates that accompanied the shift to a libertine regime centered on the individual liberty to have sex outside of marriage. To the sexual liberal, any communal or state restriction on erotic expression is presumptively repressive and therefore politically suspect. In their desire to interrogate and throw off constraints on an individual's free choice, liberals targeted laws restricting adults from consensual heterosexual relationships, and in particular laws against fornication (sex outside the marriage relationship) and adultery (sex with the marriage partner of another). As we have seen in earlier chapters, in America these prohibitions date back to the colonial period and, before that, to the common and canon law of England. Prohibitions against rape and prostitution also came in for a more muted skepticism as potentially overbroad and grounded in morality rather than tightly targeted toward acts of unmistakable coercion or exploitation.

But in the 1920s the law was slow to take up these challenges. It would be several more decades before the law embraced sexual libertinism with any fervor. Throughout the early years of the century, law enforcement tried instead to force men and women back into some version of Victorian patterns of sexual conduct, at least in public.

A first move was to distinguish the girl who surrendered to passion for love from the prostitute who sold sex for money. That such a division was necessary reflects the shift in the moral status of premarital intercourse. According to the popular wisdom transmitted in the movies, advertising, advice books, and magazines, it was "natural" for a girl to be swept away when "the real thing" came along.

In earlier periods of history the law had defined prostitution loosely as sexual promiscuity, treating prostitutes as a class of vagrants. This definition required neither a financial transaction nor pecuniary gain. In 1908 the U.S. Supreme Court stated in dictum in *United States v. Bitty* that prostitution "refers to women who for hire or without hire offer their bodies to indiscriminate intercourse with men." In the late 1910s and 1920s, however, American states consistently began to define prostitution as requiring pecuniary gain, untangling the threads of promiscuity and prostitution.

In contrast to the more forgiving attitude toward girls who gave it away, women who traded sex for money or advantage were, if possible, even more harshly condemned than before. States enacted statutes against prostitution, criminalizing specific conduct (trading sex for money) rather than a status of sexual looseness.

A new wave of antiprostitution activity rose in 1908-14 in a panic over "white slavery," or forced prostitution. Sensationalist pamphlets and books alleged that an underground traffic in women supplied urban brothels where inmates were kept in virtual slavery. Traffickers might abduct women and girls off the streets. But more threateningly, evil procurers might lure and defraud the innocent, particularly the newcomer to the city. Often these procurers were depicted as immigrants, a "foreign element" corrupting the fabric of the nation. The white slave panic was fed by the casual public sexuality of the popular culture, but also was a response to the visibility of the large vice districts in most cities where prostitution flourished openly with the protection of corrupt police and local politicians. Progressive reformers initiated elaborate investigations of these vice districts in the 1910s, hoping that publicity would generate the political will to enforce existing laws against prostitution. They also proposed preventive strategies to address the conditions that lured women into prostitution, offering "wholesome" recreational activities in working-class neighborhoods that tried to compete with the lure of the streets and the dance hall, and campaigning to raise the minimum wage for women workers. Despite fierce opposition from employers, eight states had enacted such minimum wage laws by 1913, including Massachusetts.

Among the facts uncovered and documented by the vice commission reports was that large numbers of middle-class men turned to prostitutes at least occasionally. These investigations also documented the medical consequences of commercial sex, focusing in particular on the infection of married women with venereal diseases brought home by their wandering husbands. A New York physician estimated in 1904 that 60 percent of men had at one time contracted syphilis and gonorrhea. Such alarming statistics (true or not) were publicly touted, with particular emphasis on the ravages suffered by married women. Venereal disease became yet another reason to end prostitution, and a concerted effort was made to inculcate the public with the social purity message that men, too, could and should be sexually continent.

Businessmen, lawyers, and male civic leaders had joined the old social purity coalition of feminists and clergy in the renewed campaign against prostitution in the Progressive era. The added political clout of these new allies led to enactment of laws aimed not directly at prostituted women, but at the business interests behind the commercial sex industry. By World War I, forty-four states had passed laws against white slavery going after pimps, panderers, and procurers. Some jurisdictions also attempted to prosecute patrons for prostitution, although with more limited success. The Iowa Supreme Court, for example, overturned such a statute against patrons on the grounds that men could not be guilty of prostitution. Existing laws such as those against fornication, adultery, or disorderly conduct, which could have been applied to both prostitute and patron, seldom were.

Studies of law enforcement during this period indicate that prostitutes still bore the brunt of legal sanction. Sociologist Cyril Waterman studied the disparity in the prosecution of prostitutes as opposed to pimps or procurers, and found that police arrested and courts convicted prostitutes at a much higher rate. Of 1,782 persons sentenced to prison for prostitution-related offenses in New York City over ten years, sixty-seven were men. As in the age-of-consent campaign of an earlier era, reformers' success in enacting strong prohibitory laws proved insufficient to fundamentally alter public policy absent the power to change the law enforcement infrastructure.

A successful avenue of legal attack pioneered in this period was the red-light abatement law. In 1909, Iowa enacted the first such law, a new legal tool that allowed private citizens to seek permanent injunctions against brothels and related businesses to close them down. By 1917, thirty-one other states had copied the model. The red light abatement laws went after the business end of the trade, causing landlords and brothel keepers to close up shop as soon as a citizen filed an action for injunction. Each of our exemplary jurisdictions enacted some version of this new generation of antiprostitution laws. In the early decades of the century,

Massachusetts, Virginia, Illinois, and Wyoming all passed various white slave laws against pandering and compulsory prostitution, as well as abatement laws. By 1920, the antivice campaigns had ended open prostitution in American cities. In our exemplary jurisdictions, police shut down the Chicago vice district in 1913 and the Richmond district the following year. Prostitution, however, did not go away. Rather, it changed to a decentralized, less visible trade based on streetwalkers and call girls. The invention of the automobile and the telephone allowed women to operate covertly, and by basing the trade outside of brothels, prostitution grew much more difficult to target for political purposes or police raids.

Antiprostitution probably peaked with the 1910 passage of a federal law, the Mann Act, banning "transport[ation of] a woman across state lines for immoral purposes." Originally directed at the interstate and international white slave traffic, the statutory language reached beyond the transport of women for purposes of prostitution to cover transportation for any sexual purpose, including that of consenting adults traveling interstate together. In 1917 the U.S. Supreme Court ruled that the words "immoral purpose" in the statute reached consensual, noncommercial acts, and not just prostitution or coercion. During the 1910s and 1920s federal prosecutors used the law to go after not only pimps and panderers, but also a small group of men who traveled between states with their girlfriends. Between 1910 and 1918, the Justice Department obtained almost 2200 convictions for transporting women for immoral purposes. Of the Mann Act convictions between 1910 and 1914, approximately 15 percent involved no prostitution, and 10 percent involved neither prostitution nor coercion.

To make nonmarital sex a federal crime was obviously a culturally conservative move. A Mann Act prosecution from 1917, *Caminetti v. U.S.*, illustrates the feelings of panic that the new sexual morality had set off within traditional communities and the repressive legal reaction. *Caminetti* was a fairly typical instance of sexual adventuring in any era. In Sacramento, California, two white, middle-class, married men took up with two white, middle-class, single, working women. When the parents of the young women discovered that their daughters had become involved with married men, they threatened the men, who then left the city for Reno with their girlfriends. The two couples were found in Reno and brought back to Sacramento, where the men were charged under the Mann Act, as well as with state law counts of adultery and fornication. The wives of the defendants and the parents of the young women became symbols in the local newspaper of the dangers of modern sexual mores. In sentencing the two men, the trial judge drove the point home: "[T]he laxity of social conditions and the lack of parental control made [this] possible."

Marriage, too, was affected by changes in romantic and sexual ethos in ways that implicated the law. Men and women now married after a more casual and varied experience of dating than had been allowed by the courtship rituals of middle-class Victorian culture. A typical married couple had spent time alone together, had had some chance to explore sex together, and had developed some emotional intimacy. Couples expected to continue this kind of pleasure, companionship, and romance after marriage. One of Margaret Sanger's strongest arguments for birth control was its potential to free marital sex from fears of unwanted pregnancy and thus make way for pure erotic pleasure in the marriage, an argument that accorded well with the new expectations. If the Victorian marital ideal had been based on self-control and duty, the modern marriage ideal was that of a "love match" in which sexual pleasure was a key measure of marital happiness. With eroticism as opposed to responsibility emphasized as the foundation of marriage, men and women began to marry at younger and younger ages.

The legal consequence of these youthful ventures and high expectations was that American marriages collapsed at an unprecedented rate. Between 1867 and 1929, the population of the United States grew 300 percent, the number of marriages increased 400 percent, and the divorce rate rose 2000 percent. By the end of the 1920s, one in every six marriages ended in divorce.

The reasons that husbands and wives gave for divorce in this era also reflects changed expectations. Divorcing husbands in the late nineteenth century had complained principally that their wives would not attend to domestic responsibilities. Divorcing husbands in the 1920s complained that their wives no longer were exciting or attractive, refused to have enough sex, would not settle down from lives of independent work or youthful fun, or made too many demands for money for consumer purchases. Interestingly, the complaints from wives in the divorce courts of the 1920s reflect much less change from the Victorian expectations of marriage. Women in both eras mostly said their husbands demanded too much sex or were not adequate providers.

The broadened horizon of sexual freedom affected law in other ways that damaged female interests. Having gained the right to say yes, women found they had lost some of their previous power to say no. The new sexual liberalism was an attack on sexual repression, but, as Christina Simmons emphasizes, it was more specifically an attack on women's control over men's sexuality. Angry new images of women who used sex to advantage through manipulation or blackmail replaced sympathetic Victorian images of prostitutes and promiscuous women as "lost sisters." Among this pantheon of female predators was the golddigger who married for money, and the seductress who lured wealthy men into sexual liaisons and then blackmailed them by threats of legal action to procure favorable settlements. Sisters in crime included the woman who made an engagement to marry the condition for intercourse and the wife who weaseled shopping money from her husband by promising or withholding sex. These stereotypes appeared in academic debate as well as popular culture. But their evocation proved particularly potent in arguments to weaken or dismantle protective sex laws, especially the nationwide campaign begun in the 1930s to abolish the "heart-balm" torts of seduction, criminal conversation, alienation of affections, and breach of promise to marry.

Like the Pandora image of antiquity or the shrew of seventeenth-century English gender quarrels, the popular golddigger image is paradoxical evidence that libertinism had added to women's sexual bargaining power. Once men became accustomed to the possibility of nonmarital sex with women other than prostitutes, they feared being dominated by women's capacity to grant or deny these sexual favors at will. As in the debate over raising the age of consent decades before, men responded by complaining that female sexual bargaining was a form of blackmail. Repealing the heart-balm actions was a way to scale back women's bargaining power. Worst of all, it was a move to disempowerment in a context in which the demand for marriage, which had been a kind of power, had lost much of its social support.

Woman's reluctance or resistance to sexual companionability also seemed newly suspect, and her social companions were more likely to disregard her choice to refrain from any particular sexual exchange. We can speculate that women's claims of nonconsent in rape accusations also became less believable, going as they did against the grain of altered popular beliefs about female sexual conduct.

If it was harder for women to prove they had in fact been raped, it became impossible in some parts of the country for African-American men to refute rape charges, merited or not. The epidemic of lynching that began at the end of Reconstruction as whites regained control over southern state governments and society continued with unabated ferocity into the twentieth century. Between 1889 and 1940 at least 3800 black men and women were lynched in the South and border regions. According to one recent survey, more than 700 black men accused of raping white women were lynched in the South between 1882 and 1930. And not all the killing was extralegal. Between 1908 and 1950, the State of Virginia executed forty-five black men for rape, yet not one white man suffered the same penalty for the crime.

The fear that drove the white South was that black men might claim "social equality," always understood to mean sexual access to white women. W. E. B. DuBois wrote that "[t]o the ordinary American or Englishman the race question at bottom is simply a matter of ownership of women; White men want the right to use all women, colored and White, and they resent the intrusion of colored men in this domain." Under lynch law, "rape" really meant any hint of sexual connection on any terms between a white woman and a black man. So, too, many southern states that had had no anti-miscegenation statute during slavery times enacted such laws following Emancipation. The intimacy and proximity that the unmitigated subordination of slavery easily could contain now had to be extirpated by force, whether through law or mob violence. Although rape figured large in the public justifications for lynching, less than a quarter of reported killings involved accusations of sexual assault.

The heinousness of the rape charge played in perfect harmony with the denunciations of male lust common to the sexual politics of the social purity movement, effectively blinding the nation's reform elite to the violence and desperation of the situation. WCTU leader Frances Willard, for example, on a speaking tour in the South, said in one published interview, "The colored race multiplies like the locusts of Egypt . . . The safety of women, of childhood, of the home is menaced in a thousand localities." That disregard persisted. In the first three decades of the new century, there were repeated and unsuccessful attempts to pass federal antilynching legislation. Even President Franklin D. Roosevelt, whose power and political craft revolutionized the traditional allocation of powers between the federal government and the states, did not dare to support federal antilynching legislation.

Libertinism was thus a two-edged sword for women. Women no longer had to marry to gain access to sexual satisfaction, losing the bargaining chip of social support for marriage as the base price for sexual access. But they gained access to heterosexual experiences without submitting to a legal regime in which divorce was difficult and marital rape unheard of.

## COMPETING UNDERSTANDINGS: SEX AS SCIENCE

Changed theoretical understandings of sexuality also shaped the early period of sexual libertinism. Paradoxically, theorists suggested at once that free sex expresses desirable traits of free will and action, and that sex is an uncontrollable natural drive rooted in evolutionary biology. These seemingly inconsistent understandings competed for dominance, blending in time into the weird but enduring commingling of liberty and determinism characteristic of libertine ideology. As we discuss in Chapter 12, only with the recent decay of the libertine paradigm have these competing strains become irreconcilable.

Sex as a manifestation of freedom was older than the determinism argument, invoking the political and religious radicalism of the sixteenth and seventeenth centuries. Beginning almost a century before the 1920s, romantics and free lovers had applied these principles to sex, weaving notes of individual sexual self-creation into the sober agenda of classical liberalism. This rebellious romanticism also exalted the natural. After the Enlightenment had cast doubt upon the biblical account of sexuality, sex came to be grounded in the natural order and thinkers "discovered" the naturally occurring opposite sexes.

In figuring out how these polar opposites might make a common life, sex theorists speculated that males actively and aggressively initiated, and females passively and reluctantly responded. As the libertine paradigm took on power, fueled in part by the revolutionary scientific writings of Charles Darwin, the naturalist sexual script became a new Adam and Eve story with evolution rather than God as the moving force.

In *On the Origin of Species by Means of Natural Selection* (1859) and *The Descent of Man and Selection in Relation to Sex* (1871), Darwin asserts that all living things descended by evolution from one or a few very simple forms, and explains this history with a theory of "natural selection." Darwin's work predates Mendel's genetics, so he could not explain the biological mechanism for the process he described. But to put complex theory simply, Darwin observes that organisms vary, that some variations are more suitable for survival than others in conditions of scarce resources, and that in the struggle to survive among populations the better-suited individuals will be the ones to live and reproduce. Because offspring resemble parents, favorable variations will survive and those less well-favored will die out.

Sexual theory draws most heavily from *The Descent of Man*, which was devoted to a second path of evolution, sexual selection. If success in the Darwinian measure is having your children dominate the next generation, one way is to produce the most fit children. For this path—natural selection—superior parents are favored. The other way is to produce more children, regardless of quality. For this path—sexual selection—parents with characteristics that maximize reproduction are best suited. A creature that lays more eggs, for example, is more likely to survive the evolutionary struggle than one with fewer eggs. In applying the principle of sexual selection to human behavior, Darwin focused on the characteristics that made males and females more or less successful at mate selection. Characteristics that give an individual the edge in acquiring a sexual partner could lead to superior survival if he or she selects and reproduces with a partner possessing better characteristics either for natural or sexual selection. So, for example, if breast size sexually attracts men, women with big breasts will attract more potential partners and thus be able to choose the best among them, whether from the angle of natural selection (the best provider, for example) or sexual selection (the most fertile man). In theory, her offspring should contain slightly more big-breasted females.

Darwin's theory was extended to include human psychological characteristics as well, eventually coming to explain the gender difference itself as resting on evolutionary imperative. Evolutionary biology thus supported the sexualization of identity, turning all human qualities into expressions of a primal sexual agenda.

Survival also turned out to favor the existing division of sexual labor between males and females. Sociologist Herbert Spencer, for instance, thought that women needed to reserve their vital powers in order to reproduce, and so they could not evolve intellectually. Sexual theorists Patrick Geddes and Arthur Thomson asserted that sperm tended to dissipate energy but ova conserved it, and thus concluded that the active social roles of men and the passive roles of women were sanctified by nature. After the nineteenth century had opened the whole question of the proper political and moral arrangements for sexual access, Darwinism reassigned women's sexual fate from the moral and religious order of monogamous marriage to the natural order of utilitarian mating.

Victorians recognized the implications of Darwin's theory and denied with particular fervor the suggestion that human beings descended from a common ancestor to the ape, because "apes and monkeys were supposed to be oversexed and rather obscene." Nonetheless, after Darwin, the concept of sex as the most essential of human drives and, from a materialist perspective, the most valued because of its necessity, had scientific authority. Darwin laid the groundwork for a naturalization of sexuality by which sex became an instinct, a physical phenomenon, a force that could be negotiated only, if at all, within a powerfully determined biological structure.

Moving sex away from sin or morality, and therefore away from the possibility of human responsibility, had manifest political consequences. Cast as a bedrock physical phenomenon, sex is set up to be treated as immune to human choice and therefore to cultural change. It becomes "an independent variable." Cultural institutions can affirm or ameliorate the consequences of such an independent variable, but can never do more than respond. In the modern era, this reclassification liberated sex from centuries of religious constraint. The new materialism could not, however, support an analysis of sex as a political exchange. Instead, whatever tended to encourage mating was the norm, and moral concerns like power, justice, and equality had no role.

Beyond its paralyzing impact on the idea of sexual politics, Darwinian thinking also affected larger debates about human beings and society. Just as the naturalization of sex was a two-edged sword—supporting liberation from theological and moral rigidities and, at the same time, imposing new constraints rooted in the inexorable story of evolution—Darwinian theory also offered two opposing messages about society. On the one hand, evolutionary biology could be taken to justify unequal distribution of any good or resource. "Social Darwinism" projected onto human history the same favoring of the "fit" that Darwin observed in natural selection. By contrast, the prospect of evolution also subverted a different strand of conservatism that sought to revive pre-Enlightenment claims of tradition or longevity. If nature can change, so can culture and society.

Applying the two interpretations of Darwin to sexual politics, one could conclude that sex is a blind force and the existing patterns of sexual selection a product of uncontrollable nature. Men rape, women display, all in the service of survival. And if sex is physical, there is no religious or political restraint that could legitimately govern the terms of sexual exchange. People can (and, in the interest of natural competition, should) act on whatever suits them at any given time. No particular distribution of sexual behavior is natural in the sense of eternal because nature itself changes over evolutionary time. Variation in behavior is natural, even desirable.

In the early twentieth century, two influential interpreters of Darwin, Havelock Ellis and Richard von Krafft-Ebing, produced the beginnings of modern "sexology." The new science posited sexuality as constitutive of humanness in new ways, not only as the key to the survival and progress of the species but also definitive of the personal identity of each individual. As Ellis phrased it, "sex penetrates the whole person." To Krafft-Ebing, sex was at the base of most human behavior, including learning, religion, and art. To Ellis, all of human sexuality re-volved around the aggressive male wooing the modest female in the interest of re-production. Although Ellis did not believe that this natural sexuality was congruent with monogamous marriage (the most evolutionarily fit men would be sexually restless with only one female partner), he did believe that nature tended toward monogamy as the situs for nurturing offspring. Ellis's multi-volume *Studies in the Psychology of Sex* was published in Philadelphia between 1897 and 1910.

The most influential of the turn-of-the-century sexual theorists was of course, Sigmund Freud. Reams have been written about Freud's theories, their natural history, and their political and social underpinnings. Freud was directly influenced by Ellis: He acknowledges Ellis's multi-volume *Studies in the Psychology of Sex*, in the introduction to *Three Essays in the Theory of Sexuality* (1905, 1915). The two scientists corresponded for over forty years. British sex theorist Jeffrey Weeks lo-cates the difference between Ellis and Freud in their relative commitment to the force of sexual selection. Ellis, following Darwin, remained committed to the idea that the primary essence of human sexual instinct is the drive to reproduce. Freud believed that humans originally were bisexual, and that heterosexual desire re-sulted from a complex interplay of natural and cultural forces, both of which shaped the fundamental lines of sexual desire. In bringing the cultural to the fore, however, Freud resisted making what might seem to be the obvious move to rela-tivism. Instead, Freud made a case for the universality of the dynamic wherein a young boy learns to control his sexual desire for his mother through fear of castra-tion by his father, generating the incest taboo and sexual sublimation. Freud effec-tively naturalizes the cultural, a move heavily criticized by Ellis among others, who points out that Freud's primal scene rests heavily on the cultural institution of the patriarchal family. And as in the patriarchal family, female sexual experience is largely hidden from view in Freud's work.

Darwin, Krafft-Ebing, Ellis, Freud, and their followers changed the terms in which sex was understood. Each of these pioneers concluded that the heterosexual union of dominant male and submissive female was necessary for the well-being of human beings as nature had made them. With astonishing rapidity, these ideas en-tered into the popular imagination in a simplified version that presented the sexual impulse as an insistent force not only demanding but deserving of expression. To deny or repress sexuality was unhealthy ("cruel and self-hating" in the words of Margaret Sanger), the equivalent to destroying other innate human gifts such as in-telligence, imagination, artistry, or creativity.

The new prescription of experts was a healthy indulgence of sexual desires, abandoning earlier counsels to continence and self-control. A bargaining theorist, looking at the writings without knowing the historical tale, might have predicted that the heterosexual exchange would revert to a state of nature, all competing organizing schemes—religion, ideology, morality, politics—having failed the test of science. In such a state, one would expect men to rape and fornicate, and women to try to protect their needs for support in reproduction as best they could. The females would spiral downward as one bad bargain led to another due to inferior physical strength, vulnerability to childbearing, and lack of control over the sources of ideology. Yet the disempowered female bargainers would go down to defeat with a faintly satisfied grin because the free-for-all met their constitutive sexual needs for subordination, regardless of the social cost.

As Ellis's bow in the direction of marriage's centrality reflects, however, the popular interpreters of the new theories did not sanction uncontrolled sexual license. Instead, they supported a vision of passionate union in marriage, what came to be known as "companionate marriage." Ben Lindsey, juvenile court judge and populizer of the new morality, argued to liberalize divorce and encourage contraception, practices that would allow those who had chosen unwisely to find true love through divorce and remarriage, and all spouses to pursue sexual and emotional satisfaction within the boundaries of marriage.

Finally, once real genetic knowledge came along with the work of Gregor Mendel, this materialist vision of sex opened the door to eugenics, a regime easily as repressive as moralistic sex. By observing that humans, like Mendel's sweet peas, are subject to genetic laws, the idea arose that evolution could be harnessed. By directing the genetic material at play in the heterosexual exchange— "engineering" people—the balance of desirable characteristics in the population might be skewed. Although eugenics eventually was to be identified with the nastiest of nativist and fascistic social movements, it first arose in England and the United States among reform-minded elites, intellectuals, and professionals. These Progressives, socialists, and free love advocates, including many women radicals, were key players in the eugenics movement. In 1919, Margaret Sanger wrote, "More children from the fit, less from the unfit—that is the chief issue of birth control." Sexologist Havelocks Ellis's eugenics tract, *The Problem of Race-Regeneration* (1911), was one of dozens of popularized eugenics books published.

Several developments fed the move to eugenics. First, scientists refuted an earlier orthodoxy ("Lamarkianism") that acquired characteristics could be inherited; it was now clear that the evolutionary payoff to changing environmental conditions through better education and alleviation of poverty would be limited to one generation. Even within one generation, the effectiveness of such environmental enrichment seemed limited because of the power of biological factors. Second, statisticians developed methods of measuring genetic variations, even in intelligence, which won provisional support as sound science. Promoters of the idea of an "intelligence quotient," for example, claimed that they could reliably measure the qualities that made up the human mind and gave value to its varied capacities, and then rank individuals according to their innate gifts. From the outset, the I.Q.

tests also purported to show that populations of immigrants, African Americans, and the poor were subnormal, giving a veneer of scientific validity to racist and nativist beliefs.

Having developed various "scientific" means of judging any individual's value to the species, eugenicists toyed with various schemes for motivating the "fit" part of the population—the bourgeois, the thrifty, the native—to breed. But the impracticality of such incentives soon yielded to "negative eugenics," or sterilization of the unfit. Eugenicists answered any ethical doubts about this practice on utilitarian grounds of the good they believed they were doing for future generations. If it was ethical to regulate reproduction in the interest of society, this imperative led easily into direct interference with the sexuality of the unfit. Reformers in the U.S. and Britain not only accepted and promoted eugenics ideas; by 1930 half of the states had enacted compulsory sterilization laws. These laws covered convicted criminals, but also persons considered "feebleminded" or suspected of "sexual immorality." In the first third of the century, approximately 20,000 involuntary sterilizations were performed by order of state law.

The U.S. Supreme Court upheld involuntary sterilization for eugenics purposes in 1927 in the case of *Buck v. Bell*. The State of Virginia had ordered Carrie Buck sterilized on the ground that she was feebleminded, and her mother and her infant also were feebleminded. Buck resisted the order, claiming a due process right to bodily integrity. In an opinion for a majority of eight Justices, Oliver Wendell Holmes affirmed the state's authority to sterilize institutionalized feebleminded persons on the grounds that it would serve their best interest or the interests of society. The opinion accepts without question both the scientific validity and moral correctness of eugenics:

> We have seen more than once that the public welfare may call upon the best citizens for their lives. It would be strange if it could not call upon those who already sap the strength of the State for these lesser sacrifices, often not felt to be such by those concerned, in order to prevent our being swamped with incompetence. It is better for all the world, if instead of waiting to execute degenerate offspring for crime, or to let them starve for their imbecility, society can prevent those who are manifestly unfit from continuing their kind. The principle that sustains compulsory vaccination is broad enough to cover cutting the Fallopian tubes. Three generations of imbeciles are enough.

Today, not only is eugenics discredited, but we know that the factual determinations upon which Virginia relied to sterilize Carrie Buck were unfounded. There was no feeblemindedness among the three generations of Bucks, and in any case most forms of feeblemindedness are not heritable. Buck's alleged "sexual immorality" and that of her mother (who also had borne an illegitimate child) appeared to have been her principal incapacity. Stephen Jay Gould comments bitterly on the case, "Two generation of bastards was enough."

More disturbing still, scholars now believe that Buck's foster parents had institutionalized her when she was seventeen years old because one of their relatives had raped and impregnated her. By putting Carrie away, the foster family hoped to avoid embarrassment and shield their relation from legal penalty. Notwithstanding its progressive and scientific antecedents, Buck's case reveals the danger that direct state regulation of sexuality poses for the weaker players in society. Rather than a one-on-one bargain, state-imposed eugenics brings the full force of collective social power to bear on sexual decision-making. Although the obvious target of Virginia's social interest should have been the raping relative, the path of least resistance was to bear down on the female who was the visible reproductive vehicle.

Sexual materialism affected the regime of sexual regulation in two important ways. Sex now rested on a bedrock of natural instinct, difficult to control and definitive of social differences between the sexes. Darwinian science had come to the rescue of a flagging regime of inequality imperiled by the sexual reform politics of the nineteenth century. Second, social control of sexuality took the form of eugenic sterilization. More intrusive than laws against adultery and fornication, more harsh than the regulation of prostitution on grounds of immorality and order, and more overtly sexual than prescriptions for marriage and divorce, sterilization laid on the table the issue of whether sexuality should be regulated to serve a larger social purpose.

## LIBERTINISM AS IDEOLOGY

What we call libertinism—the individualistic sexual ideology that grew out of this first popular culture, sexual revolution and the new science of sex—became the template for contemporary sexual norms. Where Victorians had stressed self-control as the measure of a man, libertinism encouraged men to act on their sexual impulses and celebrated male sexuality as natural, healthy, and irrepressible. Libertinism affirmed female sexuality too, but pictured it as passive, responsive, and tied to love and romantic commitment. Where Victorians accepted some female control over male passions as necessary and just, libertines expected women to respond to men's urgent sexual needs. Libertines ridiculed concerns about sexual aggression as prudish, and caricatured sexually withholding women. "Victorian" began its journey to becoming a dirty word.

On its surface, the new sexual morality was more egalitarian than the older world of separate spheres and double standards. Under the surface, but perhaps of more enduring political consequence, were the changes libertinism brought to the meaning of equality for women. Rather than political or economic power, women in the early twentieth century sought instead sexual liberty and the freedom to express and define themselves. The ability to choose sexual pleasure in nonmarital relationships greatly increased women's experience of personal agency. Yet this ability to choose did not necessarily mean that women were self-governing persons, nor that they possessed the power to make sexual bargains that advanced their own ends in life. Women still chose within a world of economic inequality and physical disparity with the men who were their sex partners, negotiating these private and largely unregulated bargains on terms of an imbalance of power. Consider the elaborate sexual negotiations around "treating": Who knows what sexual choices working girls would have made had they waltzed into the dance halls and amusement parks with incomes comparable to those earned by the men they went there to meet.

Further, media imagery, fashion, and style supplanted family, religion, ethnicity, and class—the traditional bases for personal identity. This allowed women to escape the control of family, but also stripped them of social allies, leaving them alone as individuals to negotiate a personal identity. And where alliance with other women in a political movement would have meant embrace of a whole agenda of social action, women acting on their own had no opportunities to exercise the virtues of rulers. In the hedonistic and materialistic world of flirting and fashion, of Darwin and Freud, sources of political commitments were few. It is not surprising, therefore, that for decades after 1920 when women finally obtained the vote, wives voted the same way as their husbands.

Because we are inheritors of the libertine revolution, we must retain a determinedly skeptical attitude toward the liberatory claims made on behalf of sexual modernity. Libertinism spoke forcefully in the rhetoric of personal freedom. If the sex reformers of the previous century had demanded an end to the double standard, advocates of sexual freedom in the next generation did too, but with a twist: Women increasingly claimed the right to adventure and liberty on the sexual terms that men traditionally had enjoyed. Historian Karen Lystra describes the change from the nineteenth to the twentieth century as a progression "away from [sexuality] as something that a woman's father owned, and then her husband, toward something that only she possessed." Pamela Haag observes that this reasoning assumes that if no particular outside party (a husband, a father, or, more broadly, the state) possesses a woman's sexual identity, then she must own it herself. Yet, Haag continues, "sexual modernization, while it conceded that women might be sexual beings, never established that women were sexual subjects, in unconditional possession even of their heterosexual desire."

Just as important, the new understanding of sexuality as a basic expression of personal liberty and a human right delegitimated democratic government. The resulting privatization and deregulation of the sexual economy paralleled a growing ideology of free trade and freedom of contract in the economic and political worlds. Instead of the optimistic hopes for a new economic order that had animated the 1880s and 1890s, the first decades of the new century were an era of economic conservatism and consolidation of power among large corporations and financial institutions. It is something of a paradox that although the 1920s were among the most liberal of times in terms of culture and intellectual thought, it was a time of entrenched conservatism in the economic and political realm. But it may be that such cultural radicalism is not anomalous, but is structurally connected to political conservatism as "compensation for lost civic hopes." Laura Engelstein makes this suggestion about pre-revolutionary Russia where, as in early twentieth-century America, the young, intellectuals, and the avant-garde turned to consumer pleasures, and particularly to sexual display, rather than to political activism. Nancy Cott has identified perhaps the most telling detail of the contradictions of this era: In 1921, the year after women gained the vote, the first Miss America contest was held.

## NOTES

The Fass quote is from Paula S. Fass, *The Damned and the Beautiful: American Youth in the 1920's* (New York: Oxford Univ. Press, 1977), 3. The Lindsey quote is from Ben Lindsey and Wainwright Evans, *The Revolt of Modern Youth* (New York: Boni and Liveright, 1925), 54, 59. The Fitzgerald quote is found in Frederick Hoffman, *The Nineteen Twenties: American Writing in the Postwar Decade* (New York: Viking, 1955), 19.

On love and marriage for nineteenth-century female pioneers, see Roberta Frankfort, *Collegiate Women: Domesticity and Career in Turn-of-the-Century America* 13 (New York: New York Univ. Press, 1977), 58–59, 73–75, 112–13. On female sexual radicalism in Greenwich Village, see Judith Schwartz, "'We Were a Little Band of Willful Women': The Heterodoxy Club of Greenwich Village," in *Passion and Power: Sexuality in History*, ed. Kathy Peiss and Christina Simmons (Philadelphia: Temple Univ. Press, 1989), 118–19; Nancy F. Cott, *The Grounding of Modern Feminism* (New Haven: Yale Univ. Press, 1987), 3, 42. On female-female relationships in the same communities, see Lillian Faderman, *Surpassing the Love of Men: Romantic Friendships and Love Among Women from the Renaissance to the Present* (New York: Morrow, 1981), 186; Blanche Wiesen Cook, "Female Support Networks and Political Activism: Lillian Wald, Crystal Eastman, Emma Goldman," in *A Heritage of Her Own*, ed. Nancy F. Cott and Elizabeth H. Pleck (New York: Simon and Schuster, 1977), 412.

The Israels quote is from Belle Lindner Israels, "The Way of the Girl," *Survey* 22 (July 3, 1909): 486.

On increases in women in the work force, see Elaine Tyler May, *Great Expectations: Marriage and Divorce in Post-Victorian America* (Chicago: Univ. of Chicago Press, 1980), 51. On African-American women in the cities, see generally Hazel V. Carby, "Policing the Black Woman's Body in an Urban Context," *Critical Inquiry* 18 (1992): 738. On middle-class black women's reform activities directed at young migrant women, see Fannie Barrier Williams, "The Club Movement Among Colored Women of America," in *A New Negro for a New Century*, ed. Booker T. Washington, N. B. Wood, and Fannie Barrier Williams (1900; rpt. New York: Arno Press, 1969), 379, 419–20; Darlene Clark Hine, "Rape and the Inner Lives of Southern Black Women," in *Southern Women: Histories and Identities*, ed. Virginia Bernhard, Betty Brandon, Elizabeth Fox-Genovese, and Theda Purdue (Columbia: Univ. of Missouri Press, 1992), 177, 186–87; Dorothy Salem, *To Better Our World: Black Women in Organized Reform, 1890–1920* (Brooklyn: Carlson Publications, 1990), 44–45.

The Addams quote is from Jane Addams, *A New Conscience and an Ancient Evil* (New York: Macmillian, 1912), 216.

On middle-class and affluent female adolescents' rebellion against Victorian social and sexual mores during the first two decades of the twentieth century, see James McGovern, "The American Woman's Pre-World War I Freedom in Manners and Morals," *Journal of American History* 55 (1968): 315–33; Rosalind Rosenberg, *Beyond Separate Spheres: The Intellectual Roots of Modern Feminism* (New Haven: Yale Univ. Press, 1982), 190–92; Lewis Erenberg, *Steppin' Out: New York Nightlife and the Transformation of American Culture, 1890–1930* (Chicago: Univ. of Chicago Press, 1981), 77–83. On personal spending patterns and shopping, see May, *Great Expectations*, 51–52.

The study on female delinquents and Yale College men is Mabel A. Wiley, *A Study of the Problem of Girl Delinquency in New Haven* (New Haven: Civic Federation of New Haven, 1915), 16–17. It is described in Ruth M. Alexander, *The "Girl Problem": Female Sexual Delinquency in New York, 1900–1930* (Ithaca: Cornell Univ. Press, 1995), 29.

On "charity girls," see Kathy Peiss, *Cheap Amusements: Working Women and Leisure in Turn-of-the-Century New York* (Philadelphia: Temple Univ. Press, 1986). On negotiating the new rules, see John Modell, "Dating Becomes the Way of American Youth," in *Essays on the Family and Historical Change*, ed. Leslie Page Moch and Gary D. Stark (College Station: Texas A&M Press, 1983), 95–102, 109, 115; Beth Bailey, *From Front Porch to Back Seat* (Baltimore: Johns Hopkins Univ. Press, 1988), 87–96.

On increases in the rate of premarital pregnancy, see Daniel Scott Smith and Michael S. Hindus, "Premarital Pregnancy in America, 1640–1971: An Overview and Interpretation," *Journal of Interdisciplinary History* 5 (1975): 537; Daniel Scott Smith, "The Dating the American Sexual Revolution: Evidence and Interpretation," in *The American Family in Social-Historical Perspective*, ed. Michael Gordon, 1st ed. (New York: St. Martin's Press, 1973); Maris A. Vinovskis, *An "Epidemic" of Adolescent Pregnancy? Some Historical and Policy Considerations* (New York: Oxford Univ. Press, 1988), 10; Daniel Scott Smith, "The Long Cycle of American Illegitimacy and Prenuptial Pregnancy," in *Bastardy and Its Comparative History* ed. Peter Laslett (Cambridge, Mass.: Harvard Univ. Press, 1980), 362–78.

On the move of men away from prostitutes in this period, see John D'Emilio and Estelle B. Freedman, *Intimate Matters: A History of Sexuality in America* (New York: Harper and Row, 1988), 234–35.

On stereotypes about sexually manipulative women, see David J. Langum, *Crossing Over the Line: Legislating Morality and the Mann Act* (Chicago: Univ. of Chicago Press, 1994), 77–96 (blackmail and Mann Act); Christina Simmons, "Modern Sexuality and the Myth of Victorian Repression," in *Passion and Power: Sexuality in History*, ed. Kathy Peiss and Christina Simmons (Philadelphia: Temple Univ. Press, 1989): 157, 165 (popular stereotypes in the culture). On the popular culture manifestations of these images, see ibid. On blackmail and the heart-balm movement, see Jane E. Larson, "'Women Understand So Little, They Call My Good Nature *Deceit*': A Feminist Rethinking of Seduction," *Columbia Law Review* 93 (1993): 374, 392–96. On blackmail and the Mann Act, see Langum, *Crossing Over*, 77–96.

Beginning in 1935, about a third of the states enacted statutes to abolish seduction and the related common-law sexual torts, in legislation commonly known as "anti-heart-balm" statutes. "Heart-balm" was a derogatory term referring to the common law sexual torts of seduction, breach of promise to marry, criminal conversation, and alienation of affections. See Nathan Feinsinger, "Legislative Attack on Heart Balm," *Michigan Law Review* 33 (1935): 979. Although the four causes of action were grouped together under the "heart-balm" label, the underlying theory of liability for each is distinct. Apparently, what linked the four torts in the mind of commentators was their focus on sexual misconduct. See ibid., 1009.

On prostitution as a species of vagrancy, see Gary V. Dubin and Richard C. Robinson, "The Vagrancy Concept Reconsidered: Problems and Abuses of Status Criminality," *NYU Law Review* 37 (1962): 102, 109–11. For early legal definitions of prostitution, see 50 Corpus Juris Secundum 800 (Brooklyn: American Law Book, 1930); 73 Corpus Juris

Secundum (Brooklyn: American Law Book, Company, 1951); 42 American Jurisprudence 260 (Rochester: Lawyers Co-operative, 1942); 63 American Jurisprudence 2d edition 364 (Rochester: Lawyers Co-operative, 1972). Early cases on the confusion over whether gain was required or not include *Commonwealth v. Cook*, 12 Met. (53 Mass.) 93 (1846); *State v. Ruhl*, 8 Ia. 447 (1859).

*United States v. Bitty* is reported at 208 U.S. 393, 401 (1908). See also *State v. Thuna*, 59 Wash. 689, 109 Pac. 331 (1910).

On the move to require pecuniary gain as an element of prostitution and the enactment of statutes criminalizing prostitution as conduct rather than status, see Thomas C. Mackey, *Red Lights Out: A Legal History of Prostitution, Disorderly Houses, and Vice Districts, 1870–1917* (New York: Garland Publishing, 1987), 54, 123.

On the vice commissions, see Mark Thomas Connelly, *The Response to Prostitution in the Progressive Era* (Chapel Hill: Univ. of North Carolina Press, 1980). For the contemporary flavor of these vice commissions, see "Five 'White Slave' Trade Investigations," *McClure's Magazine* 35 (July 1910): 348. Of our exemplary states, Chicago, Illinois, appointed a municipal vice commission and published Vice Commission of Chicago, *The Social Evil in Chicago* (Chicago: Gunthorp-Warren, 1911), and the state of Massachusetts appointed a commission that in 1914 published *Report of the Commission for the Investigation of the White Slave Traffic, So-Called* (Boston: Wright and Potter, 1914).

The Addams quote on working conditions is from Jane Addams, *A New Conscience and an Ancient Evil* (New York: Macmillan, 1912), 5, 57. On minimum wage laws and prostitution, see George J. Kneeland, *Commercialized Prostitution in New York City* (New York: Century Company, 1917), 105–6; Vice Commission of Chicago, *The Social Evil in Chicago*, 280–81. Massachusetts passed the nation's first minimum wage law in 1912, see Act of June 4, 1912, Ch. 706, 1912 Mass. Acts 780.

The Iowa abatement law is found at Laws of Iowa 1909, ch. 214. On abatement laws generally, see Mackey, *Red Lights Out*, ch. 3; Bascom Johnson, "The Injunction and Abatement Law," *Social Hygiene* 1 (March 1915): 231; and Ruth Rosen, *The Lost Sisterhood: Prostitution in America, 1900–1918* (Baltimore: Johns Hopkins Univ. Press, 1982), 28–29. On anti-vice legislation in general, see Willoughby Cyrus Waterman, *Prostitution and Its Repression in New York City, 1900–1931* (New York: Columbia Univ. Press, 1932); Joseph Mayer, *The Regulation of Commercialized Vice: An Analysis of the Transition from Segregation to Repression in the United States* (New York: Klebold Press, 1922); George E. Worthington, "Developments in Social Hygiene Legislation from 1917 to September 1, 1920," *Journal of Social Hygiene* 6 (1920): 558; Joseph Mayer, "Social Legislation and Vice Control," *Social Hygiene* (July 1919): 337; and Edward O. Janney, *The White Slave Traffic in America* (New York: National Vigilance Committee, 1911).

Antiprostitution legislation in our exemplary states include, for Massachusetts: a white slave law, Acts of 1910, ch. 424, pp. 362–65, and an abatement law, Acts of 1914, ch. 624, pp. 587–91.

For Virginia: a pandering statute, Virginia Acts of Assembly, 1910, ch. 163, p. 252; an enticement into prostitution statute, ibid., 1914, ch. 228, p. 394; and abatement laws, ibid., 1916, ch. 463, pp. 780–82, and 1918, ch. 256, p. 436.

For Illinois: white slavery laws, Laws of Illinois, p. 170 (June 9, 1909) (detention of a female in a house of prostitution); ibid., 180–81 (June 12, 1909) (pandering) (amending law approved June 1, 1908), and a multi-part statute that included abatement provisions and a criminalization of prostitution, ibid., pp. 371–74 (1915) (June 22, 1915).

For Wyoming: white slavery laws in 1890, Laws of Wyoming, ch 73, sec. 78 (1890) (enticement into prostitution) and sec. 84 (1890) (pandering), a statute to suppress prostitution, including an abatement provision, ibid., ch. 98, p. 137 (1921), and a prohibition on keeping a house of ill-fame, ibid., ch. 46, sec.1 (1921).

On the effectiveness of the abatement laws, see Mackey, *Red Lights Out*, 130. On the shutdown of the Chicago and Richmond vice districts, see Mayer, *Regulation of Commercialized Vice*, 11.

On disparate conviction rates (prostitutes vs. pimps) in New York City, see Waterman, *Prostitution*, 73–75. An example of state court decisions on patron laws is *State v. Gardner*, 174 Ia. 746, 156 N.W. 747 (1916). Waterman also reports a New York case in which a male customer was held not to be an "aider or abettor" within the language of an existing prostitution statute. See *Prostitution*, 21–22.

Dr. Morrow's estimate on men and rates of infection with venereal disease is cited and discussed in D'Emilio and Freedman, *Intimate Matters*, 204–7. On the social hygiene campaign, see Allan M. Brandt, *No Magic Bullet: A Social History of Venereal Disease in the United States Since 1880* (New York: Oxford Univ. Press, 1985).

The Mann Act is 36 Stat. 825, 1911, 18 U.S.C. Ch. 395 (*An Act to Further Regulate Interstate and Foreign Commerce by Prohibiting the Transportation Therein for Immoral Purposes of Women and Girls, and for Other Purposes*, June 25, 1910). The Supreme Court ruling is *Caminetti v. U.S.*, 242 U.S. 470 (1917). Data on number of Mann Act prosecutions is found in Connelly, *Response to Prostitution*, 56. Data on percentage of prostitution versus nonprostitution cases is found in Langum, *Crossing Over*, 75.

On the *Caminetti* prosecution, see "Prison for Diggs and Caminetti," *New York Times*, Sept. 18, 1913, p. 9, quoted in Langum, *Crossing Over*, 111.

On the new marital ideal, see Margaret Sanger, *The Pivot of Civilization* (New York: Brentano's, 1922), 140, 258. See also Margaret Sanger, *Happiness in Marriage* (New York: Blue Ribbon Books, 1931). On the lowering of the average age of marriage, see May, *Great Expectations*, 71, 76–77; on divorce rates, see 2; on reasons offered for divorce, see 100–158. The Simmons quote is from Simmons, "Myth of Victorian Repression," 170. On Simmons's interpretation of sexual liberality as a form of social control, see ibid.

On lynchings in Virginia, see Tolnay and Beck, supra, at 91–92. On capital punishment, see Eric W. Rise, *The Martinsville Seven: Race, Rape, and Capital Punishment* (Charlottesville: Univ. of Virginia Press, 1995), 120 (citing statistics gathered for the appeal by the lawyers who represented seven black men executed in 1951 for the gang rape of a white woman).

The DuBois quote is from Paula Giddings, *When and Where I Enter: The Impact of Black Women on Race and Sex in America* (Toronto and New York: Bantam Books, 1984), 61. On anti-miscegenation laws in the postbellum South, see Emily Field Van Tassel, "'Only the Law Would Rule Between Us': Antimiscegenation, the Moral Economy of Dependency, and the Debate Over Rights After the Civil War," *Chicago-Kent Law Review* 70 (1995): 873, 898; on accusations of rape in lynchings, see Ida B. Wells–Barnett, "A Red Record: Tabulated Statistics and Alleged Causes of Lynchings in the United States, 1892–1893–1894," in *Selected Works of Ida B. Wells-Barnett*, comp. Trudier Harris (New York: Oxford Univ. Press, 1991), 138, 226–39. The Frances Willard quote is from Alfreda M. Duster, ed., *Crusade for Justice: The Autobiography of Ida B. Wells* (Chicago: Univ. of Chicago Press, 1970), 151–52. On the failure to enact federal antilynching legislation, see generally Barbara Holden-Smith, "Lynching, Federalism and the Intersection of Race and Gender in the Progressive Era," *Yale Journal of Law and Feminism* 8 (1996): 31. We are indebted to Ben Brown for the insight regarding Franklin Delano Roosevelt.

The Darwin references are to Charles S. Darwin, *The Works of Charles Darwin, vol. 22: The Descent of Man and Selection in Relation to Sex* (1871; New York: New York Univ. Press, 1994).

On Ellis and Freud, see Jeffrey Weeks, *Sex, Politics and Society: The Regulation of Sexuality Since 1800* (London and New York: Longman, 1981), ch. 8.

The "sex penetrates" quote is cited in D'Emilio and Freedman, *Intimate Matters*,

225–26. The "cruel and self-hating" quote is from Sanger, *Happiness in Marriage*, 48.

On Lindsey's support for divorce and remarriage, see Lindsey and Evans, *Revolt of Modern Youth*.

The eugenics quotes of Sanger are found in Daniel Kevles, *In the Name of Eugenics: Genetics and the Uses of Human Heredity* (New York: Knopf, 1985), 90.

On the rise of "I.Q.," see generally Stephen J. Gould, *The Mismeasure of Man* (New York: Norton, 1981).

On the eugenics movement in America in the 1920s, see generally Ellen Chesler, *Woman of Valor: Margaret Sanger and the Birth Control Movement in America* (New York: Simon and Schuster, 1992), 214–17. On the move to sterilization, see Philip R. Reilly, *The Surgical Solution: A History of Involuntary Sterilization in the United States* (Baltimore: Johns Hopkins Univ. Press, 1991). On state eugenics laws and their use, see Kevles, *In the Name of Eugenics*, 107–12.

*Buck v. Bell* is reported at 274 U.S. 200, 205–6 (1927). On the factual findings of the Buck case, see Paul A. Lombardo, "Three Generations No Imbeciles: New Light on Buck v. Bell," *NYU Law Review* 60 (1985): 30, and Stephen J. Gould, "Carrie Buck's Daughter," *Constitutional Commentary* 2 (1985): 331, 337.

The Lystra quote is from Karen Lystra, *Searching the Heart: Women, Men, and Romantic Love in Nineteenth-Century America* (New York: Oxford Univ. Press, 1989), 81. The Haag quotes are from Pamela S. Haag, "In Search of 'The Real Thing': Ideologies of Love, Modern Romance, and Women's Sexual Subjectivity in the United States, 1920–40," *Journal of the History of Sexuality* 2 (1992):547. The Engelstein quote is from Laura Engelstein, *The Keys to Happiness: Sex and the Search for Modernity in Fin-de-Siècle Russia* (Ithaca: Cornell Univ. Press, 1992), 1.

On the origins of Miss America, see Cott, *Grounding*, 43–44.

# 9

## THE LAW CATCHES UP

For the first half of the twentieth century, American sex law lagged behind—or actively resisted—the sweeping changes in sexual conduct and values in the rest of society. By the time substantial legal change occurred in the late 1960s, more than 90 percent of middle-class men and half of middle-class women had had sex before marriage, and even adultery was not uncommon. Serious change was visible as early as the 1940s. Following the pioneering sexology of Havelock Ellis, Alfred C. Kinsey and a team of researchers published reports of ordinary people engaged in a wide range of illegal or disapproved sexual activities, including premarital sex, adulterous affairs, same-sex relations, patronization of prostitutes, and masturbation. This striking evidence of changed behavior among ordinary Americans bypassed moral or political debates by casting what a generation before had been acts of deviance or radicalism as normal and ordinary. Kinsey's data suggested not only that sexuality was more varied and insistent than conventional morality allowed, but that it always had been so.

This popular understanding of a natural sexual libertinism fueled the belated process of legal development. Two avenues of legal change, the American Law Institute's Model Penal Code and a series of Supreme Court decisions beginning in the 1930s, promoted decriminalization of adult consensual sexual activity in accordance with the new prescriptive naturalism championed by the sexologists.

### THE KINSEY REPORT

Kinsey purported not to be trying to spark a revolution. A university biology professor previously known for his insect studies, Kinsey said he sought to bring to the study of human sexual behavior the scientific method and moral neutrality associated with studies of animal behavior. In the late 1930s, Kinsey assembled a group of researchers that eventually grew into the Institute for Sex Research at the University of Indiana. Over more than a decade the Kinsey researchers interviewed some 18,000 men and women, the first mass investigation to empirically document American sexual habits. "Alongside this achievement," one commentator has said, "the scientific procedures of Freud's and Ellis's sexual studies appear shabby indeed."

Over time, researchers have cast harsh doubt on Kinsey's findings, particularly on his failure to abide by basic procedures of random sampling. The publication in 1995 of the broad-based, random sex survey from the National Opinion Research Center refuted many of Kinsey's findings. By 1996, the conservative, but well-respected magazine, *The Public Perspective*, could assert that "no knowledge-able person considers Kinsey's work to be survey research." In 1998, University of Houston Professor James H. Jones unveiled a massive biography, *Alfred C. Kinsey: A Public/Private Life*, in which he asserts that Kinsey was a voyeur, an exhibition-ist, a homosexual and a masochist, doing "sex research . . . [that] allowed Kinsey to transform his voyeurism into science."

But in a sense, none of this revisionism matters.

The publication of Kinsey's studies of male sexual behavior in 1948 and female sexual behavior in 1953 broke open popular debate over sexual morality. Although it was an academic study not intended for the popular market, *Sexual Behavior in the Human Male* sold 250,000 copies when first released and remained on the *New York Times* bestseller list for twenty-seven weeks. Five years later, the release of *Sex-ual Behavior in the Human Female* created a similar furor. *Time* magazine said that Kinsey had made sex talk in public acceptable: "No single event did more for open discussion of sex than the Kinsey Report, which got such matters as homosexual-ity, masturbation, coitus and orgasm into most papers and family magazines." His-torians John D'Emilio and Estelle Freedman believe that not only were Americans hungry for sexual honesty and openness, but that the cloaking of Kinsey's explo-sive data in scientific respectability allowed the popular media and the public to talk and talk and talk about sexuality without appearing prurient.

Like his sexologist predecessors, Kinsey invoked science to neutralize moral judgment. In the introduction to *Male*, Kinsey writes, "This is first of all a report on what people do, which raises no question of what they should do." Scientists, he cautioned, "have no special capacities for making [such] evaluations." Kinsey adopted the generic category of "sexual outlet" as his organizing concept and number of orgasms as his counting measure. These measures disrupted the distinc-tions that earlier sexual paradigms had drawn between marital and nonmarital sex, heterosexual and same-sex encounters, sex with a partner and masturbation or nocturnal dreams/emissions, commercial sex and noncommercial sex, sex with animals and sex with people. Any orgasm was as good as any other by these mea-sures, and no orgasmic experience was by definition more satisfying, moral, or normal than any other.

Yet Kinsey made different but equally strong value judgments, which shaped how his data were understood. Several examples illustrate this normativity. First, Kinsey defended the normality and even healthfulness of masturbation, heterosex-ual petting, and premarital intercourse as contributing to sexual adjustment and satisfaction within marriage, especially for women. He even suggested that extra-marital affairs did not always harm a marriage and might, in some instances, en-hance marital sex. Yet Kinsey's interviews did not ask about psychological well-being, and such judgments about "harm," "adjustment," or "satisfaction" are simply Kinsey's value preferences. Second, throughout *Male* and *Female* Kinsey casts as tragic and pointless anything that might limit the number of orgasms an individual enjoys during a lifetime. Included in this cast of repressive villains are social and legal sanctions against nonmarital sex, religious or moral restraints, and prejudices against nonreproductive sex like masturbation or prostitution. Such values, Kinsey dismissively concludes, originate in "ignorance and superstition" and have no rational or scientific basis.

Finally, Kinsey consistently assumes sexual behaviors that are common are also, by definition, biologically normal. Elevating biological mandate over social governance, Kinsey argued that law must change to conform to human nature as manifested in sexual practice:

> All of these and still other types of sexual behavior are illicit activities, each performance of which is punishable as a crime under the law. The persons involved in these activities, taken as a whole, constitute more than 95 per cent of the total male population. Only a relatively small proportion of the males who are sent to penal institutions for sex have been involved in behavior which is materially different from the behavior of most of the males in the population. But it is the total 95 per cent of the male population for which the judge or board of public safety, or church, or civic group demands apprehension, arrest, and conviction, when they call for a clean-up of the sex offenders in a community. It is, in fine, a proposal that 5 per cent of the population should support the other 95 per cent in penal institutions.

This evidence of a gap between ideal and reality generated no sense of moral crisis (as would have been the case in the nineteenth century), but rather argued for tolerance. Yet Kinsey's findings shocked many.

In his "snapshot" of sex in America, Kinsey found that males and females in the study had different experiences. Virtually all men had engaged in masturbation and heterosexual petting. By the age of fifteen years, most males had found some regular orgasmic outlet, whether petting or intercourse with females (including prostitutes), same-sex encounters, or masturbation. More than 90 percent of men had engaged in premarital intercourse and one half of married men had had extramarital affairs. Some 37 percent of men had had at least one homosexual experience and half acknowledged either homosexual experience or sexual feelings toward other men.

Although the women Kinsey studied had fewer sexual outlets and orgasms, three-fifths of women had masturbated and 90 percent had petted with a partner of the opposite sex. Only half of women had had premarital intercourse and one-quarter had had extramarital affairs. The average married woman experienced orgasm three-quarters of the time in sex with her husband.

Because his study indicated that men had more sexual outlets and orgasms than women, Kinsey concluded that the male sexual nature was more energetic. His surveys found that wives wanted sex less often than their husbands and that husbands wanted wives to orgasm more often. Some women said they lied about orgasm to satisfy their husbands. Yet the picture of marital sex Kinsey reported accords with the companionate ideal of shared sexual satisfaction in marriage. Kinsey's couples varied their positions for intercourse and practiced oral sex. Husbands often refrained from sex unless their wives also wanted it, which meant that Kinsey's married couples had intercourse less often than did married couples in earlier eras. Women born before 1900 reported more frequent marital intercourse and fewer orgasms than did women born after 1900. Older notions of the sexual rights of husbands and the duties of wives were fading away. Lower-class married couples in Kinsey's surveys had less varied and less mutual sex than the middle class.

Although little noted at the time, Kinsey also took issue with the idea of a vaginal orgasm. Since Freud, the existence and superiority of vaginal over clitoral orgasm had been unquestioned by scientists, doctors, and popular sex advisors. Kinsey's survey found that masturbating women climaxed as quickly as men and that women in lesbian encounters had more orgasms than women in heterosexual encounters. Kinsey argued this was proof that, contrary to popular wisdom, women were not less sexually responsive than men, but slower to climax in sexual relations with men due to "the ineffectiveness of the usual coital techniques" designed around male needs and without attention to female anatomy.

Kinsey's sample was biased toward middle-class people. This bias is significant because Kinsey found that class shaped choice of sexual outlet, especially for men. Lower-class men were much more likely to have had premarital intercourse, to have patronized prostitutes, and to have had both homosexual and extramarital experiences. By contrast, middle-and upper-class men were more likely to have masturbated, had nocturnal emissions, and petted to climax.

Some modern sex researchers question the Kinsey data, arguing that his findings must have been exaggerated given evidence of far greater sexual caution and reticence among comparable groups of people surveyed about similar issues in the 1990s. Nonetheless, in the late 1940s and 1950s, the American public embraced Kinsey as a true picture of who they were and what they wanted. Regina Morantz writes, "Relieving guilt and reassuring readers that everyone had similar sexual impulses, Kinsey's books contributed to a changing sexual climate in which ordinary people lived and worked. They probably had the same emancipating effect on the unpsychoanalyzed masses that Freud's work achieved for generations of intellectuals."

Rather than making a moral or political argument about why sexual attitudes and practices should change, Kinsey showed simply that the change had already happened. Americans either could fight the trend, or relax and go with the flow. Kinsey did more to eliminate the residuum of social conservatism than even the sexology of Ellis and Freud. Telling people that "everyone is doing it" did more to make it happen than telling them that Darwin's theory would indicate that everyone must be doing it.

As a bargaining matter, the closer society came to an unrestrained pursuit of individual sexual "outlets," the more the weaker players were exposed to the fruits as well as the impact of sexual freedom. Kinsey found, for example, that modern wives had sex less often but enjoyed it more. The transition from a Victorian notion of female passionlessness to the ideology of female sexual capacity gave women a bargaining chip by raising the value of mutual and consensual sex. Nothing in Kinsey's work, however, indicates that the ideological development should stop there. If women enjoyed sex so much while having less of it, does that mean they'd enjoy more sex even more? Kinsey does not answer that question.

## THE ROOTS OF LEGAL CHANGE

Eventually, these social changes reached the legal system. The crucial moment probably can be assigned to the 1962 release of the Model Penal Code, an academic and aspirational recasting of American criminal law. Among other changes, the Model Penal Code recommended a sweeping redefinition of sex law around a libertine model.

The Model Penal Code is a product of the American Law Institute, an elite law reform group that dates back to 1923. Although not released until the early 1960s, the Model Penal Code is rooted in the transformative cultural changes of the 1920s. From its earliest years, the Institute brought together thinkers to debate core issues of law and society, discussions that eventually would clear the path for reshaping the legal regulation of sexuality. The members debated foundational questions about the nature of law, disputes that mirrored earlier controversies in the political world dating back to Darwin's *Origin of Species*. At issue was whether there exists an ineluctable natural order that governs human society attributable to Darwinian processes of evolution, or whether society can be shaped by moral or political choices more powerful than nature. In the coming decades, the nature/culture debate would come to be applied specifically to questions of sexual morality and regulation.

The legal counterparts to the Darwinian naturalists were formalist legal scholars who believed that law was part of the natural order. Although an embrace of the messy natural arrangements of life and law hardly seems "formal," in nineteenth-century England and America the existing arrangements of power rested firmly on common law. Legal formalists saw the common law as reflecting eternal verities, coming out of the mists of time like Darwin's evolution of species, and capable of resolving every dispute between persons and between persons and the state. All that was necessary was a full understanding and preservation of formal common law principles. The proper understanding of the common law became the project of the American Law Institute, which undertook to produce magisterial "restatements" of whole bodies of doctrine (torts, contracts, etc.) designed to rationalize all common law decisions into patterns and principles such that the "natural" legal order might be discerned and applied.

In these same years, the intellectual movement later to be called "legal realism" developed in opposition to formalism. The realists believed that all law comes from official acts representing human political judgment, and not from natural order or eternal truth. The common law was simply the sum of past judicial acts, and thus no more or less legitimate or natural than the current acts of legislatures or administrative agencies. Believing in a flexible legal and social system, the realists aligned themselves with the Progressive movement in politics and activist government as a tool for reform. They supported the legitimacy of governmental regulation, particularly the New Deal.

These debates over the legitimacy of various forms of lawmaking were more than academic. Judges who preferred the common law as natural and immutable viewed regulation accomplished by legislation or administrative rule as illegitimate. For the formalist, legislation is not just another avenue for legal governance; rather, regulation disturbs the natural order of things. Relationships established by the common law, especially of property and contract, accord with the natural order and are therefore good. By contrast, efforts to restructure or redistribute those relations in pursuit of social ends such as policy, justice, or morality are, by definition, unwise, unstable, and ultimately unconstitutional. For four years after the election of President Franklin D. Roosevelt, judges of a formalist bent systematically struck down the legislation comprising the New Deal.

Notwithstanding its origins as an agency of common law formalism and the formalist conception of its ongoing restatement projects, the American Law Institute always had a strong realist strand. Among its founders was leading anti-formalist Wesley Hohfeld, and the original committee included Benjamin Cardozo, Roscoe Pound, and Arthur Corbin. This minor key of realism reflects the changing face of the legal profession. During the period from 1915 when an American Law Institute was first proposed, to the late 1920s when its work on the restatements began in earnest, the realists made substantial inroads in the legal academy and, to a lesser extent, on the bench.

A restatement of criminal law was an obvious project for the newly founded American Law Institute given the importance of criminal law to the legal system. But American criminal law was not common law but mostly statutory. Thus there was no inherently legitimate law to restate. Nonetheless, it was clear that legislatures could benefit from a model statute crafted by the best legal minds proposing ideal principles of the criminal law. Distinct from other restatements, the Model Penal Code openly substituted the brilliance of the draftsman for the winnowing process of natural selection that characterized the English common law ideal.

In 1931, the American Law Institute membership proposed to draft a model criminal code to light the way to reform of existing law. The initial proposal was for a massive empirical investigation into contemporary practices, a project that far exceeded the financial resources available during the Depression. As with so many reform projects of the early twentieth century, including the sexual revolution, the Model Penal Code was shelved until after World War II.

In 1950, the American Law Institute returned to the project. The institute formed an Advisory Council, received a grant from the Rockefeller Foundation, and, in 1952, began to work. The advisors met from 1952 until 1962. They retained a chief reporter, Columbia Law School Professor Herbert Wechsler, and assistants and consultants who submitted drafts to the advisory council for debate and direction. The advisors eventually submitted a series of tentative drafts to the body as a whole for consideration. Thirteen were considered, and, in 1962, the Proposed Official Draft was adopted.

From the outset, the Model Penal Code codifiers admitted that their project was normative and not just a descriptive compilation. In 1955, Chief Reporter Wechsler described the enterprise as "a constant preoccupation with the task of relating [the proposed] rules and principles to the fundamental moral assumptions of the society to which it belongs." Nonetheless, Wechsler was silent about the source of these "fundamental moral assumptions." Because the reporters draft the original proposals, they are the most influential players in the American Law Institute processes, but neither Wechsler nor any of the other members of the reportorial staff was a philosopher. Although the reporters consulted psychiatrists on the legal insanity sections and corrections experts on the sentencing and correction provisions, they did not consult philosophers on morality.

In later years, Wechsler would describe his own philosophy as "utilitarian in my views and approaches." But his utilitarianism sounds more like classical liberalism when he asserts that "everybody knows that a social order that doesn't provide adequate protection for personal dignity and autonomy and bodily integrity is a defective social order." Wechsler appears to have seen his particular brand of liberal/utilitarianism as an adequate source of moral insight, commenting "you don't need any sociological expertise or psychological expertise. Or any other kind of expertise."

We know more than Wechsler reveals about the moral arguments underlying the criminal sex law provisions of the Model Penal Code. One of the strongest influences on these provisions, Morris Ploscowe, laid out many of them in his treatise *Sex and the Law* (1951), published just before work began in earnest on the Code, and, indeed, the commentary sometimes sounds like a dialogue between the drafters and Ploscowe. Ploscowe's views on the nature of rape and the social realities of its prosecution are taken as givens, and most of his legislative suggestions accepted. Differences between the Code provisions and Ploscowe's recommendations call for an explanation. For example, where the Code refuses to require substantial physical penetration to charge rape, as Ploscowe had suggested, the drafters explain that the Code penalties are much less severe than the rape laws that Ploscowe analyzed in his book, and that the problem of false female testimony that Ploscowe pointed to is less serious where the fact of sexual contact is acknowledged but only the degree contested. The response to Ploscowe survives in an amended form into the official draft issued in 1962. Who was Morris Plescowe?

Ploscowe spent many years as a New York magistrate before returning to private practice and an associate professorship at New York University Law School. Perhaps because his law practice included many family law cases, he turned his scholarly attention to sexual regulation. In *Sex and the Law,* Ploscowe argues for "complete reorientation" of the criminal law of sex based on an understanding of sexuality as an intransigent natural force, an understanding Ploscowe traces to the influence of Alfred Kinsey. Noting that few branches of the law show such a wide divergence between actual behavior and established norms, Ploscowe argues for the abandonment of the effort to regulate sex altogether: "Nowhere are the disparities between law in action and law on the books so great as in the control of sex crime.... Sexuality simply cannot realistically be confined within present legal bounds."

Ploscowe did not flinch at pursuing these naturalist assumptions to their controversial conclusions. Perhaps most at odds with conventions, he justifies marriage not as the vehicle for legitimate sexuality, but rather the site for the stable rearing of children. If marriage is not needed to redeem sexuality, the relationship should not be imposed by society, and Ploscowe calls for an end to all laws that impose marriage-like obligations based on nonmarital sex, including common-law marriage, recognition of cohabitation relationships, and tort actions for breach of promise to marry and seduction. Likewise, he advocates abolishing the criminal laws of adultery and fornication: "There is no necessary relationship between mental abnormality and [those] sexual activities unless what we call 'love' is identified with and classified as a mental disease," Ploscowe explains.

Ploscowe saves his severest condemnation of existing law, however, for the subject of rape. Insisting that "large numbers of men who by no stretch of the imagination can be considered dangerous are convicted of rape," he suggests a variety of legal reforms to make rape harder to charge and harder to prove. Of the unjustly convicted, Ploscowe writes:

> They may be lacking in ethical or moral principles or a sense of social responsibility. They may be immature men who believe that sexual conquest is a sign of adulthood and virility. They may be emotionally disturbed men who are seeking an outlet for frustrations in sexual activity. They may be men who are simply following the pattern of racial or cultural behavior with which they are familiar. But they are not potential killers, potential threats to the moral integrity and honor of all women.

Ploscowe observes that "many experts [believe] rape cannot be perpetrated by one man alone on an adult woman of good health and vigor." And he quotes approvingly the musings of a judge who suggested that for every valid rape claim he saw in his courtroom, there were twelve unfounded charges.

Most unjust rape convictions, Ploscowe asserts, involve a complaining witness who knows the defendant, that is, an acquaintance rape: "At some point in the tête à tête, the man insists on having sexual intercourse, which the woman refuses. When the man attempts to impose his will a little too forcibly upon her, a charge of rape may be made." Other unjust rape convictions are those in which a woman has gotten drunk and "taken a chance that she would be tampered with sexually." Thus the bargaining chip of female sexual consent, begins to lose value as Ploscowe proposes to immunize men's forcible imposition of sexual will.

The most endemic injustice of rape law, according to Ploscowe, is the charge of statutory rape, a category of cases he describes as being too often brought against adolescent boys "who have simply followed the sexual patterns of behavior with which they are familiar in the social, cultural, educational and racial milieu in which they live," or by girls "experienced in the ways of sex" who knowingly take up with mature men. To Ploscowe's mind, it is only the mature man who seeks sex with very young girls (aged ten years and under) who manifests the "abnormal desires" from which the public truly needs the protection.

To undo these manifest wrongs in the existing legal regime, Ploscowe proposes first, to require corroboration of the rape victim's testimony, lest a man be "place[d] at the mercy of revengeful, spiteful, blackmailing, or psychopathic complainants," or be convicted "on the uncorroborated testimony of a strumpet." Second, he suggests requiring proof of more than slight physical penetration of the victim's body. Full penetration is more likely to lead to corroborating physical evidence in the form of seminal emission or injury to the woman's body. Third, he would require the victim to prove that she was sober, for "[w]hen a woman drinks with a man to the point of intoxication, she practically invites him to take advantage of her person." Fourth, he would require the complainant to show not only subjective nonconsent, but that she offered utmost resistance to the attack. And finally, Ploscowe proposes to reduce the age of consent to ten or twelve years (where it had started in the common law), and to forbid sex with a female aged twelve to sixteen years only if the girl can show she is not promiscuous.

Ploscowe's concern with where to draw the line around rape reflects what will emerge as an endemic boundary problem in a libertine regime. By separating sexual access from monogamous marriage, the line between illegitimate and legitimate sexual exchange would, by law, no longer be marked by the presence or absence of a legal formality, an objective fact. Instead, another marker such as consent or force, more subjective and reliant on the testimony of women and children witnesses, would be substituted. Line-drawing problems cannot be avoided when categorizing complex human behaviors, and especially acts that fall near the dividing line. But the problem is how to interpret new standards in a sexual world where expectations and norms also are in transition. Ploscowe's solution is to maximize sexual access and put the burden of dispute on the victim by making rape hard to plead and to prove.

Ploscowe's proposed world resembles the ungoverned state of nature latent in libertinism from Darwin's time, in which, as Thucydides put it, "the strong do what they will and the weak do what they must." Rape law is the weaker player's basic bargaining chip. If there is no effective legal control of rape, she can only hope that ideology will greatly value her consensual participation, another of her bargaining chips. In libertine times, the arguments for consideration of the other sexual bargainer must extend beyond wives to the universe of unfamiliar females, a development that requires substantial doses of good will toward females in general. Ploscowe counters this possibility, describing all women as suitable targets of the will of the stronger.

In contrast to his harsh condemnation of rape enforcement, Ploscowe supports continued and rigorous enforcement of the criminal prohibition of prostitution, rejecting any move toward decriminalization, regulation, or legalization. He argues that prostitution adversely affects public morality ("one of the cancers of our civilization") and diminishes the character of prostitutes ("broken bits of humanity"). Ploscowe's only quibble with the existing law of prostitution is that patrons occasionally are prosecuted ("The single standard may be excellent for ethics and morality; it is not necessarily a good one for the law relating to prostitution"), and that prostitution leads to police corruption. In sum, Ploscowe would maximize noncommercial sex, even where it borders on force, but he would minimize the voluntary commercial exchange of sex. Thus the only place where women openly demand compensation for sexual access would be forbidden to them.

The Model Penal Code adopted many of Ploscowe's specific proposals for changes in sex law. Like Ploscowe, the Code assumes that uncontained sexuality is both natural and morally neutral, that government's role is limited with respect to voluntary sexual exchange, and that lawmakers should be properly skeptical of claims of unwanted sexuality.

In addition to the work of Morris Ploscowe, Britain's Wolfenden Report on the laws of homosexuality and prostitution also shaped the Model Penal Code recommendations for sexual deregulation. According to Jeffrey Weeks, Britain feared for the stability of sexual virtue after World War II, in part because of revelations about several homosexual men who turned out to be Communist spies. Simultaneously, the prospect of the coronation of Elizabeth II had made the visibility of prostitutes on London streets an issue. And finally, the growth of psychiatry as an academic and popularized discourse led to a tendency to reclassify homosexuality and, to a lesser degree, prostitution, as a mental illness, rather than criminal misconduct.

As a result of these developments, in 1954 the Home Office asked Sir John Wolfenden to recommend policies to address prostitution and homosexuality. To the surprise of many Britons, the Wolfenden Committee's 1957 report recommended that homosexual and commercial sex be removed from criminal sanction so long as it was conducted in private. (Public homosexual conduct and public solicitation would remain crimes under the Wolfenden scheme.) Like Ploscowe's treatise on American law, the Wolfenden Report was explicit in its assumptions about the nature of sexuality and the role of law in enforcing sexual morality. The Wolfenden Report takes two strong positions: Society should give individuals maximum freedom of moral choice in private matters, and law can legitimately suppress public conduct for reasons of social morality. The distinction supports decriminalization of private consensual conduct and criminalization of public consensual conduct. The Report argues further that prudence dictates restraint where legal enforcement will not effectively deter conduct, and that private sexual conduct (homosexual and heterosexual, commercial and noncommercial) falls into this category. As recent commentators have pointed out, the Wolfenden Report does not go so far as to say that homosexuality or prostitution are moral acts; rather, the Committee states simply that communities are divided on the blameworthiness of such conduct. Its recommendation of tolerance rests on the classical liberal freedom even to be immoral, at least in private.

Published just as the American Law Institute debated final drafts of the Model Penal Code, the Wolfenden Report became part of the mainstream of American legal debate. English law thus continued to play its centuries-long role in the development of American thought.

## SKINNER V. OKLAHOMA: SEX AS A FUNDAMENTAL RIGHT

In the process of decriminalizing sex as a matter of social policy, the Model Penal Code also developed in dialogue with the United States Supreme Court. From the early 1940s through the 1980s, the Court decided a series of challenges to sexual regulation as a matter of constitutional right. In key cases the Court repeatedly refers to the Model Penal Code's suggested provisions and justifications concerning, for example, obscenity [*Roth v. U.S.* (1957), *Jacobellis v. Ohio* (1964), *Stanley v. Georgia* (1969) and *Miller v. California* (1973)], and abortion and sexual privacy [*Doe v. Bolton* (1973) and *Roe v. Wade* (1973)].

The constitutional argument about sexual governance slightly predates the Model Penal Code. In the 1930s eugenics case, *Buck v. Bell*, the Court had authorized legal regulation to ensure the fitness of the race. Although rooted, as sexology is, in Darwin's work, such a collectivist version of sexuality conflicts with the sexologists' interpretation of sex as an immutable individual instinct uniquely immunized from social control. From this competing perspective, collective governance is the most oppressive possible prospect threatening the individual with an overweening state. In 1942, the Supreme Court resolved the underlying tension in sex theory in favor of individualism, ruling in *Skinner v. Oklahoma* that government cannot sterilize citizens for the social good. *Skinner* is the first limit on state power to appropriate an individual's sexuality to its own ends.

The outcome in *Skinner* was far from preordained. Just fifteen years earlier the Court had approved involuntary sterilization, and it was on the authority of this earlier decision that Oklahoma had enacted the Habitual Criminal Sterilization Act at issue in *Skinner*. The Act subjected any person convicted of more than two felonies involving "moral turpitude" to sterilization. Jack Skinner had been a chicken thief from boyhood. After his third conviction for larceny, the state ordered him sterilized. He appealed.

In *Skinner*, the U.S. Supreme Court confronted in the sexual context the formalist/realist divide that had splintered the Court in earlier constitutional battles over New Deal programs. The Court's longstanding position had been that legislative interference with the economy violated the natural order of property rights reflected in the common law. Invoking the constitutional prohibitions against taking property without due process, they routinely struck down regulatory schemes. Faced with Franklin Roosevelt's court packing plan in 1937, however, the Justices changed positions ("the switch in time that saved nine") and stopped overturning New Deal legislation. Cases decided after the switch followed a new rule that legislative action would be subjected only to minimal judicial scrutiny. If any facts either known or reasonably inferable supported the regulation at issue, the Court would affirm the legislature's policy choice as constitutional. The Court reserved its more searching scrutiny for legislation that violated fundamental constitutional rights, including freedoms of expression and association, rights of political participation, rights of religious autonomy, and rights of privacy and personhood. The new standard of constitutional review made striking down the Oklahoma law more difficult.

Justice Douglas, writing for the Court in *Skinner* five years after the switch, found adequate grounds to strike down the Oklahoma statute in the distinction between those felonies that warranted sterilization and those that did not. Noting that the statute covered ordinary theft but expressly exempted white-collar offenses such as embezzlement, Douglas wrote: "Sterilization of those who have thrice committed grand larceny with immunity for those who are embezzlers, is a clear, pointed, unmistakable discrimination. . . . We have not the slightest basis for inferring that . . . the inheritability of criminal traits follows the neat legal distinctions which the law has marked between these two offenses." The Court ruled that the statute was invidiously directed at the crimes of the poor even as it exempted white-collar crimes, thus violating equal protection: "[W]hen the law lays an unequal hand on those who have committed intrinsically the same quality of offense and sterilizes the one and not the other, it has made as invidious a discrimination as if it had selected a particular race or nationality for oppressive treatment." The Court thus implicitly recognized that sexual regulation may be used as a form of political violence: "The power to sterilize . . . [i]n evil or reckless hands . . . can cause races or types which are inimical to the dominant group to wither and disappear."

Despite Douglas's strong language, the tenuousness of the larceny/embezzle-ment distinction alone might not have been enough to make the law unconstitu-tional; all legislation classifies, after all, and the "switch" cases now required the Court to defer to legislative judgments unless a fundamental right was involved. Justice Douglas thus held procreation as a fundamental right ("one of the basic civil rights of man"), and ruled that the state's direct interference in the procrea-tive capacity caused irreparable injury, "forever depriv[ing]" the criminal of "a basic liberty." Because a basic liberty was involved, the Court applied the more searching scrutiny and held that Oklahoma's incoherent selection of sterilizable crimes did not pass muster.

Concurring separately, Chief Justice Stone thought that the legislature could sterilize for one thing and not another, but still found the law fatally flawed be-cause it did not require a judicial hearing on the heritability of an individual's criminal tendencies before sterilization. Stone doubted the legislature's conclu-sion that criminal tendencies were heritable. Justice Jackson also concurred sepa-rately, agreeing with Stone, but also making Douglas's argument: "[T]here are limits to the extent to which a legislatively represented majority may conduct biological experiments at the expense of the dignity and personality and natural powers of a minority."

Stone's straightforward policy disagreement with the legislature was at odds with new constitutional doctrine of minimal scrutiny. Thus it is Douglas's and Jackson's flinching at the raw biological power of the Oklahoma law that has en-dured as the constitutional limit on sex law and policy. The fundamental rights strand of *Skinner* marked a change in constitutional law: The Court overturned its recent precedent in *Buck v. Bell*, acknowledged the dangers of political abuse of sexual regulation, and characterized the procreative aspects of sexuality in a class with human capacities such as speech that are fundamental to personhood. Res-urrecting notions of natural freedom from its pre-switch economic jurispru-dence, the Court classified sexual freedom as part of the natural order, impossible for law to constrain.

In its powerful invocation of the sanctity of the individual, *Skinner* reflects the view that sexuality is instinctive and constitutive of the self. After *Skinner*, the U.S. Constitution itself could be invoked for the idea that sex is a fundamental human right, like politics and religion. More revolutionary still, *Skinner* might be read to mean that in sex, as in conscience and belief, the individual's interests trump those of the state or society.

*Skinner* threatened to bring about the anarchic world suggested by the sexolo-gists and Judge Ploscowe, this time as a matter of constitutional doctrine. As we will see, contemporary arguments for the privileged position of pornography, even in the highly protected arena of free speech, have their roots in the exaltation of sex among human capacities so close to the surface in *Skinner*. This sweeping potential eventually would be blunted, however, by a cabining of *Skinner*. Although litigants repeatedly invoked *Skinner* in matters concerning sexual autonomy and privacy, the Court has consistently insisted the case concerns family, marriage, and procreation, not sexuality.

## THE DEREGULATION OF SEX

After *Skinner*, it seemed that state laws criminalizing adultery and fornication would be the next to fall to a constitutional challenge on fundamental rights grounds. If procreative sex is a core value, as *Skinner* seemed to say, laws forbidding people to have sex seem as obstructionist as cutting their tubes. Even conditioning reproduction on marriage restrains liberty. Yet thirty years would pass before a concerted constitutional attack on "victimless" sex crimes like fornication would be mounted.

Even without constitutional permission, however, Americans simply walked away from the criminal regulation of private, nonmarital, heterosexual sex in the decades after *Skinner*. Once male-female premarital sex grew more common and accepted, the real legal restraints were minimal. At common law a private act of fornication was no crime, and became so by statute in only some of the states. In the other states, fornication was a crime only if "open and notorious," or if it amounted to "lewd and lascivious cohabitation," which required repeated acts. Many state courts refused to convict based on three, four, six, or sporadic acts of intercourse. It had been almost a century since any state had meaningfully increased the penalties for adultery and fornication. In 1950 in Massachusetts, Virginia, and Illinois, fornication was a minor offense. Wyoming had no fornication law. Accordingly, in the mid-1950s when the Model Penal Code drafters began work on a criminal sex code, the social climate favored a loosening-up of criminal restraints and only a weak legal structure bolstered continued regulation.

Minimal as the existing laws were, the Model Penal Code proposed even greater deregulation. Sex offenses were the subject matter of Model Penal Code Tentative Draft no. 2, presented to the American Law Institute in May 1955. The draft contained sections addressing cohabitation, bigamy and polygamy, incest, sodomy, rape, and lesser sexual assaults. It served notice of radical changes to come in American sex law.

The drafters recommended prohibiting fornication and adultery only where the acts were either "open and notorious" or incestuous, which would have changed the fornication law of eighteen states and the adultery law of thirty states. Higher-ranking bodies within the American Law Institute concluded that the draft did not go far enough and recommended abolishing the laws against fornication and adultery altogether. The comments to the proposed section on adultery and fornication read like a passage from Ploscowe's treatise: Such laws rarely are enforced, and when they are, they are subject to abuse by selective prosecution and blackmail; the law has no business enforcing morality, particularly when based in religion; and finally, the law has little power to deter what Kinsey and others had described as passionate, widespread, and uncontainable premarital sex and marital infidelity. Citing the Kinsey findings, the comments observe, for example, that "[t]he extreme frequency of such behavior among otherwise law-abiding citizens suggests not only the impossibility of effective suppression but also the toleration with which such behavior is commonly viewed."

Although presented as a response to changed social reality, the radicalism of these proposals went farther than did ordinary women and men of the day. As the Institute drafted and debated, moving toward a consensus on complete deregulation, popular views of consensual heterosexual relations outside of marriage remained a confused mixture of the Victorian and the libertine, especially when it came to the behaviors acceptable for females as opposed to males:

> A double standard survived that perpetuated differences in the meaning of sexual experience. . . . Study after study of high school and college youth from the 1930's through the 1950's confirmed the existence of a double standard. The particular issues kept shifting . . . but the tension between male and female remained. Boys pushed, while girls set the line.

As a mirror of a changing world, the Model Penal Code realistically reproduced the world view of the heterosexual male, but not that of the female.

Initially, the drafters were unwilling to decriminalize private adult homosexual relations to the same extent as heterosexual relations. Advisory Council members feared that the controversy generated by such a proposal would sink the Model Penal Code project altogether. Nonetheless, the Council agreed to submit the issue to the whole body of the American Law Institute. In 1955, the Institute approved decriminalization of sodomy, taking an unprecedented but consistently libertarian position on adult consensual sex in private. The comments explain that there is no inherent harm in private consensual exchanges between adults and, citing the Wolfenden Report, suggest that such questions properly belong to the church and not to the state. The existing laws are both unenforced and unenforceable, the comments continue, risking blackmail and selective prosecution.

This willingness to revisit centuries-old moral and religious prohibitions is most obvious in the drafters' discussion of incest. Although political expediency led the Institute to vote to retain a crime of incest, the comments make clear that they regard the prohibition as having no rational basis. Perhaps there are genetic justifications, the drafters observe in a desultory way, but scientists disagree. They suggest reducing incest to a minor (third-degree) felony punishable by two to five years in prison.

The drafters were less bold regarding prostitution. If they had been consistent in their reasoning, the religious basis for the prostitution laws should have led to a recommendation for decriminalization. Yet leaning on the slender reed of venereal disease prevention, the Model Penal Code retains a crime of prostitution, albeit one punished by minimum penalty with heavier penalties reserved for pimps and others responsible for the sex business. The only innovation recommended is to reduce the punishment for patrons to a fine. The comments refer to prevailing male sexual norms in explaining this light punishment: "Imposition of severe penalties is out of the question, since prosecutors, judges and juries are likely to regard extra-marital intercourse for males as a necessary evil or even as socially beneficial."

The drafters reserved the strongest prohibitions and penalties for nonconsensual sex such as rape, i.e., sex that violates independent background norms of self-ownership. This is in keeping with the goal of detaching sexual regulation from religion, tradition, or morality. Even there, however, although the drafters acknowledge that forced sex is serious, they emphasize the undue harshness of existing law. (At the time Tentative Draft no. 2 was presented, about half of the states punished forcible rape by death and others by life imprisonment.) They also note the unjust law enforcement concerning black-on-white rape, particularly in the South.

The drafters divide the serious sexual offenses into three categories: first- and second-degree felony rape, and misdemeanor gross sexual imposition. First- and second-degree felony rape is defined as sexual intercourse against the will of the victim by means of force, kidnapping, or threat of death, serious injury, or extreme pain. Forced intercourse in marriage is explicitly excluded from the prohibition, and forced sexual intercourse by a social companion or a previous sexual partner (date or acquaintance rape) may be charged only as second-degree felony, no matter what the circumstances. Sex procured by "any threat that would prevent resistance by a woman of ordinary resolution" is not rape at all, but the lesser offense of "gross sexual imposition." Unwanted sexual touching short of penetration is a misdemeanor crime termed "sexual assault."

As Ploscowe had recommended, the Model Penal Code undermined the prohibitions against nonconsensual sex with significant defenses and barriers to prosecution. The comments identify the problems of proof in rape cases as especially severe, suggesting that women are likely to lie because of social pressures to recast a voluntary act as forced in order to preserve reputation, to revenge a failed relationship, to respond to an unwanted pregnancy, or as a means of blackmail. All offenses carry a short statute of limitations of three months as a means of requiring prompt complaint. The victim of sexual violence has no reason to delay reporting such a crime, the comments observe, and if she does delay, her motives are likely to be blackmail or her own "psychopathy," which makes corroboration imperative. No complainant can prove her case based on her testimony alone, and juries are to be instructed "to evaluate the testimony of a victim or complaining witness with special care in view of the emotional involvement of the witness and the difficulty of determining the truth with respect to alleged sexual activities carried out in private." Although the definition of felony rape mentions the victim's nonconsent, the elements of the crime emphasize proof of objective acts and evidence (e.g., presence of force, prompt complaint, and physical evidence). Although proof of victim resistance is not required, the comments assert that the degree to which the victim fights back is relevant to her credibility. Prior promiscuity bars a complaint of gross sexual imposition or misdemeanor sexual assault. If a woman was drinking when raped, she must show that she was fully unconscious before any impairment of her capacity to consent to sex is recognized.

First-degree felony rape carries a sentence of imprisonment from one to ten years minimum and life maximum. Rape by a social companion or a previous sexual partner is the lesser offense of second-degree felony rape, punished by imprisonment for one to three years minimum and ten years maximum. Nonforcible rape, or gross sexual imposition, is punished by imprisonment from one to two years minimum and five years maximum.

The draft further proposed to reduce the age of consent for statutory rape to ten years, and to prohibit "corruption of a minor" (defined as having sex with someone under the age of sixteen years, provided that the actor is at least four years older or in a fiduciary relationship with the child) as a lesser crime than rape. Persons accused of sexually corrupting a minor may defend by claiming reasonable mistake about age, so long as the child is at least ten years of age or is unchaste.

From even a short distance of history, the Model Penal Code's treatment of nonconsensual sex sounds sexist, heartless, and strangely naive. This inability to engage with rape in a fair and fruitful way was an early sign of the failings of the libertine paradigm. Over time, arguments for withdrawing government from the sexual realm as unnecessary or ineffective would prove more persuasive than any effort to guarantee that the model of free exchange was truly free.

The Model Penal Code's rape proposals had hardly surfaced in the public debate when the second wave of feminism swept into the United States, taking on rape law as one of its first targets for reform. As a result of controversy created by feminist critics, almost no state adopted the Model Penal Code's rape provisions, unlike its other proposals for sex law reform. Most states significantly rewrote their rape and sexual assault laws in the 1970s and 1980s, but under the influence of the feminist rape reform movement rather than the Model Penal Code. Most did adopt some form of the Code's grading scheme in defining prohibited acts and their penalties, ending the "either it's rape or nothing" approach of the common law.

The American Law Institute claims that thirty-four states have drawn upon the Model Penal Code to rewrite state criminal laws. Yet "drawn upon" is a phrase used loosely here. In none of our exemplary states is the law of rape harshly tilted against the complainant in the ways recommended by the Code drafters. In all four states the age of consent is higher than ten years. All four states criminalize patronizing as well as prostitution. In Virginia, Massachusetts, and Illinois (but not Wyoming), adultery and fornication remain crimes, although these laws are not enforced.

So one might argue that for all its bluster, the Model Penal Code did little to change the landscape of sexual regulation. Yet this conclusion seriously underestimates its effects. The Model Penal Code played some role in every state criminal law revision since the 1950s. Just as important, every criminal law casebook used to train the current and previous generation of lawyers includes, and often privileges, the Model Penal Code as a systematic and coherent approach to criminal jurisprudence. In the face of fifty different state schemes, national law schools sometimes teach nothing else in criminal law courses. When the Justices of the U.S. Supreme Court debated the constitutionality of various sexual regulations throughout the period 1950-80, their opinions regularly referred to the Model Penal Code's suggested provisions and justifications. As one of the chief drafters put it in 1988, "[t]he Model Penal Code has become a standard part of the furniture of the criminal law."

## ANYTHING BUT SEX: PRIVACY, REPRODUCTION, AND OBSCENITY

The *Skinner* decision could have set the U.S. Supreme Court on a course toward recognition of all private, consensual sex acts between adults as expressive of a fundamental right of sexual liberty that states could neither prohibit nor regulate. But instead, the Court indirectly embraced sexual libertinism, fighting surrogate battles over birth control and obscenity.

Birth control use among married, white, college-educated women was markedly on the rise as early as the 1920s. According to Margaret Sanger, urban immigrant and working-class women also desperately sought reproductive control, but their access to reliable birth control was limited. By the 1930s, birth control use had spread to the white working class and to African Americans. In 1942, Planned Parenthood was founded, and by 1944 there were more than 800 birth control clinics operating throughout the nation. By 1960, four fifths of all whites and three fifths of nonwhites had used contraception.

Since 1879, however, it had been a crime in Connecticut to use any drug or device to prevent conception. As of the 1940s, Connecticut's was the most restrictive birth control law in the nation. But Connecticut was not alone in legally obstructing contraception. The Sanger/Comstock battles at the turn of the century had left patchy and sporadically enforced anti-birth control and obscenity laws on the books in several states. Despite changed attitudes and patterns of birth control use, Connecticut continued to buck the trend. In 1939, the state prosecuted a family planning clinic, obtaining a ruling from the state supreme court that the state's law against contraceptive use was constitutional. Although determined to defend the law on paper, the state's policy was not to enforce the law against married couples. In 1942, in a declaratory judgment action initiated by a Yale Medical School professor, the state ruled that the law covered contraceptive use by married couples, even where a doctor diagnosed childbirth as threatening to the wife's life and health. (Typically the first step toward liberalizing a law restricting birth control or abortion is to allow for therapeutic exceptions.) Following these decisions, family planning clinics in Connecticut closed their doors, although private birth control use presumably continued. By the late 1950s, birth control activists had had enough and began a course of test cases to challenge the Connecticut law. Eventually, these test cases would foundationally change American law.

In the first round of litigation, the U.S. Supreme Court dismissed the case as nonjusticiable. The concerns of Connecticut doctors, patients, and birth control activists were "empty shadows," Justice Frankfurter wrote, because the state was not enforcing the law. Four justices dissented, including Justice Harlan, who thought the long western tradition of domestic privacy protected marital sexuality, and Justice Black, who suggested the plaintiffs just try to open another Planned Parenthood office to test the state's will.

The plaintiffs did just that in 1961. Within ten days, Connecticut closed the clinic and arrested the operators. The U.S. Supreme Court ruled in *Griswold v. Connecticut* that the state's birth control law was unconstitutional. Writing for the Court, Justice Douglas relied on "the zone of privacy created by several fundamental constitutional guarantees" to hold that the state could not prohibit the use of contraceptives by married couples, and could not punish someone who provides contraceptives or information for aiding and abetting such use. Marital sexual privacy as concerns the decision whether or not to bear children is defined as an area of "protected freedom." "Would we," the Court asked, "allow the police to search the sacred precincts of marital bedrooms for telltale signs of the use of contraceptives?" Even the dissenters agreed that the Connecticut law was "uncommonly silly," but they could find no constitutional reason that their policy preference should replace that of the state legislature.

The consequences of the decision were immediate. The Massachusetts legislature responded by creating an exception to the state's law against birth control for married people. The Supreme Court then struck down that law in *Eisenstadt v. Baird*, a 1972 case that extended *Griswold's* zone of privacy to unmarried sex. "[I]f the right of privacy means anything," the Court wrote, "it is the right of the *individual*, married or single, to be free from unwanted governmental intrusions into matters so fundamentally affecting a person as the decision whether to bear or beget a child."

The principle of *Griswold* became so much a part of mainstream sexual values that in 1987, the Senate refused to appoint federal appeals court Judge Robert Bork to the Supreme Court, in part because he did not support the outcome in *Griswold*. Bork openly derided the cultural significance of *Griswold* in his nomination hearings, dismissing the case as having been "framed by Yale professors . . . because they like this type of litigation."

Bork's opposition to *Griswold*, like that of other judicial conservatives, was more than just cranky ridicule of pointyheaded liberals. For good or ill, *Griswold*, marked the definitive end of the republic of virtue. No longer would religiously prescribed, virtuously defended, monogamous, and heterosexual marriage be immune from liberal assumptions. By breaking the tie between marriage, sex, and children, people might now marry for the explicit purpose of having more and pleasurable sex and not, as Paul said, to avoid worse sexual sins. They might marry for companionship and not, as Aquinas said, to provide the natural framework for the begetting and rearing of children. And after *Eisenstadt*, they need not marry at all if sex is the issue. Ordinary Americans had begun to renegotiate sexual practice in light of the messy reality of Kinsey's world, and *Griswold* ensured that lawmakers would be forced to face the music too.

Related developments elevated the visibility of sex in another cultural realm as well, that of speech and image. Historians D'Emilio and Freedman observe that after World War I, writers like Ernest Hemingway and William Faulkner made sexually explicit language and subjects acceptable in the realm of elite culture, subverting the connection between vice and the lower classes that had fueled Comstock's assault on French postcards and racy magazines sold from newsstands. In the famous case concerning James Joyce's *Ulysses*, a federal court ruled in 1933 that obscenity must be sought not in particular passages of a literary work, but in the dominant effect of the work. The blow struck by elite culture trickled down to the popular realm, as mainstream men's magazines like *Esquire* further pressed the limits of the sexually explicit.

A young entrepreneur, Hugh Hefner, seized the opportunity presented by these openings. In December 1953, Hefner published the first issue of *Playboy* magazine. With a first run of 70,000 copies, the magazine was selling more than a million copies per issue within a few years. By the early 1970s, each issue of *Playboy* sold six million copies and Hefner's personal fortune was approximately $100 million. Playboy was a corporate empire, housed in a Chicago skyscraper with outposts in Playboy Clubs throughout the world.

Although he was no intellectual (Hefner credited the Kinsey Reports as his greatest influence), Hefner had aspirations of doing more with his magazine than just profit from naked women. From the first issue, *Playboy* promoted a "philosophy" and sought to advise its readers on ethical and consumer as well as sexual matters. Famous for its pictures (no more explicit than under-the-table pornography of the time, but certainly more flesh than had been shown previously in mainstream magazines), *Playboy* was most influential for an overtly anti-marriage philosophy, something of a heresy in 1950s America. Cultural critic Barbara Ehrenreich calls *Playboy* "the party organ of a diffuse and swelling movement" of male rebellion against the Victorian sexual ethic of responsibility and restraint, and post–World War II ideals of breadwinning and suburban life.

Depicting the American man as the sexual and economic slave of women, the magazine encouraged men to indulge themselves in nonfamilial pursuits. As against the suburban ranch house, Hefner posed the urban bachelor pad. As against the wife for life, Hefner posed the Bunny for a night. "We enjoy mixing up cocktails and an *hors d'oeuvre* or two, putting a little mood music on the phonograph

and inviting in a female acquaintance for a quiet discussion on Picasso, Nietzsche, jazz, sex." The first issue contained an article titled "Miss Golddigger of
1953" attacking the extortionate female ethic that required marriage for sex. "All
woman wants is security," *Playboy* accused, "[a]nd she's perfectly willing to crush
man's adventurous, freedom-loving spirit to get it." If the goal of modern cultural conservatives in gender politics is to regain men's position as the natural
head of a patriarchal marriage and family structure, the *Playboy* philosophy was to
escape the domestic bondage of wives and would-be wives altogether. Although
*Playboy* would in time be seen as a rather tame rebellion, in the late 1950s and
early 1960s, the magazine was, as Hefner put it, "a symbol of disobedience, a triumph of sexuality, an end to Puritanism."

The first case challenging the very idea of criminalizing obscene literature,
*Roth v. United States,* arrived at the U.S. Supreme Court in 1957. The Court deflected the challenge, ruling that obscenity was not protected by the First Amendment. In shielding the freedom of speech and expression, the drafters of the
Constitution had not intended to cover expression of this kind. Despite the adverse outcome, the majority opinion in *Roth* carefully noted that sexual speech is
not necessarily obscene. Citing the draft definition of obscenity of the Model Penal Code, the Court limited the scope of constitutionally unprotected sexual
speech (obscenity) to material that "taken as a whole appeals to prurient interest."

With the decision that sexy was not necessarily obscene, the wall had been
breached. The Court spent the better part of the next fifteen years trying to define what it had meant in *Roth* by "appeals to prurient interest." In a 1966 case,
*Memoirs of a Woman of Pleasure v. Massachusetts,* the Court ruled that material was
obscene only if "utterly without redeeming social importance." More important,
the Court held that lay juries could not be trusted to make that judgment; obscenity was properly a question of law left to judges to determine. The Court thus
assigned itself the task of reviewing the evidence in each obscenity case, and the
Supreme Court movie theater was in business. Meanwhile, in *Stanley v. Georgia*
(1969), a bookie inadvertently caught with pornographic materials when the authorities searched his home for gambling materials had his obscenity conviction
overturned on privacy grounds. By resting its ruling on the enduring respect for
the privacy of the home, the Court in *Stanley* created the possibility of a regula-
tion-free zone in the home for any kind of consensual sex. But over time *Stanley,*
like *Skinner,* would be closely limited, entering the limbo of Supreme Court cases
too hot to overrule and too hot to follow.

After seven years of watching dirty movies, the Supreme Court took another
stab in 1973 at defining obscenity on something other than a case-by-case basis.
In *Miller v. California,* the Court ruled that the government could regulate expression if, "to the average person applying contemporary community standards, the
work, taken as a whole, appeals to the prurient interest, depicts or describes in a
patently offensive way sexual conduct as specifically defined, and, taken as a

whole, lacks serious literary, artistic or political value." In a companion case, the Court began the process of confining *Stanley* to its facts, sending *Paris Adult Theater I v. Slaton* (1973) back to the state courts for a decision whether, under the new standard, a commercial theater could screen obscene films if it did not publicly advertise. In subsequent years, this process continued as the Court upheld municipal use of zoning to restrict the location of pornographic movie houses, whether the films shown were legally obscene or not.

As the Supreme Court grew more conservative in the mid-1970s and early 1980s, the deregulation of sexual speech and expression ground to a halt. The conservative justices were willing to let local standards drive the decision whether and when to prosecute the production, sale, distribution, and possession of sexually explicit materials. The liberal justices withdrew into dissent in obscenity cases after *Miller*, throwing up their hands and arguing that no nonarbitrary distinction could be drawn between permissible eroticism and impermissible obscenity. Meanwhile, in the world outside of the Court, sex materials grew markedly more available and graphic in the 1980s, and many fewer obscenity prosecutions were mounted.

An important exception concerned sexual materials involving children. In *Ferber v. New York* (1982), the Court unanimously upheld a New York criminal law that restricted the distribution of child pornography, obscene or not, as a means of protecting child performers from the sexual abuse involved in the making of such materials. Although the challenged law could reach speech and images that were not obscene, the Justices agreed that sexually explicit material made with child performers enjoys no First Amendment protection. *Ferber* is perhaps better understood as a case about child labor or child abuse and not an obscenity ruling.

Adult heterosexual conduct, like sexual expression, also grew more public as law backed off here as well. Heterosexual litigants desultorily sought to attack the remaining laws against adultery and fornication through various constitutional challenges in the 1970s and early 1980s, but the lower courts continually ducked the issue under various procedural guises. Gays and lesbians fought the real sexual freedom campaign in the courts through challenges to state sodomy laws. This campaign culminated in 1985 in the Supreme Court decision in *Bowers v. Hardwick*. Not mounted as a test case, *Bowers* arose when Georgia police inadvertently came upon two men having sex in the bedroom of a private home and arrested them for sodomy. Despite powerful facts—a private home, police invading the bedroom, consensual acts between adults, a law whose enforcement would prohibit sex absolutely to homosexual people—the Supreme Court rejected the sexual freedom claim. After *Bowers*, the impetus for heterosexuals to press for a fundamental right to be sexual—a constitutional claim implicit in the logic of *Eisenstadt* and *Skinner*—faded. Many states had liberalized or repealed laws against fornication, adultery, or sodomy, and no state meaningfully enforced the remaining laws against heterosexuals.

Decriminalizing nonmarital sex was not the same, however, as accepting it as an ordinary human activity governed by ordinary legal rules. Nonmarital sex fell into a kind of state of nature, outside of civil society and ungoverned by law or morality. In this world of unregulated sex, the pornographer was indeed the philosopher.

## NOTES

The evidence on rates of premarital sex comes from Alfred C. Kinsey et al., *Sexual Behavior in the Human Male* (Philadelphia: W. B. Saunders, 1948) and *Sexual Behavior in the Human Female* (Philadelphia: Saunders, 1953).

The "shabby indeed" comparison of Freud and Ellis with Kinsey comes from Paul Robinson, *The Modernization of Sex: Havelock Ellis, Alfred Kinsey, William Masters, and Virginia Johnson* (New York: Harper and Row, 1976), 43–44.

The "no single event" quote is from *Time*, Aug. 24, 1953.

The observation that Kinsey allowed Americans to "talk dirty" without reprobation is from John D'Emilio and Estelle B. Freedman, *Intimate Matters: A History of Sexuality in America* (New York: Harper and Row, 1988), 286–87.

Kinsey's disavowal of moral judgment is from *Male*, 7. On Kinsey's counting method, see *Male*, 3–5, 7. The single exception to orgasm as the counting measure was experiences of heterosexual petting, which were counted even absent orgasm. For Kinsey's avowed disinterest in psychological well-being, see *Female*, 328–30, 385–88, and *Male*, 593. On the restraints on orgasm that originate in "ignorance and superstition," *Male*, 203. On the danger of jailing virtually all men for their sexual practices, see *Male*, 392.

On the public controversy surrounding the Kinsey reports, including the Rockefeller Foundation funding decision, see Regina Morantz, "The Scientist as Sex Crusader: Alfred C. Kinsey and American Culture," *American Quarterly* 29 (Winter 1977): 561, 575. On the effect of exposure to the Kinsey reports on sexual attitudes, see ibid., 583 n. 55, citing Leo P. Crespi, "Youth Looks at the Kinsey Report," *Public Opinion Quarterly* 12 (Winter 1948): 687; Harold F. Giedt, "Changes in Sexual Behavior and Attitudes Following Class Study of the Kinsey Report," *Journal of Social Psychology* 33 (1951): 131; C. Kirkpatrick, Sheldon Stryker, and Philip Buell, "An Experimental Study of Attitudes Towards Male Sex Behavior with Reference to Kinsey's Findings," *American Sociological Review* 17 (Oct. 1952): 580.

For survey data on men's range of orgasmic outlets and rates of premarital sex, see *Male*, 219, 551–52, and fig. 145. For data on married men's rate of extramarital affairs, see ibid., 585; for data on men's homosexual experiences, see 610, 623, 650.

For survey data on women's range of orgasmic outlets and rates of premarital sex, see *Female*, 142, 233, 286; for data on married women's rate of extramarital affairs, see 416; for data on married women's orgasms in marital sex, see 356.

On the comparisons between the sexualities of married men and married women, see ibid., 352–53, 375, and *Male*, 563–82, esp. 571. For Kinsey's findings on married women's sexuality in older and younger generations, see *Female*, 358–59, 362–65. For survey data on sex in lower-class marriages, see *Male*, 363–74, 386.

On clitoral orgasm, see *Female*, 163–64, 374, 468. In this attack on the patriarchal construction of "sex" as heterosexual intercourse, Kinsey anticipated the feminist critique still almost two decades in the future. See, e.g., Susan Lydon, "The Politics of Orgasm," in *Sisterhood Is Powerful: An Anthology of Writings from the Women's Liberation Movement*, ed. Robin Morgan (New York: Random House, 1970), 197.

On comparative premarital sexual experiences among middle-and lower-class men, see *Male*, 335–63, esp. 347–55, and 374–84, 551–57.

For speculation that Kinsey exaggerated, see Edward O. Laumann, John H. Gagnon.

Robert T. Michael, and Stuart Michaels, *The Social Organization of Sexuality: Sexual Practices in the United States* (Chicago: Univ. of Chicago, 1994) (conducted by NORC, the National Opinion Research Center at the University of Chicago). The NORC researchers criticize Kinsey for constructing his sample entirely from volunteers, arguing that this procedure biases the findings upwards by self-selecting for people with a demonstrated strong personal interest in the thing being studied, notably, sexual behavior (35, 44-45). This bias undermines the degree to which the Kinsey findings can be generalized to the population at large.

The "relieving guilt" quote is Morantz, "Scientist as Sex Crusader," 582.

On initial proposals for an American Law Institute, see N. E. H. Hull, "Restatement and Reform: A New Perspective on the Origins of the American Law Institute," *Law and History Review* 8 (1990): 55; Daniel J. Klau, "Note: What Price Certainty? Corbin, Williston and the Restatement of Contracts," *Boston University Law Review* 70 (1990): 511, 516.

The description of the formalist idea of common law is drawn from Herbert Wechsler, in Norman Silber and Geoffrey Miller, eds., "Toward 'Neutral Principles' in the Law: Selections from the Oral History of Herbert Wechsler," *Columbia Law Review* 93 (1993): 854

On legal realism, see generally Laura Kalman, *Legal Realism at Yale, 1927-1960* (Chapel Hill: Univ. of North Carolina Press, 1986).

On the early proposals for the Model Penal Code project, see Herbert Wechsler, "Model Penal Code," *Columbia Law Review* 68 (1968): 1425, 1426.

Weschler's "constant preoccupation" quote is from Wechsler, "The Model Penal Code," in *Crime, Criminology and Public Policy: Essays in Honour of Sir Leon Radzinowicz*, ed. Roger Hood, (New York: Free Press, 1974), 419, 425-26.

On the use of experts in the Model Penal Code process, see Hon. Shirley S. Abrahamson, "Refreshing Institutional Memories: Wisconsin and the American Law Institute," *Wisconsin Law Review* (1995): 1, 14-16; Sanford H. Kadish, *Blame and Punishment: Essays in the Criminal Law* (New York: Macmillan, 1987), 237.

Weschler's description of his own philosophical views is from Silber and Miller, eds., *Oral History of Herbert Wechsler,* 869.

Ploscowe's influential book on sexual (de)regulation is Morris Ploscowe, *Sex and the Law* (New York: Prentice-Hall, 1951). Ploscowe was chief reporter for the Model Penal Code sections on criminal sentencing. The "complete reorientation" quote is on p. 281; the "disparities between law in action and law on the books," 155; the "cannot realistically be contained" quote, 281.

On deregulating nonmarital sex, see ibid., 1-2; on love as a mental disease, 164. The quote concerning the over-enforcement of rape laws, 187; the quote on doubt that a healthy woman can be raped, 165-66; the reference to the judge who sees twelve unfounded rape charges for every meritorious one, 165-66; the "tete a tete" quote, 170; the quote concerning the fact that a drunk woman has "taken a chance," 175; on "abnormal desires" and the definition of statutory rape, 170, 175, 178, 181-82, 184, 193; on age of consent, 172-79, 190-94.

For Ploscowe's rape reform proposals: The requirement of corroboration is found in ibid., 194, see also 189; the "strumpet" quote, 190; the requirement of more than slight penetration, 192; the requirement of sobriety, 175, 192; the requirement of utmost resistance, 191; the argument for reduction in age of consent, 178-79, 193-94.

The Thucydides quote is from *History of the Peloponnesian War*, transl. Rex Warner (Harmondsworth: Penguin Books, 1972), 360.

Ploscowe on prostitution is found in *Sex and the Law,* 265, 268, 270.

A divorce lawyer, Ploscowe wrote a book for popular audiences and columns for a

New York legal newspaper recounting anecdotes of bloodthirsty wives leading lives of idle luxury on unearned alimony, tales that apply to the world of marriage the images of harpies and golddiggers applied to single women in the 1920s. For Ploscowe on alimony abuses, see Ploscowe, "Alimony," *Annals* 383 (May 1965): 13, and Ploscowe, *The Truth About Divorce* (New York: Hawthorn Books, 1955).

The Wolfenden Report is published as Committee on Homosexual Offenses and Prostitution, the Wolfenden Report (1957; New York: Stein and Day, 1963), 52. On the Report process, see Jeffrey Weeks, *Sex, Politics and Society: The Regulation of Sexuality Since 1800* (London and New York: Longman, 1981), 239-44.

The Wolfenden Report's discussion of sexual conduct that cannot be deterred by law is found at The Wolfenden Report, supra, at 52, and was cited in the Model Penal Code. On homosexuality in particular, see The Wolfenden Report, supra at para. 61.

The drafting of the Model Penal Code began in 1952. The proposed official draft of the Model Penal Code was adopted on May 4, 1962, see American Law Institute, Model Penal Code (Proposed Official Draft, 1962). The revision of the Commentaries began in 1976, and the official draft is published with those revised comments. See American Law Institute, Model Penal Code (Philadelphia: The Institute, 1980). Unless otherwise noted, we use the official draft and revised comments, and reference it as "Model Penal Code" or simply by section number. Early drafts of the Code that contain important sex law proposals are *Tentative Drafts Nos. 2, 4, American Law Institute, Model Penal Code* (Philadelphia: The Institute, 1954). In addition, the American Law Institute Proceedings, including crucial decisions to accept or reject recommendations of the drafters, are reported as American Law Institute Proceedings. We also reference these throughout.

Commentators on The Wolfenden Report's moral stance on homosexuality include Larry Cata Becker, "Exposing the Perversions of Toleration: The Decriminalization of Private Sexual Conduct, the Model Penal Code, and the Oxymoron of Liberal Toleration," *Florida Law Review* 45(1993): 755, 769 n.44. The statement in the Report that communities do not agree on the blameworthiness of certain conduct is found at The Wolfenden Report, supra, at para. 355. The Comments to the Model Penal Code also echo this position. See generally Model Penal Code sec. 213.2 cmts.

For cases in which the U.S. Supreme Court refers to Model Penal Code's suggested provisions and justifications, see, e.g., *Roth v. U.S.*, 354 U.S. 476, 488 n.20 (1957) (obscenity); *Jacobellis v. Ohio*, 378 U.S. 184, 190 n.6 (1964) (obscenity); *Stanley v. Georgia*, 394 U.S. 557, 567 n.10 (1969) (obscenity); *Doe v. Bolton*, 410 U.S. 179, 182, 192 (1973) (abortion) and id. at 204 (Appendix B) (same); *Roe v. Wade*, 410 U.S. 113, 139, 152 n.50 (1973) (abortion); *Miller v. California*, 413 U.S. 15, 20 n.2 (1973) (obscenity).

*Skinner v. Oklahoma* is reported at 316 U.S. 535 (1942).

The "switch in time" reflected not simply political pressures on the Court. It also grew out of changed views of the proper role of courts vis a vis legislatures, and new ideas about what economic liberty requires in an era of mature industrial capitalism. See Laurence H. Tribe, *American Constitutional Law* 769 (2d. ed., Mineola, N.Y.: Foundation Press, 1988). The *Carolene Products* footnote on fundamental rights reads, "There may be a narrower scope for operation of the presumption of constitutionality where legislation appears on its face to be within a specific prohibition of the Constitution, such as those of the first ten Amendments." *United States v. Carolene Products Co.*, 304 U.S. 144, 152 n.4 (1938). Elsewhere the Court has held that in defining fundamental rights, it will look to "principle[s] of justice so rooted in the tradition and conscience of our people as to be ranked as fundamental," and hence "implicit in the concept of ordered liberty." See *Palko v. Connecticut*, 302 U.S. 319, 325 (1937) (Cardozo, J.).

The "wither and disappear" quote from *Skinner* is at 316 U.S. 535, 541-42 (1942).

The technical holding of the case is reported at 316 U.S. 535, 541 (1942). The concurring opinions in *Skinner* and quotes therefrom are at 316 U.S. 535, 543-45 (1942) (Stone, C. J., concurring); 316 U.S. 535, 546 (1942) (Jackson, J. concurring).

The cabining of *Skinner* to procreation and not sexuality was final in *Bowers v. Hardwick*, 487 U.S. 186 (1986), in which the Court defined *Skinner* as being about procreation, implicitly rejecting its relevance to the question of whether there existed a fundamental right to sexual expression violated by the prosecution of a homosexual man for private, consensual, adult acts of sodomy. See id. at 190.

Morris Ploscowe discusses the increasing refusal of states by the middle of the twentieth century to enforce their own fornication laws in Ploscowe, *Sex and the Law,* supra at 145, 153. This also is evidenced in our exemplary jurisdictions. As noted in the text, Wyoming did not treat fornication as a crime. Massachusetts law (ch. 272, sec. 18) punished a single act of clandestine fornication, but the punishment was three months imprisonment or $30. Illinois required open or notorious fornication (ch. 38, sec. 11-8), and then only imposed six months imprisonment or $500 fine. Virginia law (sec. 18.2-344) punished a single act of clandestine fornication by a fine of $20. See Robert Veit Sherwin, *Sex and the Statutory Law in all 48 States: A Comparative Study and Survey of the Legal and Legislative Treatment of Sex Problems* (New York: Oceana Publications, 1949): pt. 1, chart 5 at 83-85.

The Model Penal Code proposal to deregulate adultery and fornication is found at sec. 213.6 cmts. at 430-39. The decision of the Institute to overturn the drafters' proposal and move to complete decriminalization is reported at American Law Institute Proceedings 83-88 (1955). The "extreme frequency" quote is from id. at 437. The number of state laws that would have been affected by the proposed deregulation is described at sec. 213.6 cmts. at 430-31. The nonenforcement of existing laws is recounted at id. at 434-36. The quote on the persistence of the double standard is from D'Emilio & Freedman, supra, at 262.

On the 1955 American Law Institute vote to support decriminalization of private, adult homosexual relations, see American Law Institute Proceedings 131 (1955) and sec. 213.2, cmts. at 372. On the rationale for such a move, see sec. 213.2, cmts. at 362, 365-76.

The proposal on incest is found at sec. 230.2, at 397. The discussion of the Institute's skepticism about the reasons for the prohibition is found at sec. 230.2 cmts. at 402-08.

On the prostitution proposals, see American Law Institute, Model Penal Code sec. 207.12, at 167-69 and cmts. at 169-82 (Tentative Draft No. 9, Philadelphia: The Institute, 1959). The "a necessary evil" rationale for the decision to punish patronizing by fine and not as a crime is at id. at 180.

The rape proposals were first presented to the Institute as sec. 207.4 (Rape and Related Offenses), Tentative Draft No. 4, and considered at the May 1955 meeting of the Institute. See American Law Institute Proceedings 105-27 (1955).

On the grading scheme finally adopted, see Model Penal Code, Part II, vol.1, at 271-72 (Introductory Note to Article 213). First and second-degree felony rape are defined at sec. 213.1 at 274. The definition incorporates the exclusion of rape in marriage, see sec. 213.1(1), and also the downgrading of rape by a prior social acquaintance or sexual partner to a second-degree felony, see sec. 213.1(1). The rationale for the spousal exclusion is described at sec. 213.1 cmts. at 341-46. Gross sexual imposition is defined at sec. 213.3. Sexual assault (unwanted touching short of intercourse) is defined at sec. 213.4. The exclusion of promiscuous complainants is found at sec. 213.6(3) and cmts. at 419-20.

The drafters emphasize the importance of "objective" factors that will corroborate the rape victim's testimony about her subjective lack of consent at sec. 213.1 cmts. at

307. On the requirement of corroboration, see sec. 213.6(5), which bars liability in rape if the victim's testimony stands alone. The drafters justify this unusual burden of proof by describing their "effort[s] . . . to avoid making the imposition-consent inquiry entirely on a subjective basis and seek[ing] objective indicia to support the necessary finding of compulsion." Sec. 213.1 cmts. at 307. Victim resistance is not an element of the crime of rape, but has evidentiary relevance. See sec. 213.1 cmts. at 306–07. On the requirement of prompt complaint (i.e., the statue of limitations), see sec. 213.6(4) and cmts. at 420–21. On the jury instruction requirement, see sec. 213.6 cmts. p. 422. The citation to Sir Matthew Hale is at id. at 428.

On the proposed penalty for first-degree felony rape, see sec. 213.1(1) cmts. at 308. On the proposed penalty for second-degree felony rape, see sec. 213.1(2)(a) cmts. at 312.

On the reduction of the age of consent to ten years, see sec. 213.1(1)(d). For the definition of corruption of a minor, see sec. 213(3) and cmts. at 323–24, 378. On the penalties for same, see sec. 213.3(2) and cmts. at 376, 384–85. The mistake of age defense is provided for at sec. 213.6(1) and cmts. at 413–17.

The seriousness of sexual intercourse obtained by force, threats or certain "fundamental deception[s]" is acknowledged at American Law Institute Proceedings 241 (1955). On the state of rape law at the time early drafts of the Code proposals were presented, see id. at 241 & n.94. On the drafters' concerns about the racial unfairness of rape law enforcement, see sec. 213.1 cmts. at 281 & n.27.

Comments on the proof problems in rape cases are found at American Law Institute, Model Penal Code section 207.4, at 241 (Tentative Draft No. 2, Philadelphia: The Institute, 1954) and sec. 213.1 cmts. at 302–03. The prompt complaint requirement is from sec. 213.6(4) and cmts. at 420–21. The "vindictive complainant" quote is from sec. 213.6 cmts. at 421. The requirement that a woman lose consciousness from drink or drugs before she can claim incapacity to consent is found in the definition of rape at sec. 213.1(1)(c) and cmts. at 319.

The dialogue between the Model Penal Code drafters and Ploscowe concerning degree of penetration required is found at American Law Institute, Tentative Draft No.4, sec. 207.4 & cmts. at 244 (1955). In the official draft, the revised version of the exchange is found at id. at sec. 213. cmts. 347–48.

On the rape reform movement, see generally Leigh Bienen, "Rape III—National Developments in Rape Reform Legislation," *Women's Rights Law Reporter* 6 (1980).170 (surveying various reformations in modern rape law). On the lack of success of the Model Penal Code proposals for rape law, see Richard A. Posner and Katharine B. Silbaugh, *A Guide to America's Sex Laws* (Chicago: University of Chicago Press, 1996): 5–7).

For the claim that 34 states have followed the Model Penal Code, see ibid. Part I, vol.1, p. xi (Foreword). In his introduction to a retrospective consideration of the Model Penal Code on its 25th anniversary, Dean Richard Singer reflected that "nearly forty states have recodified their criminal laws, using the Code as the lodestar." Symposium, The 25th Anniversary of the Model Penal Code, "Introduction," *Rutgers Law Journal* 19 (1988): 518.

The rape (and sexual assault) statute in all four states: Illinois: Ill. Ann. Stat. ch. 720, para. 5/12-12, 5/12-13, 5/12-14, 5/12-15, 5/12-16 (enacted 1961). Massachusetts: Mass. Gen. Laws ch. 265 sec. 22 (enacted 1974); ch. 272, sec. 3 (enacted 1978); ch. 272, sec. 53 (enacted 1943). Virginia: Va. Code Ann. secs. 18.2-61 (enacted 1950), 18.2-67.1-5 (enacted 1981). Wyoming: Wyo. Stat. secs. 6-2-301-303,-305 (enacted 1982).

In all four states the age of consent is higher than ten years. Illinois (17 years): Ill.

Ann. Stat. ch. 720, paras. 5/12-16 (enacted 1961). Massachusetts (16 years): Mass. Gen. Laws ch. 265, sec. 23 (enacted 1697); Mass. Gen. Laws ch. 272, sec. 35A (enacted 1955). Virginia (15 years): Va. Code Ann. secs. 18.2-61-63 (enacted 1950). Wyoming (18 years): Wyo. Stat. sec.14-3-105 (enacted 1957) (felony for any person to take immodest, immoral, or indecent liberties with any person under eighteen). See also Wyo. Stat. sec.6-2-303 (enacted 1982) (felony to subject a person under twelve to sexual intrusion or sexual contact if actor is at least four years older than victim); Wyo. Stat. sec.6-2-304 (enacted 1982) (felony to subject person under sixteen to sexual intrusion if actor is at least four years older than victim).

All four states criminalize patronizing as well as prostitution. Illinois: Ill. Ann. Stat. ch. 720, para. 5/11-14 (enacted 1961) (prostitution and soliciting); Ill. Ann. Stat. ch. 720, para. 5/11-18 (enacted 1961) (patronizing). Massachusetts: Mass Gen. Laws ch. 272, sec.53A (enacted 1983) (prostitution and patronizing). Virginia: Va. Code Ann. sec. 18.2-346 (enacted 1950) (prostitution and patronizing). Wyoming: Wyo. Stat. secs. 6-4-101 (enacted 1982) (prostitution); Wyo. Stat. secs. 6-4-102 (enacted 1982) (patronizing). In all four states, both prostitution and patronizing are misdemeanors.

In Illinois, Massachusetts and Virginia (but not Wyoming), adultery and fornication remain crimes, although these laws are not enforced. Illinois: Ill. Ann. Stat. ch. 720, para. 5/11-8 (enacted 1961) (fornication is misdemeanor; must be open and notorious); Ill. Ann. Stat. ch. 720, para. 5/11-7 (enacted 1961) (adultery is misdemeanor; must be open and notorious). Massachusetts: Mass. Gen. Laws ch. 272, sec. 18 (enacted 1692) (fornication is misdemeanor); Mass Gen. Laws ch. 272, sec. 14 (enacted 1978) (adultery is felony). Virginia: Va. Code Ann. sec. 18.2-344 (enacted 1950) (fornication is misdemeanor); Va. Code Ann. sec. 18.2-365 (enacted 1950) (adultery is misdemeanor).

The "standard part of the furniture" quote is from Symposium, The 25th Anniversary of the Model Penal Code, "Introduction," *Rutgers Law Journal* 19 (1988): 518, 521.

On the growth of Planned Parenthood and the spread of clinics and contraceptive use, see Linda Gordon, *Woman's Body, Woman's Right: A Social History of Birth Control in America* (New York: Penguin Books, 1977), 341-90; Abraham Stone and Harriet Pilpel, "The Social and Legal Status of Contraception," *North Carolina Law Review* 22 (1944): 212, 215. On the percentage of white, college-educated women in the 1920s using contraception, see James Reed, *From Private Vice to Public Virtue: The Birth Control Movement and American Society Since 1830*, at 124 (New York: Basic Books, 1978). The 1960 data cited by D'Emilio and Freedman is found in Pascal K. Whelpton et. al., *Fertility and Family Planning in the United States* 34, 303-04 (Princeton: Princeton Univ. Press, 1966). Margaret Sanger describes lack of contraception for urban immigrant and working-class women in Margaret Sanger, "My Fight for Birth Control (1931)," in *Women's America: Refocusing the Past*, 340, Linda K. Kerber & Jane Sherron De Hart, eds., 3d ed., (N.Y.: Oxford Univ. Press, 1991). On birth control use among African-Americans, see Jesse M. Rodrique, "The Black Community and the Birth Control Movement," in *We Specialize in the Wholly Impossible: A Reader in Black Women's History*, 505, Darlene Clark Hine, Wilma King & Linda Reed, eds. (Brooklyn: Carlson Publishing Company, 1995).

On the Connecticut birth control fight leading up to the *Griswold* case, see generally Mary L. Dudziak, "Just Say No: Birth Control in the Connecticut Supreme Court Before *Griswold v. Connecticut*," *Iowa Law Review* 75 (1990): 915; David J. Garrow, *Liberty and Sexuality: The Right to Privacy and the Making of Roe v. Wade* (New York: Lisa Drew Books, 1994).

The state supreme court decision upholding the Connecticut law is *State v. Nelson*, 126 Conn. 412, 11 A.2d 856 (1940). Connecticut prosecuted the clinic as an accessory to the crime of use by its patients. Interestingly, sale or distribution of contraceptives was not itself a crime.

The 1942 declaratory judgment action by a Yale medical school professor was *Tileston v. Ullman*, 129 Conn. 84, 26 A.2d 582 (1942).

The test cases in the late 1950s were *Buxton v. Ullman*, 147 Conn. 48, 156 A.2d 508 (1959), appeal dismissed, 367 U.S. 497 (1961), reh'g denied, 368 U.S. 869 (1961); *Trubek v. Ullman*, 147 Conn. 633, 165 A.2d 158 (1960), appeal dismissed, 367 U.S. 907 (1961); *Poe v. Ullman*, 367 U.S. 497, 501-02, 508 (1961).

Justice Frankfurter's "empty shadows" quote is from *Poe v. Ullman*, 367 U.S. 497, 501-02, 508 (1961). The dissenting opinions are reported at ibid., 508 (Black, J., dissenting); ibid., 509 (Douglas, J. dissenting); ibid., 522 (Harlan, J., dissenting); ibid., 555 (Stewart. J., dissenting).

*State v. Griswold* is reported at 151 Conn. 544, 200 A.2d 479 (1964), rev'd sub nom *Griswold v. Connecticut*, 381 U.S. 479 (1965). The "sacred precincts" language is from ibid., 485-86. The dissenters' "uncommonly silly" language is found at ibid., 527 (Black, J. and Stewart, J., dissenting).

Robert Bork discussed the *Griswold* decision in Robert Bork, "Neutral Principles and Some First Amendment Problems," *Indiana Law Journal* 47 (1971): 1, 7, 12. On opposition to Bork's nomination based on his *Griswold* position, see generally Michael Pertschuk & Wendy Schaetzel, *The People Rising: The Campaign Against the Bork Nomination* (St. Paul, MN.: Thunder's Mouth Press, 1989); Patrick B. McGuigan & Dawn M. Weyrich, *Ninth Justice: The Fight for Bork* (Washington, D.C.: Free Congress Research & Education Foundation, 1990). For Bork's response, see generally Robert H. Bork, *The Tempting of America: The Political Seduction of the Law* (New York: Free Press, 1990). Bork's "Yale professors" remark is quoted at *Nomination of Robert H. Bork to be Associate Justice of the Supreme Court of the United States: Hearings Before the Senate Comm. on the Judiciary*, 100th Cong., 1st Sess. pt.1, at 116, 241 (1987).

*Eisenstadt v. Baird* is reported at 405 U.S. 438 (1972). The crucial "right of the individual" language from the opinion is found at ibid., 453 (emphasis original).

The appeal of the obscenity conviction involving Joyce's *Ulysses* is reported at *United States v. One Book Called "Ulysses,"* 5 F. Supp. 182 (S.D.N.Y. 1933), aff'd 72 F.2d 705 (2d Cir. 1934).

On the *Playboy* empire, see generally Gay Talese, *Thy Neighbor's Wife* (Garden City, N.Y.: Doubleday, 1980). On *Playboy* as a cultural phenomenon, see Barbara Ehrenreich, *The Hearts of Men: American Dreams and the Flight From Commitment* ch. 4 (Garden City, N.Y.: Anchor Press/Doubleday, 1983). The "jazz and Nietzsche" quote is found at Hugh Hefner, "The Playboy Philosophy," *Playboy*, Jan., 1963, at 41. Hefner's "a symbol of disobedience" claim is quoted in Talese, supra at 106. The "all woman wants is security," quote is from Bob Norman, "Miss Golddigger of 1953," *Playboy*, Dec. 1953.

The *Roth* test is set out at 354 U.S. 476, 485, 488 n.20, 489 (1957). *Memoirs of a Woman of Pleasure v. Massachusetts* is reported at 383 U.S. 413 (1966). The Supreme Court movie theater is described in Bob Woodward & Scott Armstrong, *The Brethren: Inside the Supreme Court* 198 (New York: Simon and Schuster, 1979). *Stanley v. Georgia* is reported at 394 U.S. 557 (1969). *Miller v. California* is reported at 413 U.S. 15 (1973), and its test is set out at ibid., 24.

*Paris Adult Theater I v. Slaton* is reported at 413 U.S. 49 (1973). As an example of the withdrawal of the liberal Justices into dissent in obscenity cases after *Miller*, see, e.g., ibid., 73 (Brennan, J., joined by Stewart, J., and Marshall, J., dissenting).

On pornography in the 1980s, see D'Emilio & Freedman, supra at 328. *Ferber v. New York* is reported at 458 U.S. 747 (1982).

*Bowers v. Hardwick* is reported at 487 U.S. 186 (1986).

# 10

## THE LIBERTINE REGIME

By the 1970s, libertinism had evolved from an outlaw philosophy to a norm. After the Kinsey Report, the Model Penal Code, and the Supreme Court's constitutional imprimatur, libertine sexual deregulation became the conventional wisdom with which any alternative would have to contend. As a regime of sexual governance, libertinism is answerable, like each of the prior regimes we have considered, to political judgment. How does libertinism resolve each of the fundamental issues of political judgment: What can we know, what are people like, and what is a good political order? How does it measure up against the standards of human flourishing, equality and autonomy, and hedonistic satisfaction by which we judge a good regime?

Despite protestations of neutrality and universality, the libertine model of sexual regulation never rested on an incontestable "what everyone knows to be right." As Chapter 9 reflects, libertinism was a mixture of classical liberal individualism and utilitarian sexual hedonism. In this mixture, sexual philosophy was but a subcategory of mid-twentieth-century political thought.

Liberal/utilitarian political thought started from the tolerant, secularized, freedom-loving, and optimistic individualism we call classical liberalism. By the nineteenth century, liberalism was confronted with the claims of the third school of western political thought, utilitarianism. In emphasizing the well-being of the whole population and the transfer of goods from one person to another to increase the collective good, utilitarianism can fairly be described as the philosophy most supportive of the modern European and American welfare states. Beginning around John Stuart Mill's time, and for more than a century in the West, utilitarianism overtook liberalism as the dominant (although not the only) source of political justification. This shifted the emphasis in political decision-making from freedom to material well-being, and from the individual to the society as a whole.

Unlike the work of Tocqueville, which came early in the life of the virtue republic, and unlike Mill, who was one of the prime architects of the movement for female equality, liberal-utilitarian sexual libertinism actually preceded the theory that would justify or explain it. Little had been done to draw together the two competing strands of western political theory until the publication in 1971 of Harvard philosopher John Rawls's *A Theory of Justice.* Rawls is credited with reviving liberal political theory for the first time since Mill, animating a rights-based individualism that had languished during the period of utilitarian dominance. Rawls, however, is not a pure liberal, but rather blends the individualism of classical liberalism with some utilitarian collectivism. (After Rawls, the most individualistic strands of classical liberalism migrated to the philosophy we will call libertarianism.) Rawls's drafts had been circulating among academic philosophers since the early '60s.

A *Theory of Justice* attempts to specify the minimum terms of a defensible political arrangement. Rawls's contribution is to suggest that people establish their governing principles and institutions by imagining a political world without knowing what their place in it will be. They will not know if they are young or old, rich or poor, and so on. This ignorance will correct for transparent exercises of power and self-interest, Rawls argues, and so the principles agreed upon by this procedure will be just. From this position of ignorance, Rawls predicts, people would make two basic arrangements for their collective lives: (1) each person should enjoy the most extensive liberty compatible with a similar liberty for others, and (2) social and economic inequalities are to be arranged so that they are reasonably expected to be to everyone's advantage. Self-consciously rejecting the utilitarian past, Rawls asserts that the overall well-being of society doesn't count, because no one would want to sacrifice his or her well-being simply to raise the well-being of others.

The flood of political writing that followed A *Theory of Justice* interpreted these two principles to require an individualistic approach to issues of physical security, speech, belief, and expression (the scheme of most extensive liberty). However, despite Rawls's protestations, his theory seems to require something of a utilitarian economic collectivism, where no one gets richer than others unless those riches also benefit the poorest. Rawls's approach does not dictate complete sharing, but merely assumes economic equality as a starting point. Thereafter, if one individual invents something or devises a way of doing things that expands the pie, the inventor may keep an unequal share of the profits, so long as everyone's economic well-being also is somewhat improved. Rawls's philosophy uncannily mirrored the post-New Deal understanding of law and politics. The market economy may be regulated in the interest of the nation and to protect the poorest, but the individual exercise of fundamental liberties is protected from government interference by the most stringent of standards.

Unlike Tocqueville and Mill, Rawls says very little about sex. But the revival of rights-based individualism reflected in Rawls's work was applied to the problem of sex by philosopher Thomas Nagel in an essay titled "Sexual Perversion," published in 1969. Despite the title, Nagel is actually proposing a general theory of sexual conduct, transcending conventional understandings of "perverted" and "normal" sex. He places sex somewhere between hunger and love, denying that sex is merely an appetite immune from moral judgment and also denying that sex must express another attitude, such as love. Instead, Nagel describes sex as an attitude toward another person, an attraction to a fusion of their physical or social attributes, including appearance.

For Nagel, the appropriate sexual exchange is mutual, reciprocal, and interdependent. Nagel portrays sexual desire as involving a complex series of layered mental perceptions, happening in three stages: (1) one person is aroused, then the object of arousal is aroused independently; (2) the initiator perceives the follower's arousal and the initiator is further aroused by the awareness that the follower is independently aroused; and (3) the follower perceives that the initiator is aroused, leading the follower to feel even more aroused, which, in turn, inspires the initiator to arousal by its effect on the follower. At this last stage, the initiator reaps the harvest of having the desiring will of another respond to his or her willed desire. Applying this test to actual sexual practices, Nagel concludes that sex acts that sidestep this reciprocity of wills, like sexual engagement with animals or children, or sadism and masochism, are perverted, but that freely willed homosexuality, for example, probably is not.

Nagel stops short of concluding that perverted sex is immoral in the traditional sense, speculating that people's sexual practices might be more like their health or beauty practices, better or worse for the actor, but if worse not descending to immorality. He also refuses to judge whether perverted sex is bad sex in the sense of unenjoyable sex, and concludes that even perverted or bad sex may be better than none.

Nagel's philosophical interest in sex parallels Rawls's project in trying to marry the strands of an idealistic individualism and a hedonistic utilitarianism. In Rawls's public world of government and business, classical liberalism found its home in Rawls's first principle, the realm of most extensive liberty, and utilitarianism in the second principle of shared fruits of economic cooperation. By comparison, in Nagel's world of partnered sex, individualism explains the crucial role of the independent development of desire and its free exchange between two separate persons. In Nagel's theory, even the mechanism of arousal is in part (after the initial response to the physical self of another) an act of almost disembodied sexual will. Indeed, the free invocation of sexual desire through the focus on the desiring will characterizes Nagel's unique construct. After the initial response to the other's physical self, the utilitarian sexual hedonism in Nagel's blend surfaces again at the end of the essay when he refuses to allow his concept of unperverted sex as an exchange of wills to be used to restrict or even condemn as "immoral" pleasurable acts of sex in the real world regardless of their failure to live up to his standards.

The uncertainty reflected in both of these attempts to synthesize philosophies was also manifest in life and law. Classical liberalism took the form of deregulated sexual individualism, but utilitarians split. In the early years of the libertine paradigm, the utilitarian concern with collective well-being took the form of a residual Victorian social purity, valorizing the community of marriage, the family, and

the religious community, forbidding prostitution, embracing eugenics, and enforcing the Mann Act. Meanwhile, utilitarian hedonism took the form of a self-
justifying sexual pleasure, confusingly allied to individualist classical liberalism
more often than to its collectivist utilitarian sister.

Some of the complexity of this philosophical picture can be explained by the
order in which libertinism emerged, with popular culture leading and law and
philosophy trailing behind. Long before libertine theorists valorized sexuality, the
popular culture had made the word "sexy" a new adjective for describing something irresistibly attractive. To be influential in the popular culture did not require
a majority in the legislature, consensus among philosophers, or the stamp of approval from elite culture. With so much being negotiated in the decentralized and
fluid space of daily life, libertinism had no shared structure of belief, and the
emerging attitude and way of life was inherently unstable. In practice, libertinism
embraced a classical liberal approach to sexual regulation, embodied in the Model
Penal Code and *Griswold v. Connecticut*, and at the same time a utilitarian hedonism,
reflected in Kinsey's love affair with the orgasm and the sexual exaltation of the
*Playboy* philosophy. Like Rawls's theory, libertinism always was vulnerable to the
internal contradiction of these disparate influences. When libertinism came under
attack, as we will see in Chapter 11, the classical liberals and the utilitarian collec-
tivists each split off from the unstable libertine alliance.

These diverse philosophical roots contributed to libertinism different and
sometimes inconsistent assumptions about the fundamental questions of knowledge, personhood, and politics. Regarding knowledge, libertines at first claimed to
be skeptical about the possibility of sexual understanding. The strongest version of
this skepticism was the claim that we cannot know about the sexual experiences of
other people, and so there is no basis on which to decide between competing
claims of the sexual good. This skepticism was the strongest fuel for sexual deregulation. Justice William O. Douglas, dissenting in *Miller v. California*, muses that, "[t]o
many the Song of Solomon is obscene. I do not think we, the judges, were ever
given the constitutional power to make definitions of obscenity." Comments to
the Model Penal Code provision proposing deregulation of adultery note that "it
must be recognized, as a practical matter, that in a heterogeneous community such
as ours, different individuals and groups have widely divergent views of the seriousness of various moral derelictions." Morris Ploscowe comments that "[a]dul-
tery and fornication are practiced by normal and abnormal individuals alike."

Other libertines were agnostic rather than skeptical, simply asserting that
knowledge might be possible, but no sure answers had emerged. Ploscowe notes
(and the Model Penal Code cites his view) that:

> Until late in the last century the stock explanations for homosexuality and
> sodomitic practices were excessive masturbation or appetites jaded by normal
> means of sexual expression.... [Although] science today offers an explanation of
> homosexuality ... students of homosexuality disagree. Some believe that biolog-

ical and constitutional factors predominate . . . some scientists . . . regard the homosexual as an intersex. . . . [A]nother scientist declared that homosexuality is nature's way of redressing the male-female balance.

The Model Penal Code also includes an extended comment on the moral ambiguity of various forms of adultery:

> The enduring affair is properly regarded as a graver threat to the home and family than the occasional or transitory infidelity which Kinsey found in half the married men's lives. But the difficulty in defining the situation is formidable . . . if we undertake to punish mistress-keeping, we can hardly overlook the at least equally offensive and dangerous character—the Don Juan or Lothario.

When libertines turned to law reform, the position of uncertainty was useful in sidestepping the looming conflict between the remnants of social purity on the statute books and the private practice of libertinism. Lawmakers found it politic both to refuse to repeal sexual restrictions and to refuse to enforce them. In this climate of caution and hypocrisy, libertines found it easier to sell deregulation as an expression of skeptical tolerance rather than an exaltation of sexual fulfillment. Political theorist Michael Sandel calls this the invocation of the "sophisticated" version of political judgment. Advocates of unpopular lifestyles seek a "thin and feeble" form of respect in the virtue of free choice in light of uncertain knowledge, and do not try to convince their opponents of the moral value of the conduct they choose.

But the argument eventually shifted away from cautious uncertainty about knowledge to a confident certainty in the good of sexual fulfillment. In a development running from the early free love movement through the sexual self-actualization of the 1920s and the *Playboy* philosophers of the 1950s, culminating in the explosion of sexual consumerism in the 1960s and 1970s, libertinism came to rest on affirmative assertions of the value of sexual fulfillment itself. Hedonistic libertines claim that they can know the good (a traditional utilitarian assumption, but one completely at odds with either liberal skepticism or agnosticism), and that sexuality is an intrinsically good aspect of human nature and community.

Although divided about knowledge, libertinism spoke in a single voice about personhood. Libertines believe that personhood is organized on an individual basis. This is most clearly drawn in *Eisenstadt v. Baird*, the Supreme Court decision that distinguishes individuals even in a marriage:

> The married couple is not an independent entity with a mind and heart of its own, but an association of two individuals each with a separate intellectual and emotional makeup. If the right of privacy means anything, it is the right of the individual, married or single, to be free from unwarranted governmental intrusion into matters so fundamentally affecting a person as the decision whether to bear or beget a child.

Hedonists also honor personhood as a situs of self-actualization, whether spiritual and emotional, or material and physical. Romantics, such as the free lovers, emphasize personal growth and fulfillment, a version of personhood in which sex is a path to higher pleasures. Materialists simply construe persons as units of physical pleasure. The difference between free love romanticism and blunt materialism surfaces in Ploscowe's book. Unlike the free lovers, Ploscowe sees people as incapable of virtue: "The flesh has always been weak. . . . Men and women copulate in sovereign disregard of penal statutes."

Given hedonism's roots in the collectivist philosophy of utilitarianism, the prominence of the individual in hedonistic libertinism is a puzzle. Nagel's picture of two individuals weaving a web of sexual arousal that begins in their hedonistic physical selves, but soon evolves into respect for one another's free will, could have bridged the gap. As we will see in Chapter 11, however, the decay of libertinism cast shadows on this happy picture of the marriage of individual and collective goods. Feminists and others began to talk about sexual pain as well as pleasure, requiring the utilitarian to argue for the sacrifice of one individual's sexual pleasure in light of the just claims of a pained other. Because utilitarianism must recognize the pains of one as well as the pleasures of another, the hedonists resorted to ever more elaborate descriptions of the pleasures of sex to outshout the critics or romanticized what were at bottom physical transactions to avoid the outcome of the pain-pleasure calculus.

Once law caught up, the choice of deregulating sex rather than suppressing it reveals the third of the assumptions of libertinism—its politics. Here, libertinism mostly follows classical liberalism. The Wolfenden Commission concluded, for example, that it is not the state's role to impose a particular morality on individuals. Ploscowe agrees that state action is not only improper, but ineffective: "There is little that police, prosecutors, and courts can do." The Model Penal Code adopts both positions: The state should not act, and if it does it will not be effective. The drafters write that it is "inappropriate for the government to attempt to control behavior that has no substantial significance except as to the morality of the actor." Such matters, they conclude, "are best left to the religious, educational and other social influences."

Not neutral on any of the foundations of moral prescription, libertine sexual deregulation rested on: (1) skepticism about or agnosticism among various schools of sexual knowledge, or, inconsistently, on the knowability of the good of sex; (2) assumptions of individualism in personhood, either optimistic or pessimistic; and (3) suspicions of the propriety as well as the effectiveness of using the state to enforce sexual limits. Does libertinism satisfy any definition of a good regime? From a moral perspective, is sex in itself such a value that it preempts all criticism of its delivery system?

## JUDGING LIBERTINISM

In its initial commitment to skepticism about sexual knowledge, libertinism begins from a premise different from that of virtue theories. Virtue theories hold that it is possible to know the sexual good not only for oneself, but also for other persons and for the whole of society. This self-confidence is true of the classical virtue thinkers of the ancient world and of the Christian virtue traditions associated with Augustine and Aquinas. Dialogue and reason, not skepticism or even agnosticism, was the ancients' answer to competing claims of truth. Christians, by contrast, looked to faith and revelation for knowledge of the good. The sexual epistemology of libertinism is the historical product of the violent religious conflicts of the Reformation, resolved when irreconcilable differences gave rise to norms of tolerance rather than agreement about the truth. To the ancients and Christians, libertines would appear derelict in their moral duty for forgoing the search for truth regarding a human capacity as important as sexuality. Libertines might respond that if something as sacred as religious belief and observation is a subject for tolerance, sexual tolerance is easily justified.

To the libertine, sexual truth is elusive because people are physically separate and psychologically opaque to one another. Virtue theories, by contrast, emphasize human similarity. Given that all people share a common nature—the species with speech and reason, for example, or creatures of God's will—their well-being, even regarding something as complicated and subjective as sexuality, can with adequate effort be discerned and understood. Moreover, people can be shaped in their desires through culture and education. Accordingly, the community, whether it be the family, church, popular and civic culture, or the state, can create better persons by inculcating better forms of sexuality. To the ancients, better forms were those that led one's eyes upward to the good (in Plato's *Symposium*, sex is an avenue to love of the good) or created occasions for self-mastery and the mastery of others (like sexual friendship between men), and those forms that advanced proper household management (like sex with one's wife). To Christians, the better form of sex is marital and reproductive sex, which contains the temptation to sin and manifests in a material form the spiritual union between Jesus and the church. Virtue republicans valued sex for its role in preserving civic virtue and order in a disorderly democratic world.

Romantic and hedonistic libertinism holds that the good can be known, as virtue ethics does. But neither romantic self-fulfillment nor physical sensation qualifies as an acceptable definition of the good under the premises of civic virtue ethics. To a philosophy that values politics, community, and reason, ends such as self-involvement and physicalism are base purposes.

Libertinism accords best with modern liberalism, in its Rawlsian compromise of libertarian individualism and utilitarianism. Yet, like classical liberalism, some strands of libertinism are skeptical about the possibility of sexual knowledge. Such skepticism is not itself a moral stance: Thoroughgoing skepticism leaves people in the dark about the best or even better forms of sexual relationship to seek. Rather, skepticism gets its moral clout from the role it plays in containing political violence and promoting political tolerance, which are perhaps the principal historical achievements of the liberal tradition. In the history of the United States, libertine skepticism can take credit for encouraging sexual tolerance, in turn lessening the suffering of people who desire same-sex relations or sex outside of marriage, and those who want to escape lifelong marriage. Jailing, blackmail, stigmatization, psychiatric coercion, relational misery, and sexual frustration all have been eased by that toleration. Even the morality of tolerance could be contested, however, for it places physical and psychic peace above the right or the good as a political value.

Nonetheless, tolerance promotes classical liberal values of individuality, autonomy, and freedom. Sexual desire, like belief and conscience (the principal concerns of classical liberalism) is bounded by the individual human body. Sexuality, like belief and conscience, often eludes reason and will, and cannot be proved empirically. Autonomy thus seems the proper framework for such an individualistic and inexpressible decision. Finally, libertinism provides the highest degree of sexual freedom. Like classical liberalism, which celebrates the individual's effectiveness in devising and executing his or her life plan, this version of libertinism allows the individual to execute sexual plans with minimal interference.

Most of the interference that libertines fear comes from the state rather than the community. Indeed, both the Wolfenden Commission and the Model Penal Code affirmatively embraced private institutions of sexual oppression, including shaming, stigma, theories of deviancy, and silencing. Homosexuals should hide themselves and stay out of the parks; prostitutes should be banished from the streets and bars; psychologists should be called upon to "cure" homosexuality and "save" failing marriages. In this focus on governmental restraints on freedom, libertinism follows the norms of classical liberalism.

The confidence of hedonistic and romantic libertines in the good of sex threatens classical liberal values, but accords with utilitarianism. Utilitarianism depends upon the measurement of experienced pains and pleasures. To the extent that libertinism equates all sex with pleasure, whether physical pleasure or the emotional highs of self-expression and romantic fulfillment, it gains a potent utilitarian justification. This backup position has done great service in current popular debates over sexual politics. If deregulation is likely to produce more sexual exchanges between women and men, and if sex is an unalloyed good, then the libertine regime also must be good by a utilitarian measure.

The rub comes when the utilitarian confronts the argument that libertine sex creates more pain as well as more pleasure. Utilitarians weigh each person's pleasure and pain separately, but add them up collectively in making a moral judgment. Accordingly, if some sex is good and some not good, then the utilitarian takes no position either for or against libertine sexual arrangements, but tries to determine which way the balance tips. As an example, the argument for punishing adultery is that it undermines marriage and the family, institutions regarded as healthful for the society as a whole. To a classical liberal, communal interests are an insufficient basis for imposition of penal sanctions on an individual. A utilitarian might argue that restraints on the freedom of some persons carry a cost in fearful expectations that tips the balance toward freedom, regardless of the cost to the collective well-being. But the utilitarian and liberal would come to the same outcome by quite different paths.

Interestingly, in its divide between the value of the romantic soul and the value of the orgasmic body, hedonistic libertinism reproduces a division in utilitarianism between the rigid calculus of Jeremy Bentham and the nuanced hierarchy of pleasures described by John Stuart Mill. Although both Mill and Bentham recognize psychological as well as physical pleasures, Bentham simply counts the utility of all pleasures equally and would not value self-expression more than orgasm. Mill's theory of developed pleasures, by contrast, fits more comfortably with the romantic sexuality of the free love movement than the orgasm worship of modern libertinism.

Although traditional utilitarian theory cannot judge a libertine regime on its face as either good or bad without more information about actual pains and pleasures, the strand of utilitarian theory that Rawls blended into liberalism has norms and assumptions more amenable to libertinism. The blend of classical liberalism and utilitarianism that makes up modern liberalism avoids the dispute between utilitarian knowledge and classical liberal skepticism. Materialistic on both sides, the blend treats people's expressed preferences as the equivalent of knowledge such that whatever people say they want and need is taken to define their good. The role of the state is to create enough freedom for people to realize those preferences even as it provides them enough economic security to protect against the worst pains.

Finally, regarding politics, insofar as regulation is required to realize its ends, utilitarianism does not distinguish the state from other agents of pleasure or pain. By comparison, the libertine emphasis on public tolerance, which is tolerant of private oppression, violates that norm. Modern liberals share the classical liberal's heightened fear of the state, recasting it within the utilitarian's pain/pleasure calculus as increased fear. But modern liberals do not make the classical liberal category distinction between public and private. Accordingly, one might envision a set of facts so onerous that the modern liberal could be teased apart from the libertine. For example, in a developed economy, sexual reproduction at an early age often disqualifies a young mother from an independent economic life, consigning her to a life of poverty and dependency.

Classical liberal theory would not allow the state to interfere with the sexual choices of a young person who is past the age of reason. Modern liberalism might permit regulation (in the form of a stricter law against statutory rape, for example), weighing the onerous consequences over a whole life against a few years of fear of prosecution.

Even more-sex-is-always-good libertinism is vulnerable to utilitarian arguments. A utilitarian might argue, for example, that unlimited sex has downsides—disease, for example, or the perverse way that an unlimited supply of anything good diminishes both desire and satisfaction. Mill's developed pleasures calculus suggests the possibility that concentrating on one pleasure, like sex, narrows and channels human possibilities so greatly that the pleasure seeker is obsessed, mentally ill or abnormal. Such an argument rests on some agreement about flourishing and normalcy. If people's desires for pleasure must be circumscribed so as to preserve their capacity for pleasure, then the pain/pleasure analysis begins to sound like virtue ethics.

Libertinism changes shape so easily that it is hard to capture the paradigm long enough to evaluate it. At one extreme, libertinism is a subordination of communal order to the claims of individual pleasure. At the other, it is a disguised tolerance of disorder in the name of peace and freedom. In between are the innumerable shades that we have tried to sketch above. It may be that the libertine century is still too close to allow us to see its outlines in full.

Because libertine theory is so protean and opportunistic, its effect on bargaining is also hard to evaluate. Rawls's exercise in neutrality seems likely to produce the best possible conditions for just and reasonable bargaining, because in setting the ground rules no one is allowed to know where they will end up in the social order. Optimally, this includes knowing whether they will be male or female. As applied to sexual bargaining, Rawls's theory has been interpreted to allow individuals to conclude whatever sexual agreements they choose, protected by the laws against physical predation. Yet Rawls's image of a universe of individual actors, each pursuing life plans unhindered by others, misses big pieces of the problem of *sexual* bargaining. Unlike behaviors of traditional concern to classical liberals—religious worship, or going about the public streets, for example—sexual actors cannot achieve their ends by acting as disconnected units requiring only to be left alone in their pursuit of liberty, protected from one another physically by law. The desire of many people is for partnered sex. To achieve these sexual ends, the players must have a framework for cooperation with one another. More problematic, to achieve their individual sexual ends, they must be able to act collectively to restrain the other players in their free action.

In addition, even in philosophers' thought experiments, only women get pregnant, only women give birth, and only women nurse infants. Accordingly, while somewhat protected by Rawls's regime, women come to the sexual bargaining table at a *natural* disadvantage. (These natural facts, hidden in Rawls's theory, are also completely concealed in Nagel's imagined one-night stand of mutual desire.) A woman must bargain away the disadvantage. Over numbers of encounters, the disadvantage of always having to bargain away the natural state begins to add up. In each succeeding bargain the woman comes to the table relatively weaker and weaker. The solution to this natural inequality of individuals is collective action (like support for childbearing and childrearing), but this coercion violates Rawls's commitment to the most extensive liberty possible. Women might invoke the second principle that economic inequality be permitted only to the extent that the benefits are shared. Yet men could answer that the strength they gain by being free of reproduction is natural, like beauty and intelligence, and immune from the second principle. Or they might offer an unequal share of the surplus they earn by being free of reproduction, contending that any transfer payment improves the woman's natural state.

Finally, Rawls's vision of the world of free action ignores the critical role of ideology in bargaining. By immunizing speech in the scheme of most extensive liberty, Rawls licenses the loudest shouter. Weaker players often gain bargaining power by advancing a vision of desirable behavior that protects them. Throughout history this has included Christian celibacy, courtly love, egalitarianism, manly self-restraint, and companionate marriage. These ideological supports work because they shut off competing visions of legitimate sexual transactions, leaving some loud shouters alone in the wilderness. Consider the ideological success of the nineteenth-century age-of-consent campaign, when almost no legislator was willing to step forward to embrace pedophilia. During that uneasy silence, adult women grew in power and the young were protected.

If there are pitfalls for the weak even in Rawls's protective and ambitiously egalitarian philosophy, hedonistic libertinism makes bargaining even harder for the weak. Because the pleasure of sex is valued above all things, any resistance is unnatural and illegitimate, and pain and cost are discounted. Finally, romantic libertinism, which elevates sex beyond the physical into a path of self-definition, leaves virtually no room for bargaining. Even the force of consent, which any ordinary understanding of "self"-definition would prize, must be constrained. The benefit of the doubt must fall on the side of more sex lest an opportunity for sexual realization be missed out of an excess of concern for consent.

From pleasure, a disregard for pain. From romance, a deafness to the will of the object of desire. From freedom, less and less choice for the weak. Half classical liberal, half utilitarian, libertinism lacks the template of fair evaluation of earthly delight that is the core of utilitarian morality. In the end, it is most at home in its father's arms as the product of classical liberal individualism and the elevation of freedom above all other claims.

## NOTES

Rawls sets out his original position scheme for political formation in *A Theory of Justice* (Cambridge, Mass.: Belknap Press of Harvard Univ. Press, 1971), 12. Representative works that interpret Rawls to treat some human characteristics as deserving of the most extensive liberty, but treat economics as shared fruits, i.e., more collectively, are John E. Roemer, *Theories of Distributive Justice* (Cambridge, Mass.: Harvard Univ. Press, 1996);

Joel Feinberg, *Social Philosophy* (Englewood Cliffs, N.J.: Prentice-Hall, 1973); J. H. Wellbank, "Bibliography on Rawlsian Justice: 1951-1975," *Philosophical Research Archives* 2, no. 1102 (1976).

Thomas Nagel's "Sexual Perversion" was originally published in 1969, and is reprinted in Thomas Nagel, *Mortal Questions* (Cambridge: Cambridge Univ. Press, 1979), 39.

Justice Douglas in *Miller* on the Song of Solomon is reported at 413 U.S. 15, 37, 46 (1973) (Douglas, J., dissenting). Comments to the Model Penal Code provision proposing deregulation of adultery are found at American Law Institute, *Model Penal Code* (Philadelphia: The Institute, 1980), sec. 213.6 cmts. at 430-39. Ploscowe on adultery and fornication among "normal and abnormal individuals alike" is found at Morris Ploscowe, *Sex and the Law* (New York: Prentice-Hall, 1951), 164.

Ploscowe on varying views of the origins of homosexuality is in ibid., 211. The Model Penal Code reference is found in American Law Institute, *Model Penal Code*, sec. 213.2 cmts. at 368.

The Model Penal Code on the moral relativity of adultery is found in ibid., sec. 213.6 cmts. at 437, 439.

Michael Sandel on "thin" justifications and "sophisticated" tolerance is found in "Moral Argument and Liberal Toleration: Abortion and Homosexuality," *California Law Review* 77 (1989): 521.

The quote from *Eisenstadt*, 405 U.S. 438, 453 (1972) (emphasis original).

Ploscowe on people's incapacity for virtue is found in *Sex and the Law*, 271, 275, 281.

On lack of enforcement of sex crime laws, see Committee on Homosexual Offenses and Prostitution, *The Wolfenden Report* (1957; New York: Stein and Day, 1963); Ploscowe, *Sex and the Law*, 278, and American Law Institute, *Model Penal Code*, Tentative Draft No. 4 (Philadelphia: The Institute, 1954), sec. 207.1, at 205, and sec. 207.1, at 207.

Mill's "more developed pleasures" utilitarianism and Bentham's "rigid calculus" can be taken from Jeremy Bentham, eds. H. L. A. Hart and F. Rosen, *An Introduction to the Principles of Morals and Legislation* (New York: Oxford Univ. Press, 1995) and John Stuart Mill, *Utilitarianism and On Liberty* (Garden City, N.Y.: Doubleday, 1961).

On unlimited access dulling the appetite, see Henry Sidgwick, *The Method of Ethics* (New York: Macmillan, 1901).

Among the feminist critics of Rawls are Linda R. Hirshman, "Essay, Is the Original Position Inherently Male-Superior?" *Columbia Law Review* 94 (1994): 1860; Susan Moller Okin, *Justice, Gender and the Family* (New York: Basic Books, 1989); Carole Pateman, *The Sexual Contract* (Stanford: Stanford Univ. Press, 1988); Moira Gatens, *Feminism and Philosophy* (Bloomington: Indiana Univ. Press, 1991), 65-66.

## 11

## THERE'S NO SUCH THING AS FREE LOVE

In 1982 and 1983, feminist lawyer and scholar Catharine MacKinnon shot across the bow of the libertine consensus. "[S]exuality is to feminism what work is to marxism," she wrote. Adapting the approach of Foucault and the social constructionists to the analysis of heterosexual sexual relations, MacKinnon argued that sexuality is a social institution and not a natural phenomenon, and described the particular social relations creating heterosexuality as relations of dominance and submission. Powerful players create a sexuality that eroticizes hierarchy, she wrote, and also persons of "masculine" and "feminine" identities to act out these sexual roles. By fusing "normal" sexuality with these relations of power, men face the choice of dominance or celibacy, and women the choice of submission or celibacy. To the extent that people choose to be sexual rather than celibate, they reinforce gender hierarchy. MacKinnon thus situated heterosexuality at the heart of women's oppression.

The MacKinnon essays are not the only, or even the first, manifestation of tensions in the happy picture of libertine sexuality. Within the free and easy political and cultural movements of the 1960s, the persistence of a gender hierarchy grounded in sexuality ("The only position for women in the Black Power Movement is prone") fueled the rebirth of feminism. A generation of activist women, already attuned to structures of oppression, applied their civil rights and pacifist politics to their own condition. From the outset this new wave of feminists argued for at least one non-libertine legal position regarding sex, seeking both stronger rape laws and more aggressive and effective law enforcement against rape.

But MacKinnon subjected not just force and violation, but also consensual sex to the standards of power and justice. MacKinnon challenged the popular feminist tenet that rape is an act of violence and not an act of sex by refusing to credit the distinction, arguing that some violence is sex and vice versa. By questioning whether consent really marks the line between moral and immoral sex, her analysis brought rape and heterosexual intercourse into troublingly close relation. From this angle, it no longer was so easy to consider oneself a political liberal or a sexual libertine and also a feminist. And it became difficult for sexual libertines to distance their conduct from rape by the easy invocation of consent. This challenge to libertine sexual standards set the stage for what would emerge as a bitterly divisive conflict among feminists and liberals over sexual politics in the 1980s.

MacKinnon challenged all of the libertine assumptions. When she criticizes an erotic of dominance and submission, she assumes that some knowledge of the sexual good is possible. The skepticism of libertine sexuality, by contrast, took it as gospel that no one can know the sexual pleasure of anyone else and that only the individual can decide what his or her sexual needs are. MacKinnon's emphasis on political equality challenges the hedonistic version of personhood and its claim that pleasure outweighs the abasement of oneself or another. Some of MacKinnon's opponents take her stance to be anhedonic and thus hostile to sexual pleasure: "My Mother Liked to Fuck," sex radical Joan Nestle asserts in an attack on the position, implying that anyone who would question her mother's pleasures does not. MacKinnon's analysis assumes the social construction of sexuality, which weakens the libertine's political arguments that sex should remain unregulated. If nature determines what is sexy, then "doing what comes naturally" means being free to follow one's essential nature. Alternatively, if no one can know what is sexually good for anyone else, being left alone to seek out one's greatest pleasure is freedom. By either measure, state imposition of sexual standards is repressive. In the social constructionist model, by contrast, the lack of state regulation does not necessarily signal freedom, but only that private relations of power have been left untouched. If a stronger player needs a partner to play a particular sexual role in order to have pleasure, he can use his power to cause a weaker player to give it to him. The stronger player is also empowered to use persuasion rather than force to cause the weaker player not simply to obey, but to share the stronger's ideas about what is sexy. Such a world is different from, but no less "constructed" or more "liberated" than a world controlled by state or communal authority. In denying the automatic equation of non-regulation with freedom, MacKinnon posits that some apparently liberated settings can be oppressive, just as some restraints can be liberating. Both positions are incoherent to the libertine.

This corrosive refutation of the underpinnings of the libertine sexual paradigm coincided with other cracks in the structure. Outside the sexual realm, radical thinkers challenged the metaphysical assumptions of liberalism, further straining the alliances between feminism and liberalism or libertarianism. As we saw in Chapter 6, Mill's argument for the fundamental similarity of the sexes framed the development of modern feminism. Rawls did not distinguish between men and women when he described the people who would set forth the basic rules of political justice. Yet in the late twentieth century, a growing body of feminist thought openly challenged the assumption that men and women are the same and the liberal version of equality as applied to gender. Feminists observed that in many human pursuits, if women are treated the same as men they tend to end up on the bottom. If equality meant sameness, they concluded, women might be allowed to behave like men, but would be penalized insofar as they failed to resemble the male norm.

In a case decided in the mid-1970s, the Supreme Court ratified this pessimistic reading of the meaning of liberal equality for gender, holding that a disability insurance policy that excludes pregnancy from coverage does not make a gender-based distinction. The line that such a policy draws is between pregnant people and non-pregnant people regardless of gender, the Court reasoned. Critics of the ruling pointed out that if female workers must forgo childbearing to enjoy equality in employment benefits with their male peers, what it means to be a "worker" is, implicitly, to be a man. So, too, workplaces structured such that no normal parent can raise decent children likewise assume a male worker, because the employer expects that someone other than the employee will take primary responsibility for child care.

Feminists pushed the insight further, noting that not only employers, but also liberal philosophers consistently failed to ask what liberal justice might mean for the heterosexual couple and the family. In the mid-1980s, sociologist Lenore Weitzman concluded in *The Divorce Revolution* that the modern regime of family law is too liberal, freeing men from material and moral responsibility for their spouses and children. Political philosopher Susan Moller Okin concluded, in *Justice, Gender and the Family* that the modern family is not liberal enough, preserving hierarchical virtue republican family relationships and expectations. Taken together, both analyses paint a picture of illiberal private families nestled within a too-liberal public culture, or Tocqueville's model of democratic society thriving 150 years later.

A critical aspect of the libertine paradigm of sexual regulation was the abandonment of marriage as the condition for heterosexual access. Consistent with this position, libertine regimes struck down or did not enforce laws against fornication and adultery. Beginning in California in 1969, states also changed divorce law to make exit from marriage easier. No-fault divorce, today available in some form in all of the states, allows dissolution not only in cases where both spouses want to end the marriage, but also where the spouse seeking divorce has violated the marriage contract and the spouse seeking to preserve the marriage has not. Between 1960 and 1990, the divorce rate doubled to about 40 percent of all first marriages, although in recent years the rate has begun to drop slightly.

Marriage is indeed an anachronism in a philosophical tradition that makes individual choice (and not formal status or any communal institution) the focus of sexual decision-making, and that elevates hedonistic satisfaction over other moral claims. If men and women choose to have sex and stay together, good for them; if not, too bad. In either event, there is no reason for the state, church, or society either to encourage or discourage marriage. Further, if a norm of equality requires that males and females be treated as though they are the same in all meaningful respects, including in sex, female vulnerability to pregnancy and childbearing must be regarded either as a personal choice unrelated to gender, or as a natural disability (like short stature or limited ambition) that politics has no business trying to ameliorate. Childrearing responsibilities, too, must be seen as individual matters to be worked out by consensual arrangement, not subjects for political resolution.

Compared with the monogamous, patriarchal marriage that dominated earlier sexual paradigms, the libertine vision of marriage as personal choice appears both liberating and egalitarian. Contrary to this happy picture, however, Okin argues that existing family arrangements do not conform to any liberal ideal but are, instead, hierarchical hangovers from the past.

Negotiations theorist Rhona Mahony builds on Okin's analysis. According to Mahony, girls raised in illiberal families expect less of themselves, and so pursue educational avenues predictably ill-suited for the technological world of good jobs and without the expectation of lifelong earning in the labor market. As adult women, they make the "rational" decision to sacrifice the poor prospects they have created for themselves in exchange for the lesser share of a man's larger pie, and so go on to marry older or more ambitious men. Within such marriages, spouses do not equitably pool their resources for investment in the education or career strategies that would enhance the wife's economic power as much as the husband's. Married women either quit their marginal jobs to stay home and raise children, or routinely sacrifice work, education, and leisure to perform a disproportionate share of the household maintenance and child care. Recently, economic analyst Edward McCaffery has illustrated how the entire American tax system is designed to produce that same set of female "choices," taxing the income of the second earner at the high marginal rate of the first earner and thus making it unprofitable for a lesser earner to work at all. Add to this the 1997 gender gap in wages of 30 percent, and the incentives for married women not to work mount.

Wives often fail to exercise the divorce option because they are economically dependent. With no good alternative to the negotiated agreement of hierarchical marriage, wives have less than equal power in their families. Children learn injustice in such families, a setting that shapes their character for future citizenship within public institutions.

Okin prescribes a rigorous regime to enforce equality in marriage: public education for gender equality, household wages for stay-at-home wives, public child care for equal access to jobs and politics, more economic sharing at divorce. Yet the illiberal family cannot easily be reformed within the libertine regime. If the law tries to require marital equity, when marriage is an individual choice and no one must marry for sex (or is even subject to strong legal incentives to do so), men might choose not to marry at all. Once in, spouses are free to exit if not satisfied with the deal for any reason.

In her opening blast against libertine divorce, Lenore Weitzman describes the consequences of this free entry and exit from marriage. In earlier historical periods, liberal divorce was a woman's solution and not a woman's problem. Nineteenth-century feminists struggled to liberalize divorce in response to the plight of wives of batterers, alcoholics, adulterers, and spendthrifts. As it happened, the triumph of no-fault divorce a century later was not motivated by feminism but was instead a law reform response to fraud and collusion. By revealing how the no-fault policy hurt women, however, *The Divorce Revolution* caused a revolution in feminist thinking.

Instead of a happy world of self-actualizing divorce, Weitzman argued, men were leaving and not paying enough support to keep their families out of poverty, even as they themselves rose by every economic measure after divorce. Weitzman's own data has been challenged, but better-designed studies confirm the pattern she describes. In the first year after divorce, men's income increased 13 percent and women's income declined 13 percent, a gap of 26 percent altogether. A second and longer-term study showed an eventual disparity of 52 percent among white divorced couples.

Okin and Weitzman had thus exposed the soft underbelly of the libertine marriage. Without state enforcement of laws against fornication and adultery, men had less reason either to marry or to stay married. If they did marry, they wanted some payoff in the form of an unequal share of the surplus of the joint enterprise. Having gained the upper hand, many husbands still found the deal unsatisfactory and sought exit. Bargaining theory predicts this outcome. Where the players start out unequal, the outcomes will be unequal. The libertine regime did not lead to equality in the sexual relationship of marriage, just as it did not establish workplace equality.

Outside of marriage, society began to witness the consequences of a sexual state of nature. The idea that consensual sexual exchanges apart from marriage should create any moral obligations of decent, fair, or noninstrumental conduct fell out of vogue. The law treated reprehensible and harmful personal conduct in intimate relationships as largely beyond the reach of not only criminal, but also civil law. Fraud, extortion, and negligence—all conduct that is subject to civil (and, in some instances, criminal) legal liability in nonsexual transactions—was lawful in sexual relationships. Courts cited the need to respect sexual freedom and individualism (usually described in the case law as "privacy") as the reason for refusing to intervene. In 1998, when the long-married President of the United States was accused of having a sexual relationship with one of his employees, a White House intern, defenders argued that his behavior did not amount to legally prohibited sexual harassment and therefore was beyond even moral judgment.

Men did better than women even in the pleasures of sex. With the emergence of the companionate ideal in the early part of the century, erotic mutuality was the libertine norm. Yet what seemed a romantic and hopeful vision of partnered satisfaction supported a new ideology of female subordination. Freudian-influenced sex "experts"—psychiatrists, physicians, and marriage counselors, as well as popular media advisors—told women that vaginal orgasm during heterosexual intercourse was the mark of a sexually and psychologically healthy woman.

Clitoral orgasm was immature and represented the female's refusal to accept that she lacked a penis (or, by extension, a man's place in the world). A mature, "well-adjusted" woman surrendered to femininity, transferring the seat of her genital pleasure from the active clitoris to the responsive vagina. Only the vagina, which functioned by accepting the activity of the male organ and was satisfied by being filled up, was the truly womanly genital. Tocqueville's counsel to the American girl to surrender her independence and voluntarily assume the subordination of womanhood found an updated and specifically sexual language in mid-twentieth-century psychoanalytic sexology.

Yet in the years following World War II American women had a hard time adjusting to their Freudian femininity. Female frigidity was a significant problem. The diagnosis was female dysfunction rather than unsatisfying male sexual partners, or a new script for heterosexual sex.

The Masters and Johnson findings first published in 1966 definitively refuted the Freudian explanation. The researchers found that women's orgasmic capacity is greater than that of men; that women are capable of multiple orgasms; that scientific instruments can detect only one kind of female orgasm, and it is clitoral; and that female orgasm is more intense when the clitoris is directly stimulated than when orgasm is achieved through vaginal intercourse. In short, it was not female psychology or anatomy that left women nonorgasmic, but what men and women were doing in bed. The male preference for vaginally centered sex caused female frigidity, and the cure for the problem was to reframe sex around female preferences, and the clitoris in particular.

The Masters and Johnson findings fueled an influential rethinking of heterosexuality in popular culture. If most women could be orgasmic if sex was done differently, then the new Battle of the Sexes was to be fought in the bedroom, where couples had to negotiate what they did when they had what they called "sex." For previous generations, "sex" between males and females had meant vaginal intercourse and its preliminaries. With the rediscovery of the clitoris and its role in female sexual response, intercourse no longer could be seen as the natural expression of two physically complementary bodies. Rather, vaginal intercourse was a socially constructed preference of no innate primacy, at least if the goal was mutual sexual pleasure rather than reproduction. Further, if men's and women's sexual needs were not naturally complementary, mutuality would require bargaining over who did what and for how long, who would go first, and so on. Finally, if the ideal of simultaneous orgasm was unrealistic, then men and women would have to consider how to take turns in giving and receiving pleasure. The romantic imagery of being swept away sexually on one tidal wave of passion—a remarkably durable fantasy, as evidenced in the popular culture of film and novel—foundered on a more material, more political reality.

For women, the sexual goal was clitoral stimulation, which meant negotiating for cunnilingus and positions for intercourse that permitted direct clitoral touching (i.e., not the missionary position). For men, the debunking of the myth of the vaginal orgasm allowed them to concentrate more on nonvaginal sex, fellatio in particular.

But, as Barbara Ehrenreich points out in her history of the popular sexual culture of the 1970s and 1980s, the move to oral sex was not automatically reciprocal between heterosexual partners. As reflected in the popular genre of sex books of the era—explicit manuals like *The Sensuous Woman* and *The Joy of Sex*, surveys like *The Hite Report*, collections of personal experiences like *My Secret Garden* and *For Yourself*, and above-ground pornography, such as the film *Deep Throat*—negotiating for oral sex emerged as an issue of power in the male-female relationship. A 1975 sex survey of 100,000 mostly white, mostly middle-class, mostly married women conducted by *Redbook* magazine found, for example, that 85 percent of women practiced fellatio. Yet men were not reciprocating the favor. Shere Hite's 1976 study found that only 42 percent of women were reaching orgasm through cunnilingus. Hite drew a political lesson from this data: Women's lack of social power was translating into a lack of sexual power, resulting in fewer orgasms and less pleasure. Even if women were willing to bargain away their physical and economic security and make themselves sexually available without any collateral relational demands, even sexual pleasure was not certain. This, too, required bargaining.

More recent surveys of sexual satisfaction show that male-female sex is still more satisfying for men than for women. Some 75 percent of men, but only 29 percent of women, report that they always reach orgasm during sex with a partner of the other gender. To an overwhelming degree, vaginal intercourse remains the most common heterosexual practice, indicating that the conventional sexual script has changed very little. There is suggestive evidence that women regularly lie about orgasm to men, leading men to believe they are more satisfying partners than they really are. Women as a group, for example, quite accurately estimate the percentage of their male partners who reach orgasm during sex, but men significantly overestimate the percentage of their female partners who do so.

Private relations of inequality spilled over into the public sphere. A thriving industry of savagely violent and abusive pornography took root in the soil tilled by early libertine-era constitutional decisions expanding the scope of the First Amendment. As more women entered waged work for longer periods of their adult lives, and as women workers sought and took on positions of authority in the workplace, sexual harassment became an increasingly serious problem. Yet among libertine purists, women who criticized pornography or resisted sexualization in the workplace were caricatured as frigid and Victorian, implicitly threatening them with the choice between celibacy and submission.

Feminists proposed law reforms to resist these most public practices of dominance heterosexuality, that is, pornography and workplace sexual harassment. Sexual harassment violated the equal employment laws, MacKinnon and other legal scholars proposed, and MacKinnon and her colleague Andrea Dworkin urged legislatures to enact statutes that would allow persons harmed by pornography to seek damages from the makers and distributors. Both ideas ran headlong into the defenses of the libertine paradigm. As to pornography, the defenders said we cannot know what gives other people sexual pleasure, sexual pleasure is a paramount good, people will use pornography or forgo it depending upon their own, internally constructed sexual preferences, and people need access to all kinds of ideas to develop and express fully individualized personhood. Sexual minorities argued that in a world that repressed the practice of their sexual nature, only a libertine regime of free speech allowed them at least the consolations of fantasy and masturbation. Cast in legal language, libertine defenders claimed any restriction of pornography violated the constitutional protection of free speech and, at their most extreme, asserted that such limitations raised the prospect of totalitarianism. Pornographers became this generation's version of the political dissidents persecuted and jailed in other eras for their dangerous ideas. Instead of Emma Goldman, Hollywood presented Larry Flynt.

The move to make sexual harassment unlawful evoked similar responses. Critics insisted that one cannot know whether another person is interested in a particular sexual interaction unless one asks, that legally imposed silence or restraint will lead to less sex when more sex is a paramount good, and that people can fend off harassers depending upon their own, internally constructed sexual preferences. Legal critics said that to regulate sexual harassment is to violate the protections of free speech and privacy and to threaten totalitarianism or, at the least, Senator Joseph McCarthy's witch hunts. Sexual harassers became the real victims, persecuted by zealous and repressive feminists hostile to the natural and normal desires of heterosexual males.

Interestingly, however, the legal move against sexual harassment fared better than that against pornography, both with lawmakers and in public opinion. Sexual harassment in the school or workplace is now firmly established in federal and state law as a form of gender discrimination and a ground for tort liability. By contrast, despite grass-roots campaigns in various cities to enact local ordinances and legislative efforts to establish new civil rights protections in federal and state law, the law governing pornography is little changed since the 1970s. What has shifted is both the popular and elite debate around the issue. Many legal scholars who were traditionally considered liberals have refused the bait of free speech absolutism, opening the way for a more nuanced consideration of the constitutional meaning and social price of pornography. Although ultimately struck down by a classically liberal Supreme Court, a law to limit access to pornography on the Internet did pass the Congress.

There are both obvious and subtle explanations for the different outcomes. First, statutory regulation of pornography is widely targeted (as statutes usually are), whereas for historical reasons, the civil rights laws depend on case-by-case determinations, resembling the one-on-one tort model that fits comfortably with the individualistic assumptions of the liberal state. Second, bringing sex into the workplace subjects sex to the ordinary standards of justice applicable to other aspects of public life, including norms against discrimination in hiring and firing. Treating someone sexually to the detriment of his or her position as a worker resembles the kind of injury the law already has the tools to remedy. Finally, the greater acceptance for rules against sexual harassment reflects prudery and a persisting attachment to the idea that sex belongs only in the private sphere. By dragging sexual dominance out of the bedroom and into the office, the harasser subjects himself to censure for having acted in a "crude" and "vulgar" way in public. Although pornography, too, is publicly displayed, its presence is somewhat concealed by specialty stores, clubs, and theaters, as well as merchandising practices. In addition, pornographic materials are purchased in the marketplace but intended for consumption in the home, allowing pornography to retain its private coloration. Despite the vast size of the commercial enterprise involved in its production and distribution, the use of pornography continues to be seen as a fair strategy in the unregulated private world of sexuality. So long as sex remains hidden, experienced in a solitary encounter, or cloistered within the family or confined to the home, public standards of justice will not apply.

Libertine sex, however, has spilled out of the bedroom to mark the lives of innocent bystanders in other troubling ways. Research shows that children of divorce as a group fare worse than those whose parents do not divorce. Incest and child sexual abuse are more prevalent when a child lives with someone who is not his or her natural parent. Children of single mothers are disproportionately poor, involved in crime, and unsuccessful in school. Single mothers are disproportionately dependent upon public assistance, an increasingly inadequate and humiliating form of economic support.

Finally, the 1980s witnessed the emergence of a new, fatal venereal disease risk, HIV/AIDS, transmitted by both homosexual and heterosexual activity. Researchers at the National Opinion Research Center (NORC) of the University of Chicago report that almost a third of Americans have changed their sexual behavior to avoid infection, using monogamy or selectiveness almost as often as condoms, which are supposed to promote safer sex without limiting sexual activity. As we write, promising developments in medical care have opened the possibility that HIV-infected people can survive the disease. Nonetheless, it is difficult to deny that HIV/AIDS changed the conversation about sex.

All told, the cracks in the libertine regime have grown too wide to ignore. People have begun to question whether the individual is, in fact, the only relevant consideration in questions of sexual morality. Perhaps sexual and reproductive strategies should be subject to social needs and constraints. Responses are proliferating. The question now is whether the cures may be worse than the disease.

## BACK TO THE FUTURE: REVIVING THE VIRTUE REPUBLIC

Cultural conservatives respond to the down side of libertinism by proposing to revive various aspects of the republic of virtue. If popular mores are any guide, this virtue revival would not be quite the step backward that a sex-saturated media would suggest. Updates of the Kinsey research in the 1990s reveal that a majority of Americans order their sexual relations in less than libertine ways. Researchers at the NORC launched an ambitious study of sexual practices in 1992, focusing on a randomly selected and nationally representative group of some 3500 adult women and men. This is the first study whose size allows for good comparison with Kinsey's findings some forty years before. Although between two-thirds and three-quarters of heterosexual women and 80 percent or more of heterosexual men have intercourse before marriage, reflecting a real revolution in premarital sexuality, once married they tend to report themselves as faithful and sexually moderate. Only 10 percent of women and about 25 percent of men engage in adultery. Most married couples have sex about twice a week, and married people have more sex than unmarried people living without a partner. Vaginal intercourse remains overwhelmingly the most common heterosexual practice, followed by oral sex, which has become a somewhat more ordinary part of the sex life of heterosexual couples.

When libertinism was young and its social consequences not fully manifest, criticism from defenders of sexual virtue were marginal in the cultural debate. Two social experiences, however, combined to revive cultural conservatives' voice in debates over sexual policy—the sympathetic portrayal of yuppie single motherhood in the media and the rising rates of single motherhood among the poor. Interestingly, both involve libertine female sexual behavior perceived as being out of control. Although early pioneers like Kinsey and Hefner thought that women would be freed by libertinism from social and legal strictures on their sexuality, we have shown that libertinism always rested on a male norm. Thus the regime failed to confront fully the persisting sexual double standard or the historical imperative to control and restrain female sexuality. Yet libertinism always contained the possibility of female independence, if not equality. The indisputable evidence of this was the rising rate of single motherhood.

With the poor single mother, racism combined with growing hostility to the poor to support a serious assault on libertine sexuality, at least as linked to reproduction. The second flash point was a purer example of the alliance of libertinism and feminism. A statistically small but highly visible group of mature, self-supporting, and unmarried women began to have babies and raise them alone, threatening the linkage of reproduction, female monogamy, and male claims on women and children through marriage. Opposition to single motherhood emerged as the organizing axis of the virtue revival. Linked to positions against abortion and sex education, the virtue revival seeks to restore monogamous heterosexual marriage and to contain female sexuality within it.

On many fronts society hopes to discourage the poor from reproducing by

criticizing their sexual behaviors as irresponsible, and, by reducing or withholding welfare benefits for their children. Recent welfare and health and educational
policy reforms focus on getting poor men back into the role of economic provider and household head, discouraging sexuality among teenagers, and deterring births in economically dependent families.

Although the campaign against young, poor, single mothers recalls the eugenics movement, which categorized some human babies as "unfit" or at least undesirable, no one argues that the poverty and feeling of abandonment that often
accompanies fatherlessness is anything but terrible for children. In bargaining
terms, too, although specific circumstances may make dual parenting undesirable,
on its face, for a woman to bear alone the full financial and emotional cost of
childrearing seems like a bad sexual bargain.

Single parenthood is not so costly, however, when it takes place among the
educated elite, many of whom responded with angry indignation when
then-Vice President Dan Quayle criticized the single parenthood of Murphy
Brown, whose television character is a single, fortysomething, news broadcaster of
substantial means. Although Quayle explicitly based his criticism on the social
consequences of single parenthood among the poor, critics and later proponents
took Quayle to be a critic of any refusal to marry as a condition of sex and childbearing. In these terms, single parenthood threatens the institution of male dominance. Murphy Brown was having sex without dominance. If she could get away
with it, what reason would she (or any economically independent woman) have
to step into that yoke?

This interpretation of the patriarchal agenda of the virtue revival is buttressed
by the fact that Quayle was understood to be heavily influenced by William Kristol, his chief of staff, a man who is now an influential conservative political commentator. Kristol is the author of a lucid, but little noted essay arguing for the
necessary subordination of American women in marriage. In "Women's Liberation: The Relevance of Tocqueville," Kristol asked:

> Supposing women were liberated—what then? Is there no danger the leaders
> of the women's revolution will, like other revolutionaries, according to
> Tocqueville, go beyond what is reasonable and fail to secure happiness and vir-
> tue?

Although other factions of the virtue revival rely openly on religion to oppose
single motherhood and nonmarital sex as sins, and religion historically has been a
powerful force for confining heterosexual sex within marriage, Kristol apparently
realizes that invoking the deity in a secular state is a costly move. Like Tocqueville,
Kristol advises instead that Americans look to democratic virtue for guidance,
and specifically to Tocqueville's vision of the virtuous democratic republic for
"an understanding of women's place in post-revolutionary America—an understanding that accords with their true interests and with the interests of men and
society."

Tocqueville, Kristol says, would not approve of women's liberation or libertine sexual behavior, which Kristol describes as a social order in which the "character of men and women will and should become less distinct." Tocqueville would tell us that this unisex world is dangerous because women shape mores, and without their moral tutelage there is nothing to control the democratic, materialist quest for individual well-being: "Insofar as women's liberation liberates women's passion for material well-being side by side with men's, women will no longer shape the mores that can save Americans from the dangers to which the passion for well-being exposes them." Thus, Kristol advises, women must be taught "to grasp the following three points: the necessity of marriage, the importance of good morals, and the necessity of inequality within marriage."

Marriage revival is not by definition a regressive development for women. Okin's just and liberal relationship, for example, might mark a progressive move toward equality and flourishing within heterosexuality for women. Kristol is not, however, arguing for Okin's egalitarian marriage. He explicitly rejects any such image of the appropriate relationship between women and men. According to Kristol, male androgyny, even a mild form of androgyny, is dangerous to democracy. The just and caring men that Okin seeks will not be "sturdy and intractable," and thus will be unable to resist the "form of despotism that democratic nations need fear, the schoolmaster state." Kristol asks, with only faintly disguised contempt,

> Why do "caring" men deserve the epithet "feeble"—at least from a political point of view? Because caring men are not intractable, and it is male intractability that underlies the love of independence. That love blocks the road that equality opens up toward the terrible new form of servitude.

Kristol concludes that "[m]ale intractability, even irrational male aggressiveness, seems to be useful" to our democracy, in the same way as female submission is useful.

Given that women who share Okin's aspirations will not submit willingly to sturdy and intractable (not to mention irrational and aggressive) males, Kristol says that women must be educated to this submission. Women must be convinced that marriage is necessary because men are stronger and, being stronger, they are "likely to enjoy their liberation at the expense of women." Accordingly, women should recognize that they will be dominated anyway, and so marriage is in their self-interest. Kristol's evaluation of the impact of libertinism is a little raw, but not far from our own analysis. In light of men's advantage in the libertine world, they can extract a high price for their willingness to marry and restrict their rapaciousness. Kristol concludes from this that women must accept that "[t]he price [they] . . . pay for marriage and morality [is] submission to the husband within the family." Echoing Hobbes, Kristol asserts that every association must have a head, "and it seems natural, at least in the sense of necessary, that the man be the head."

Seen against this well-worked-out political theory, Murphy Brown's fictional pregnancy threatened Kristol and other cultural conservatives. Rather than educating women to the selfless and altruistic necessity for their subordination to men in marriage and sex, it gave them an example of freedom from such subordination. Buttressed by the market economy and the laws against physical violence, Murphy Brown could form a family without submission.

The focus on Murphy Brown also illuminates the sexual dominance payoff to men of the virtue revival. Not only would men regain the female asset each of them had been able to deploy in their competition with one another before women moved out of the private world, but a whole category of players (and thus a source of fear) would be removed from the realm of competition. Finally, the beautiful, successful, and intelligent Murphy Brown would indeed be a worthy object for the exercise of male dominance. In a recent radio essay, David Brooks, an editor of Kristol's conservative magazine, *The Weekly Standard*, explains why any man would want such a wife:

> A decade ago, I sat at a table with a group of famous male economists and philosophers. We were talking about whether it was better to marry a Democrat or a Republican. We all chose Democrat. If you marry a Republican woman, we felt, she'll end up with a helmet-headed hairdo, Mamie Eisenhower's wardrobe and she'll want to name your daughters Chastity and Temperance. That stereotype, which was never very fair, is blown away these days ... [Now Republican women] tend to be successful lawyers, economists, teachers and journalists.

Not only that, but they have learned their Tocquevillean lesson of the separate spheres. Although in 1996, Brooks does not talk about submission as frankly as Kristol did, he says Republican women are appealing marriage prospects because "[m]any of them have suspended their careers so they can stay at home with young children. . . . They use a modern sensibility to see the virtues in old-fashioned manners [where] [m]en and women can occupy different roles."

Quayle's speech elicited a storm of criticism from the libertine establishment. Not attuned to the full dimensions of Kristol's political theory, libertines simply focused on how such criticisms might limit their sex life, invoking as gospel the libertine assumptions of sexual skepticism, hedonism, and individualism. In a representative article, *New York Times* culture critic Jan Hoffman described Quayle as asserting that "only people married (to each other)—or animals on PBS—should have sex," allowing the absurdity of this notion to speak for itself.

The virtue revivalists have some good arguments against this blind fury. Kristol anticipated that a libertine relationship between players of unequal strength and social position would result in dominance anyway. If so, what greater political virtue can be claimed by libertinism over more repressive sexual orders, apart from more and better sex?

At this point, libertines could either grasp the nettle of inequality and give it palatable justification, or abandon an absolute position against regulation, construct a norm of a just and nonhierarchical heterosexuality, and collectively enforce it through, among other social technologies, the coercive power of law. Both developments are characteristic of contemporary political theory as Rawlsian libertinism has begun to weaken.

## THE FREE-FOR-ALL

The first move—to justify inequality—is the clearest alternative to the virtue revival and takes the form of sexual libertarianism. This reflects the break in theory between classical liberalism and the Rawlsian liberal-utilitarian blend. Having taken up the task of justifying existing inequality, sexual libertarians end up advocating tolerance of an almost unlimited potential inequality.

Harvard philosopher Robert Nozick provides the overall framework for the libertarian purification. Just as Rawls's untidy liberal theory overall framed the libertine sexual bargain of the 1970s, Nozick's powerful arguments against economic and political redistribution of the natural order justified the existence of unequal sexual relationships as the necessary price of freedom in the succeeding decades. Published in part as a response to Rawls's argument for economic redistribution, Nozick's 1974 *Anarchy, State and Utopia* became the intellectual template for the contemporary libertarian revival.

Nozick defends a minimalist state whose principal function is to prevent assault and murder. People begin with their natural fates. From that starting point, any consensual transactions and only consensual transactions are defensible. Nozick assumes that we can know the good, that the good is the individual exercise of an untrammeled will consistent with protection for one's material self, that people are naturally separate physical beings, and that a good politics is the absolute minimum of cooperation that individuals would agree to in light of their natural starting places.

Nozick's libertarianism is devoted to protecting the inequality that results from market transactions. Libertarians justify unequal market outcomes (such as the gender gap in wages) on the grounds that the consensual transactions of the market process are pure. If women are paid less, this means they start from a position of less market value. The sexual transaction by contrast involves differences grounded in physical nature. Although Nozick does not directly address sexuality, if physical nature is an ineluctable inequality, the libertarian must defend the inequality in the sexual bargains that stem from that unequal starting place or explain why the state should step in and enforce an unnatural equality.

The obvious comparison is to differences in physical strength. With respect to unequal strength, Nozick and most libertarians do support a redistributive and egalitarian structure in the form of the laws against violence, which assign a monopoly of force to the state. Nozick argues that government can monopolize deadly force between naturally unequal physical players because free individuals in the state of nature would have formed a series of protective associations to defend themselves against each other, culminating in the state's monopoly on force. For the libertarian, the basic criminal law thus bears the legitimating mark of the consent of each and every individual, even if it involves state coercion.

It is not clear, however, that the narrow libertarian prohibition on the use of physical force by private actors means that sexual violence as such is prohibited. Nozick's assumption of the inviolability of the autonomous individual might make rape immoral, but cooperating with others to prohibit rape violates the rapist's individuality.

To make rape illegal in the minimal state, sexual access must be analogized to life and freedom from pain, which are the interests that Nozick assumes will drive people to form the imaginary cooperative associations that justify the state. If people would not all agree to organize to protect themselves against rape, there is no consensual story to tell to justify the state, and the state's prohibition on rape overreaches.

Nor is rape law necessarily justified by the less individualist Hobbesian strain of libertarianism. Hobbes held that government legitimately monopolizes force because the state of nature is so nasty that even the strongest prefer government to the threat posed by conditions in the state of nature. Here, too, the application of the basic insight to the specific case of rape is contestable. In a world of radically unequal players, the stronger can rape without danger of being punished by the weaker. Why shouldn't stronger players motivated only by self-interest want to take advantage of their greater physical strength? Hobbes's prediction that this would produce anarchy is not necessarily true if the weaker are much weaker and can readily be identified by, say, gender characteristics. If neither retaliation nor anarchy is the price, neither Hobbes nor Nozick offers a convincing account of the reasons why self-interest would lead the stronger to restrain themselves from rape or any other one-sided coercion.

Lacking a compelling philosophical reason, the libertarian support for rape laws seems more a result of political expedience than conviction. Perhaps it is not surprising, then, that rape remains a severe problem under the libertine regime. Nor is it surprising that rape is common in those purely consensual social relationships most resembling the libertarian ideal. According to the most conservative data (that of the NORC researchers), 22.8 percent of adult women reported in 1992 that they had been forced by a man or men to do something sexually that they did not want to do. Most often the man who forced them was someone they knew well, were in love with, or were married to. Only 2.8 percent of men in the study said they had ever forced a woman into a sexual act.

If the libertarian argument for restraining sexual violence is shaky, nothing in the philosophy addresses the remaining physical inequalities between men and women associated with pregnancy and nursing. To the libertarian, natural disadvantages in personal resources (e.g., unequal intelligence, energy, beauty, or charm) create no basis for redistributions that would impair individual liberty.

Because of the natural disadvantages of pregnancy and nursing, women in a purified libertine order would be systematically disadvantaged in reaping the fruits of
sexual cooperation with men. To compensate, they would be pressed to enter
into contracts of inequality, just as William Kristol hopes they will.

To take the position that vulnerability to pregnancy is just the female's bad fortune is harsh and perhaps not palatable in a world of superficial equality norms.
Accordingly, politically savvy libertarians make ameliorative arguments based on
evolutionary biology in defense of inequalities in male-female sexual relationships.
Because human beings reproduce sexually, requiring both male and female genetic
material, there is a biological necessity for paired sexual opposites. From this natural fact, a school of political thought known as sociobiology justifies as biologically
innate a persistent pattern of gender hierarchy and a broad range of behaviors associated with human sexuality. According to the standard sociobiological script,
women inherit a weaker sex drive, can reproduce only a limited number of times
in a lifetime, but know that the offspring they bear are their genetic issue. Men, by
contrast, have an innately powerful sex drive, relatively unlimited power to inseminate many females during a lifetime, but have little assurance of their genetic connection to the offspring born to the women around them. These promiscuous
males and passive females must pursue different sexual and reproductive strategies
if each wishes to pass down genes to the next generation. Males must inseminate as
many females as possible, but cooperate in the support and rearing only of their
own offspring; females must be choosy, trading sexual access for support and cooperation from the males in childrearing.

The invisible hand of natural selection supports these gendered agendas by pre-
ferring dominant men with powerful sex drives who are both promiscuous and
jealous, and restrained, manipulative females who are able to withhold sex as a bargaining strategy. It is from the sexual bargaining between these pairs, the story goes,
that the persistent cultural pattern of male domination and female subordination
arises in all its iterations. In the course of human evolution males raped, competed
with other males, and sought to control female sexuality through cultural institutions such as monogamy, the double standard, marriage, jealousy, sequestration, and
repression of female carnality. Females mated with males under these conditions to
obtain protection and food during childbirth and nursing. Females who pursued
this strategy survived to reproduce, and thus the genetic inclination to engage in
such arrangements gradually concentrated in the female population through the
generations. By this evolutionary story, what appears to political thinkers to be the
desperate grasping of systematically disempowered players is transformed into the
natural preference of the human female for a sexuality organized around relations
of dominance and submission. To criticize or attempt to reshape these sexual arrangements thwarts natural desires and is doomed to fail as contrary to human nature and biological imperative.

It is political thinkers more than scientists who take the evolutionary account to describe not just the human condition, but human well-being. To criticize or attempt to reshape the innate harmony of gender-unequal sex thwarts natural desires and is doomed to fail as contrary to human nature and biological imperative. Even among political thinkers, however, some, like legal economist Judge Richard Posner, depart from the "just-so" quality of the sociobiological account. Posner describes the evolved sexual strategies of men and women in such a way that conflict seems unavoidable. Posner's males desire the most offspring with the least responsibility and fidelity, but the females desire the most commitment to their limited offspring. In addition to painting a picture of competing ends, Posner's respect for human rationality leads him to acknowledge that females are capable of strategic thinking to advance their different sexual and reproductive agenda.

All these theories ignore the obvious problem that even if the sociobiological description of human desire and psychology were true, natural realities long have been taken as the starting and not the stopping place of moral theory. Moralists have not stopped trying to explain why murder is bad, nor have states and societies ceased trying to use communal institutions to discourage the act, because people are inclined by nature to kill one another. Any rich concept of human "nature" allows us to criticize physical coercion and sexual dominance, and seek to extirpate it. Still, despite its stunted vision of human possibility, sociobiology is more palatable than the bald libertarian assertion that "might makes right," and it remains the most common metaphysical argument for the gender hierarchy perpetuated by the libertine state.

Finally, Rawlsian liberals did not just relinquish the sexual field to the virtue theorists and the libertarians. Liberals are struggling to adapt the insights of feminism to find an adequate liberal approach to private relations of sex and family. A key issue has been the unyielding defense by many liberals of violent and degrading pornography. In a recent article, "John Stuart Mill and the Harm of Pornography," liberal philosopher David Dyzenhaus argues for separating the values of liberalism as a transhistorical theory from the historical assumptions that drive modern liberals to defend pornography. Dyzenhaus's goal is to ally liberalism with the feminist critique of pornography. Beginning with Mill's liberal classic, *On Liberty*, Dyzenhaus notes that Mill recognized the harms from private as well as public oppression. Indeed, Dyzenhaus points out, Mill introduces *On Liberty* as concerned with "the nature and limits of the power which can be legitimately exercised *by society*" (emphasis in Dyzenhaus), and he traces a concern with private oppression running throughout Mill's essay. "Social tyranny," Mill tells us, is "more formidable than many kinds of political oppression, since, though not usually upheld by such extreme penalties, it leaves fewer means of escape, penetrating much more deeply into the details of life, and enslaving the soul itself." Pornography (and, one may project, other consensual but exploitative sexual arrangements), Dyzenhaus continues, operates in this fashion by constructing a vision of sexuality inextricably intertwined with dominance, such that people cannot even imagine true sexual autonomy.

Lost autonomy is a harm that liberals can understand. Building on Mill's recognition of the harms of private oppression, Dyzenhaus observes that Mill accepted government restraint of individuals when they seek to harm important interests of fellow citizens. If citizens must be restrained, Mill actually preferred public regulation to private regulation, because, "while penalties attached to political oppression are extreme, the oppression itself is overt and thus transparent to the oppressed." According to this reading of liberalism, Dyzenhaus argues, restraint of government is not an end in itself but simply a means to be evaluated according to the core values of the philosophy, such as autonomy. This undermines the libertarian claim for the political value of the minimal state. Dyzenhaus thus separates liberalism from libertarianism, and with it sexual libertinism, preserving liberalism as a possible source of insight into a new paradigm for sexual governance after libertinism. A variation of the goal-directed analysis of pornography has come from moderate legal scholars who contend that the First Amendment is intended only to protect speech necessary for democratic self-governance.

Dyzenhaus does not represent the mainstream liberal position, which is better represented by philosopher Ronald Dworkin, who argues that censorship, even of pornography, reflects an unacceptable disrespect for the autonomy of the individual. In Dworkin's domain, it is respect rather than sex that justifies political tolerance of pornography. For American Civil Liberties Union president Nadine Strossen, pornography is good because sex is good, and she sprinkles her defense from constitutional doctrine and abstract principles of free expression with tales of visits to live sex shows. In recent work, Thomas Nagel blends the two arguments, contending that censorship of pornography is wrong all out of proportion to the actual harm it does. Any censorship expresses an unacceptable vision of the way in which humans can be treated, and any effort to censor pornography is particularly disrespectful because it is so difficult to know anything about the sexuality of others. "[P]eople cannot understand one another's inner lives by consulting their own emotional reactions to what other people do." Nagel's argument from skepticism is particularly disappointing, because his earlier essay, "Sexual Perversion," was so central to the contemporary effort to describe and understand sex rather than to throw up one's hands in skeptical helplessness.

Recently, philosopher Joshua Cohen has made a claim for sexual freedom even more ambitious than Strossen's. Cohen addresses pornography as part of a defense of a broad doctrine of free speech, but he acknowledge the power of the moderates' claim that the political and constitutional protections of speech should not extend beyond that necessary to protect the degree of political debate essential to a self-governing people. Yet Cohen argues that pornography should be protected from regulation because sexual expression amounts to a moral compulsion, in a category with bearing witness in religion or creating an artistic thing of beauty. After the election of 1996, Ronald Dworkin struggled to defend pornography even as he advocated restraint of citizen expenditures for political speech in the name of campaign finance reform, creating pressure for a unique category for sexual speech.Unlike Dworkin, Cohen doesn't hide sex behind the shield of speech; he protects speech by asserting the value of sex. Cohen's erection of sex over politics enables him to abandon his First Amendment commitments in areas such as campaign funding (where he, too, supports government regulation), whereas Dworkin is harder pressed to reconcile his acceptance of regulation of political speech with his support of unfettered sexual expression as an expression of a generalized respect. In this liberal defense of libertinism, Dworkin's "sophisticated" defense of free speech collapses into Cohen's elevation of the hedonistic value of pornographic excitement. In response to the allegations of sexual misconduct by a married President in 1998, much popular commentary has taken a similar line, arguing that sex is singular. Accordingly, commentators insist that to make sexual misconduct part of a political judgment is illegitimate.

Pornography matters from a bargaining standpoint because, like workplace sexual harassment, pornography is ideologically directed toward disempowering the weaker player. Cohen finesses the issue, invoking incoherent arguments from female sex radicals that pornography allows for "rethinking subversive possibilities for sexuality and identity within the terms of power itself." Nagel, however, is honorably explicit about the price in sexual power that tolerance for pornography and sexual harassment extract:

> I believe that it is a very deep and essentially inevitable result of the longstanding inferior social and economic and interpersonal status of women in our culture, as in every other, that simply *being a woman* is instinctively felt to be a worse thing than being a man . . . But I think the wish to improve it by the device of interfering with the sexual fantasy life and sexual expression of heterosexual men, so long as they do not directly harm specific women, is unwise and morally obtuse.

Similarly, regarding sexual harassment, Nagel's position is that the sexual desires of heterosexual men are simply more important than the harm they cause:

> The toleration of sexual feelings should include a certain margin of freedom for their expression, even if it sometimes gives offense, and even though it will often impose the unpleasant task of rejection on its target.

Insofar as there is an unavoidable minimum of cost to the sexual transaction, the burden is properly placed on the weaker player.

The sexual scandal surrounding the President ignited a previously marginal movement to repeal the sexual harassment aspects of the Civil Rights Act. Libertine theorists, including legal commentator Jeffrey Rosen of the formerly liberal, now "post-ideological" magazine, *The New Republic*, had been trying for years to create a groundswell for repeal or narrowed definitions of sexual harassment in law. Thwarted by a unanimous Supreme Court application of the law in the most recent sexual harassment cases, Rosen, and *New Yorker* magazine legal analyst Jeffrey Toobin reopened the subject of repeal as part of a perceived social revulsion against punishing a popular President for sexual misconduct. Toobin was particularly exercised over Yale University's prohibition of faculty-student sex, enacted in the aftermath of an incident involving a 17-year old freshman failing mathematics and the 31-year old math teacher she sought out for help.

As against these efforts to justify sexual inequality as women's fate (whether political or evolutionary), virtue ethicists and their improbable allies, the bargaining theorists, take another road. Virtue ethicists seek to construct a theory of sexuality that aspires beyond nature as imperfectly revealed by sociobiology or libertarianism, and beyond hierarchical religious tradition as imperfectly disguised by the Tocquevillean revival. Bargaining theorists are figuring out how to get there. Our version of such a theory is the subject of the two following and final chapters.

## NOTES

See Catharine A. MacKinnon, "Feminism, Marxism, Method and the State: An Agenda for Theory," *Signs: Journal of Women in Culture and Society* 7 (1982): 515; Catharine A. MacKinnon, "Feminism, Marxism and the State: Toward Feminist Jurisprudence," *Signs: Journal of Women in Culture and Society* 8 (1983): 635.

On the origins of the modern feminist movement in the civil rights movement and the new left, see generally Sara M. Evans, *Personal Politics: The Roots of Women's Liberation in the Civil Rights Movement and the New Left* (New York: Alfred Knopf, 1979).

A utilitarian could accommodate MacKinnon's critique of hedonism by conceding that for highly developed creatures like human beings, the pain of political submission outweighs sexual pleasure grounded in domination and submission, or that pleasure falsely experienced is not valuable. But refined hedonism is not the version embraced by sexual libertines. An understanding of personhood that is principally physical cannot place much value on nonphysical goods such as dignity, or even on an accurate perception of the political world in true consciousness.

Joan Nestle, "My Mother Liked to Fuck," in *Powers of Desire: The Politics of Sexuality*, ed. Ann Snitow, Christine Stansell, and Sharon Thompson (New York: Monthly Review Press, 1983), 468.

John Rawls does recognize the reality of sexed bodies and sexual reproduction in a few passages about the family. See Rawls, *A Theory of Justice* (Cambridge, Mass.: Belknap Press of Harvard Univ. Press, 1971), 7, 463, 490.

The Supreme Court's decisions that pregnancy discrimination is not sex discrimination are *Geduldig v. Aiello*, 417 U.S. 484 (1974), and *General Electric v. Gilbert*, 429 U.S. 125 (1976). Congress overturned these cases in enacting the Pregnancy Discrimination Act, Pub. L. No. 95-555, 92 Stat. 2076 (1978).

Lenore J. Weitzman, *The Divorce Revolution: The Unexpected Social and Economic Consequences of Divorce for Women and Children in America* (New York: Free Press, 1985); Susan Moller Okin, *Justice, Gender and the Family* (New York: Basic Books, 1989).

Data on the current divorce rate is reported in U.S. Bureau of the Census, *Head Count: The Changing American Household*, Washington, D.C. (1996).

On the family as a "school for injustice," see Okin, *Justice, Gender and The Family*, 17-23. On the relationship between power in the family and labor market position, see

Rhona Mahoney, *Kidding Ourselves: Babies, Breadwinning, and Bargaining Power* (New York: Basic Books, 1995). On the failure of women in college to pursue traditionally high-paid fields of study, such as science and engineering, see Dorothy C. Holland and Margaret A. Eisenhart, *Educated in Romance: Women, Achievement, and College Culture* (Chicago: Univ. of Chicago Press, 1990):

> When the women in our ethnographic sample began their college careers, they had reputa-
> tions as good students, and approximately half said they would major in a math-or sci-
> ence-related field. All stated that they expected to pursue a career after graduating from
> college . . . [L]ess than a third of these bright and privileged women met their own expec-
> tations for their future. By the time they left college, they had arrived at practices—to put
> the outcome in terms of the critical educational and feminist literature—that are key to
> sustaining women's subordinate positions in society. Most had ended up with intense in-
> volvements in heterosexual romantic relationships, marginalized career identities and infe-
> rior preparation for their likely roles as future breadwinners.[8]

On tax policy and its effects on women's status, see generally Edward J. McCaffery, *Taxing Women* (Chicago: Univ. of Chicago Press, 1996).

All liberal thinkers in the Anglo-American tradition, from Tocqueville to Mill, argue that the family is crucial to the development of morality in citizens, implicitly resisting Plato's argument for abolishing the family. These earlier philosophers, however, ac-cepted the gender hierarchy of the traditional family in its relationships and practices, even if, after the Enlightenment, they sought to defend it not as a patriarchy, but as a community built on altruism and complementarity (i.e., consent).

On the no-fault divorce reform, see Herma Hill Kay, "An Appraisal of California's No-Fault Divorce Law," *California Law Review* 75 (1987): 291; Herma Hill Kay, "Equal-ity and Difference: A Perspective on No-Fault Divorce and Its Aftermath," *Univ. of Cincinnati Law Review* 56 (1987): 1.

Lenore Weitzman's data on the gender gap in income after divorce has been revised. Better research is Greg J. Duncan and Saul D. Hoffman, "A Reconsideration of the Economic Consequences of Marital Dissolution," *Demography* 4 (Nov. 1985): 485-97 (reporting first years after divorce), and Annemette Sorenson, "Estimating the Eco-nomic Consequences of Separation and Divorce: A Cautionary Tale from the United States," in *Economic Consequences of Divorce: The International Perspective*, ed. Lenore J. Weitzman and Mavis Maclean (New York: Oxford Univ. Press, 1992), 263 (longer-term results).

Although we argue that men are exiting from even illiberal marriages, statistics show that wives file for divorce more often than husbands. See Frank F. Furstenberg, Jr., and Andrew J. Cherlin, *Divided Families: What Happens to Children When Parents Part* (Cam-bridge, Mass.: Harvard Univ. Press, 1991), 22. Lenore Weitzman found similar patterns; Weitzman, "Child Custody Awards: Legal Standards and Empirical Patterns for Child Custody After Divorce, Support and Visitation," *Univ. of Calif. at Davis Law Review* 12 (1979): 473, 516, n.122. Weitzman and other commentators read these numbers as indi-cating that women are the innocent parties in marriages destroyed by infidelity or abuse. Others, like Gay C. Kitson and Marvin B. Sussman, believe that women have less hope for the survival of the marriage. Kitson and Sussman, "Marital Complaints, Demographic Characteristics, and Symptoms of Mental Distress in Divorce," *Journal of Marriage and Family* (Feb. 1982): 87. In any event, although divorce reformers antici-pated that greater sexual equality would liberate some women to end marriages, they failed to anticipate that men, too, would be liberated by the new regime, and that men's liberty would be an important cause in women's and children's impoverishment.

Martha Fineman argues that women's economic hardship after divorce is caused by gender-neutral division of marital property and not by no-fault divorce rules. See Mar-tha Albertson Fineman, *The Illusion of Equality: The Rhetoric and Reality of Divorce Reform*

(Chicago: Univ. of Chicago Press, 1991), 32-34. Marsha Garrison has shown that in making the discretionary decision on an "equitable" division of marital property, judges value prior economic contributions more than any other factor, a pattern that strongly favors men. See Garrison, "How Do Judges Decide Divorce Cases? An Empirical Analysis of Discretionary Decision Making," *North Carolina Law Review* 74 (1996): 401, 455-57.

An example of the current criticism of the consequences of libertinism, especially for children, is Barbara Dafoe Whitehead, "Dan Quayle Was Right," *Atlantic Monthly,* April 1993, p. 47.

On the use of claims of sexual privacy to bar legal remedy for sexual wrongdoing, see generally Jane E. Larson, "Women Understand So Little, They Call My Good Nature 'Deceit'": A Feminist Rethinking of Seduction," *Columbia Law Review* 93 (1993): 374; Martha Chamallas, "Consent, Equality, and the Legal Control of Sexual Conduct," *Southern Calif. Law Review* 61 (1988): 777.

For a discussion of Freud and the vaginal orgasm, see Barbara Ehrenreich, Elizabeth Hess, and Gloria Jacobs, *Re-Making Love: The Feminization of Sex* 52 (Garden City, N.Y.: Anchor Press/Doubleday, 1986), 52. An example of the popularized psychoanalytic sexual advice of the mid-century is Hendrik M. Ruitenbeek, ed., *Psychoanalysis and Female Sexuality* (New Haven: College and Univ. Press, 1966), 11-12. On female dysfunction in the 1950s, see Ehrenreich et al., *Re-Making Love*, 51-52.

On Masters and Johnson's rediscovery of the clitoral orgasm, see William A. Masters and Virginia E. Johnson, *Human Sexual Response* (Boston: Little, Brown, 1966). The debunking of the myth of the vaginal orgasm should not have been news in 1966. Alfred Kinsey had concluded in 1953 that "in spite of the widespread and oft-repeated emphasis on the supposed differences between female and male sexuality, we fail to find any anatomic or physiological basis for such differences." Alfred C. Kinsey et al., *Sexual Behavior in the Human Female* (Philadelphia: Saunders, 1953), 641. On the effects of Masters and Johnson's findings on popular culture, see Ehrenreich et al., *Re-Making Love*, 69, 72-73.

On the heterosexual "oral sex wars," see ibid., 82. The *Redbook* survey is reported at Robert J. Levin and Amy Levin, "Sexual Pleasure: The Surprising Preferences of 100,000 Women," *Redbook*, Sept. 1975. The *Hite Report* is published as Shere Hite, *The Hite Report* (New York: Macmillian, 1976). For Hite's political analysis of women's lack of orgasm through cunnilingus, see 233.

Popular sex advisors of the libertine era included J., *The Sensuous Woman* (New York: Dell, 1969); Alex Comfort, *The Joy of Sex* (New York: Simon and Schuster, 1972); Hite, *The Hite Report*; Nancy Friday, *My Secret Garden* (New York: Pocket Books, 1974); Lonnie Garfield Barbach, *For Yourself* (New York: Anchor Press/Doubleday, 1976). As an educator on fellatio, the film *Deep Throat* (Vanguard Film Productions, 1972) was a cultural phenomenon.

The definitive survey of sex practices and values in the 1990s is Edward O. Laumann, John H. Gagnon, Robert T. Michael, and Stuart Michaels, *The Social Organization of Sexuality: Sexual Practices in the United States* (Chicago: Univ. of Chicago Press, 1994) (conducted by the National Opinion Research Center (NORC) at the University of Chicago). For data cited on heterosexual practice, see 97-100; on lying about orgasm, 115. In relying on a random sample (and not volunteers), the NORC study may be more reliable than the Kinsey research. Both studies, however, used interviewing to gather data, raising questions about whether people are truthful about their sexual histories, desires, or views when face-to-face with a researcher.

On the size of the pornography industry, see a 1997 *U.S. News and World Report Special Report*, Feb. 10, 1997. The report revealed that Americans in 1996 spent more than $8 billion on hard-core videos, peep shows, live sex acts, adult cable programming, sexual devices, computer porn, and sex magazines (44).

On the sexual harassment cause of action, see Catharine A. MacKinnon, *Sexual Harassment of Working Women: A Case of Sex Discrimination* (New Haven: Yale Univ. Press, 1978). On the antipornography ordinance, see Andrea Dworkin and Catharine A. MacKinnon, *Pornography and Civil Rights: A New Day for Women's Equality* (Minneapolis: Organizing Against Pornography, 1988); Paul Brest and Ann Vandenberg, "Politics, Feminism and the Constitution: The Anti-Pornography Movement in Minneapolis," *Stanford Law Review* 39 (1987): 607. For the theoretical work of MacKinnon's collaborator, Andrea Dworkin, on pornography, see Andrea Dworkin, *Pornography: Men Possessing Women* (New York: Perigee Books, 1981).

Larry Flynt, publisher of Hustler magazine, is glamorized as a political hero in *The People v. Larry Flynt* (Columbia Pictures, 1996).

The U.S. Supreme Court recognized the sexual harassment cause of action under Title VII in *Meritor v. Vinson*, 477 U.S. 57 (1986). See also Title VII, 42 U.S.C. sec. 20000e-2(a)(1) (1994), and the Equal Employment Opportunity Commission guidelines on sexual harassment at 29 C.F.R. sec. 1604.11(b) (1985). Interestingly, however, sexual harassment on the street—another public venue—is not unlawful. But see Cynthia Grant Bowman, "Street Harassment and the Informal Ghettoization of Women," *Harvard Law Review* 106 (1993): 517. As an example of the resistance to legal regulation of workplace sexual harassment, see Lloyd R. Cohen, "Sexual Harassment and the Law," *Society* (May/June 1991): 8-13.

Among the liberal legal scholars arguing for a more nuanced position on the constitutional meaning and social price of pornography, see Fred Schauer, *Free Speech: A Philosophical Inquiry* (Cambridge: Cambridge Univ. Press, 1982); Cass Sunstein, "Pornography and the First Amendment," *Duke Law Journal* (1986): 606. The Communications Decency Act, a law to limit access to pornography on the Internet, did pass the Congress, only to be struck down as unconstitutional by the U.S. Supreme Court. See *Reno v. American Civil Liberties Union*, 65 U.S. Law Week 4715 (June 26, 1997), striking down the Communications Act of 1934, secs. 223 (a, d), as amended 47 U.S.C. sec. 223 (a, d).

Concerning changes in attitudes and behavior among heterosexuals in response to HIV/AIDS, see ibid., 432-37; on the emotional and cultural effects of HIV/AIDS for heterosexuals, see generally Katie Roiphe, *Last Night in Paradise* (New York: Little, Brown, 1997).

Details from the NORC study on the moderation of American heterosexual practices are from Laumann et al., *Social Organization of Sexuality*, 86-93, 102-7, 114, 203, 214-19.

On racial readings of the rhetoric against single motherhood, see generally Rickie Solinger, *Wake Up Little Susie: Single Pregnancy and Race Before Roe v. Wade* (New York: Routledge, 1992), on the enduring differences in public policy response to black and white teenage pregnancy, beginning in the 1920s and continuing through the present.

William Kristol's reading of Tocqueville and the modern women's movement is William Kristol, "Women's Liberation: The Relevance of Tocqueville," in *Interpreting Tocqueville's Democracy in America*, ed. Ken Masugi (Savage, Md.: Rowman and Littlefield, 1991), 480; on the risks of modern feminists disregarding the demands of democracy, see 480-81, 489, 491; on the dangers of androgyny, 485; on male intractability and the risks of the schoolmaster state, 485; on the necessity of inequality in marriage, 492-93.

David Brooks on Republicans versus Democrats as marriage prospects is found at National Public Radio, "All Things Considered," June 19, 1996, Transcript No. 2249-7.

Jan Hoffman's reading of Dan Quayle on Murphy Brown is found at Jan Hoffman, "Television, TV Shouts 'Baby' (and Barely Whispers 'Abortion')," New York Times, May 31, 1992, sec. 2, p.1.

Robert Nozick, Anarchy, State and Utopia (New York: Basic Books, 1974), supports a minimal or "night watchman" state whose narrow purposes include a monopoly on force—which, presumably, includes a prohibition against at least forcible rape. Nozick's argument against redistribution is found at ibid., 160, 168, 170.

The modern data on incidence of rape is reported at Laumann et al., Social Organization of Sexuality, 335, 335-39.

The standard sociobiological argument on sexual difference is authoritatively stated in Donald Symons, The Evolution of Human Sexuality (New York: Oxford University Press, 1979). Sociobiology rests on the highly contested premise that observation of nonhuman animal behavior (particularly primate behavior) provides direct insight into human nature, and that human social institutions can be traced back to biological bases. See Edward O. Wilson, Sociobiology: The New Synthesis (Cambridge, Mass.: Belknap Press of Harvard Univ. Press, 1975), 2 ("Sociobiology is defined as the systematic study of the biological basis of all social behavior"). Much of sociobiology rests on observation of animals, particularly primates, whose behavior is then analogized to the human environment. The most detailed and influential critique of sociobiology as bad science is by philosopher of science Philip Kitcher, Vaulting Ambition: Sociobiology and the Quest for Human Nature (Cambridge: MIT Press, 1984).

In the past decade, primatologists have disproved the sociobiological story of passive females and promiscuous males as having been based on evidence gathered using distorted observation methods. The revelation of bias and bad science in early primate studies has "revolutionized the entire field of evolutionary biology and the study of the evolution of behavior." Jane Lancaster, Introduction to Female Primates: Studies by Women Primatologists, ed. Meredith F. Small (New York: A. R. Liss, 1984), 4. On primate field studies showing a range of female behaviors not predicted by the standard sociobiological account, see, e.g., Sarah Blaffer Hrdy, The Woman Who Never Evolved (Cambridge, Mass.: Harvard Univ. Press, 1981), 59-130; Barbara B. Smuts, Sex and Friendship in Baboons (New York: Aldine, 1985), 81-122, 235-60; Sarah Blaffer Hrdy, "Female Reproductive Strategies," in Small, ed., Female Primates, 104; Barbara B. Smuts, "Sexual Competition and Mate Choice," in Primate Societies, ed. Barbara H. Smuts, Dorothy L. Cheney, Robert M. Seyfarth, Richard W. Wrangham, and Thomas T. Struhsaker (Chicago: Univ. of Chicago Press, 1986), 385, 392-99; Meredith F. Small, Female Choices: Sexual Behavior of Female Primates (Ithaca: Cornell Univ. Press, 1993).

Richard A. Posner's use of sociobiology is found in Sex and Reason (Cambridge, Mass.: Harvard Univ. Press, 1992).

David Dyzenhaus, "John Stuart Mill and the Harm of Pornography," Ethics 102 (April 1992): 534.

Compare Dworkin on pornography, Ronald Dworkin, "Liberty and Pornography," in The Best American Essays, 1992, ed. Susan Sontag (Boston: Houghton Mifflin, 1992), with Dworkin, "The Curse of American Politics," New York Review of Books, Oct. 17, 1996. Nadine Strossen's defense of pornography is published as Defending Pornography: Free Speech, Sex, and the Fight for Women's Rights (New York: Scribner, 1995).

Thomas Nagel's argument against censorship is published as "Personal Rights and Public Space," *Philosophy and Public Affairs* 24 (1995): 83. The "people cannot understand one another" quote is on p. 102.

Joshua Cohen's defense of pornography is published as "Freedom, Equality, Pornography," in *Justice and Injustice in Laward Legal Theory*, ed. Austin Sarat (Ann Arbor: University of Michigan Press, 1996), 129.

On renewed arguments to repeal or restrict the sexual harassment cause of action, see Jeffrey Rosen, "When Reckless Laws Team Up," *New York Times*, Jan. 25, 1998; Jeffrey Toobin, "The Trouble With Sex," *New Yorker*, Feb. 9, 1998.

# PART FOUR

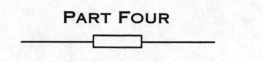

# HARD BARGAINS

## 12

## THE RULES OF THE GAME

Unsolved problems of a decaying paradigm often illuminate the way to the new. We argued in Chapter 11 that none of the contenders to replace the libertine regime satisfies the claims to autonomy and equality for at least half of the population. The contenders see deeply into the failings of the present order, yet remain selectively blind to defects in their own positions. Virtue revivalists see the perils of freedom but not the injustice of sexual dominance and subordination. Libertarians ignore the effects of unequal initial positions within their model of private ordering and unfettered freedom. Sociobiologists offer a disrespectful vision of sexual harmony that calls for females to be natural slaves. Liberals maintain an unstable and incoherent compromise of libertinism in private and statism in public.

Feminism has not produced a fully adequate alternative, either. The feminist critique, now more than 150 years old, spotlights the centrality of sexuality to women's equality claims. But the movement has not translated this insight into a consistent sexual position, leaving women in the double bind of identifying as sexually male or acceding to an outdated protectionism. Faced with the issues of pornography and prostitution, for example, feminists divide right down the middle. On other issues, the majority of feminists lean libertine in some cases, as in opposing the punishment of pregnant women for fetal alcohol damage, and protectionist in others, as in supporting laws for registering sex offenders upon release from prison.

The feminist failure to translate its critique of libertinism into a coherent sexual politics is not surprising. The classical liberalism of Elizabeth Cady Stanton and John Stuart Mill was the intellectual wellspring of Anglo-American feminism. Yet the purest expression of classical liberalism is a libertine sexual politics, with all its blindness to the natural and social inequalities that feminism seeks to overcome. Marxism, which radical and socialist feminists also claim as an intellectual antecedent, subsumes sexual politics to class politics: Marx treated the sexual relationship as natural, an exception to his criticism of naturalizing relationships of power generally; Engels traced the origins of sexual inequality to male control of private property, assuming, apparently, that sexual oppression is not a problem for the property-less proletariat.

Although feminists criticize these aspects of liberal and Marxist political thought, they have not answered the foundational questions of human nature, knowledge, and the good essential to a fully worked-out sexual philosophy of their own. Catharine MacKinnon defends a purely critical stance as an adequate feminist sexual policy and practice:

> [T]o consider "no more rape" as only a negative, no more than an absence, shows a real failure of imagination. Why does "out now" contain a sufficiently positive vision of the future for Vietnam and Nicaragua but not for women?

This critical "no more" position states an agenda of nondomination, and feminism has steadily pressed that agenda into the sexual realm with profoundly positive gains for women's well-being. Lacking a positive theory of human sexual well-being, however, feminists cannot always explain how a nondomination standard would apply to a specific and contested issue. Unsatisfied with the "out now" program, for example, people repeatedly press MacKinnon in her public appearances to answer specific questions such as whether there can be nondominating heterosexual intercourse in a society of gender inequality, or whether the exchange of money in the sex industry ameliorates or enlarges the dominance element in the commercial sexual exchange. In sum, feminism addresses women's lives but has not produced either its own sexual philosophy or a concrete political strategy. None of the other candidates on the table—leftover liberalism, libertarianism, virtue revival, or sociobiology—meet the basic standards of personhood if both women and men are taken into account.

As libertinism decays, we propose a new paradigm of sexual regulation. In Chapter 2, we set out our tentative theoretical assumptions for this work. The legal and philosophical history set out in Chapters 3–11 highlighted the forms of sexual exchange and the forces of society and nature that such a paradigm must address. In this chapter, we revisit our initial assumptions against the background of that history and flesh them out as the foundation for our proposal. In Chapter 13 we make detailed proposals for a new legal approach to the foundational issues of heterosexual regulation: rape, prostitution, adultery, and fornication.

## THE BARGAINING APPROACH TO SEXUAL REGULATION

### An Imperfect Theory

Ours is not a perfectly consistent or universally applicable sexual theory. Given the variety in human sexual personhood, practices, and desires, no sexual theory in history has achieved such universality and perfection. Sex is simply too fluid for perfect theory.

This disclaimer is necessary because some contemporary thinkers argue against tolerance of any imperfection in political sexual theory. In light of sexual variety, they claim, an imperfect scheme might mistakenly produce one undesirable instance of sexual repression. Given that any political theory, like any legal regime, occasionally generates a wrong result, this zero tolerance standard must be defended. Such hypervigilance against repression rests on the classical liberal belief that the willing, self-creating aspects of personhood matter more than the communally responsive or virtuously self-sacrificing aspects of the person. Among the possibilities of liberal freedom, moreover, they contend that sexual freedom is central to human self-creation and definition, more important than democratic politics or communal responsibility.

We cannot satisfy the zero tolerance standard and promise that no good sexual encounter will ever be prohibited or deterred by our proposals. Nor can we be confident that if our proposals are adopted, police and prosecutors, judges and juries, lawmakers and scholars will respect our underlying commitments in all instances. What we do know with perfect confidence is that an argument against theory on the grounds that it is imperfect allows the nontheorist to ignore the actual consequences of his or her perfectionism for actual lives. This argument of intolerable mistakes makes it impossible for there to be any law at all. Such so-called intellectual rigor amounts to no more than a green light for the sexual aspirations of the stronger player.

### A Sexual Theory That Has Learned the Historical Lessons of Knowledge, Personhood, and Politics.

Our premises are that knowledge, including knowledge about sex, is possible; that sexual personhood is a mix of the physical, the mental, and the cultural; that male-female sex is political; and that much of sexual politics is worked out in discrete instances of one-on-one bargaining outside the public eye. Our inquiry into history has ratified these assumptions, and the accumulation of human experience recorded there answers some of the questions that our assumptions allow us to ask: What do we know about sex? What kind of sexual people are we? What does political and moral analysis require of sexual governance? And, what kinds of governance will be effective given the nature of sexual exchange?

### What we know

Every scheme of sexual regulation known to history, even the most avowedly skeptical, has rested on some theory of the sexual good. All of the ancient schemes assumed a version of the sexual good: stable reproduction of the patriarchal family in Greek and Jewish law; control over the self and dominance of female subjects in accordance with the natural order in Aristotle; transcendence of the sexual body as a liberation from worldly claims among early Christians. Plato explored the erotic as an avenue to the contemplation of the pure form of the good in the *Symposium*. In the *Republic*, he linked the sexual good to the political good, recommending group sex and anonymous parentage to divert loyalty from the family to the polis.

Aquinas argued that reproduction is the good end of sex, which became Roman Catholic doctrine. The birth of modernity in liberal political theory and

Protestant religion uncoupled the sexual good from reproduction. Liberalism found full sexual expression only in the individualism of the libertine twentieth century, when it became technologically possible to sidestep the natural reproductive consequences of male-female sex. But Protestantism immediately and profoundly changed European sexual thought, allowing conjugal sex as a Christian sexual good, and leading to the idealization of companionate sex in the bourgeois marriage.

English colonists in America transplanted this Protestant ideal of conjugal sexuality as well as remnants of patriarchal feudalism, a mixture that would frame the legal regulation of sex in America until the middle of the nineteenth century. The racialized sexual regimes of the slaveholding colonies and states rested on an ultimately failed effort to renew the ancient ideal of sexual flourishing for a patriarchal elite. Considering the new nation in its post-revolutionary transition, Tocqueville gave conjugal sex a secular justification as the civilizing force that would bring order to the unruly males of the democratic experiment. This ideal of sexual virtue in a democratic republic created the distinctive culture of virtue republican America.

Both the social purity and free love movements of nineteenth-century England and America invoked the romantic and idealistic vision of the sexual good latent in Protestantism and the Enlightenment. Free lovers saw sex as the path to earthly delight and self-actualization. Social purists had no less lofty an ideal of the sexual good, imagining an end to sexual pain and the creation of true sexual community between women and men. Free love sought to pursue eroticism wherever it could be found, so that marriage no longer was necessary for sexual access. Social purity sought to repress painful sex wherever it might be found, meaning that marriage was not sufficient for sexual access. In both ideals, sex with dignity and mutual pleasure was the goal for the male-female union.

The twentieth-century hope for a sexual regime that could stand free of any moral vision of the good, made manifest in the proposals of the Model Penal Code, is a long-delayed product of the classical liberal commitment to tolerance. Yet if the ideology of libertinism insisted that particular sexual arrangements be immune to moral judgment, the regulatory philosophy ultimately rested on the premise of hedonistic pleasure. So important was the good of physical pleasure in sex that the regime sacrificed other goals such as bodily security, social equality, and protection of the young.

In sum, however much they differed, each historical regime understood itself as advancing an idea of the sexual good. Our proposals, too, rest on a particular vision of the sexual good.

### What it means to be a person

History supports a pluralistic concept of political and sexual personhood. Ancient pagan cultures honored people for their capacity to recognize the good and to live a life that fully used their capacities. The ancients especially honored people's natural sociability and their capacity for reason. Philosophers such as Aristotle produced a list of human virtues, like courage, loyalty, and practical wisdom, that expressed those capacities.

Classical liberal understandings of human beings as mainly material creatures destabilized this ancient vision of virtue. However, no satisfactory moral theory since ancient times has been able to do without some version of reason and sociability as definitional of what it means to be a person. Even John Rawls rests his modern theory on the two assumptions that people are "rational" in that they use their intelligence to realize their ends, and "reasonable" in that they desire to live cooperatively with others on terms that all can accept. To both ancients and moderns, this innate sociability includes sexual desire for others, as well as the capacity for more enduring forms of intimate community.

History also gives strong evidence that, however culturally constructed and malleable sexual desire may be, there is some natural minimum of heterosexual desire within the human population (although not necessarily within each individual). For a brief period (at least in terms of historical time) during the nineteenth century, "true women" were thought to lack much innate sexual desire of any kind. Yet in most eras of western history, both women and men have been recognized as feeling powerful sexual drives, very often for each other.

To this enduring picture of reason, sociability, and desire, modernity added new aspects of personhood. Hobbes and Locke recognized that regardless of sociability, people also are physically individual and self-actualizing creatures who seek their own good. Given these strongly self-directed impulses, it is unnatural, or at least imprudent, to make political arrangements without the consent of the governed. Enlightenment political philosophers, as well as the new sciences of psychology and sexology, emphasized people's moral individualism. This extension of the principle restrained not only political authority but also social coercion, a realm where much of sexual governance takes place. Even utilitarianism, which at the bottom line is collectivist, honors the individual by allowing each to count as one, and none as more than one.

The foundational notion of each one seeking his or her own good also supports the egalitarianism historically linked to liberalism, because it undermines the concept of some persons as natural rulers and some as natural slaves. Although classical liberalism started from Hobbes's premise that each person is strong enough or clever enough to kill another, egalitarianism has found many expressions, including the Protestant belief that all people have equal access to the wisdom of the Bible, and the secular equality of modern liberal states resting on each person's capacity to plan his or her own life. In societies that survived the vicious racial and religious hierarchies of personhood pursued as state policy in the twentieth century, the prudential claims of equality have enjoyed a quiet revival. The alternatives proved, as Locke predicted, simply too murderous to tolerate.

Finally, feminism has added the strand of female personhood and equality. Women now are recognized as possessing the aspects of personhood, such as reason, sociability, and individuation. Women think as well as feel, dominate as well as nurture, establish community with others as well as suffer their fates alone. These arguments for female personhood also argue for female equality, at least outside a scheme of Hobbesian equality of physical strength.

What endures, however, is the debate about whether women desire subordination, either as natural slaves in an evolutionary hierarchy or as relational angels in a virtue regime. We argue that history does not support these ambitious claims of natural psychological difference. Moreover, we argue, political theories of natural inequality have produced such intolerable outcomes in history that even the "unnatural" commitment to political equality in the face of actual inequalities seems preferable. But the most powerful argument against the claim of natural inequality is made by Mill: Every behavior that sociobiologists and virtue revivalists invoke as proof of female difference can be explained as the behavior of moral equals acting strategically to advance their interests under conditions of disempowerment. Until society witnesses female behavior under conditions of physical and economic security, and equal ideological and social standing, arguments that women naturally desire inequality are dangerous speculation.

The person that emerges from western history is complex and plural, with origins in both biology and culture. Excepting only the traditions of racial and gendered hierarchies of personhood, we take from this history that any theory of personhood adequate to shape heterosexual governance must respect a range of human capabilities from the physical to the cognitive, psychological, and emotional. Any adequate system of governance must rest on the shared aspects of human nature and the commonalities of the human condition, and yet respect moral and physical individuation.

## What is the sexual good

From these judgments about what we can know about sex and human nature, we draw our sexual morality. From the ancient world we learn that a good sexual regime accepts the social nature of human sexuality. People want sex with other people, and the sexual community created by this desire often engages much more about the persons involved than their bodies. Because people are sexual and sociable by nature, sexual sacrifice should not be the ordinary human condition, and we thus reject the ideal of a celibate life for any but a few unusual people. Most people will and should be sexual, and a good society will help them express this aspect of themselves. Because we believe that some minimum of sexual desire will be for people of the other sex, provision must be made for the specific realities of male-female sex.

Aquinas teaches us that moral sex between males and females requires full awareness of what may be required for the raising of children. When people have heterosexual intercourse, the society has a stake in the potential for reproduction. Effective contraception does not remove society's claims. People risk pregnancy for many reasons apart from lack of technological alternatives, and even planned-for offspring require support for many years after their creation in the sexual union.

From the tradition of Christian chastity we learn that people are not only physical creatures, but also spiritual and moral selves. The Protestant ideal of romantic love counsels us to honor the companionate aspects of the sexual union. From libertinism and its classical liberal and utilitarian antecedents we learn to recognize the powerful draw of physical pleasure in sex and to respect individual agency. Finally, feminism teaches us to respect the moral equality of all persons, despite actual differences in size, strength, and vulnerability to childbearing, and notwithstanding an embedded social hierarchy.

Although the language of moral philosophy is always of the good, we must also "give injustice its due," as the late philosopher Judith Shklar expressed it. Any definition of the good includes a rejection of what is not good. In determining what is not good, we take note of the many instances in which history talks back to philosophers and governors, as human experience refutes wrongly held moral and political convictions. Rawls calls this the process of reflective equilibrium, by which people test their theories against the moral lessons of their experience of life. Human experience, for example, refutes Aristotle's belief that women, slaves, and particular racial groups are animals, Augustine's vision of sexuality as a corruption of human nature, Aquinas's narrowing of the valid purposes of heterosexual union to reproduction, the Puritan belief that individuals live only for God or the community, Tocqueville's belief that companionship is a substitute for justice, Kinsey and Hefner's faith that more sex is necessarily better sex or a better life, and the sociobiological belief that some people are genetically programmed to the advantage of those in power.

## THE TECHNOLOGIES OF SEXUAL GOVERNANCE

Just as every society assumes some understanding of the sexual good, every society establishes some political means of sexual governance, what we call a "regime." Existing debates about sexual regulation mostly focus on direct acts of government, specifically prohibitory and regulatory law, but ideology and schemes of private ordering also are critical tools for sexual governance. Throughout our account of history we have focused on this relationship between public governance and private ordering, specifically the patterns of one-on-one bargaining over the conditions of sexual access between women and men.

Under each regime of sexual regulation in history the players bargained.

Shakespeare's play *Romeo and Juliet*, for example, is a window into the burgeoning Renaissance development of youth bargaining with their parents to choose their own mates rather than serve the interests of their families for aristocratic alliance or economic advantage. The diaries and correspondence of Victorian men and women reveal that premarital sex was not always a natural and spontaneous expression of youthful love and lust, but an occasion for elaborate negotiation grounded in differing social positions. Often women tried to hold out for promises of marriage or commitment before consenting to intercourse. Court records of nineteenth-century seduction cases reveal that some men lied, gambling that a woman's fear of reputational exposure or his superior social or economic status would insulate him from accountability for this deception. In the libertine era, *The Rules*, a controversial book on how to catch a husband by being hard to get, brings to light the unwritten tradition of strategic female wisdom about sexual bargaining during courtship. *Playboy* is a glimpse into the parallel tradition of libertine male sexual strategies.

Law, technology, ideology, and collective action all structure sexual bargaining. Through these avenues, a weaker player can mitigate her vulnerability, although these techniques also may enable the stronger to extend his natural and social advantages.

In relying on interpretation and persuasion, ideology is not the rule of law, but has been a powerful ally throughout history in advancing women's interests under conditions of legal and social disadvantage. The Protestant ideal of conjugal companionship, for example, softened the excesses of private power within marriage. So, too, the aspiration to companionate marriage affected political arrangements, as in Mill's arguments for sex equality on the grounds that a subordinated woman is an unfit life companion. Ideologies of celibacy, chivalry, manly self-restraint, superior female virtue, companionate marriage, and gender equality all have affected sexual bargaining.

Ideology, however, can be turned against the weak. Consider the transformation of courtly love, arguably the first cultural moment in western history to pose some alternative to pure sexual conquest. Directed at the strong, the courtly love in its pure form enjoined the lover to a Platonic affection with no sexual content. Such an ideal of love requires recognition of the other person as fully human. In the succeeding centuries, however, the ideology of romance was turned against the weak to justify the residuum of inequality by recasting conquest as swooning consent. By the twentieth century, the "search for the real thing" became a psychological version of coverture, in which the well-being of the weaker player is not bargained for, but yielded in the romantic aspiration that the strong will look out for her from motives of altruism. So far, no amount of divorce, abandonment, and impoverishment has been adequate to shake this romantic ideology.

In recent decades, cultural conservatives and sexual libertines in concert have invoked the ideology of romance to stave off feminist moves to strategies of law and collective action in support of female sexual bargaining power. Women who are strongly self-protective in sexual bargaining are labeled unromantic, asexual, or man-hating, and thus threatened with a life of loneliness and sexual frustration.

These contemporary arguments boil down to the contention that women should not be trying to bargain about sex. The ideology of romantic love, once an enhancement of women's status in sex, now diminishes her strength.

Sexual bargainers also act collectively. Through activism on issues of rape, seduction, prostitution, pornography, and the campaign against continued tolerance of a double standard, nineteenth- and twentieth-century women sought to close off other sexual avenues and force men to bargain with them for sexual access at the price of greater sexual mutuality. Nineteenth-century feminists were the first in history to begin collectively to challenge the notions of sexual obligation that justified rape, involuntary childbearing, and joyless sex as conditions of marriage. So, too, women lobbied for other legal concessions regarding the marriage bargain during this era, including property and child custody rights and the right of exit through liberalized divorce.

Only one current sexual theory—the most extreme version of sociobiology—rules out bargaining in the sexual exchange. Other understandings, like Christian doctrine, may assume that God has dictated a certain sexual order and that any other strategy is heretical. Classical virtue ethics might criticize as immoral a sexual bargain that violates a person's natural use as, for example, women bargaining for equality when, as Aristotle said, their "voices naturally lack authority." But even these theories at least acknowledge the possibility, if not the optimality, of sexual bargaining.

All four categories of sexual acts we consider in detail throughout this book—rape, prostitution, adultery, and fornication—have been subject to bargaining throughout history. And in each instance, the law has established the parameters of those negotiations. All sexual bargaining takes place in the shadow of the law. Seen in this light, we may recognize all sex law as a restraint on liberty, especially of the stronger player.

Without law, forcible rape, for instance, is a subject of bargaining only in the most limited and Hobbesian sense that characterizes a concession made under threat of death or violence as "consent." So, too, the common law doctrine that treated marriage as an irrevocable consent to sex limited sexual bargaining to the initial decision to marry or not, thereafter seriously restricting the possibilities for sexual bargaining within the relationship. Such restriction on marital sexual bargaining amounted to a license to rape.

The law of statutory rape seeks to protect children completely from the one-on-one power dynamic of private sexual bargaining. Given that adults as a class have more bargaining power than children, the ongoing policy debates over the age at which young people graduate from this legal protection can be seen as efforts to strengthen or weaken the sexual bargaining position of adults who seek sexual access to the young. Moreover, in gender terms, if children are no longer available as sexual partners for heterosexual adults (typically, adult men), the bargaining position of adult women is strengthened. Men must then negotiate with women for heterosexual access, usually at a higher price than the weaker child could demand.

Between adult women and men, the continuum from gross sexual impositions by force or threat, to sex obtained by fraud, extortion, or emotional pressure, to freely willed sexual exchanges reveals endless occasions for bargaining and an infinite variety of possible arrangements. All efforts to broaden legal definitions of sexual coercion—for example, reforming rape laws, allowing women to sue for seduction in their own name, or creating a sexual harassment cause of action—are efforts to strengthen the structural bargaining position of the weaker player to such negotiations.

Early in history, the laws of rape and seduction were little concerned with the girl or woman herself, but existed to protect the interests of fathers and husbands from the sexual claims of other men. With the birth of romance in courtly love, and as reinforced by Reformation and Enlightenment individualism, the sexual players themselves self-consciously sought to take control over sexual bargaining, whether for marriage or for nonmarital sex. As sexual access came to be seen as within the control of the woman and a matter principally concerning her personal interests rather than the interests of her family or male guardian, crimes such as rape and seduction also were reconceived as assaults on the woman herself. Only when rape and seduction served to strengthen women's interests vis à vis men (as opposed to strengthening fathers, husbands, and masters against sexual trespassers) did these legal limits became controversial as restraints on liberty.

Laws against prostitution attempt to close off avenues for sexual access outside the complex social bargains of marriage or other consensual unions. Feminist criticism of prostitution focuses on the harm done by openly privileging male social and economic superiority in the sexual exchange. As MacKinnon puts it, "if being so vulnerable that anything anyone will pay to do to you can be done to you is consent, prostitution is consensual." Prostitutes dissent, arguing they are making the best bargain they can make. Seen as a bargaining matter, the effect of forbidding prostitution is clear. Money has disproportionate value because it is fluid and fungible. Limiting the negotiability of currency in the sexual market renders the currency of currency less powerful. If money cannot be offered outright, the male-female sexual negotiation must be disguised. For example, a date uses both money and time, and thus the price goes up. Accordingly, the laws against prostitution are important not only for what they seek to prohibit directly, but also for their indirect effect on the availability of prostitutes as cheap, mostly female sexual labor, lowering the price for the rest of the sexual work force.

The laws of fornication and adultery made the formality of marriage rather than individual consent the condition for lawful sex between women and men. Heterosexual access is very costly under these laws; in the absence of divorce, serious enforcement of the prohibitions made lifetime servitude the price of heterosexual satisfaction. In modern times, some states have repealed these laws outright.

In the other states in which such laws remain on the books, they are not enforced. Courts today acknowledge that there is virtually no possibility that heterosexual consenting adults would be prosecuted for fornication or adultery. Reflecting this judgment, no national crime statistics report includes a category for consensual sex crimes between heterosexuals.

Yet even when not criminally enforced, the fornication and adultery prohibitions continue to have legal consequences that affect sexual bargaining power. Courts have held, for example, that a state fornication statute bars a partner infected with a sexually transmitted disease from suing her lover in tort. Other states refuse to protect unmarried couples under the marital status category of fair housing laws if a criminal fornication law exists. Where fornication is illegal, long-term cohabiting couples may be denied the property rights associated with marriage, even if they could establish meritorious claims in contract or restitution. The Internal Revenue Service penalizes unmarried but cohabiting taxpayers living in states where fornication statutes are still on the books by denying them a dependency exemption. In some states, a man who fathers a child in an adulterous relationship may not claim any parental rights if his lover's husband chooses to accept the child as his own. In each instance, although the sex involved is not illegal enough for the state to prosecute directly, officials use illegality as a reason for denying any incidental legal claim involving the disfavored relationship. The withdrawal of civil law from nonmarital or adulterous relationships reestablishes a partial state of nature between the parties, and thus diminishes the bargaining power of the weaker player.

Nonmarital sexual relations are cast even further beyond the pale by refusal to enforce basic prohibitions of force and violence in sexually intimate relationships, hence the political centrality of efforts to enforce the rape and fraud laws between social acquaintances. So, too, the passion and provocation defenses to murder provide a violent sex partner with a cheaper shot at the physical integrity of the other player by reducing the possibility of a murder conviction. Under these circumstances, the bargaining stance of the stronger player is much enhanced and a near state of nature is sometimes achieved.

For 6000 years of recorded western history, no political regime, and certainly no regime of sexual regulation, recognized females as full and equal participants in the basic goods of citizenship. Although the Roman *lex julia* included rape among the forbidden transactions of force and fraud, Christian Europe did not know of meaningful prohibitions against rape in the interest of the female members of society until the late middle ages, when the church imposed itself on behalf of its chaste sisters. As liberal individualism and democracy swept Europe from the Protestant Reformation in 1511 to the French Revolution almost 300 years later, women did not preach, vanished upon marriage, and neither voted nor governed. Among the godly in Puritan New England, only a woman was ever hanged for adultery. In democratic America, Tocqueville thought that women should sacrifice themselves in marriage to keep unruly men in order. No American sex code until the mid-nineteenth century included husbands in its prohibition of adultery (unless they were having sex with someone else's wife). In 1962, respected lawyers and law professors of the American Law Institute recommended that criminal law recognize women's tendency to lie about rape.

Although liberal individualism began to press the system of male dominance as early as the 1780s, long after women achieved suffrage in the United States, the private precinct of the bedroom was the last bastion of gender inequality. When modern feminism put the justice of sex back on the table in the 1960s, it was the Millian concept of women as free-acting individuals in the male model of democratic citizenship that persuaded. Equality meant that women were free to bargain for what they desired, including sex. Because the recognition of women's citizenship stopped at the fact of bargaining, rather than the process or outcome, it missed the predictable consequence of a downward spiral. In our own times, males not only are larger, stronger, and immune from pregnancy and childbirth (the physical bargaining advantages), they are richer (owning more assets and earning more income), more powerful (dominating the spheres in which social power is wielded), and the beneficiaries of millennia of assumptions that they belong on top. Under these circumstances and absent extraordinary strategies, in any unstructured sexual bargaining process females will come out behind and on the bottom. They will exchange sexual access under terms of emotional, physical, and financial disadvantage, bear the greater burden of the reproductive consequences of heterosexual intercourse, and spend more of their capacities and opportunities to obtain a lesser sexual deal.

Liberals recognized the effect of unbalanced bargaining in the economic realm decades ago. But when women make similar complaints about sexual bargaining, liberals invoke theories of the special philosophical place of sexual expression or paralyzing fears of state oppression. Inequalities of either starting or ending position have no normative role in libertarian or sociobiological theory. Virtue revivalists acknowledge the downward spiral that threatens the weak, but urge women to pay for protection by surrendering equality. Feminists are ambivalent about bargaining, favoring free sexual choice but also recognizing women's vulnerability to sexual violence in a lawless world and to exploitation in one-on-one bargains with men. Too often, however, feminist thinking about sexual choice substitutes agency (the feeling of acting for oneself) for power (the capacity to influence one's own circumstances and those of others). Choosing among a range of insecure and costly sexual encounters may give women the illusion of choice, but such bad bargains do not lead to self-determination or freedom. Our proposals take as a core premise that a good regime of sexual governance will seek to assure flourishing freedom, and equality for both women and men.

History tells us that most sex between women and men takes place in private, dispersed and unofficial circumstances. In a variety of settings from the soulfully intimate to the grimily commercial, private actors seek to come together to accomplish their sexual ends—some complementary, some conflicting. They do so through a series of decentralized and subtle interactions almost entirely beyond the power of the state to regulate directly. Yet most existing legal thinking on sexual regulation focuses exclusively on the prescriptive model of state-enforced prohibition. In the past decade or more, feminist scholarship has broadened the working definition of "regulation" to include the delegation of sexual governance from the state to private communal institutions, such as the family. But there remains that vast world of non-criminal, non-familial sexual exchanges effectively out of reach of law and community.

Accommodating this reality of private ordering requires a new technology of sexual regulation. By seeking to use law to structure private bargaining rather than control outcomes directly through legal prohibition or penalty, our goal is to encourage the sexual flourishing of individuals through the vehicle of their own perceived needs. Our prescription corrects through empowerment for any preferences that represent the players' mistaken confusion of their interests with their limited prospects. We believe structured bargaining can do effectively what law might otherwise be capable of only by aggressive intrusion and crude prohibition.

We use the bargaining model because it helps us understand the sexual world better and because it brings a much broader range of sexual exchanges into the realm of communal decisionmaking and everyday politics. But we also favor private ordering because it respects individual liberty and autonomy, and because it acknowledges the plurality of definitions of the sexual good. Thus a regulatory strategy of structured bargaining goes some distance toward answering legitimate fears of an overweening state knocking on the bedroom door, although to those who place unrestricted individual sexual expression over any communal or other personal interest, no limit, however flexible, could be justified.

We have some experience from labor law relying on a bargaining model between strong and weak players. After an unregulated period during America's early industrialization, the economic collapse of the 1930s brought to power a progressive government that sought to ameliorate the inequalities between labor and capital by providing a legal framework for the weak to bargain collectively through unions. Although fears of violence and revolution as well as aspirations for economic justice motivated the passage of the Wagner Act in 1936, the resulting regime of labor law and the union movement it supported allowed workers to strike employment bargains that narrowed the gap between rich and poor without leading to Stalinism, as many at the time predicted.

The labor regime added to people's dignity and was flexible enough so that after some forty years, workers could abandon collective bargaining when they no longer perceived it to be in their self-interest. The balance tipped in the early 1980s when pro-business interests altered the baseline distribution of bargaining chips, removing the right to strike with the massive use of replacement workers. Replacement workers would not have been available, however, if a critical mass of workers had not decided to abandon collective action for one-on-one bargaining.

The many decades of industrial peace and parity accomplished by the labor regime is evidence that bargaining in a context of cleverly devised and narrowly targeted public structures to support the weaker player and push the parties toward agreed-to social ends can work. Bargaining fosters the dignity and self-respect associated with advancing one's own ends, even as it avoids the worst outcomes of libertinism. In addition, bargaining is flexible over time, allowing the parties to revisit their agreements as conditions change.

What we propose, then, is a legal framework to balance the bargaining power of the stronger and weaker players in the heterosexual exchange. Through this regulated regime of private ordering, we come as close as possible to satisfying the goods of all three philosophical regimes: human flourishing, autonomy and equality, and hedonistic satisfaction.

## NOTES

On Marx's naturalization of the sexual relationship, see Karl Marx, *The German Ideology: Marx and Engels, Collected Works* (New York: International, 1975), 31. On Engels, see Friedrich Engels, *The Origin of the Family, Private Property and the State,* ed. Eleanor Burke Leacock (New York: International, 1972).

The "no more rape" quote is from Catharine A. MacKinnon, *Feminism Unmodified: Discourses on Life and Law* (Cambridge, Mass.: Harvard Univ. Press, 1987), 219.

Rawls's "rational" and "reasonable" assumptions are found in John Rawls, *Political Liberalism* (New York: Columbia Univ. Press, 1993), 50.

On women's place in the Hobbesian scheme of physical strength, see Linda R. Hirshman, "Material Girls: A Game Theoretic Version of the Social Contract Exercise with Women Present" (Ph.D. dissertation, Univ. of Illinois at Chicago, 1994).

The "give injustice its due" quote is from Judith N. Shklar, "Giving Injustice Its Due," *Yale Law Journal* 98 (1989): 1135.

The "reflective equilibrium" idea is from John Rawls, *A Theory of Justice* (Cambridge, Mass.: Belknap Press of Harvard Univ. Press, 1971), 48-51.

On women's voices lacking authority, see Aristotle, *Politics,* 1260a20.

As an example of the admission that there is no chance of a heterosexual being prosecuted for fornication or adultery, see, e.g., *Doe v. Duling,* 782 F.2d 1202, 1206 (4th Cir. 1986). As examples of a fornication law being used to bar tort recovery for disease transmission, see, e.g., *Doe v. Roe,* 841 F. Supp. 444, 446 (D.C. Cir. 1994) (using Virginia law, court allows defense that where plaintiff engaged in fornication, he or she prohibited from recovery in tort for transmission of a venereal disease); *Zysk v. Zysk,* 404 S.E.2d 721 (Va. 1990) (same). As an example of a fornication law being used to exclude unmarried cohabitants from protection under "marital status" provisions of the fair housing laws, see, e.g., *State v. French,* 460 N.W.2d 2, 5-6 (Minn. 1990). As an example of a court using a fornication law to deny any contract remedy to long-term cohabitants, see, e.g., *Hewitt v. Hewitt,* 77 Ill.2d 49, 394 N.E.2d 1204 (Ill. 1979). Federal tax law denies the dependency exemption to unmarried cohabitants at Sec. 152(b)(5) of the Internal Revenue Code of 1986, U.S. Code Title 26, as amended through Dec. 31, 1994. On this differential tax treatment, see generally William V. Vetter, "I.R.C. Section 152(B)(5) and Victorian Morality in Contemporary Life," *Yale Law and Policy Review* 13 (1995): 115. An unmarried man may be denied paternity rights if the husband of the mother chooses to recognize the child as his own; see *Michael H. v. Gerald D.*, 491 U.S. 110 (1989).

# 13

## HARD BARGAINS

In 1879 Mabel Loomis Todd wrote in her diary:

> The night brought us very near to each other. The physical effect of our close communion was unlike anything I ever experienced—it was enjoyment, and yet it was hard for me to feel the same kind of intensity as before—it was a thrilling sort of breathlessness—but at last it came—the same beautiful climax of feeling I know so well.

When women and men choose one another, sex, like other forms of human cooperation, benefits both. Sex thus resembles the classic of game theory called the Battle of the Sexes in which cooperation is everyone's preferred strategy, and the only issue is how a man and a woman will divide the surplus of their social cooperation. Yet our assurance that both men and women gain something by sexual cooperation cannot be the last word on the morality or politics of their dealings. Lovers will divide all the good and bad that their union creates and, in the world as we know it, will do so mostly by private bargaining. This heterosexual bargaining takes place between naturally and socially unequal players. Where the strong rule, the outcome of such an exchange is predictable: Weaker players face the choice of accepting a bargain of sex on bad terms, or living a solitary life on better terms but with no sex. Each is a hard bargain.

We propose to change these bargaining outcomes, specifically to divide the surplus of male-female sexual cooperation more equitably. We conclude from history that direct prohibition of sexual conduct is effective only at the margin, opens the door to arbitrary and discriminatory enforcement. By contrast, law has powerful oblique effects on heterosexual bargaining, often regulating indirectly what it cannot reach directly. Because the conventional model of sexual regulation has been prohibitory, in past regimes these bargaining effects have been mostly incidental rather than intended. We intend to invoke law's bargaining effects directly.

Game theory seeks to explain bargaining effects, working from the insight that the initial distribution of power between the players determines bargaining outcomes. A hungry person will work more cheaply than someone with savings in the bank. With the help of theory, we have shown how particular legal regimes affected sexual outcomes. We can use that knowledge strategically to predict future bargaining outcomes and design legal reforms that will accomplish intended ends by structuring the largely hidden world of sexual bargaining.

Our proposal has two goals: to establish baselines that moderate the downward spiral of unequal bargaining, and to allow for wide play in sexual choice and preference. What follows is both an agenda for practical legal reform and an outline for a broader intellectual project. Although we believe our approach could be applied broadly to sexual governance, we do not address every aspect of heterosexual connection, much less human sexuality generally. Our recommendations address only the four areas of male-female exchange on which we have focused throughout this book—rape, prostitution, adultery, and fornication. At some points our analysis remains tentative and stops at suggestion rather than conclusion. What this rough draft of a sex code does do fully is demonstrate our principal theoretical claim—that structured bargaining can regulate male-female sexual exchange in the interest of political and moral values of flourishing and equality, and at the same time assure individual autonomy and liberty.

Although our focus on bargaining is novel in contemporary sexual theory, there is nothing revolutionary in the proposals that follow. The past includes many grand sexual experiments, from the radical celibacy of early Christians to the radical erotic of free lovers. It may be that risk and idealism promises new solutions to old problems, but it is hard to escape the fact that none of these utopias transformed heterosexual relations in deep and enduring ways. We retain some established rules from past sexual regimes and discard others. We import legal mechanisms from other areas of beneficial human cooperation, such as the market, which, like male-female sex, work mostly by private bargain. We opened our review of sexual regulation by speculating that theories of the unique nature of sexuality were not on their face convincing. Nothing in our historical survey or philosophical analysis has led us to believe that sexual bargaining does not respond to law, or that eroticism and emotions are exempt from the ordinary rules of human behavior. The most unsettling aspect of our proposals may be our insistence that sex laws be enforced as written, abandoning the current practice of adopting sweeping restrictions for symbolic and political gain and then shying away from the controversy that might result from enforcing those limits.

## RAPE: THE BASELINE

Forcible rape is the direct use of superior power to bypass consent and gain sexual access. When men and women come together to negotiate the exchange of sexual access, the law against rape is a key determinant of the initial distribution of their sexual bargaining power. In his economic analysis of sexual regulation, *Sex and Reason*, Judge Richard Posner suggests that men will rape more when the bride price is high. Conversely, men should marry more if the cost of rape is high.

Direct historical evidence of the struggles between individual men and women that ended in rape is scarce. But history does offer plentiful proof that rape law establishes the relative power of men and women in bargaining for consensual sex. Ancient societies treated rape as an injury to the victim's father, guardian, or husband, and provided him strong redress, including rights of private violence. Wives, daughters and female slaves in elite households thus enjoyed strong, albeit secondhand, bargaining power in their sexual dealings with predatory males. This power was not an extension of the females' sexual will; to the contrary, patriarchs often used rape law to separate their women from desired sexual partners. But a woman under such a regime could at least deny sex to some men, even if she lacked the autonomy to grant access to others. This describes, for example, the white woman in the antebellum South, whose sexual position was more secure and dignified than that of an enslaved woman explicitly denied the protections of rape law, or even of a free black woman, who was regarded by social custom as simply "unrapeable."

Beginning in the late middle ages, European law reconceived rape as a protection of female bodily integrity, placing the right to invoke the law in the hands of the victim. Perhaps because this law redistributed power from men to women (instead of from man to man, as the ancient law did), the law was weakly enforced. With women given some power to act in their own sexual interests, the fear arose that victims would manipulate this power by lying to protect reputation, wreak revenge, or blackmail innocent men. Nowhere other than in the law of rape is the redistributive agenda of strengthening the weaker player in male-female sex more visible.

The political struggles in the nineteenth and twentieth centuries, first to strengthen, then to weaken, and again to strengthen rape law likewise track gender politics. In our own era, male-female sexual bargaining takes place against the backdrop of libertine deregulation in which the mutuality of consent has replaced the formality of marriage as the baseline for sexual access. By replacing marital status with free sexual contract, libertinism freed people to negotiate endlessly varied, one-on-one sexual bargains. In this free market regime, rape law is the only broad legal constraint on heterosexual sex.

Free market systems ordinarily offer strong limits on access (e.g., private property) as a precondition for secure dealing. Thus a strong rape law should be the foundation of the libertine regime. But one reason people are willing to accept strong protection for private property is that they can expect to be a buyer or a seller at different times. As we have seen, men and women are not similarly situated with respect to the law of rape; even if victims may be of either sex, offenders are almost invariably males.

If the stronger player cannot just take sex but must get consent, and the mere possibility of mutual pleasure is not enough to justify the sex in every instance, the stronger player must concede that the partner he wants may have a different sex-

ual agenda. (This analysis does not change if males and females always seek different sexual ends, or do so only sometimes.) He will have to go some distance
toward satisfying her ends if he wants her agreement to cooperate. (The desiring
weaker player must also do so, but she never has the option of using superior
force.) Bargaining for consent thus begins. Perhaps he must make himself a more
agreeable companion, or promise her more mutuality of pleasure, or agree to
forego sex with others, or use a condom.

Attaching legal consequences to particular forms of sexual access thus functions
as a price increase. This insight illuminates the stakes in ongoing debates over sex
policy such as whether silence should be treated as consent or not. Those favoring
a requirement of explicit and affirmative consent seek to raise the price of sexual
access; those opposing, to lower it.

In sum, rape law is the baseline: It establishes a level of permissible sexual conduct below which no private agreement can fall, no matter how superior the bargaining position of the stronger player. We propose to raise the baseline price of
sexual consent by requiring an affirmative "yes" as the condition for intimate access between adults. In order to bar the use of the natural social advantage of age in
sexual bargaining, we propose to constrain older men and women from seeking
sex (consensual or not) with girls and boys. But we also would remove some conduct that involves no categorical abuse of authority, but is nonetheless prohibited
as "statutory rape," from the reach of the law altogether.

To the degree that past rape reforms have begun from or continued the common law understanding of rape as forcible sexual imposition, they do not corre-
spond to modern understandings of what is right and wrong about heterosexual
conduct. Violence is bad, but force and threat are just one manifestation of a larger
category of bad behavior—refusal to respect another's autonomy. Legal scholar
Stephen Schulhofer argues for reconceiving the range of punishable sexual impositions that current law typically tries to shoehorn into the category of rape as a
more nuanced range of offenses against autonomy. His alternative places consent
rather than force at the center of criminal sex law.

Sexual line-drawing balances the risk of deterring wanted contacts against the
risk of encouraging unwanted contacts. Where the conduct interferes minimally
with the victim's bodily integrity and decisional autonomy, we conclude the risk
should fall on the side of encouraging more sexual contacts, even at the risk of allowing some undesired intrusions. So, for example, a person may not want a business acquaintance to hold her hand and look meaningfully into her eyes when she
offers a handshake, but if he does this, even without her consent, the interference
with her control over her sexuality is relatively minor, albeit annoying. (As a technical matter, any unconsented touching is a civil battery and, depending on the
circumstances, may also amount to sexual harassment.)

Schulhofer argues that a focus on autonomy suggests different rules about what
constitutes consent with respect to minor as opposed to significant intrusions on

the body. For minor intrusions on the body, such as an unwanted kiss or hug, consent should be presumed and a clear "no" required to prove criminal interference with sexual autonomy.

If, however, what is at stake is intimate access to the body—the genitals and other sexualized parts of the body, such as breasts, buttocks, and crotch—any mistake is far more consequential. If a person is touched or penetrated in these places without consent, her interest in controlling access to her sexuality is profoundly impaired. Where the unwanted intrusion is significant and/or directed at the sexual body, such as penetration of the vagina, anus, or mouth, or grabbing of the breasts, buttocks, or crotch, only positive and clear agreement to such contact should suffice. Silence and ambiguity would be construed against the intruder.

Note that Schulhofer's theory includes sexual contact that is not forced or threatened, but still may not be consensual. Such cases involve what is perhaps the ordinary instance of acquaintance rape where a woman remains silent or is ambiguous about her unwillingness, or where her consent is equivocal and a man simply proceeds on the theory that "she didn't say yes, but she didn't say no, either." The libertine position is that adults should bear the burden of explicit rejection in all cases. Schulhofer suggests to the contrary that where sex is taken peaceably but without unequivocal consent, the sexual imposition is still a crime, although a lesser wrong than forced sex. We agree.

Sexual contact obtained by force or its threat, or without clear and affirmative consent, violates the victim's right to bargain for the conditions of sexual access. Yet the character of injury in forced sex is both different and greater than in nonconsensual sex. In forced sex, the violent party extracts more benefit from the sexual transaction than the party who acts simply without consent. The violent party gets the conscious participation of the disempowered partner or the sick thrill of forcing the victim to witness her own domination. Because this violence not only violates sexual autonomy, but also threatens public order and social norms of peaceability and respect for the physical boundaries of the body, the strongest criminal sanctions should apply. Force and threat most strongly restrain the human freedom to bargain and should be prohibited in all instances.

The lines drawn by this allocation of the burdens of consent, ambiguity, and silence are clear and intuitive and present no fairness problems. The rules follow conventional understandings of the zones of the body as well as commonsense rules of respectful conduct, and thus are comprehensible to the lay person. By forcing the stronger player to bargain with the weaker for an explicit consent, we begin to ensure mutuality as a condition for all adult sexual exchanges. Each party will get a fair and reliable chance to ask for something of what he or she wants from the sex, even if we cannot assure that the benefits of cooperation will always (or even usually) be divided equally. Under our proposed rules the weaker player can extract a higher price for sexual consent than under a narrower definition of rape as a prohibition on force, or even coercion. At the same time, our proposed rules allow for lively and diverse range of sexual bargains, not imposing any single vision of "good" sex between adult men and women.

## SEX WITH CHILDREN

Along with force, among the most egregious of bargaining imbalances is the adult who seeks sex with a child. In childhood and adolescence, a few years represents a lot of development, and age differences can mean great differences in reason, judgment, and power. Yet from ancient Athens to the present day, western society has had a social norm favoring the pairing of older males with younger females. Recent studies document that to some degree this norm still holds. Researchers find that at least half of the babies born to minor women are fathered by adult men. When we consider only unmarried mothers under the age of eighteen years, 21 percent of babies born to these girls and young women involved a male partner at least five years older. The youngest mothers, those fifteen years and younger, are the most likely to have had an adult male partner. Almost 40 percent of fifteen-year-old mothers had a partner aged twenty years or older. In these male adult-female child pairings, the age inequality magnifies the risk of gender inequality in the heterosexual exchange.

Children are so comparatively disempowered in their dealings with adults that adult-child sexual transactions can be compared to those obtained by the use of force as distortions of an ideal of equal bargaining power. Moreover, the consequences of adult sex with adolescents and children affect society generally. For these reasons, we suggest the act should be criminal. Thus we would continue the existing legal doctrine known as "statutory rape," that is, laws that treat as the equivalent of forcible rape even consensual sex with an underage person. But we would limit the common law definition of statutory rape to reach only the adult who has sex with an underage person, excluding from punishment the younger partner in adult-child sexual contact (consistent with current law), and the case of sex between two underage persons (contra current law). For purposes of this narrowed doctrine of statutory rape, we would define the age of consent as sixteen years. An adult is a person who has reached the age of majority, which in all states is eighteen years.

The traditional rationale for treating consensual sex with an underage person as rape is that the child, like an unconscious adult, is not mentally or morally competent to consent. The incapacity of age principle applies broadly in Anglo-American law: Minors, for example, are not legally bound to perform contractual promises. We follow this tradition and modify our preference for bargaining as the principal means for regulating male-female sex. The young can neither fully reason about nor bargain effectively for their flourishing or their pleasure. Where natural facts (immaturity and childhood) dictate that fair bargaining cannot take place between identifiable groups of people, both virtue ethics and utilitarianism counsel us to abandon the liberal preference for contract in favor of status-based rules that assure the substantive best interests of both the young and of society.

To set an age of consent—that is, to define who is a "child" or "underage"—is a historically contingent question, and differs depending upon the sphere of activity at issue. If ten years was considered "mature" in 1650 for sexual purposes, this might not be mature in a developed industrial economy where education can last for a quarter-century or more, or in a world in which life expectancy has doubled for males and tripled for females. But if, for pragmatic reasons, the law must draw a bright line, what is the age below which we doubt that a young person benefits from heterosexual contact with an adult?

We already have concluded that the choices made by the young are not the best guide to their sexual well-being. We propose therefore to substitute our adult judgment for theirs and ask what degree of sexual experience is good for the young. This judgment will differ depending upon which of the three western philosophical traditions we invoke for the analysis. Virtue ethics would support sexual restraints on the young until they have completed many of the educational and developmental tasks of adolescence. In this tradition, adult society is morally obligated to supervise the upbringing and development of the young. The need for a long period of education and work apprenticeship to prepare for citizenship in our complex economy and state is a virtue ethics argument for a relatively high age of consent, perhaps eighteen years or more.

Utilitarianism would argue for an earlier age of consent given the reality that young bodies feel desire and are capable of sexual pleasure. As the age of puberty drops from generation to generation, so, too have other signs of maturity, including the appearance of sexual urges. Reasoning from this capacity for physical pleasure, a utilitarian might suggest that the age of consent mirror puberty, perhaps eleven or twelve years, or even younger.

The utilitarian analysis is obscured, however, by the difficulty of accurately weighing the sexual pleasures and pains of young females as distinguished from males. When researchers talk to adolescent girls about sex with boys and men, they find that girls seldom express positive feelings about desire or pleasure. Although a large percentage of teenaged girls are sexually active, many describe pleasure as something that their partners get from them, or as something that they get from giving pleasure to others. Sex is a way to get male affirmation, romance, or relational security at a time in life when a sexualized peer culture causes girls to suffer insecurity and diminished self-image. Girls recognize that they are objects of male desire, and so they try to negotiate fulfillment of their emotional needs through sex.

If the girls were simply indifferent, the sum of adult male pleasure might tip the utilitarian calculus in favor of adult-child sex. But the dangers of abuse, fears of pregnancy and reputational exposure, along with the lack of fulfillment of romantic fantasies associated with sex for girls, can make the act a positively traumatic experience, offsetting the hedonistic payoff in sex that utilitarianism recognizes. Further, rape and coercion is not an uncommon sexual experience for teenaged girls: In one study, 29 percent of teenaged mothers reported having had sexual intercourse as a result of physical force. And even if sexual victimization and trauma are not the ordinary experience, we are cautious in light of the heavy weight of female silence on the key issues of desire and pleasure in toting up the utiles. At the least, we know that sex for adolescent females is not an innocent experience of uncomplicated lust as sometimes portrayed.

Liberalism would favor maximum freedom with a low age for consent, tolerating inappropriate adult–child sexual transactions at the margins in order to avoid reining in the freedom of youth and those adults who seek sex with them. Some liberals argue that the young are in fact capable of good sexual choices. Often this argument is bolstered by an appeal to the hedonic strain of libertinism that holds sex to be so enjoyable that its value outweighs even the risk of imperfect consent. Or liberals may sacrifice the young by overvaluing early signs of autonomy or overstating fear of the state in order to prevent creating any precedent for restricting adult sexuality. In either case, our commitments to more than just a facade of sexual autonomy and mutuality, and our vision of sex as part of a rich realization of human capabilities, leads us to reject these positions.

We have chosen sixteen years as an appropriate age of consent in an effort to balance protection for immaturity and respect for the complex developmental tasks of adolescence with the pleasure demands of the maturing body and erotic imagination and the practical problems of enforcement. Because it tells a young person a lie about what it takes to succeed in the world, adult sex with much younger partners, even those over the formal age of consent, is usually an act of wrongdoing. The wrongdoing is particularly acute for young females, who are largely newcomers to the world of achievement through education and work. Since the feminist movement opened up the world of waged work to large numbers of women in the late twentieth century, women have to face the realities of formal work. Such work is often difficult, it is arduous, it is imperfectly rewarded and rewarding, and the rewards take a long time to come. The young are tempted to fantasize that there is a way around this hard job of life. One of the deepest rooted female fantasies is the fantasy of escape through alliance with an established male—a prince, in the fairy tales. In reality, however, such alliances rarely operate to rescue the weaker player. The older adult may be married or may go through a number of younger sexual partners before finding, if he ever does find, one worth sharing his adult power with. And this says nothing of the ignobility of avoiding the hard work of life. We draw the legal line at a place much less protective than the moral ideal, but we have no illusion that the age of consent answers the important moral questions of sex and power.

In many states, the law already forbids adult–child sex, but the prohibition is barely enforced. There has been a revival of interest in enforcing statutory rape laws in recent years, another sign of the breakup of the libertine paradigm. But where such prosecutions have been undertaken, the motive behind enforcement, in our judgment, often misses the mark.

The prohibition of adult–child sex should be enforced consistently and even-handedly, respecting the law as written. Too often, however, prosecutors screen out the typical cross-age sexual partnering and reserve their attention for the politically popular case, or move to enforce the law only when the child becomes pregnant and threatens to become a public responsibility. When rape law is thus manipulated for other political agendas, the legitimacy of a principled ban against adult sexual access to children is eroded. Nor, we believe, should a ban on adult-child sex be used to deter pregnancy outside of marriage or to enforce an ideal of marriage as the only permissible sexual relationship. Recently, for example, prosecutors in several jurisdictions offered to dismiss statutory rape charges if the adult man married the teenaged girl he had impregnated. In addition, we would reject the traditional common law defenses of mistake of age and promiscuity of the victim. Mistake of age is like silence in rape cases: Depending on where the burden of mistake is placed, either some older persons will have sex with partners too young to be proper sexual players, or, alternatively, some older persons (and their young partners) will miss the chance to enjoy some acceptable sexual experiences. Because our goal is to impose a duty of care on the stronger player, we expect the older person to discover the age of any potential sex partner. As to the younger player's "promiscuity," our proposal does not rest on the value that a child places on himself or herself as reflected in prior sexual behavior. Nor do we value only sexually innocent children, a position that limits legal protection to kids lucky enough never to have been harmed by sex before. The entrapment defense remains available in cases of gross unfairness to defendants.

Finally, children should never be treated as criminals for making the bad sexual choice to deal with an adult. The core of the incapacity of age idea is that children are not competent to defend their own interests against predatory adults in an unregulated marketplace, sexual, economic, or otherwise.

Consistent with our focus on bargaining power, we propose to exclude sex between underage persons from the category of statutory rape, and indeed from the reach of the law altogether. We disagree with prosecutors in one jurisdiction who plan to charge as rape the contact between an eleven-year-old girl who "taught" an eight-year-old boy how to have sexual intercourse, even though law enforcement officials acknowledge that the older girl probably is herself a victim of prior sexual abuse. This is not because we regard sex between the young as either moral, wise, or a social good, or because we are not willing to see a female as a rapist. Instead, we are consistent in our adherence to the logic of the legal concept of incapacity, which intends to prevent the young from being held to bad decisions that will have enduring life consequences. This rationale argues for not judging the young in their sexual dealings as we would adults, extending this protective rationale even to perpetrators and not just to victims. Adults should not punish the sexually active young, but seek to restore young people to the path of flourishing, equality, and community membership.

## FORNICATION

Fornication is the offense of sex outside of marriage. American law typically characterizes only heterosexual couplings as fornication; same-sex acts are treated as the more serious crime of sodomy, although by technical definition same-sex acts are also fornication because they take place outside of marriage. Even during this era when libertinism dominates both popular and intellectual culture, courts and legislatures have not definitively deregulated fornication. State and federal law continues to disadvantage nonmarital sexual partners in tax, housing, insurance, public benefits, family property, inheritance, and so on. Fornication remains a crime in about half of the states, but law enforcers have simply stopped enforcing those laws as written, an equivocation explicable more by political interest than philosophical principle.

The ancient world forbade elite women nonmarital sex so as to prevent men from sexual trespass on one another's property. But since the advent of Christian power in Europe, fornication laws pressed men as well as women into marriage as the only legitimate sexual relationship. Given natural and social vulnerabilities in sex and reproduction, the weighty and mutual obligations of socially enforced marriage was a better outcome than most women could have expected from sexual bargaining on their own. Although the elevation of status depended on the content both of marriage and the nonmarital state (which varied over time and from place to place), we conclude that laws against fornication generally elevated the status of women in history by increasing the price that men paid for heterosexual access. For example, when women acted collectively in the social purity movement to close nonmarital sexual avenues, forcing men to marry for sex, the redistribution of power inherent in their agenda of enforced laws against fornication, as well as seduction, prostitution, and adultery, elicited powerful resistance. The redistribution of power also explains for us the hypocrisy of American fornication laws, which are ubiquitous, yet little enforced in most historical periods.

We propose to deregulate simple fornication, which we define as consensual, nonmarital sex untainted by coercion, disparate age, or other categorical bargaining imbalances. We take this stand even though restrictions on nonmarital sex historically have enhanced women's bargaining power. Rather than try to force sexual actors into marriage, we choose to modify the anarchic state of nature that characterizes nonmarital sexual bargaining. To limit consensual sex between men and women to the enduring and complex relationship of marriage (as fornication laws do) substantially injures liberal values of autonomy and individualism, diminishes the sum total of sexual pleasure in the world, and discourages the sociability and community vital to human well-being. Moreover, once sexual exchange outside marriage is a better alternative to the negotiated agreement to marry, there will be less need for women to seek refuge in marriage, and marriage itself should change. In bargaining terms, the better the sexual state of nature, the less oppressive marriage can be.

Some moral arguments against fornication can be easily dispensed with, while others require more careful response. Fornication is not intrinsically immoral to the liberal or utilitarian. Fornication is freely chosen, which satisfies the liberal concern for autonomy, and the act brings pleasure, which justifies it on utilitarian grounds. Fornication *might* be immoral to the liberal or utilitarian if the act ran afoul of some other relevant concern. For example, a liberal might object to the use of force or fraud to induce consent to sex. Or a utilitarian might count not just the sexual pleasure of the fornicators, but also any pain caused by the exploitation that may accompany sex with few legal constraints. But these caveats apply only to special instances of fornication, and not to the category.

Cultural conservatives do take a categorical stance against fornication, arguing that the act weakens the motivation to marry, encourages the early sexualization of children, and economically burdens society with dependent unmarried mothers and their children. William Kristol argues in addition that women must play their Tocquevillean role of moral compass to save the democratic republic by reining in their fellow citizens through sexual virtue. We argue below that neither a virtue ethics approach nor a concern for women's natural and social inequalities leads to a categorical condemnation of fornication. If fornication is reframed as a question of creating intimate community, virtue ethics can approve of the sociability of sexual community outside of marriage, and yet still provide for the complex social claims that may grow up around such relationships. Care and support of dependent children can be addressed through laws and social programs narrowly directed at them, and not by regulating the sexual conduct of all adults.

An intriguing and unexpected argument against fornication comes from feminist and Kant scholar Barbara Herman. Immanuel Kant is an improbable authority for a feminist, because his writings include large doses of eighteenth-century misogyny. Nonetheless, Herman cleverly notices that Kant's ideas about male-female sex strikingly resemble those of one of libertinism's fiercest critics, modern feminist theorist Andrea Dworkin. Kant says:

> Taken by itself [sexual love] is a degradation of human nature; for as soon as a person becomes an Object of appetite for another, all motives of moral relationship cease to function, because as an Object of appetite for another a person becomes a thing and can be treated and used as such by every one.

Compare Dworkin, who says:

> It is especially in the acceptance of the object status that [the sexual woman's] humanity is hurt; it is a metaphysical acceptance of lower status in sex and in society; an implicit acceptance of less freedom, less privacy, less integrity.

Herman reminds us that in Kantian terms, making another person—a separate individual capable of rational thought and free will—into an object for one's own desire is immoral, even if "the pleasures of sex lead women to volunteer to be treated as things." To Kant, the thingness is more important than the pleasure.

The libertarian strain of libertinism sees an easy answer to sexual objectification. If one is concerned with women's dignity and freedom, her consent ("women volunteer to be treated as things") squares the moral circle. People routinely agree, for example, to labor for one another. But Kant asserts that in sex, unlike in employment, the urgency of desire leads us to purge the relationship of all regard for the other as a person. And he further argues that it is immoral even to ask to use another person in such a way. We cannot ask, and the object of our desire cannot grant it, just as people cannot sell themselves into slavery.

But if sexual desire is objectifying and no private agreement to objectification is possible, then celibacy looms. Herman is unwilling to accept this gloomy fate. In the place either of celibacy or immoral private agreements of objectification, Herman invokes Kant's solution of marriage. In marriage, the objectification inherent in sex can be contained and diluted to an acceptable moral level, because the sexual partners have other ways to ensure a secure moral regard for each other's life.

This still leaves the argument that if sex needs an agreement like marriage to be moral, such agreement could be the subject of private bargain. Why is state-defined marriage necessary? According to Kant, most human needs cannot be solved by private agreement. Agreements are nothing more than a claim on the other person's future compliance and, as such, cannot exist outside the state's machinery of enforcement. Such contracts are not immoral, as the contract for mutual sexual slavery would be, but they are unenforceable and hence impractical. Herman points to the many abuses of sexual dealing outside of marriage or the law, and concludes with Kant that we should not place much faith in the moral reliability of private bargains. Here, Herman invokes the dark vision of the sexual state of nature, particularly for women who are vulnerable by their physical nature to both force and reproduction. Given this, Herman not only prescribes the highly protective bargain of marriage, but invokes the state to enforce it. If there is only one moral sexual bargain (marriage), it follows from her argument that laws against fornication should be universal and vigorously enforced.

The weak point in this argument is the contention that sex is different in kind (and not just in degree) from other human interactions about which the law leaves people free to make a variety of private arrangements. Herman does not specify exactly what it is about objectification in sex that distinguishes it from other human activities. People participate in a range of human relationships in which they make claims to the body and personality of others: assault and battery, friendship, family, partnership, employment, slavery, random proximity on the street. Moral societies use formal law as well as informal social norms to restrain the dangers of objectification that Kant identifies in such claims. In the Anglo-American legal system, for example, you cannot touch someone without their consent. Social norms disparage people who put their own interests before those of their friends. Modern states no longer permit unlimited family authority, recognizing wives and children as having rights apart from husbands and parents. The law places fiduciary duties on partners and professionals, and requires some degree of reciprocity in employment, ruling out slavery and the more savage exploitations of wage labor. Police arrest those who expose their genitals to random strangers on the street.

To argue for the proper relational setting for heterosexual access within this exemplary range of possible arrangements, then, we must first understand what sex between men and women is like from a moral standpoint. Andrew Dworkin asserts that the physical asymmetry of heterosexual intercourse ("The woman could not take him over as he took her over and occupy his body physically inside") means that no equal exchange is possible. Thomas Nagel concludes that sex involves the risk of objectification, but can be saved from "perversion" by invoking the free will of the object of one's desire, specifically, the sexual will. Nagel condemns sex with another person unless the desire is or could be mutual. Sex avoids perversion (if not aspiring to morality) insofar as it recognizes the dignity of the other person's desire as an exercise of their Kantian will.

We, too, see sex as involving core issues of human personhood. Yet nothing we have seen in the history of sexuality indicates that heterosexual conduct is unique and deserving of a degree of state protection markedly greater than any other human interactions, as Herman suggests. We take a less absolute position concerning heterosexual intercourse than Andrea Dworkin, believing that in some legal and social contexts, women can bargain for male-female sex in ways that ameliorate their inferior gender status.

Like Nagel, we would place sex firmly in the midst of other human relations as serious but not singular. We are more demanding than Nagel, however, in recognizing that even where sexual desire is both mutual and authentic, moral interests other than the free will of the parties can become involved. These also merit protection. Sex takes place in many settings outside the anonymous singles bar that provides the context for Nagel's 1969 analysis. (And we are duly chastened by the rapidity with which the respectful Nagel of "Sexual Perversion" evolved into the Nagel of the 1990s who defends all forms of pornography and cavalierly assigns the pain caused by egregious sexual harassment to the weaker player in the interest of protecting the sexual free will of the stronger.)

Seeking a path between Herman's morally ambitious aspiration to marriage and Nagel's elevation of a mutual if casual encounter, we propose to leave simple fornication to private bargaining. Like our rape proposal, however, our rules require significant reworking of both criminal and civil law. Because we are pessimistic about the ability of the pure exchange of sexual desire to respect personhood, and because we recognize that fornication slides easily into much more complex and consequential relationships, we propose additional regulation when sex comes to involve cohabitation, economic dependency, or the formation of joint life plans.

Long–term fornication relationships between men and women historically were called concubinage. Like marriage, although with lesser rights, such arrangements protected women from humiliating or impoverishing sexual bargains, for which they traded sexual access and, typically, sexual exclusivity. The historical practice of regulating concubinage rests on the judgment that when sexual exchange forms the foundation for a social community, minimal conditions of political fairness should apply.

In many states today, the ancient structure of concubinage would actually be an improvement on the punitive, discriminatory legal treatment of enduring but nonmarital sexual unions. Some jurisdictions recognize no legal claims whatsoever arising from sexual communities outside of marriage, casting such complex arrangements as nothing more than unlawful fornication or the equivalent of prostitution. By withholding civil law from these relationships, even private bargains between the parties cannot be enforced as contracts. Other states recognize some claims of cohabitants, but only if the couple has expressly contracted for mutuality in their relationship. The most equitable states recognize not only express contracts but also implied contracts and claims for equitable remedy. A few states take an alternate approach and recognize cohabitant unions as common-law marriages. In this unsettled legal climate, if men and women cohabit or ally sexually over many years, there is no certainty that any Kantian responsibilities for the "person as a whole" will be exchanged or be enforced.

One step toward a more just sexual community would be to treat contracts of care, even where sexual access is part of the consideration, as enforceable contracts. This was the issue presented by the so-called California "palimony" case, *Marvin v. Marvin* (1976). After *Marvin*, and in those states that followed this leading case, sexual partners may agree, orally or in writing, to bind themselves to responsibility for the other's well-being, usually in the form of shared property or an obligation of support when the relationship ends. The *Marvin* court was extraordinarily careful, however, to insist that sexual services could provide none of the value that the parties exchanged in making an agreement for a common life. The court engaged in this fiction to avoid any implication that its decision either condoned fornication and prostitution, or cheapened traditional marriage.

We see no reason why sex should be ruled out as motivation for an exchange between intimates. Apart from an analysis that treats sex as distinct from all other human transactions (which we have rejected), and in a secular state (which we inhabit), there is no reason either to penalize nonmarital sex or to channel people into traditional marriage. When fornication is accompanied by a web of other commitments and dependencies, the law at least must allow individuals to guard their interests by contract and not force them into the state of nature. Accordingly, and in contrast to the existing law's refusal or, at best, reluctance, to enforce contracts within avowedly sexual relationships, we propose that express promises between cohabitants or long-term lovers—whether written or, as will be more common, spoken—be enforced with particular fidelity. Like the rape rule that "no means no," sexual bargains such as "yes, if you support me" or "yes, if you leave me all your money when you die" should be accepted as fair trades. This new rule would require not legislation, but changes in both contract doctrine and case law.

Unlike express contracts, implied agreements (in fact or in law) force courts to make not just controversial policy decisions, but also complex factual judgments. An agreement for sexual community is implied in fact if sexual partners behave as if they intend some sharing agreement to pertain. We propose that implicit agreements be liberally interpreted based on all the facts of a nonmarital sexual union. Using a couple's course of conduct over time to establish an agreement to share might be confused with common-law marriage, but the two approaches differ. Common-law marriage, recognized in only a small minority of the states, requires the parties to hold themselves out to the world as married. Our proposal would routinely enforce mutual understandings between openly unmarried people.

The more ambitious aspect of our concubinage proposal concerns agreements implied in law. We propose the enactment of a statute in each state that would require sharing in some nonmarital sexual relationships, whether or not the parties agreed or expected to do so. The statutory concubinage contract would be triggered in the following circumstances:

(1) the couple have been sexually involved for a specified duration of time; and
(2) one of the following occurs:
　(a) there is a substantial difference in the assets of the two parties; or
　(b) one party leaves a job and devotes himself or herself to the domestic well-being of the couple; or
　(c) one party leaves a geographical location in response to the other's job or family situation; or
　(d) one party leaves an educational pursuit before graduation and devotes himself or herself to the domestic well-being of the couple, or takes a job while the other person continues his or her education.

If these requirements are satisfied, we propose that the following responsibilities and rights arise:

(1) economic support if the relationship ends as may be needed for rehabilitation and education; and
(2) equitable property division, including shares of pension, insurance, public benefits, or investments; and
(3) rights to a pro rata share of inheritance when one party dies, even if the relationship ends before death; and

(4) rights to an amount of property representing the costs of care when ill or disabled.

Although we would impose these statutory rights and duties without consent, we would allow the parties to waive them following full disclosure of assets and by explicit agreement concluded before the triggering act or acts. Waiver qualifies the protection offered by the legal status of concubinage, yet it encourages bargaining. (For bargaining purposes, the content of the statutory agreement is less important than its existence.) As in our rape proposals, the proposed statute places the burden of silence or ambiguity about relational expectations on the stronger bargainer. The risk of triggering the agreement may motivate the stronger player to explicitly bargain for a waiver, offering, perhaps, a less attractive but nonetheless beneficial deal. With such bargaining, rational self-regard may begin to replace romantic fantasies (usually the province of the weaker), bringing into the open the real conditions under which sexual access is being traded. If even a bad sexual bargain is better than none from the point of view of the weaker player, we have nothing further to say. In keeping with our commitment to liberal autonomy, a brisk acquaintance with the consequences of one's choices is all we would ask the coercive state to do in this adult, consensual setting.

Both libertarians and cultural conservatives will likely oppose this concubinage proposal. A conservative will object that the proposal legitimates prostitution and channels people away from marriage. As to the prostitution claim, Nagel provides an answer: In long-term alliances, it is usually the case that the parties exchanged sexual access based on mutual sexual desire and not just money. In the statutory scheme, this assumption is embodied in the requirement of a passage of time before the implied agreement even threatens to kick in. Thus the ancient distinction between prostitutes, who have sex with anyone who offers the price, and concubines, who ally with one person for an extended period, remains a morally meaningful distinction.

The argument that marriage is derogated rests on the idea that formal marriage has such unique merit that the law should press people into it. In a secular state, marriage cannot be defended as God's command, and so for policy purposes we must find marriage's merit in social function. The secular moral argument for marriage is Herman's, which, as we have seen, depends upon an understanding of male-female sex as singularly consequential among human relations. To the extent that a sexual alliance comes to resemble the complex and morally charged relationship that concerns Herman, our concubinage scheme addresses many of her concerns for mutual care without forcing people into a status rooted in religion and historically associated with inequality.

The libertarian should support enforcement of express agreements of concubinage as part of the libertarian commitment to private ordering. A libertarian might object to a statutory agreement of concubinage, however, as a restraint on human freedom, asserting that the weaker player should defend her own sexual interests by, for example, holding out for marriage before consenting to sex. A principled libertarian should also oppose formal marriage, insisting that people make their own version of intimate community by private bargain every time. In any event, because our scheme provides for waiver, the libertarian can object only to shifting the burden of silence onto the stronger player. Accordingly, the libertarian analysis reduces to the position that a person who does not affirmatively bargain for a good deal remains silent or equivocal and instead is either in a weak bargaining position or a fool. In either case, the libertarian would not help the weak or foolish by providing status protections.

Indeed, there is some evidence that the weaker players in long-term nonmarital unions tend to be weak and foolish. They are weak in that they do not seek and hold strong labor market positions, do not resist pressure to bear more than a fair share of domestic labor, and are willing to sacrifice individual self-interest to the interest of the community or the other partner. They are fools in that absent any enforceable agreement or status, they trust that the pairing is an altruistic partnership.

But libertarian counsel to pull oneself up by the bootstraps and refuse to make sexual bargains under terms of disadvantage is flawed, because it assumes that solitary action is the only autonomous, self-respecting option available. This contention is at the core of the libertarian approach to sex law. Even a liberal like Nagel in his later work recommends that working women deal with harassing employers and coworkers by "taking care of themselves." Yet challenging a more powerful person at the risk of one's livelihood may be stupid, rather than self-regarding behavior. Indeed, an effort to go it alone may be the best evidence that a weakling is also a fool in that she deludes herself into thinking she can get a decent sexual bargain despite her initial position of weakness. Rather than foolish independence, we urge weaker players to act collectively through the democratic process to enact laws like our concubinage proposal that stake out alternative default positions from the predictable downward spiral of an unregulated world of private bargains.

### ADULTERY

The offense of adultery has been defined variously as sexual contact with a married woman by a man not her spouse (the ancient and common law formulation), or sexual contact by any married person with someone not his or her spouse (the modern, gender-neutral formulation). Throughout western history, marriage served as a frame for Christian doctrine concerning permissible sex, a guarantor of property rights and legitimacy for inheritance, and, more recently, a vehicle for the romantic ideology of companionate marriage. The law of adultery defended all these values and functions, and also had multiple bargaining effects on sex between men and women.

Like laws against fornication, making adultery unlawful restrains heterosexual liberty in the interest of marriage. Ordinarily, such support for marriage would benefit women. But the ancient and common law definition of adultery strengthened the bargaining position of husbands and weakened that of wives and lovers. Prior to modern reform, divorce law, for instance, allowed a husband to discard an adulterous wife (and denied her either a marital property share or child custody rights), but forbade the wife any parallel right to leave and punish a straying husband. So, too, the social tolerance for male infidelity allowed a married man to keep a mistress and yet plead no power to marry her, weakening that women's sexual bargaining position as well as that of the wife. By contrast, wherever women tried to attack the double standard in law and custom—in the social purity movement, or in "fault" divorce rules that penalized adulterous spouses in marital property division—women's sexual bargaining power was enhanced and that of married men diminished.

During the libertine period many states deregulated adultery, and where criminal laws against adultery remain today they are rarely enforced. Other legal rules that once gave bite to the obligation of marital fidelity also have been repudiated or fallen away: A husband no longer has a right to sexual services from his wife, as at common law; divorce no longer depends exclusively upon spousal fault; and the common law torts defending marital sexual exclusivity such as criminal conversation and alienation of affections have been abolished.

Beginning from our premise that sexual justice has no necessary reference to marriage, it is tempting to equate fornication with adultery as a consensual act of pleasure and mutuality, presumptively good for human flourishing, and therefore neither immoral nor (at least in a good state) unlawful. But the relational contexts of fornication and adultery differ. Adultery involves betrayal of a promise of fidelity, and simple fornication does not. Accordingly, our proposals to regulate the two sexual relationships also differ.

Framing the issue presented by adultery as a "betrayal of a promise of fidelity" adopts a particular perspective on marriage, implying that the relationship is a private agreement. Historically and currently, however, the marital obligation of fidelity derives principally from the state. Marriage is not a contract, but rather a status that one contracts into. No one must marry, but if they do they must abide by the state's definition of the duties and rights of the relationship. Neither spouse can renounce marital duties and rights. A spouse may choose not to enforce his or her marital rights to full advantage, but only willingness to continue the renunciation assures the other spouse's freedom. Even a prenuptial agreement, which looks contractual, is enforceable only if a court determines first that its provisions do not injure the institution of marriage. This model of marriage as a status relationship powerfully limiting individual freedom of action endured even throughout the libertine period.

In asking whether adultery should concern the law, we must first decide what model of marriage to subscribe to. Should we abolish marriage as a status, leaving men and women (and other groupings of intimates) free to contract for any model of sexual community? Or should the state create multiple models of marriage from which people may choose? Less radically, should the state definition of marriage evolve to accommodate changed values, including an abolition of the requirement of sexual fidelity?

We do not subscribe to the religiously grounded notion that marriage is necessary for moral sex, but we would not abolish marriage as a form of sexual community. For natural or social reasons, physical pleasure and emotional intimacy between women and men often requires an enduring and complex relationship. A publicly created and recognized marital status assures social support for a serious promise of commitment to the well-being of another adult. This still leaves unanswered the question whether marriage, conceived as a mutual commitment to one another's well-being, should include an obligation of sexual fidelity. We propose to restore to marriage a nonnegotiable duty of sexual exclusivity. Although moral sex does not require a commitment of the duration or depth of marriage, we conclude that people who choose marriage want sexual exclusivity so that the status protects them from the vagaries of the sexual market with all its physical and emotional risks. Although 25 percent of American men and 10 percent of American women reportedly commit adultery today, a great majority of people also think it is wrong. If concubinage is regulated, as we propose to do, people can choose from a graduated series of relational obligations, with marriage as the most comprehensive.

Despite the evidence that sexual fidelity is expected in marriage, under current law that expectation carries no legal weight. There are a variety of mechanisms through which lawmakers could give weight to a duty of sexual fidelity. These include reinvigoration of the criminal law of adultery; forced divorce in any marriage in which adultery occurs; a lesser share of marital property for an adulterous spouse upon voluntary divorce, or creation of a civil action for personal injury in the hands of the wronged spouse.

We propose the latter two options. If one spouse breaches a promise of sexual exclusivity, the wronged spouse suffers a personal loss to dignity and reputation, may experience emotional and mental distress, risks exposure to sexually transmitted disease, and may be deceived about his relationship to the children in the family. Yet these injuries are to the person and not to society. Framed as an injury to the person rather than the state, the most appropriate remedy for adultery is civil compensation, either in the form of a "bonus" in the division of marital property upon divorce or death, or a tort action for money damages available either during the ongoing marriage or after divorce.

It is conventional wisdom among legal scholars that the use of fault determinations at any stage of marital dissolution will encourage divorcing parties to perjure themselves. Before the no-fault divorce reforms, commentators describe divorce proceedings as almost invariably corrupt and perjurious. This fear of perjury reflects a broader presumption that disputes between sexual intimates are categorically different from other human conflicts, and present unique and difficult proof problems not easily handled by the existing tools of legal truthfinding. Yet experience belies this conventional wisdom. Several states currently factor some element of fault into the division of marital assets at divorce. Lawmakers in these jurisdictions presumably find ordinary legal processes adequate to the task of adjudicating accusations of marital wrongdoing. We propose that all states adopt the rule that adultery constitutes marital fault, and that fault affects property division at divorce or death.

The second prong of our proposal is to create a tort of adultery. This will, perhaps, generate even more skepticism. Perhaps compensation between spouses makes sense at death or after divorce, but if we presume a sharing model of marriage, is it meaningful to order one spouse to pay damages to another during an ongoing marriage? We argue that there is nothing incongruous about the transfer of assets from one spouse to another during an ongoing relationship. This legally describes, in fact, what happens in the designation of marital property under both common law and community property regimes, although these property interests ordinarily are not liquidated until the marriage ends in either death or divorce. Legal scholar Joan Williams proposes that family property routinely be divided during the course of marriage, with the practical effect of giving each spouse greater power to manage that property unilaterally. A wealth of research shows that the degree of family decision-making power a spouse exercises depends on the amount of property he or she controls. Thus a transfer of assets from an adulterous spouse would shift power between married people and, given that men have a higher rate of marital infidelity, the greater measure of that shift would be from husband to wife.

We have argued consistently that political justice in the male-female sexual exchange must be separated from marriage. Part of this agenda is the legal privatization of adultery, shifting its regulation from criminal to civil law. We also see real practical advantages in a civil remedy for adultery. The injured spouse can decide whether and when to invoke the law, depending upon subjective perceptions of harm, the existing balance of bargaining power within the marriage, and the available nonlegal avenues for redress. Our proposal avoids the hard bargain offered by the current law by which a betrayed spouse must either accede to betrayal or sacrifice all other marital interests in the blast furnace of divorce. The civil law remedy of tort dignifies, and at the same time moderates, spousal outrage at the uncivil act of adultery.

## PROSTITUTION

The illegality of prostitution is perhaps the most contested question of heterosexual regulation. The law, however, reflects little of the intellectual ferment that has bubbled around this issue since the emergence of the libertine paradigm. With only one exception, all states prohibit prostitution as a crime; the outlier, Nevada, delegates the power to regulate to the county. State criminal laws define prostitution variously as selling sex (reaching wholly private conduct) or soliciting the sale of sex (focusing, as the Wolfenden Report suggested, on the public nuisance aspects of prostitution). Some, but not all, of the states also make patronizing a prostitute a crime, although nowhere are patrons prosecuted in the same numbers or with the same vigor as prostitutes. All of the states also make it a crime for third parties to profit from prostitution, including business agents (pimps), solicitors (panderers), recruiters, and those who rent real property for the purposes of prostitution.

As in rape, it is impossible to analyze the sexual relationship of prostitution and ignore its demography. The prostitution relationship today, and in the known past, consists to a marked degree of adult male patrons of adult female prostitutes, and of male and female child prostitutes. Likewise, there are striking racial and ethnic divisions in prostitution, with white men comprising most of the patron class, and nonwhite women a disproportionate part of the sex workers. In the ancient world, prostitutes virtually always were foreigners or slaves. Thus any useful analysis of prostitution must deal with it as a social practice with an enduring division of roles based on gender, age, race, and ethnicity.

From a bargaining perspective, prostitution strengthens the position of the woman or child selling the sex. The prostitute gains economic advantage from sexual access that she otherwise might be pressured by force or need into giving away. This individual advantage comes at the expense of the patron, but also at the expense of the collective bargaining power of women in dealing with men who seek female sexual cooperation. Apologists sometimes claim that prostitutes spare others the full weight of male desires. But prostitutes in fact damage the interests of nonprostitutes, bidding down the price of heterosexual access. Nonprostitute women are not paid for each discrete instance of sexual cooperation with a man. But over the longer term, a web of economic, social, and emotional exchanges can grow up around an intimate male-female relationship, which usually represents more gain to the woman than the money exchanged in the commercial sex transaction. Moreover, prostitution is a standing offer to violate the marriage contract of sexual fidelity, and thus particularly injures the interests of wives. Where prostitution is curtailed, wives are better situated to force their husbands to bargain with them for sexual access. These conflicts of interest explain the persistent failure of the two groups of women to ally, despite repeated attempts in history.

Expansive as the current regime of prostitution prohibitions is, not every instance in which sex is exchanged for money violates the law. If the exchange of sex for money is posed as a condition of employment, it amounts to sexual harassment. But the penalty imposed on the employer who imposes or tolerates an illegal sexual condition of employment is civil and not criminal. If the worker chooses to comply and does not complain, the law does not enter in. Outside the workplace, using economic pressure to gain sex is ordinarily neither rape nor prostitution. If, for example, a wealthy man threatens to evict his girlfriend from the apartment that he pays for unless she consents to particular sex acts, current law will treat her "consent" as valid.

By contrast, the prostitute's consent to the sale of her sex is not an effective defense either to her criminal liability nor to that of her customer. The law against prostitution prohibits all parties in all circumstances from making the frankly commercial sexual bargain.

Each aspect of the prostitution transaction—the sex part and the commerce part—is analogous to something the law does not otherwise meaningfully restrict (fornication and wage labor), but taken together the acts are unlawful. If sex is not unlawful and the exchange of sex for money is not per se unlawful, why is selling sex a crime? Neither lack of consent nor commodification are adequate explanations. The rule is incoherent. Yet this incoherence concerning sex and money has led neither to deregulation, nor to a more consistent explanation for continuing the policy of criminal prohibition.

Based on our earlier analysis of rape, the problems of child prostitution and coerced prostitution are easy to resolve in ways consistent with larger structures of consent and coercion in Anglo-American law. Coercion into prostitution amounts to rape, as does even a voluntary prostitution arrangement between an adult and an underage girl or boy. Neither act is meaningfully consensual. The principle is clear, but the application is likely to be murky. The pressures that lead an adult, adolescent, or child into prostitution may not easily fit into existing legal categories of coercion. Fraud, extortion, and exploitation of psychological and emotional needs, especially if there is a history of sexual abuse, bring many women, girls and boys into the trade.

Feminist scholars Mary Louise Fellows, Beverly Balos, and Margaret Baldwin propose the creation of a civil cause of action to allow a prostitute to recover money damages from a pimp for coercion into prostitution. Florida enacted such a law, and similar legislation was proposed in Minnesota. These laws define "coercion into prostitution" to include not simply force and threat, but also threat of legal complaint or report of delinquency, extortion, blackmail, and threat of legal interference with a mother's relationship with her children. Sexual "bargains" that exploit the prostitute's emotional or economic needs also are defined as coercive, including isolation from speech or communication with others, exploitation of a condition of developmental disability, or the need for food, shelter, safety, or affection, or any promises of marriage. We support these expansions of the legal definition of coercion as they apply to the specific realities of the social practice of prostitution, and also the move to civil rather than criminal remedy.

The nut of the issue comes, however, when we consider the fully voluntary choice of an adult woman to work as a prostitute, and the choice of an adult man to patronize her. Criminalizing these choices amounts to a significant restraint on the liberty of both parties. In light of our goals to encourage sexual flourishing consistent with a plurality of desires and the moral equality of all persons, what is the best policy?

We propose to decriminalize adult, consensual prostitution, removing all criminal laws (including those against soliciting, patronizing, living off the earnings of a prostitute, etc.). We propose instead to regulate sex commerce through existing labor laws, protecting prostitutes as workers and treating pimps and patrons as employers. Prostitution would be an illegal labor contract, subject to the civil and administrative penalties already applicable to, for example, child or sweatshop labor. A patron or pimp who makes an arrangement for prostitution would be penalized like the employer who seeks to employ workers underage, in unsafe working conditions, or at below minimum wage rates. Treating prostitution as socially undesirable labor is the best response to an activity that fits uncomfortably into even in our pluralistic scheme of values.

The change from a framework of criminal prohibition to labor regulation would transform law enforcement. Only the employer and not the worker could be prosecuted for violating the law. We recognize that the prostitute would be affected indirectly by the effort to prevent customers from buying sex, even if she is not penalized for entering into the prohibited work arrangement. However, unlike the current treatment of prostitutes as criminals, workers employed in violation of labor laws are not punished or stigmatized, even if the goal of the laws may be abolition of the worker's job. Thus prostitutes could demand payment for work performed under an illegal contract, protest harsh working conditions, or unionize without suffering legal penalty, even though their employment would remain illegal.

This cautious legal response to the sexual relationship of prostitution reflects the tentative and conflicting philosophical guidance to be found in the three traditions on which we rely. Where there is no clear consensus on the immorality of a sexual relationship, our default position—out of liberal regard for individual decision-making and the plurality of sexual values—is not to enforce direct rules. But where a class of sexual transactions raises ubiquitous moral problems from a virtue ethics, liberal, or utilitarian perspective, or unequally distributes bargaining power, we are willing to regulate these relationships. The question is whether prostitution is such a risky class of transactions.

Libertarians, including a feminist wing, condemn criminalization of prostitution as based on indefensible remnants of Christian religious doctrine and fears of female promiscuity. They argue that sexual services should be available in the marketplace as are the means to satisfy other basic physical needs such as food or shelter. A closely related position, most powerfully advanced by prostitutes on their own behalf, is that criminalizing the sex trade unfairly restricts women's economic opportunities. Selling sex is among the highest-paid of female occupations, and women should be allowed to use their bodies and labor to greatest personal advantage. Illegality arguably reinforces entrenched traditions by which, throughout western history, other people have controlled female sexuality. Consistent with this reasoning, prostitute organizations like COYOTE in the United States endorse removal of all laws penalizing women and youth in prostitution. They also oppose regulation of the trade, a position based on past experience, particularly in Britain and European countries, in which humiliating medical inspection and licensing policies were adopted not to make sex work safe for prostitutes, but to make prostitution safe for men and society. Although some prostitute organizations endorse the current criminal penalties directed at trafficking and procuring, as well as enforcement of laws that protect prostitutes from fraud, deceit, and compulsion, other prostitute advocacy organizations want no state or police involvement in any aspect of the trade.

Virtue ethics easily interferes with consensual arrangements if they impair human flourishing, no matter how freely consented-to or economically advantageous the arrangement. Being in control of one's self and sexuality is one aspect of a flourishing life, but the only dignified set of terms on which one moral person should yield to another is when the exchange is substantively equitable. Our understanding of the virtue ethics requirement of substantive equity in sexual exchange emerges from the debate in the classical world concerning sex between adult men and boys. (Recall that in the ancient world, sex with women was not accorded the same moral weight because the female role was to serve; boys, on the other hand, would mature into men and potential citizens, and their dignity thus merited regard.) According to contemporary analysts of ancient Greek homosexuality, it was morally questionable whether a man should ask a boy to play the role of a woman (the penetrated, or ruled) in homosexual intercourse. Being on the bottom was undignified. The moral standard emerged that such sex should take place only in the broader context of a relationship of tutelage, and that a boy should be sexually used by an adult man only until he reached a certain age, at which point he should assume his proper position on top as a sexual ruler.

For virtue ethics, it is damning that the overwhelming majority of men who patronize prostitutes are never themselves in the position of being prostituted; they are always the buyers of sex, and the women and youth are always the sellers. Prostitution thus lacks the marker of virtuous political exchange—that the parties have a turn at being both the ruled and the ruler. It is only in marriage or noncommercial relationships of mutual desire (as Herman and Nagel prescribe) that the male and female participants take turns sexually. Some argue that the imbalance of prostitution goes even deeper, reinforcing other ancient norms by which women exist to serve male needs and desires, denying their moral personhood altogether. Prostitution in the current world is, in fact, tainted by ancient oppressions of women, leading dissenting prostitute advocacy organizations, such as WHISPER in the United States, to seek the outright abolition of prostitution. WHISPER sees prostitution as a crime against women, rejects the notion that women freely choose prostitution from among other economic alternatives, and denies that working in the trade is an avenue of female agency or independence.

Even if the imbalance of power in the sexual relationship of prostitution is one-sided, enduring, and partakes of a naturalized hierarchy among persons, is prostitution different in this regard from wage labor or other relationships of sale or exchange that involve the body? With this question we move again to the liberal analysis of prostitution and personhood. It is a key debate within liberalism to distinguish wage labor (which is morally acceptable) from slavery (which is not). The classical liberal philosophers agreed that one may not alienate the entirety of one's own body and personality through enslavement, even if the enslaved consents freely to the subjection. Hegel perhaps best explains this powerful exception to the defining liberal commitment to individual autonomy. Because the moral personality requires a physical embodiment in this world, the body comes to stand for the self, he writes. "Therefore, these goods, or rather substantive characteristics, which constitute my own private personality, and the universal essence of my self-consciousness are inalienable and my right to them is imprescriptible."

Wage labor, by contrast, can be a moral arrangement for the liberal, because a person may alienate a part of her bodily self (her labor) and do so temporarily (for an eight-hour day) without alienating herself entirely. The wage labor relationship also carries with it other indications of reciprocity, in that the employer must compensate the worker for her time, energy, and loss of autonomy by paying wages. Political theorist Carole Pateman argues that prostitution is fundamentally different from wage labor, because, when sex becomes a commodity in the capitalist market so, necessarily, do bodies and selves. "The prostitute cannot sell sexual services alone; what she sells is her body." Pateman argues that to sell one's sex is to sell one's body, as well as the sexual self that is core to moral personhood. This argument invokes an ancient concept of personhood by which we honor people because they possess reason and spirituality and are not just material beings. Nineteenth-century romanticism added emotion and creativity to this idea of a person, and beginning with the free love movement, sexuality, too, became a core aspect of the self. By this rich understanding of personhood, we cannot separate our sex from our beings in the same way that we can separate our labor from our selves.

As for individualist liberalism, prostitution fails under the terms of Barbara Herman's and Thomas Nagel's Kantian sexual ethics. Herman would have it that a person has enduring concern for the whole life of a sexual partner, Nagel, that he or she cares about the other person's desire. The prostitution relationship is the antithesis of Herman's durable and multifaced relationship. The point of the commercial sex relationship is that the payment of money justifies the patron's right to use the prostitute instrumentally, and this limits the responsibility he must take for any consequences to her. Nor can the prostitution relationship survive even Nagel's greater tolerance for casual, nonmarital sex. The exchange of sex for money substitutes nonsexual consent for sexual consent, thereby negating the mutuality of desire that Nagel would require. The prostitute does not make her sex available to the patron because she feels desire for him, but because she wants his money. Nor does the patron fundamentally seek the prostitute's desire for him; he is purchasing the right to use her for a limited period of time and for his own purposes. He desires her pleasure only if he needs that display for his pleasure.

We are reluctant to rely on Nagel's ethics alone, however, because, as we noted in our refusal to make marriage a condition of sexual access, we disagree with analyses that treat sex as a human activity fundamentally different in kind from all others. Many human activities take place because money is offered. Yet the proffer of money to substitute for mutual desire in a sexual transaction pushes our classification of sex as just another activity very hard. In the end, we do regard sex as somewhat different, if only in degree rather than kind, and we think sex requires a high degree of respect, more than, say, professional sports, to which it is so often compared. Our moral concern about prostitution is reinforced, moreover, because prostitution does not simply fail Kantian standards; it is a sexual relation that positively flouts the Kantian attention to moral individuality. Indeed, some patrons derive pleasure from the fact that the prostitution relation violates these boundaries. Evidence from patrons suggests that commercial sex is often pleasurable because there are no strings attached, because the patron enjoys dominion over rather than mutual regard for the body and desire of the prostitute, and because the sex is instrumental and one-sided.

If prostitution is of uncertain moral status, its bargaining effects are unambiguous, and this drives our proposal to regulate commercial sex as a labor issue. First, prostitutes gain in individual bargaining power at the expense of women as a group. Like strikebreakers where a union is on the scene, prostitutes find a market because there are things non-prostituted women will not do without pay or at a low price. We argue that it is because some women can demand more from sex than a market that exists for prostituted women. This reflects different conditions and power within the group of women.

Tolerating prostitution lets the most starving worker set the prevailing wage. Other women can bargain up from there, but their opening position is weakened. And if prostitution lowers the price of sexual access to women, it is the kind of competition that politically organized women will act collectively to restrain, just as organized labor lobbies hard for minimum wage laws. If it is in the interest of the weaker sexual players to act collectively to raise the price of sexual access (for example, by strengthening rape law or requiring an implied contract of concubinage), another means is to use law to close off avenues by which the stronger gain access to defectors from the collective strategy. Defectors may be women willing to have sex in unacceptably dangerous and degrading conditions, or who demand only limited monetary compensation for sexual access, a resource the stronger control more of by virtue of social advantage.

Thus we explain the historic anti-prostitution stance of organized women in America as predictable cartel behavior. Through collective action—typically, campaigns to criminalize or eradicate the prostitution trade—women as a political group founded on common sexual interests seek to limit the competition. Shutting down prostitution works like a union contract, not only raising the wages for all workers by the power of the collective, but also preventing the strong from making private bargains with the weakest workers in order to drive down the price and undermine the collective's power and discipline. Thus there will be rifts in female solidarity whenever the issue of prostitution arises.

Many throughout our nation's history have accused organized labor of undermining the individual's right to work, and of racketeering and violence in their discipline of strikebreakers and free riders. So, too, many attack organized women's anti-prostitution activism on similar grounds. It cannot be disputed that organized labor achieved tremendous gains in wages and working conditions for the economically weak. But their success rested in part, for example, on attacks on groups of disempowered laborers brought in to break strikes and a determined campaign to exclude women workers from union ranks because women would drive wages down.

An analysis of anti-prostitution as collective bargaining should not shield this political strategy from criticism for its historic or current abuses. But understanding the logic of that position sharpens understanding of the debate over prostitution. Our bargaining analysis focuses not simply on the individual woman sex worker and her liberty or exploitation, but on her role within the larger economy of sexual labor and her impact on the political strategy of female cooperation.

Second, it is a labor issue that the working conditions of prostitution are unacceptably dangerous to the employees (whether they contracted to be there or not). This reality presents a straightforward utilitarian argument for regulation, at least to improve working conditions. Prostitution creates an environment in which women are at great risk of being harmed through violence, economic exploitation, substance abuse, and psychological diminishment. Sometimes it is glibly asserted that prostitutes do nothing that married women do not also do, but the comparison gravely understates both the work and danger associated with the sex industry. Prostitutes, on average, have sex with strangers four times a day, amounting to more than a thousand sexual encounters with non-intimates each year. Prostitute women and youth are raped and beaten by customers in far greater numbers than are other women and children. These numbers are not surprising considering that each sexual encounter with a prostitute sets up a state of nature in which the prostitute exposes herself physically in a covert setting. Even legalizing prostitution would not eradicate this reality nor, given the numbers of encounters with total strangers, reduce the danger even to the level of domestic violence and child abuse generally.

Yet the current policy of criminal prohibition cannot survive utilitarian scrutiny, either. Criminalization has led to widespread police corruption and sexual abuse of prostitutes. Because the trade is stigmatized and unlawful, workers are effectively denied the protection of the laws against sexual assault, battery, and fraud. Even murders of prostitutes elicit noticeably less response from law enforcement than killings of other citizens. Illegality drives much of the industry into the shadows, shielding business and employment practices from scrutiny under ordinary legal standards.

Our proposal treats prostitution as a social practice and not a natural and enduring fact. It is not necessary that prostitution exist, and it is possible for the trade to be regulated, transformed, and even abolished. We take no position on what the ultimate best policy would be, but argue that a first step toward a more just system of law is to take prostitution out of the state of nature and into the ordinary world of civil law.

## NOTES

The excerpt from Todd's diary is quoted in Peter Gay, *The Bourgeois Experience: Victoria to Freud, vol. 1: Education of the Senses* (New York: Oxford Univ. Press, 1984), 84. Mabel Loomis Todd, a resident of Amherst, Massachusetts, was married to David Todd and carried on an adulterous affair with Austin Dickinson, the married brother of poet Emily Dickinson.

The discussion of rape and bride price comes from Richard A. Posner, *Sex and Reason* (Cambridge, Mass.: Harvard Univ. Press, 1992), 384.

On the gender divide in rape law, although one can imagine exotic fact patterns involving female rapists, real instances of this are so rare as to be meaningless in making political judgments. In the 1970s and 1980s, many states made their rape statute gender-neutral both as to victim and rapist, and broadened the conduct prohibited to sexual assault, including penetration of the sexual organs of another with an object and coerced oral sex. Women have sexually assaulted men in both of these latter ways; most women prosecuted for raping men, however, participated with a group of men in a gang rape against a male victim.

Our proposal for reconceiving rape law is based on the work of Stephen J. Schulhofer in "Taking Sexual Autonomy Seriously," *Law and Philosophy* 11 (1992): 35-94.

The claim that at least half of teenaged mothers have adult male partners is documented in M. Males and K. S. Y. Chew, "The Ages of Fathers in California Adolescent Births, 1993," *American Journal of Public Health* 86 (1996): 565-68 (mothers aged 10-18 years and fathers aged 19 years or older) (1996); D. J. Landry and J. D. Forrest, "How Old Are U.S. Fathers?" *Family Planning Perspectives* 27 (1995): 159-161, 165 (mothers aged 15-19 years and fathers aged 20 years or older). The 21 percent figure for unmarried minor mothers with substantially older partners is documented in Laura Duberstein Lindberg, Freya L. Sonenstein, Leighton Ku, and Gladys Martinez, "Age Difference Between Minors Who Give Birth and Their Adult Partners," *Family Planning Perspectives* 29 (1997): 61-66. The 40 percent figure for mothers 15 years and younger is on p. 66.

In our exemplary jurisdictions today, the age of consent is 17 years in Illinois, Ill. Ann. Stat. ch. 720, paras. 5/12-16 (enacted 1961); 16 years in Massachusetts, Mass. Gen. Laws, ch. 265, sec. 23 (enacted 1697); Mass. Gen. Laws, ch. 272, sec. 35A (enacted 1955); 15 years in Virginia, Va. Code Ann., secs. 18.2-61,-63 (enacted 1950); and 18 years in Wyoming, Wyo. Stat., sec. 14-3-105 (enacted 1957) (felony for any person to take immodest, immoral, or indecent liberties with any person under 18). See also Wyo. Stat., sec. 6-2-303 (enacted 1982) (felony to subject a person under 12 to sexual intrusion or sexual contact if actor is at least four years older than victim); Wyo. Stat., sec. 6-2-304 (enacted 1982) (felony to subject person under 16 to sexual intrusion if actor is at least four years older than victim).

The examples we cite of misguided prosecutions under current laws of statutory rape are reported in Jim Chilsen, Associated Press, April 27, 1997 (residents of Port Washington, Wisc., pressuring district attorney to dismiss rape charge against 18-year-old man who impregnated 15-year-old girl because he offers to marry her); Matt Lait, "Agency Helps Some Girls Wed Men Who Impregnated Them," Los Angeles Times, Sept. 1, 1996, p. 1 (social workers encourage marriages between pregnant minors and adult men who impregnate them; some girls as young as 13 years affected).

The question of whether statutory rape laws will deter teenaged pregnancies is different from the question whether such laws will protect minors from sexual exploitation and abuse. Some researchers into adult male-female child pairings are skeptical about whether statutory rape laws will deter teenaged births; see, e.g., Patricia Donovan, "Special Report: Can Statutory Rape Laws Be Effective in Preventing Adolescent Pregnancy?" *Family Planning Perspectives* 29 (1997): 30-34, 40; Lindberg et al., "Age Difference Between Minors," 66. Even some who question whether statutory rape enforcement can lead to fewer teenaged births believe, nonetheless, that some version of these laws is necessary to protect minor girls from being exploited or coerced in their sexual decision-making. See, e.g., Michelle Oberman, "Turning Girls into Women: Reevaluating Modern Statutory Rape Law," *Journal of Criminal Law and Criminology* 85 (1994): 15. C.f. Lindberg et al., "Age Difference Between Minors," 66 (would confine interventions to prevent adult-child sex to the youngest girls).

Statutory rape remains the single general check in the law on adolescent heterosexual sex. By the late 1970s, teenaged girls no longer could be classified as "delinquent" solely on the grounds of sexual activity. Pregnant girls and young mothers could stay in school. Minors had access to contraception, and even to abortion in some states. Where access to abortion is restricted by the requirement of parental consent, the state must provide a judicial bypass mechanism. On delinquency, see *In Re Gault*, 387 U.S. 1 (1967) (minors in delinquency proceedings have some due process rights). On access to school, see Title IX of the 1972 Educational Amendment Act (pregnant or married students, as well as mothers, may remain in school). On contraception and abortion, see *Eisenstadt v. Baird*, 405 U.S. 438, 453 (1972) (unmarried people have a right to contraception); *Roe v. Wade*, 410 U.S. 113 (1973) (women have right of abortion); *Carey v. Population Services International* (1977) (minors may buy over-the-counter contraception); *Bellotti v. Baird*, 443 U.S. 662, 821 (1979) (parental consent statutes without judicial bypass and confidentiality provisions unconstitutional); *H. L. v. Matheson*, 450 U.S. 398 (1981) (parental notification laws justified by "State's interest in full-term pregnancies"). These legal developments decreased the penalties for minors' sexual activity, but did not overturn statutory rape laws nor erase the idea that sex with underage females was a greater social problem than sex with underage males. In 1981 the U.S. Supreme Court upheld a law prohibiting sexual intercourse with a female under the age of 18 years. The state had no comparable law protecting minor males, although underage boys could violate the law against sex with minor girls. See *Michael M. v. Superior Court of Sonoma County*, 450 U.S. 464 (1981) (state has sufficiently compelling interest in preventing teenage pregnancies to justify gender-specific statutory rape laws).

On the lack of pleasure in sexual intercourse for many adolescent girls, see Michelle Fine, "Sexuality, Schooling, and Adolescent Females: The Missing Discourse of Desire," *Harvard Education Review* 58 (Feb. 1988): 29. An anecdotal but insightful account of female adolescent sexuality is Naomi Wolf, *Promiscuities: The Secret Struggle for Womanhood* (New York: Random House, 1997). Wolf argues that girls are initiated into sexuality at too young an age, without respect for the development of their own sexual identities as women. Sharon Thompson has collected a rich selection of sex stories from a more numerous and diverse population of teenaged girls in Sharon Thompson, *Going All the Way: Teenage Girls' Tales of Sex, Romance, and Pregnancy* (New York: Hill and Wang, 1995). Although Thompson finds that some teenaged girls are able to manage heterosexual intercourse for their own ends, other girls are devastated by the romantic disappointment and abuse they encounter in sexually active peer relationships. Psychologist Mary Pipher in *Reviving Ophelia: Saving the Selves of Adolescent Girls* (New York: Ballantine Books, 1994) recounts the struggles of adolescent girls both to mature into their identities as sexual women and to avoid sexual predation, which she argues is endemic among teenagers. Research confirms that sexual violence is common among teenagers. See Kristin A. Moore, Christine Nord Winquist, and James L. Peterson, "Nonvoluntary Sexual Activity Among Adolescents," *Family Planning Perspectives* 21 (1989): 111; Debra Boyer and David Fine, "Sexual Abuse as a Factor in Adolescent Pregnancy and Child Maltreatment," *Family Planning Perspectives* 24 (1992): 7.

There is a debate on whether men or women get the better of marriage. Barbara Ehrenreich argues that the economic benefits of marriage for women and their children make the arrangement more advantageous to them than to men:

> The fact that, in a purely economic sense, women need men more than the other way round, gives marriage an inherent instability. . . . It is, in retrospect, frightening to think how much our sense of social order and continuity has depended on the willingness of men to succumb in the battle of the sexes: to marry, to become wage earners and to reliably share their wages with their dependents.

Barbara Ehrenreich, *The Hearts of Men: American Dreams and the Flight from Commitment* (Garden City, N.Y.: Anchor Press/Doubleday, 1983), 2-3. George Gilder, on the other hand, argues that without stable unions with women, men cannot be civilized. See George F. Gilder, *Men and Marriage* (Gretna: Pelican, 1986) and *Sexual Suicide* (New York: Quadrangle Books, 1973). Richard Posner and other scholars influenced by sociobiology, and law & economics contend that both spouses are equally advantaged because of gains through the specialization that is characteristic of domestic unions. See, e.g., Richard A. Posner, "Conservative Feminism," *Univ. of Chicago Legal Forum* (1989): 191; Richard Posner, *Economic Analysis of Law*, 3rd ed. (Boston: Little, Brown, 1986), 127-30.

The judgment about Kant as a "misogynist" comes from Barbara Herman, "Could It Be Worth Thinking About Kant on Sex and Marriage," in *A Mind of One's Own: Feminist Essays on Reason and Objectivity*, ed. Louise M. Antony and Charlotte Witt (Boulder, Colo.: Westview Press, 1993), 49, 50. Herman also says, "Kant has dreadful things to say about women." Herman notes the connection between Dworkin and Kant (51 n. 2). The comparative Kant and Dworkin quotes come from Immanuel Kant, *Lectures on Ethics*, transl. L. Infield (New York: Harper and Row, 1963), 163, and Andrea Dworkin, *Intercourse* (New York: Free Press, 1987), 140-41.

Kant on marriage is found in *Philosophy of Law*, sec. 24, p. 110, sec. 25, p. 111; Kant, *Lectures on Ethics*, 166-67. Kant on the role of law in creating the conditions for moral use is found in *The Metaphysical Elements of Justice (Rechtslehre)* (1797) transl. John Ladd (Indianapolis: Bobbs-Merrill, 1965), secs. 1-9. Kant does not allow one to consent to be freely used by another for metaphysical reasons, in order to protect the maximum life-long exercise of independent human reason.

Thomas Nagel discusses fornication and sexual morality in "Sexual Perversion," in *Mortal Questions* (Cambridge: Cambridge Univ. Press, 1979), 39.

*Marvin v. Marvin* is reported at 18 Cal. 3d 660, 665, 684, 557 P.2d 106, 110, 122, 134

Cal. Rptr. 815, 819, 831 (1976) (implied contract can be enforced provided the consideration is not sexual services).

As examples of the refusal of some jurisdictions to enforce even express contracts between cohabitants, see, e.g., *Rehak v. Mathis*, 239 Ga. 541, 542, 238 S.E.2d 81, 82 (1977) (cohabitation is immoral consideration and cannot support contract); *Hewitt v. Hewitt*, 77 Ill. 2d 49, 66, 394 N.E.2d 1204, 1211 (1979) (contradicts public policy to recognize mutual property rights between unmarried cohabitants); *Davis v. Misiano*, 373 Mass. 261, 263, 366 N.E.2d 752, 754 (1977) (woman has no right to support in absence of marriage). For a discussion of the cases generally and the underlying contract doctrines, see Ellen Kandoian, "Cohabitation, Common Law Marriage and the Possibility of a Shared Moral Life," *Georgia Law Journal* 75 (1987): 1829; Clare Dalton, "An Essay in the Deconstruction of Contract Doctrine," *Yale Law Journal* 94 (1985): 997, 1095-113.

For an argument that common-law marriage should be revived to protect women's interests, see Cynthia Grant Bowman, "A Feminist Proposal to Bring Back Common Law Marriage," *Oregon Law Review* 75 (1996): 709. Many other nations have laws to protect long-term sexual intimates. See, generally, Grace Ganz Blumberg, "Cohabitation Without Marriage: A Different Perspective," *UCLA Law Review* 28 (1981): 1125, 1170-78 (laws of Israel, Cuba, South Australia, Ontario, etc.).

On the enforceability of prenuptial agreements (and an argument against them from a feminist perspective), see, generally, Gail Frommer Brod, "Premarital Agreements and Gender Justice," *Yale Journal of Law and Feminism* 6 (1994): 229 (trend is toward enforceability of such agreements).

On feminist support for the idea of "contractual marriage," see, e.g., Marjorie M. Schultz, "Contractual Ordering of Marriage: A New Model for State Policy," *California Law Review* 70 (1982): 311. For a critical view of the same, see Jana B. Singer, "The Privatization of Family Law," *Wisconsin Law Review* (1992): 1443.

For a thoughtful examination of the reasons for and against a formal status of marriage, see Kandoian, "Cohabitation." We have argued that law should not use marriage as the basis for establishing or regulating heterosexual sexual relations. Martha Fineman goes further to argue that heterosexual relationships should not be the basis for family formation. Rather than construct rules to protect women who choose interdependence in patriarchal marriage, she argues, family law should be linked directly to the parent-child unit, most often a mother and child. See Martha Albertson Fineman, "The Neutered Mother," *Univ. of Miami Law Review* 46 (1992): 653, 665.

There is support among some feminists for a return of a measure of marital fault in divorce. See Barbara Bennett Woodhouse, "Sex, Lies, and Dissipation: The Discourse of Fault in a No-Fault Era," *Georgetown Law Journal* 82 (1994): 2525 (with comments by Katharine T. Bartlett) (Symposium: Divorce and Feminist Legal Theory). Only fifteen states have "pure" no-fault laws—laws that abolish all fault-based grounds for divorce and make "marriage breakdown" the sole basis for divorce. See Herma Hill Kay, "Beyond No-Fault: New Directions in Divorce Reform," in *Divorce Reform at the Crossroads*, ed. Stephen D. Sugarman and Herma Hill Kay (New Haven: Yale Univ. Press, 1990), 191. Fault has been expressly retained as a factor in spousal support and/or property distribution in twenty-two states and the District of Columbia. See ibid., 211 n. 18. Accord Barbara Bennett Woodhouse, "Property and Alimony in No-Fault Divorce (II)," *American Journal of Comparative Law* 42 (Supp. 1994): 175, 183 (reports to XIVth Congress of the International Academy of Comparative Law) (substantial minority of states, approximately one-quarter, regard economic and marital fault as relevant to property distribution). See also David Gruning, "Property and Alimony in No-Fault Divorce (I)," *American Journal of Comparative Law* 42 (Supp. 1994): 147 (fault in the community property states).

On the percentage of American men women who report having extramarital sex, and their views of the act, see Edward O. Laumann, John H. Gagnon, Robert T. Michael, and Stuart Michaels, *The Social Organization of Sexuality: Sexual Practices in the United States* (Chicago: Univ. of Chicago Press, 1994), 22, 212–16, and tab. 5.14.

On the relationship between income contribution and family power, see generally Susan Moller Okin, *Justice, Gender and the Family* (New York: Basic Books, 1989). Some of the research is Glenna Spitze, "Women's Employment and Family Relations: A Review," *Journal of Marriage and Family* 50 (1988): 595, 601–3 (employed wives exercise more power in family decisions than unemployed wives, at least in money decisions); Philip Blumstein and Pepper Schwartz, *American Couples* (New York: Morrow, 1983): 53–56 (in heterosexual couples, the comparative income power of the partners establishes family power); Dair Gillespie, "Who Has the Power? The Marital Struggle," *Journal of Marriage and Family* 33 (1971): 445 (the higher a husband's income and social status, the more family decision-making power he exercises).

For a capable summary of the libertine-regulationist debate on prostitution, see Sibyl Schwarzenbach, "Contractarians and Feminists Debate Prostitution," *NYU Review of Law and Social Change* 18 (1990-91): 103. For a flavor of the libertine position, see, e.g., Lars Ericsson, "Charges Against Prostitution: An Attempt at a Philosophical Assessment," *Ethics* 90 (1980): 335, 355; David Richards, "Commercial Sex and the Rights of the Person: A Moral Argument for the Decriminalization of Prostitution," *Univ. of Pennsylvania Law Review* 127 (1979): 1195, 1269–70, and see, generally, David A. J. Richards, *Sex, Drugs, Death, and the Law: An Essay on Human Rights and Decriminalization* (Totowa, N.J.: Rowman and Littlefield, 1982). For a flavor of the feminist-regulationist position, see Carole Pateman, *The Sexual Contract* (Stanford: Stanford Univ. Press, 1988), and Roger Matthews, "Beyond Wolfenden?: Prostitution, Politics and the Law," in *Confronting Crime*, ed. Roger Matthews and Jock Young (London and Beverly Hills: Sage, 1986), 198.

On the racial demographics of prostitution, see D. Kelly Weisberg, *Children of the Night: A Study of Adolescent Prostitution* (Lexington, Mass.: Lexington Books, 1985), 87–88.

On the "sex work as legitimate employment" position, see, e.g., "World Charter of Prostitutes' Rights," International Congress for Prostitutes' Rights, Amsterdam, Feb. 1985, reprinted in Gail Pheterson, ed., *A Vindication of the Rights of Whores* (Seattle: Seal Press, 1989), 40. The strongest position against regulation of any form is that of COYOTE/National Task Force on Prostitution, in Frédérique Delacoste and Priscilla Alexander, eds., *Sex Work: Writings by Women in the Sex Industry* (Pittsburgh: Cleis Press, 1987), 290 ("no mutually voluntary aspects of prostitution should be criminal, including relationships between prostitutes and third-party managers"). The dissenting position from within the prostitute community is that of WHISPER. See, e.g., Sarah Wynter, "WHISPER: Women Hurt in Systems of Prostitution Engaged in Revolt," in ibid., 266.

On the proposal for a civil action for coercion into prostitution, see Margaret A. Baldwin, "Strategies of Connection: Prostitution and Feminist Politics," *Michigan Journal of Gender and Law* 1 (1993):65, 71–73 (Symposium Issue on Prostitution: From Academia to Activism). Two states have enacted laws providing for such a cause of action. See, e.g., Fla. Stat. Ann. ch. 769.09 (Harrison 1992); Minn. Stat. sec. 611A.81 (1994). See discussion of Florida statute in Baldwin, "Strategies of Connection," 71–73.

On the experiences and self-understandings of men who patronize prostitutes, see Harold R. Holzman and Sharon Pines, "Buying Sex: The Phenomenology of Being a John," *Deviant Behavior* 4 (1982): 89. There are female patrons of male prostitutes; see Cecilia Karch and G. H. S. Dann, "Close Encounters of the Third World," *Human Relations* 34 (1981): 249–68 (describing North American female customers and black male prostitutes in Barbados), but the rarity of the relationship is its most notable characteristic. Perhaps it is possible to imagine a world in which women patronize male and child prostitutes to the same degree that men currently patronize female and child prostitutes. But there is no moment in western history when this has been the pattern, and no reasonable foreseeability that such a pattern will emerge in the world as we know it.

As an example of the Enlightenment philosophical consensus that enslaving oneself is not a permissible political liberty, see, e.g., Georg Wilhelm Friedrich Hegel, *Philosophy of Right* (1821), transl. T. M. Knox (Oxford: Clarendon Press, 1952), 52-53.

Carole Pateman's position on regulating prostitution is succinctly stated in "Defending Prostitution: Charges Against Ericsson," *Ethics* 93 (1983): 561, 562. See also Pateman, *The Sexual Contract* (Stanford: Stanford Univ. Press, 1988), ch. 7.

For a description of the working conditions of prostitutes, see Phillipa Levine, "Prostitution in Florida, A Report to the Gender Bias Study Commission of the Supreme Court of Florida" (Sept. 1988), summarized in Ricki Lewis Tannen, "Report of the Florida Supreme Court Gender Bias Study Commission," *Florida Law Review* 42 (1990): 803. On the number of "tricks" an average prostitute turns, see Matthew Freund et al., "Sexual Behavior of Resident Street Prostitutes with Their Clients in Camden, New Jersey," *Journal of Sex Research* 26 (1989): 460, 465 (average of slightly more than four customers per day). On violence, child abuse, and rape of prostitutes, see Mimi H. Silbert and Ayala M. Pines, "Occupational Hazards of Street Prostitutes," *Criminal Justice and Behavior* 8 (1981): 395, 397 (70 percent raped by customers and 65 percent beaten by customers). Prostituted women and adolescents have histories of very high incidences of early sexual experience and childhood sexual assault. See Weisberg, Children of the Night, 108-10; Jennifer James and Jane Meyerding, "Early Sexual Experience and Prostitution," *American Journal of Psychology* 134 (1977): 13, 38 (65 percent of sample had been raped, 85 percent before the victim was 15 years of age).

For a useful discussion of the view of prostitution as a fact of nature, see Laurie Shrage, *Moral Dilemmas of Feminism: Prostitution, Adultery, and Abortion* (New York: Routledge, 1994), 81-98.

A considered argument for a progressive policy of legal but regulated prostitution ("radical regulationism") is Matthews, "Beyond Wolfenden?" Matthews's guidelines for legislation are: (1) a clear commitment to general deterrence; (2) the reduction of annoyance, harassment and disturbance; (3) protection from coercion and exploitation; and (4) the reduction of the commercialization of prostitution (204).

# 14

## CONCLUSION

Sex is political. It is one kind of society that human beings create. Thinking about sex is thinking about the real and ideal organization of human beings in sexual society. Rape is a sexual association of force, like the state of nature. With civil peace, people establish a market economy of sex in prostitution. Sex organized into marriage establishes a polity based on kinship. Sex between individuals, and without force, payment, or kinship negotiations, creates a society of gift or barter.

The western political tradition is rich in resources for understanding each of these political relationships. Although the heterosexual relationship has not been treated as a subject for political analysis concerning two equal players, male-female sex has not been immune from political theory. Throughout history, the needs and beliefs about sexuality and community of the dominant male player, from the Jewish patriarch to the *Playboy* philosopher, shaped sex theory, as it did theories of representation or property ownership. Greek virtue offered sex as self-control; Christian salvation offered chastity and then conjugality; classical liberalism offered opposite sexes and a withdrawal of community and politics from the family and sexuality; and Victorianism offered the redemption of the private through virtue. Our own century differs from the preceding millennia because libertinism aspired to extend sexual citizenship to females as well as males. Only living with libertinism has revealed how political arrangements continue to favor the males.

We have traced the history of heterosexuality as an institution of political organization and governance. We have demanded of each historical regime that it account for itself according to the accepted standards of political thought, departing from the tradition only by asking in every instance about the philosophical standing of both male and female players. In Chapters 12 and 13 we set forth our own theory of heterosexuality as a political relationship that treats males and females as full political actors, using the idea of structured bargaining to negotiate a passage between unbridled individualism and moral tyranny. We address the many ways sexual community may be established (force, sale, and gift/barter) with our proposals for legal rules governing rape, prostitution, fornication, and adultery. We suggest a new structure of sexual regulation that maximizes the possibilities that the players will enjoy the benefit of a good life, as the western tradition has come to view one.

Speculating about the sexual lives that our proposal would encourage, we believe people will have fewer sexual encounters than in the heyday of libertinism. Young people under the age of sixteen years would be urged against sexual activity in the interest of sparing them the burdens of reproduction or the distractions of emotional excesses during the long developmental period necessary for a prosperous and competent adulthood. Enforceable criminal sanctions would forbid adults from using their powerful but temporary bargaining advantage of age and authority to conscript the young into sexual service.

Once past the age of sexual majority, consensual sexual exchanges between males and females would be left unregulated within the boundaries of consent and community. A vigorous definition of consent would place the burden of silence or ambiguity on the more powerful player, usually the male. That subset of sexual transactions in which a man thinks a woman's silence means consent would move from the currently permissible to the potentially criminal, a heavy deterrent. Those unwilling to take the chance will either hold off or ask. Where asking elicits affirmative consent, the sexual encounter will go forward. When nonconsensual encounters are discouraged but more open sexual conversation encourages negotiation for consent, we cannot say whether the balance will mean more or less sex.

It is possible there will be fewer enduring but nonmarital heterosexual relationships under our concubinage proposal. Either the stronger and richer player will break off a relationship rather than become liable for economic sharing, or the weaker player will not be tempted to make a foolish bargain because she has been confronted with the stronger's lack of regard for her well-being. On the other hand, the law's power to stabilize such relationships by mutual obligation may make informal but lasting unions more sturdy. Short-term, nonmarital sexual relationships between men and women also may become more common because such encounters do not trigger obligations.

We can predict less adultery. Adulterers who think they won't be caught, like any violators, will not be deterred. Among rational players, however, some adulterous activity will be deterred because the injured spouse will have civil remedies both at divorce and in lieu of divorce. With concubinage in place, which promises economic sharing but no necessary expectation of sexual fidelity, there may be less marriage.

We predict less commercial sex over time, even though prostitution would be decriminalized. Strict application of the prohibition of consensual sex between adults and children, even prostitute children, would deter child prostitution. The labor regulation model would open patrons, pimps, club owners, landlords, and others on the business end of the sex industry to repeated and potentially harassing civil penalties. Because our scheme would not subject prostitutes themselves to legal sanction, their bargaining power should increase in the short term, resulting in higher prices for sexual labor. It is possible this economic advantage would bring more prostitutes into the market, in turn pushing prices down again. But the continual disruption of the business will, over time, make sex work less attractive employment. We expect no overnight transformation of prostitution, but a slow reorganization and dissipation.

By itself, less heterosexual intercourse is no reason to reject our proposals. If "more is always better" were the governing insight where sex is concerned, the war in Bosnia, with its attendant epidemic of rape as a tool of genocidal control, would be a model of sexual society. It is an enduring paradox of human nature that the openness of libertinism and the pleasure in utilitarianism produces the insight that more sex is not necessarily better sex. Recognizing this phenomenon, virtue ethics theories do not automatically assume more is better. Even the libertarian urge for more freedom does not embrace more freedom for the stronger when the tradeoff is less freedom for the weaker, unless we reduce the libertarian insight to an embrace of anarchy or a theory that rests on might making right.

Although the pleasures of sex are felt in the most intimate parts of the body and spirit, in the end sex takes much of its value from the fact that it involves at least one other human being. A human being is a creature of speech and reason, and, as such, a creature of politics. In this fundamental sense, we have sex in public.

# INDEX